Cross-Cultural Understanding

Arranged and edited by

Filmer

F. S. C. NORTHROP

HELEN H. LIVINGSTON

Yale Law School

Harper & Row, Publishers

New York, Evanston, and London

Cross-Cultural Understanding:

ᒪᒍᒪᒍᒪᒍᒪᒍᒪ *Epistemology in Anthropology*

The reciprocal relationship of epistemology and science is of note-worthy kind. They are dependent upon each other. Epistemology without contact with science becomes an empty scheme. Science without epistemology is—insofar as it is thinkable at all—primitive and muddled.

—Albert Einstein

LIBRARY OF CONGRESS CATALOG CARD NUMBER: 64-10591

E-O

Dedicated to

FRAY BERNARDINO DE SAHAGÚN (1500–1590), Franciscan Missionary, Father of Anthropology in the New World. He devoted sixty years of his life to understanding from the inside, in the light of their philosophy, the culture of the ancient Mexicans. He collected hundreds of pre-Columbian texts in the Náhuatl language; he examined them with a critical eye and, finally, offered to his contemporaries a living image of the life and thought of the pre-Hispanic Mexicans in his *General History of the Things of New Spain*, a masterpiece and example of anthropological research for generations to come.

Preface

At the request of the late Dr. Paul Fejos, the twenty-first symposium of the Wenner-Gren Foundation for Anthropological Research was organized by its chairman under the provisional title "The Determination of the Philosophy of a Culture." The members met from September 16 to 26, 1962, at the Foundation's European Conference Center in Burg Wartenstein, Austria. With the exception of Chapter 1 and Part IV, the papers were prepared and distributed before the symposium began. No paper was either read or summarized by its author at the conference. Instead, each contribution was studied by the conference members before the session in which it was discussed. This procedure acquainted the members with a critical examination of their respective contributions during the first six days of the symposium and left the last four days for the consideration of certain topics arising from the discussions. Space does not permit the publication of all these sessions. The members of the symposium selected those which comprise Part IV. They also appointed the Editor, who was Rapporteuse of the symposium, to prepare their revised manuscripts for publication and see this book through the press. Finally, after many suggestions, they proposed and agreed upon *Cross-Cultural Understanding: Epistemology in Anthropology* as the most appropriate title.

During the discussions of the Mexican and African cultural philosophies described by Dr. León-Portilla and Mr. Janheinz Jahn, the remarkable objectivity and proven practicality of the anthropological understanding of ancient Mexican culture by the sixteenth-century Fray Bernardino de Sahagún became evident. This is why, after discussions led by Professors Yamamoto and Maquet and Mr. Klausner, concerning some contemporary theoretical and practical difficulties in cross-cultural understanding, the symposium members unanimously voted the dedication to Fray Bernardino de Sahagún and invited Dr. León-Portilla to write the dedicatory page.

The aforementioned necessary omission from this book of some important discussions is mitigated in part by the fact that tapes for all the thirty-five sessions are on file in the New York office of the Wenner-Gren Foundation. A speaker's index for each tape includes some brief notes on the speaker's remarks which are not to be considered a verbatim report. Among the major topics discussed are the following: (1) "Some Examples of Paintings by Primates and Humans," as shown and described by Dr. Eibl-Eibesfeldt; (2) "The Difficulty in Cross-Cultural Religious Understanding: An Oriental View of Christianity," by Professor Tatsuro Yamamoto; (3) "Cross-Cultural Operational Definitions," with discussion opened by Professor Jacques J. Maquet.

We thank Mrs. Laurie Montanye of the Foundation for transcribing two of the tapes. Our special gratitude goes to Rollins College for a grant which covered all editorial expenses during the final nine months of the manuscript's publication and indexing.

Since the symposium occurred, the remarkable event that was Paul Fejos has perished. The eternal object, which is all that he was and did, remains. For this the members of the symposium, and all others whose privilege it was to know him, are lastingly grateful.

F. S. C. NORTHROP Symposium Chairman
HELEN H. LIVINGSTON Editor

March, 1964

Contents

PREFACE   *vii*

CONTRIBUTORS   *xiii*

Introduction

1. The *Raison d'Être* of the Inquiry   *3*
   F. S. C. Northrop

2. Some Epistemological Remarks on the Cultural Philosophies
   and Their Comparison   *13*
   Jacques J. Maquet

Part I

3. Philosophy in the Cultures of Ancient Mexico   *35*
   Miguel León-Portilla

4. Value Conceptions in Sub-Saharan Africa   *55*
   Janheinz Jahn

5. Popular Buddhism in Northeast Thailand   *70*
   William J. Klausner

6. Recent Studies on the Japanese National Character   *93*
   Tatsuro Yamamoto

7. The Common Elements in the Philosophy of Matrilineal
   Societies in India   105
   U. R. Ehrenfels

8. Scheduling   125
   Charles F. Hockett

Part II

9. Some Old Ideas About the Human Brain from a Recent
   Point of View   147
   Valentino Braitenberg

10. Communication and Meaning—A Functional Approach   162
    Donald M. MacKay

11. A Historical Introduction to the Postulational Foundations of
    Experimental Epistemology   180
    Warren S. McCulloch

12. Toward a Deductively Formulated and Operationally Veri-
    fiable Comparative Cultural Anthropology   194
    F. S. C. Northrop

13. The Burmese Language: An Epistemological Analysis   223
    Khin Maung Win

14. Structural and Dynamic Elements in the Greek Conception
    of Physical Reality   237
    S. Sambursky

15. The Theoretical Constructs of Western Contractual Law   254
    Joseph C. Smith

16. Status and Contract in Primitive Law   284
    E. Adamson Hoebel

Part III

17. Experimental Criteria for Distinguishing Innate from Cul-
    turally Conditioned Behavior   297
    Irenäus Eibl-Eibesfeldt

18. Distinguishing Differences of Perception from Failures of
    Communication in Cross-Cultural Studies   308
    Donald T. Campbell

Part IV

19. The Relevance of Neurophysiology for Anthropology   339

20. Free Will and Causal Prediction   356

21. Some Practical Implications   365

INDEX   385

Contributors

BRAITENBERG, Valentino, Professor of Cybernetics, Department of Theoretical Physics, University of Naples, was trained as a neuropsychiatrist in the University of Rome. Dr. Braitenberg's research, carried out in Italy, Germany, and the United States, has been mainly concerned with the problem of translating the structure of animal nerve nets into functional schemes.

CAMPBELL, Donald T., Professor of Psychology, Northwestern University, where he has been since 1953, received his Ph.D. (1947) from the University of California, Berkeley. His fields of specialty include social science research methodology, theory of social attitudes, and an area which he calls "the comparative psychology of knowledge processes," of which the present chapter is illustrative. He is the author of some seventy articles in psychology and related social sciences.

EHRENFELS, U. R., Professor and head of the Department of Anthropology, University of Madras, is presently guest professor at the Süd Asien Institut der Universität Heidelberg. He studied philosophy, Islamics, and anthropology after travels in the Near East and India, where he settled in 1938. He pursued field research, especially in Kerala, Assam, and East Africa. Publications include *Mother-Right in India* (1941), *Kadar of Cochin* (1952), *North-South Polarization* (1957), and *Light Continent* (1960).

EIBL-EIBESFELDT, Irenäus, Research Associate, Max-Planck-Institut für Verhaltensphysiologie, received his Ph.D. in 1950 from the University of Vienna. Since 1957, Dr. Eibl-Eibesfeldt has been Scientific Director of the International Institute of Submarine Research, Vaduz. His research in ethology, especially of vertebrates and marine biology has taken him on expeditions to the Indian Ocean, Caribbean Sea, Galapagos Islands, South America, and other places. Publications include *Galapagos* (1960) and "Angeborenes und Erworbenes im Verhalten der Säugetiere," *Zeitschrift für Tierpsychologie*, Vol. 20.

HOCKETT, Charles F., at Cornell University since 1946, and Professor of Linguistics and Anthropology since 1957, received his B.A. and M.A. degrees in Ancient History at Ohio State University and his Ph.D. in Anthropology in 1939 from Yale University. The author of many articles on linguistics, language and culture, and language and human origins, his books include *A Course in Modern Linguistics* (1958), *A Manual of Phonology* (1955), with Robert E. Pittenger and John J. Danehy, *The First Five Minutes: A Sample of Microscopic Interview Analysis* (1960).

HOEBEL, E. Adamson, Professor of Anthropology, University of Minnesota, studied anthropology at Columbia University and later law and jurisprudence at the University of California as an Inter-Disciplinary Fellow of the Social Science Research Council. A specialist in primitive law, he has done field work among the Cheyenne, Comanche, and Pueblo Indians with special reference to problems of legal and political control of behavior within the tribal setting. He is the author of *The Law of Primitive Man: A Study in Comparative Legal Dynamics* (1954) and (with Karl N. Llewellyn) *The Cheyenne Way: Conflict and Case Law in Primitive Jurisprudence* (1941).

JAHN, Janheinz, studied literature at the Universities of Munich and Perugia. With his translation into German of African and Afro-American poets and writers, he proceeded to specialize in neo-African culture and literature and became a cofounder of the African literary journal *Black Orpheus*. His major anthropological book, *Muntu: An Outline of Neo-African Culture*, has been translated into several languages, as has *Through African Doors*.

KLAUSNER, William J., B.A. (Phi Beta Kappa), LL.B. and M.A. (Southeast Asia Area Studies) from Yale, was admitted to the Connecticut Bar in 1953. A Ford Foundation grant (1955–1957) permitted village research studies in northeast Thailand. Since 1959 he has been a Program Specialist for The Asia Foundation with special responsibilities in the spheres of Buddhist and rural programing. He is the author of several articles including "The Northeast Thailand Migration Problem" and "Guide for Rural Workers" in *Social Science in Thailand* (1960).

LEÓN-PORTILLA, Miguel, Professor at the Faculty of Philosophy and Letters, National University of Mexico since 1957 and Director of the Inter-American Indian Institute since 1960, Dr. León-Portilla received his M.A. in Philosophy from Loyola University of Los Angeles and his Ph.D. in Anthropology from the National University of Mexico.

He is the author of many articles published in Latin America, the United States, and Europe. His books include *The Mind of Ancient Mexico* (Spanish eds. 1956, 1959; English ed. 1963) and *The Broken Spears* (1962), also published in Spanish, German, and Italian.

LIVINGSTON, Helen H., Assistant in Research and Secretary to Professor F. S. C. Northrop since 1948, she was the Rapporteuse of the Wenner-Gren Foundation for Anthropological Research Symposium No. 21. Upon its conclusion, she was elected Editor of this volume by the contributors.

McCULLOCH, Warren S., a Staff Member, Division of Sponsored Research, Research Laboratory of Electronics at Massachusetts Institute of Technology since 1952, received his B.A. from Yale in 1921, M.A. in 1923, and M.D. in 1927 from Columbia University. Dr. McCulloch taught at Yale University and the University of Illinois. A member of the American Academy of Arts and Sciences, the American Mathematical Society, the American Neurological Association, the American Physiological Society, and others, he is the author of over a hundred articles on the functional organization of the brain.

MACKAY, Donald M., Granada Professor of Communication and head of an interdisciplinary research team at the University of Keele, Staffordshire, England, since 1960, was graduated in Natural Philosophy from St. Andrews University and received his Ph.D. from the University of London, where he was latterly Reader in Physics. His research interests have moved from radar and electronic analogue computing, by way of information theory, to the organization of the brain as a communication system. Publications include (with M. E. Fisher) *Analogue Computing at Ultra-High Speed* and scientific papers on information theory, experimental psychology and physiology, theory of automata, and philosophy of science.

MAQUET, Jacques J., Professor at the École Pratique des Hautes Études of the University of Paris, first studied philosophy and particularly epistemology in Europe and at Harvard University then specialized in Social Anthropology at the University of London, where he received his Ph.D. He spent eleven years in tropical Africa as a field anthropologist, was head of a research center in social sciences in Rwanda, and Professor of Anthropology at the University of the Congo, Elisabethville. His books include *The Sociology of Knowledge* (1951), *Aide-mémoire d'ethnologie africaine* (1954), *Ruanda* (1957), *The Premise of Inequality in Ruanda* (1961), and *Afrique, les civilisations noires* (1962).

NORTHROP, F. S. C., Sterling Professor of Philosophy and Law, Emeritus, Yale University, and Elizabeth Morse Genius Visiting Professor, Rollins College, for the winter term 1962–1963, received his B.A. from Beloit College, M.A. Yale University in Economics, and

Ph.D. from Harvard University in Philosophy in 1924. A member of
the Yale faculty since 1923, he was also on the faculty of the Graduate
School and the Law School. The author of many scientific, philosophical, and legal articles, his books include *The Meeting of East and West*
(1946), *The Logic of the Sciences and the Humanities* (1947), *The
Complexity of Legal and Ethical Experience* (1959), and *Philosophical Anthropology and Practical Politics* (1960).

SAMBURSKY, S., Professor and head of the Department of History
and Philosophy of Science, Hebrew University, Jerusalem, he studied
mathematics, physics, and philosophy in Berlin and Koenigsberg, where
he received his Ph.D. Since 1928 he has been a member of the academic staff of the Hebrew University. Experimental physicist (atomic
and molecular spectroscopy), his main field of research is Greek scientific thought. His publications include *The Physical World of the
Greeks* (1956), *Physics of the Stoics* (1959), and *The Physical World
of Late Antiquity* (1962).

SMITH, Joseph C., Assistant Professor of Law, University of British
Columbia. Professor Smith received his B.A. from Brigham Young
University, LL.B. from the University of British Columbia, 1960, and
LL.M. from the Yale Law School, 1961. He was awarded the Rowell
Fellowship in International Law and received the Felix Cohen Prize
in legal philosophy while at Yale.

WIN, Khin Maung, Lecturer in Philosophy at the University of
Rangoon, he received his B.A. (Honors) in Philosophy from Rangoon
University, an M.A. and Ph.D. from Yale University. He is currently
teaching Eastern and Western philosophy. He has translated two
books into Burmese, one on logic and the other on Indian philosophy.

YAMAMOTO, Tatsuro, Professor and Chairman of the Department of
Oriental History at the University of Tokyo, was graduated from the
Tokyo Imperial University. He has studied and traveled in Vietnam,
Cambodia, Thailand, the United States, France, and India. In 1952
he was awarded the Japan Academy prize for the study of Vietnamese
history. Visiting Professor at Yale University for the first term 1962–
1963 and at Cornell University, the second term, his writings include
"Origin of the Words Tung-yang (Orient) and Hsi-yang (Occident),"
in *Toyo Gakuho* (1933), research on Vietnamese history (1950) and
Views on History (1957).

Introduction

The Raison d'Être
of the Inquiry F. S. C. NORTHROP

1

In a final reflection on his own experience as a mathematical physicist, Albert Einstein expressed the conclusion which appears on the title page of this book.[1] This conclusion tells us that science neglects epistemology at its peril. In the same year, Clyde Kluckhohn, writing as a cultural anthropologist, affirmed that "there are no organized groups of human beings without their own philosophy. . . . If the behavioral facts are to be correctly understood, [their] philosophy . . . must also be known."[2] This statement affirms that philosophy is a universal category of cultures and that any other factor, be it universal or provincial, of a particular culture is misunderstood unless it is interpreted in terms of that particular people's specific philosophy. The present book, as its title indicates, combines these two conclusions of Einstein and Kluckhohn and pursues some of the consequences.

The current state of the Kluckhohnian culturally anthropological part of the inquiry is the theme of the next chapter and Part I. The Einsteinian epistemology of mathematical physics and the more mature scientific method which it entails, for both (1) the physical anthropology of human nervous systems, including recent communication science, and (2) a more objective comparative cultural anthropology, are the concern of Parts II, III, and IV.

The cultural philosophies and current anthropological methods are put first. Otherwise, the epistemology of this book would be little more than "an empty scheme." For the same reason, cul-

tural examples of each of the two parts of the complex epistemology of mathematical physics appear in Chapter 13 by Professor
Khin Maung Win of Burma and Chapters 14 and 15 by Professor
S. Sambursky of Israel and Professor Joseph C. Smith of Canada
respectively.

Parts III and IV then pursue some of the operational and other
consequences of relating the epistemology and its scientific method
of Part II to the cultural anthropological materials and methods of
Part I. More especially, in Part III the chapter by Dr. Eibl-Eibesfeldt is concerned with experimental criteria for distinguishing
physically anthropological innate human behavior from that which
is artifactually self-determined or culturally conditioned. Then,
within the latter, the psychological expert in cross-cultural perception tests, Professor Donald T. Campbell, directs attention to
experimental procedures which may permit the confirmation or
disconfirmation of whether a particular people's cultural philosophy falls within one or another of the epistemological possibles
described in Part II.

The fact of self-determinated, as well as culturally conditioned,
human behavior raises the question of free will in its relation to
the mechanically causal prediction upon which scientific method
generally, and especially that of the complex epistemology of Part
II, rests. This is why, as the prepared papers of the symposium in
Parts I, II, and III were being discussed, the theme of Chapter
20 in Part IV became evident as a topic which must be pursued
later in the general discussion.

It is to be noted that the first three chapters in Part II are by
the two medically trained experimental neurophysiologists, Drs.
Valentino Braitenberg and Warren S. McCulloch, and the communication scientist Professor Donald M. MacKay. All three are
experts in the epistemology, method, and mechanical theory of
modern physics in its recent cybernetic extension to neurophysiology and communication science.

Their chapters may be viewed, therefore, as an attempt to
throw light on the following question: What is there about the
neurophysiology of any healthy human being which makes cultural anthropology possible? More specifically, what, viewed neuro-
physiologically, in the light of the recent teleologically mechanical
theory of the nervous system, the McCulloch-Pitts theory of
"trapped universals," and communication science, makes it pos-

sible for the motor responses and cultural artifacts of the people of a particular culture to be a function of not merely the facts of the moment as given in their sensory stimulation, but also "their own" remembered, intercommunicated, and shared philosophy? Cautions, concerning what in these recent cybernetic neurophysiological developments is relevant and what may be ignored by anthropologists, set the opening theme of the symposium's overall discussion, which appears as Chapter 19 in Part IV.

Professor MacKay's expertness in communication science obviously has much in common with Professor Hockett's anthropological competence as a linguist. This is why, notwithstanding previous references to it, Professor Hockett's chapter is put at the end of Part I, near Professor MacKay's. The reader will find these connections reinforced in the discussion in Chapters 19 and 20 of Part IV.

It is to be noted that there is a difference between Einstein's and Kluckhohn's statements of the interdependence of science and philosophy. Einstein restricts his statement to that particular branch of philosophy called epistemology—the science whose business it is to investigate knowing *qua* knowing. Kluckhohn refers to philosophy in general.

Since the language of Einstein's physics is mathematical and mathematicians found, at the beginning of this century, that the skills of the philosopher with his formal logical calculi are interdependent with those of the mathematician, Einstein's use of the word *epistemology* must be regarded as including that branch of twentieth-century philosophy called symbolic, or mathematical, logic. The central importance of scientific theories being formalized in such a mathematical, or logical, calculus, if they are to be epistemologically unequivocal and meet the methodological criteria of modern natural science, will become evident in Professor Braitenberg's and other chapters in Part II and in the discussion in Chapter 19 of Part IV.

Mathematics is important for both epistemology and anthropology in another respect. As Willard Gibbs noted, "Mathematics is a language." Moreover, modern mathematicians and symbolic logicians have shown that its logical syntax is often not that of ordinary languages. So great is the difference that Whitehead, who pioneered with Bertrand Russell in the study of these matters, said to the writer in the early 1920s, "One cannot be too suspicious

of ordinary language in science and philosophy."[3] These considerations suggest that describing a culture with any ordinary language,
or with linguistic categories abstracted largely if not solely from
the world's ordinary languages, may distort and misrepresent any
culture in which, as is happening everywhere today, artifacts deriving from the epistemology of non-Aristotelian Western mathematical physics and its mathematical language and logic play a
significant role. This is one of many reasons why the professional
mathematical physicist and historian and philosopher of science,
Professor S. Sambursky, is an indispensable contributor to Part II
of this inquiry.

Kluckhohn's less epistemologically focused statement of the interdependence of science and philosophy is confirmed so far as
cultural anthropology is concerned by the contributors and their
respective chapter titles in Part I. They show that one can approach the mentality of a people and cultural philosophies, both
systematically or by way of their value norms, religious ceremonies,
their comparative legal norms, their linguistic categories, their
economic ways, their music, or the dance. Only occasionally, and
often more covertly than explicitly, do the chapters in Part I refer
to the epistemological manner in which the cultural content of
what they describe is known and conceived by the people in question or by the observing anthropologist.

This is why it is important that the cultural anthropologists
in this book (1) be born, or expert, in diverse cultures which
collectively encircle the earth, and (2) their specialized anthropological interests refer to as many different aspects of cultural
activity as possible—aesthetic, historical, systematically metaphysical, practical, economic, and linguistic as well as ethical and legal.
Mexico's Professor Miguel León-Portilla insures that cultures
which take painting and the passionate existential commitment of
the bullfighter as philosophically primary are not left unrepresented.
Similarly, Mr. Janheinz Jahn speaks, not only as one of the most
incisive and penetrative of the younger contemporary West German minds, but also for the drumbeats and dancing of several
Sub-Saharan African tribes and the philosophical conception which
their art forms and value norms express. An Austrian cultural background, informed initially by the influence of a scientifically distinguished father, and followed by several years' residence and
anthropological research in South India, given especially to the

study of matrilineal societies, comes to expression in Professor Ehrenfels' chapter. Dr. Khin Maung Win guarantees, as does the lawyer William J. Klausner, that the dominantly Buddhist people of Southeast Asia, between China and India, for whom religion traditionally had philosophical primacy, are not overlooked. They also illustrate the difference between (1) looking at a Buddhist Burmese village from the standpoint of a native-born believing Buddhist, nurtured by a mother's bedtime stories in his language, and then epistemologically trained as a philosopher in the recent West; and (2) seeing a similar Buddhist Thai village through the eyes of an American contractual lawyer, who later specialized in Southeast Asian Area studies, speaks Thai, is married to a Thai, and has lived in a Thai village for some seven years. The reader may find the chapter by the historically disciplined expert on Japan and Eastern Asian culture, Professor Tatsuro Yamamoto, of similar interest. There he summarizes the results of studies of Japanese mentality by Japanese anthropologists who use some recent methods of American social scientists. Professors E. Adamson Hoebel and Charles F. Hockett represent United States anthropology and insure that attention is given to the linguistic and the legal factors in culture, and that theoretically analytic and deductive as well as inductive anthropological methods are included. Professor Jacques Maquet wears several cultural and professional hats. By birth and early education he is a Belgian. He has a Ph.D. from Harvard University in sociology, specializing in the sociology of knowledge. Anthropologically he is Belgian, French, American, and British trained, focusing on Africa and implemented by several years with the Ruanda people in the Congo. Only by such diversity in national and cultural backgrounds and interests can the risk be lessened of taking as the elementary, or causally, primary concepts of all cultures those factors in human experience which are regarded as elemental in the nation, culture, or professional educational background of the observing anthropologist, or cultural philosopher.

These cultural anthropologists do more, however, than sample the present state of their science and recent methods for determining the cultural mentality or philosophy of a given people. All are also seeking more adequate theoretical concepts and methods. In fact, Professor Maquet actually initiates here the enterprise which the title of this book describes. This is why his chapter is put next in the Introduction section rather than in Part I, where it might equally appropriately fall. His application of epistemology to anthropology occurs when, drawing upon his expertness in the sociology of knowledge, he applies a preliminary epistemological analysis to Kluckhohn's thesis that philosophy is a universal cultural category and to the present methods of cultural anthropology including his (Professor Maquet's) own. His conclusions, nonetheless weighty even though they are modestly "tentative," must be allowed to speak for themselves. It sufficeth here to note but one thing. At the very least, his chapter shows from within cultural anthropology itself that epistemology is as important for this science as Einstein and other natural scientists have found it to be for mathematical physics. Thus he points up the over-all *raison d'être* of this book. *It anticipates that the interdependence of the skills of the epistemologically expert philosopher of science and those of the scientist is going to take on, in the decades ahead, the same importance in cultural anthropology (and ipso facto, in the social sciences and humanities generally) that similar collaboration between such philosophers and mathematical physicists has taken on since the century's opening.*

Why this indispensability of epistemology for any science that is not to remain "primitive and muddled"? Two relevant answers merit brief attention. One has to do with the nature of any scientific enterprise; the other with Einstein's own experience between his discovery and his publication of the Special Theory of Relativity.

The universal scientific reason becomes evident when one notes what the words *science* and *epistemology* mean. Any scientific inquiry is an exercise in human knowing, and the special science whose business it is to investigate human knowing *qua* human knowing is epistemology. Always, therefore, any science whose primary concern is some subject matter other than human knowing *qua* human knowing is the combination of the subject matter of that particular science and epistemology. Hence, not merely the "notable interdependence of science and epistemology," but also the "well-nigh unthinkable" notion of the one without the other. Nevertheless, since there is no point in human knowing except as it is the knowing of a specific something, Einstein's observation that epistemology without science is merely an empty scheme is correct also.

Einstein's personal experience of the necessity of epistemology for physics has to do with the relation between the directly observable data of the Michelson-Morley experiment of 1885 and Newton's claim that in the mathematically physical postulates of his mechanics he had introduced no hypotheses, but had, instead, deduced the assumptions of his theory from the directly inspectable experimental data.

Unfortunately, the space and time assumptions of Newton's theory, when supplemented electromagnetically by Maxwell, entailed a result other than that given in the Michelson-Morley experiment. Einstein's problem, therefore, was to find a way of reconciling the Michelson-Morley experimental data with the assumptions of Newton's mechanics and Maxwell's electromagnetics for that tremendous range of directly observable experimental data with respect to which both these theories had been empirically confirmed. Einstein's Special Theory of Relativity does precisely this.

Even so, he told the writer, he did not feel justified in publishing this theory upon his initial discovery of it, because of Newton's aforementioned epistemological account of the relation between the experimental data and the space-time assumptions of the Newtonian theory. The reason for this hesitancy to publish was twofold. First, Einstein's Special Theory entailed a rejection of Newton's universal postulates concerning space and time. Second, the experimental data confirming Newton's theory are repeatable today and therefore hold as much for Einstein as they did for Newton. Consequently, if the epistemological relation between Newton's experimental data entails Newton's postulates concerning space and time, Einstein must accept these postulates also, and, therefore, cannot reconcile the Michelson-Morley experiment with Newtonian mechanics and Maxwellian electromagnetics by substituting the space-time postulates of the Special Theory of Relativity for the quite different ones of Newton and of Maxwell. This would be warranted only if a fresh epistemological analysis of human knowing, not merely in physics, but also with respect to the ordinary man's directly sensed simultaneity of spatially separated events, showed Newton's epistemological theory of the relation between the directly observable data of ordinary and mathematical physical knowledge and the postulates of Newton's theory to be erroneous.

Einstein became convinced that such is the case by two independent means. The first was his own fresh epistemological examination of anyone's knowledge of the publicly meaningful simultaneity of spatially separated events.[4] It showed, as it will show anyone who examines the matter with epistemological care, that, although one senses the simultaneity of spatially separated events, such sensed simultaneity does not provide a meaning for public nowness for spatially separated events, but gives instead a simultaneity that is one thing for one person and a different thing for a person but a quarter of a mile away from him, even when both are at rest on the same physical frame of reference.[5] Einstein's other independent confirmation came from his reading of Hume's epistemological examination and description of what the senses give us. In this description Hume pointed out that we do not sense any relation of necessary connection. But, logical implication between the directly sensed data of an experiment and the postulates of Newton's theory is one of the strongest instances of necessary connection of which the mind is capable of conceiving. It follows, therefore, that no sensed data given by either ordinary observation or any physicist's experiments can logically imply, and thereby insure the deduction of, the postulates of any scientific theory from the experimental data. Instead, the deductive logic of both the ordinary person's and the mathematical physicist's belief in public time runs only in the converse direction, from the assumptions of the belief or theory to the ordinarily or experimentally sensed data. Newton's epistemological description of his knowledge in the science of mechanics is, therefore, erroneous.

Forthwith Einstein had two independently confirmable warrants for publishing his Special Theory of Relativity in 1905. Thus also did he personally experience the interdependence of the skills of the epistemologically trained philosopher of science and those of the scientist.

That the same may be true for cultural anthropology is suggested even by Kluckhohn in a reason which he gives in support of his conclusion that philosophy is a unique universal cultural category. This reason is that: "There is much more to social and cultural phenomena than immediately meets the ear and eye. . . . The 'strain toward consistency' which Sumner noted in the folkways and mores of all groups cannot be accounted for unless one postulates a more or less systematic pattern of reaction to experience as a characteristic property of all integrated cultures. In a certain deep sense the logic (that is, the manner of interpreting relationships between phenomena) of all members of the human species is the same. It is the premises that are different."⁶ The problem immediately arises concerning how, for the people of a particular culture, the anthropologist can know with scientific warrant that he has determined "their own" philosophical premises, or even whether this is humanly possible, unless anthropologists and epistemologists collaborate in an epistemological analysis of both the subject matter and the methods of anthropology, after the manner in which Einstein, both independently and in conjunction with his study of Hume, did this with respect to the ordinary person's and mathematical physicist's knowledge of the publicly meaningful simultaneity of spatially separated events.

The timeliness of the next chapter should now be evident. Its point of departure has been put concisely by Kluckhohn in the opening paragraph of his classical study, "The Philosophy of the Navaho Indians":

> The publication of Paul Radin's *Primitive Man as a Philosopher* did much toward destroying the myth that a cognitive orientation toward experience was a peculiarity of literate societies. Speculation and reflection upon the nature of the universe and of man's place in the total scheme of things have been carried out in every known culture. Every people has its characteristic set of "primitive postulates." As Bateson has said: "The human individual is endlessly simplifying and generalizing his own view of his environment; he constantly imposes on this environment his own constructions and meaning; these constructions and meanings are characteristic of one culture as opposed to another."⁷

FOOTNOTE REFERENCES

1. Schilpp, Paul A. (ed.), *Albert Einstein: Philosopher-Scientist*, Library of Living Philosophers, Evanston, Ill., 1949, vol. 7, pp. 683–684.
2. Kluckhohn, Clyde, "The Philosophy of the Navaho Indians," in F. S. C. Northrop (ed.), *Ideological Differences and World Order*, Yale, New Haven, 1949, pp. 356, 358.
3. For reasons, see Northrop, F. S. C., *Man, Nature and God*, Simon & Schuster, New York, 1962, p. 100.

4. Einstein, Albert, *The Theory of Relativity* (4th ed.), Methuen, London, 1921, ch. 8.
5. Northrop, F. S. C., *op. cit.*, note 3, pp. 211–212; see also Paul A. Schilpp (ed.), *The Philosophy of Alfred North Whitehead*, Library of Living Philosophers, Evanston, Ill., 1941, vol. 3.
6. Kluckhohn, Clyde, *op. cit.*, note 2, pp. 357–358.
7. *Ibid.*, p. 356.

Some Epistemological Remarks on the Cultural Philosophies and Their Comparison JACQUES J. MAQUET

2

This paper is concerned with some epistemological questions raised by the comparison of cultures from the philosophical angle. As it is written for a discussion in a symposium, I have not hesitated to put forward very tentative views, hoping to reap the benefit of criticism by colleagues.

Is Philosophy a Universal Category of Culture?

It is now commonly accepted by anthropologists that philosophy is a universal category of culture. That is to say, in any particular social heritage, there is a philosophy which is transmitted from one generation to the next, just as a certain type of family, cooperative patterns, and technological skills are parts of the culture of any society.

The admission of a category to the dignity of a cultural universal is usually founded deductively and inductively, but even if the latter reasoning is emphasized, the former is clearly more convincing. From a certain conception of the nature of man and society, it is deduced that any society, if it is to survive, must encompass in its culture a certain "aspect" or "compartment," for instance, the organization of the distribution of consumer goods. Such an organization being what is usually defined as an economic system, it is concluded that economy is a universal category. Then, it is added, we could reach the same conclusion inductively, as all the societies studied up to now present indeed an economic organization.

The affirmation that any people has a philosophy rests upon the same kind of reasoning, but here the inductive confirmation can hardly exist, as many of the societies known up to now, particularly the nonliterate ones, are devoid of any expressed philosophy. The deductive reasoning goes somewhat along the following lines. Rules of behavior are set by any society for its members in order to regulate their interpersonal relations; people have traditional ways of dealing with their physical environment; rituals are built around birth, puberty, death; members of a particular group exhibit patterned attitudes when confronted with disease, natural catastrophes, sorcery, and so on. All these observable phenomena must be explained, justified, and supported by a system of ideas concerning the world, the place of man in the world, his destiny, the nature of reality, the ultimate values. This system of ideas is a philosophy or a world view, in the sense that it attempts to determine what human, social, and physical reality means. However crude and uncritical it may be, it is knowledge: to observe data—external or internal, but distinct from the observer —and say what they are.

Up to this point, it is postulated that the phenomena the anthropologist observes—behaviors and objects—make sense for the culture bearers only because they correspond and are in harmony with their knowledge of man and nature. If philosophy is to be a universal compartment of culture, it must be further postulated that no society could survive without a system of explanation. This amounts to the assertion that there is in human society a "natural" need to understand. This affirmation is not always clearly stated, but it seems necessary if one wants to postulate a priori the universality in culture of the philosophical category. We shall call a *cultural philosophy* this philosophical part of a culture.

May a Cultural Philosophy Be Implicit?

In fact, there are nonliterate societies in which a world view is expressed with the scope and richness of a Western philosophical system. The Dogon, in the Niger valley, studied by Marcel Griaule and his students, provide certainly one of the best examples of an expressed, but esoteric, philosophy. But such cases are rare. Most of the time, we find only some scattered views on the world in rituals, proverbs, tales, or historical traditions. Even if put together, they do not constitute a philosophical system. Because of the very frequent absence of an expressed philosophy in nonliterate societies, Clyde Kluckhohn and others have put forth the concept of a covert or implicit philosophy.

If I may quote myself, "That covert part of a culture is partly or totally implicit in the sense that these fundamental conceptions and values remain for the culture bearers unexpressed or even unconscious. They are thus reached by induction, some by immediate inference from observation, some by a process encompassing several stages of abstraction."[1] Again:

They are located, so to speak, on different levels of abstraction. Some are arrived at by immediate inference from observation, as when we say, for instance, that for [the Ruanda] "the invisible world is a fearful reality." This statement may be immediately inferred from the behavior of the Ruanda people: their words, when they tell us their beliefs about the action of the spirits of the dead, and their behavior, if they are threatened by them. On the other hand, a statement such as "strictly contractual relationships are inconceivable for a [Ruanda]" is much more abstract because it is reached by successive stages from an analysis of the political organization of Ruanda.[2]

We shall come back later on to the inductive processes by which philosophical propositions are inferred from observed behavior. I would like to stress here the consequences of the covert character of the philosophy of many nonliterate cultures.

First, such an implicit philosophy does not belong to what Professor Hockett calls, in Chapter 8, the "two equally objective views that can be taken towards the life of any human community." It is not a part of the outside view "whose frame of reference is that of physics," as the philosophical propositions are not to be found formulated in the culture of the community; neither is it a part of the inside view, which is the view the members of a community have of themselves, as the covert philosophy is postulated by the anthropologist, but not expressed by the people themselves. Thus we arrive at the somewhat disturbing conclusion that the covert philosophy of a society, i.e., the set of inferences drawn by an anthropologist, cannot be said to be a part of that culture.

This, as such, does not have any negative bearing upon the validity of the inferences, but entails a second important consequence. It is that the implicit philosophy is not to be considered as a reconstruction of a system existing somewhere in that culture, either in esoteric traditions known only by a few initiates or in a forgotten past. The implicit philosophy is a research tool made by the anthropologist in order to connect and summarize different pieces of knowledge unrelated in the culture, and still more to gain a deeper insight into the behavioral patterns by seeing them as expressing one or a small number of unique and unstated premises, and finally to be able to predict some conducts and reactions. Although an implicit philosophy, through the functions just mentioned, is very close to the culture from which it is inferred, it remains external to it, is not a part of the social heritage of that society. Its function is analogous to that of, say, the Oedipus complex in the explanation of some particularities of the psychological setup of an individual. The Oedipus complex is a theoretical construct which may be a key permitting one to understand parts of the patient's behavior and to predict it in a certain measure; but this useful tool for the psychiatrist remains external to the patient.

Thirdly, the implicit philosophy is not to be expressed with concepts and categories taken from the culture studied. The anthropologist does not attempt to build a system of meanings which could be accepted by the members of the society he studies as their philosophy; he tries to build a system which is meaningful and useful to him and other anthropologists. His attitude is to be compared to the attitude of the student of biological or natural phenomena; the atomic theory is not to be understood by electrons. This consideration could perhaps alleviate the scruples of anthropologists who apologize when expressing the implicit philosophy of a non-Western people in Western terms. Concepts and categories used should be scientifically good, adequate, useful, operational for the constructs one wants to build; it does not matter if they are Western or not. If the anthropologist's reasoning does not permit him to infer from behavioral patterns some principles under which different observations can be subsumed, it is not because his tool is Western, but because it is inadequate. A biological theory, whatever its origin, Western or not, must use the conceptual language of its origin in accounting for all biological phenomena, Western or not.

We can answer now the questions formulated in the first two headings of this chapter. There is a cultural philosophy wherever a system of knowledge concerning the world and man is found expressed in a culture. This knowledge is a part of the inside view which a community has elaborated. When reporting such a philosophy, the anthropologist must be careful not to introduce concepts alien to it. The difficulties of translation are great. By a conceptual analysis, the observer attempts to establish the differences between the original concept used in the culture studied (which is expressed in the language of that culture) and the concepts in his own language and culture which are most akin to it. He will also attempt to follow the paths of the reasoning process which may be very different from the ones he uses in his own way of thinking. Such a transposition of a philosophy from one universe of thought to another can never be a complete success, but it should be attempted. Not to try it would be to give up any hope of communication between different cultures.

When no philosophical views are to be found expressed in a culture, we must conclude, I am afraid, that there is no cultural philosophy in that culture. Certainly a covert philosophy may be inferred from the observable behavioral patterns. Such a philosophy is not implicit in the sense that it is contained in the culture but in the sense that an external observer may integrate under its principles some traits of the culture. It is an *as if* construct. The behavioral patterns of a group of animals, chimpanzees, for instance—but also less "anthropomorphical" animals, such as a pack of wolves—can also be related to some world views assigned by the observer to the group. It may be said, for instance, that chimpanzees react to each other *as if* they recognized the authority of the strongest male, or *as if* the animals of other groups were enemies. It does not mean that authority and hostility are concepts of chimpanzees, but that by projecting his concepts, the observer is able to summarize different behavioral patterns and to relate them to a few principles of explanation.

To sum up, only an expressed world view may be said to constitute a cultural philosophy; implicit philosophies are useful constructs devised by an outside observer, but they are not part of the social heritage of the observed society. Consequently, it does not appear that philosophy may be considered as a cultural universal.

From now on, we shall use the term *philosophy* to denote expressed philosophy and the term *philosophical construct* to denote what has been called implicit or covert philosophy.

Epistemological Status of a Cultural Philosophy

Let us start with some fragments of an anthropological text on the material world as seen by an African people. It is one of the many similar reports to be found in anthropological literature. I have written it after a field study in Ruanda.

The world in which men are placed and which they know through their senses was created *ex nihilo* by *Imana*. The Ruanda word *kurema* means to produce, to make. It is here rendered "to create" because our informants say that there was nothing before *Imana* made the world. This belief concerning the origin of the material world is universal and clear. To any question on this point, the answer is ready.

The [Ruanda] assert that we do not see the whole of the material world which was created at that time. The world of our experience is flat; its limits are far away and made of fences like the ones we see around kraals. On these fences there is a big rock which is the sky we see. Beyond the rock, there is another world (*ijuru*) similar to our own, with hills, trees and rivers. This world may be said to be heavenly only in the sense that it is above the sky: it is not a paradise but rather a richer duplicate of our world. Under the soil on which we tread there is yet another world (*ikuzimu*) also conceived as similar to our own. . . .

In essentials our world was created as we see it now, but there have been some changes in the course of its history. . . . This, and a belief that the world is now slowly degenerating, getting old (people's stature is decreasing, cows give less milk), suggest that the Ruanda conception of the universe is not a wholly static one. The world does not remain the same, it is in process of evolution. However, when direct questions are asked, it appears that this conception of the life of the universe has not been the subject of speculation and is not of great importance to the [Ruanda].[3]

This description of a part of the Ruanda cultural philosophy belongs clearly to what Professor Northrop calls the natural history period of anthropology. The observer has attempted to express with the concepts of his culture the knowledge of the physical world that the Ruanda people have. If we admit that the basic unit of study remains for a large section of anthropology the culture of a particular society, such descriptions keep their usefulness.

On this level, the validity of the description rests upon the proper use of the field techniques of research. However, even at this stage, so close to the raw data of observation, the anthropologist chooses certain facts and neglects others. He is guided in his selection by his own conception of what is relevant to a view of the physical world; he asks questions only on certain points. Quite often, the "theory" under the description rests on uncritical common-sense conceptions. Progress consists in the awareness of that and in the replacement of these naive conceptions by hypotheses drawn from a theory.

This requirement is still more imperative when we pass from the description and analysis of a particular culture to the stage of the comparison of cultures. And obviously, anthropology is primarily concerned with the study of society and culture and not with the description of particular cultures. Such description is a first stage, an indispensable one, which must be overcome. It is only then that anthropology may claim to be a full discipline of knowledge.

At that comparative and synthetic level, anthropology verifies the characteristics of Western knowledge. As Professor Northrop has made clear in *The Meeting of East and West*, Western knowledge proceeds by a priori hypotheses controlled a posteriori by indirect verification. "The logic of the verification, even when it is empirical and experimental, is as follows: The theory is proposed; logic is applied to its basic assumptions and to their operationally determined empirical content. . . . [Thus] the consequences of the theory are deduced. These consequences are then put to the test of ordinary or experimentally controlled observation."[4]

To sum up, descriptions of cultural philosophies belong to the descriptive stage of anthropology, which is already dependent upon a theory, even if it is a not too consciously expressed common-sense conception. The criteria of validity are the same as those used for the description of any other aspect of a culture.

Before discussing in a more detailed manner some epistemological questions pertaining to the theoretical aspect of anthropology, let us consider the philosophical constructs.

Epistemological Status of a Philosophical Construct

From the Ruanda political behavior, we may infer a philosophical principle that I have called "the premise of inequality." Let us see how it has been reached.

An anthropologist can observe only the behavior of people engaged in particular social relations. A meets B and they interact in a certain way; then A meets C and they behave in another way. Later on, different roles will be distinguished in each individual: A is the father of B and the lord of C. A behaves the same way with respect to all the males who call him "father" and in a different way vis-à-vis all the people who call him "lord." And all the other "fathers" have much the same behavior as regards their sons and all the other "lords" as regards their inferiors. The role of father and the role of lord may be described. We are already on a certain level of abstraction.

The roles of the lord and his inferior may be isolated in a feudal institution existing in Ruanda. In this institution, the lord –inferior relation is hereditary. The lord's role appears protective and profitable. The anthropologist observes that protection is not restricted to a certain field, but potentially encompasses the whole of the inferior's life; that protection is not manifested by a set of particular obligations for the lord. It is up to the latter to decide the extent of his protection. The profits consists of dues and tribute labor provided by the inferior at the superior's discretion. The inferior role is complementary. Behavioral patterns of the two roles may be summed up by the words *paternalism* and *dependence*.

This is only a generalization of observations. Upon that basis, the anthropologist reasons as follows. When paternalism and dependence define permanent reciprocal roles, the relation is different from what it is when they express the transitory roles of a father and his young son. In the latter case, it is known that the son will grow up, and, one day, even if he has to wait until after his father's death, he will be equal to what his father was. But the inferior is not supposed to grow up; he will always remain in the dependent position. This implies that there is a fundamental inequality between the two persons, and this inequality is transmitted from generation to generation. The anthropologist concludes that the feudal relationship, as it exists in that society, supposes the underlying belief in the fundamental inequality of men. This schematized example makes clear that the principle of inequality does not belong to the culture of Ruanda: it is a logical inference drawn from observed facts by an anthropologist, and it has perhaps never been expressed by a member of the society.

Such a construct belongs to the theoretical level of anthropology; it "asserts more than observation gives, and is not verified directly. . . ."[5] It cannot be said to be true or false; it is a tool which is useful or not.

Its first utility is to *summarize* in a convenient form a certain number of observations which, at first sight, were not related. Various political behavioral patterns appear to be unified as expressions of the same general principle. Second, these conducts are *explained* as follows: Ruanda people behave *as if* they believed in the fundamental inequality of men and wanted to translate this belief in their social relations. Third, by assuming that the same principle will be applied also to behaviors other than the observed ones, it is possible to *predict* different ones.

It is also by the predictive function of the inferred principle that we will be able to verify its validity. The principle of inequality is now considered as a premise. That is to say, the anthropologist is going to deduce some consequences from the nonegalitarian proposition. In the Ruanda case, I have expressed these consequences as "a set of theorems, by which is meant general propositions or statements which are not self-evident." They are:

THEOREM I. When two persons are involved in any kind of social relation, it is their mutual hierarchical situation which is regarded as the most relevant element of the relation.

THEOREM II. As in almost any human relation, there is some superiority of one actor over the other; as that aspect is always stressed and as inferiority relations are patterned on intercaste relations, paternalistic and dependent attitudes were to be found in almost every human relationship in Ruanda.

THEOREM III. As the superior–inferior relations are patterned on the father–son model, there is no private sector in the life of the inferior vis-à-vis his superior.

THEOREM IV. Strictly contractual relations are not possible. To enter into a contract implies that the intended parties were previously independent of one another and equal, conditions that are very rarely realized in Ruanda.

THEOREM V. With such socially accepted conceptions about inequality, those who occupy the superior position in most of the social relations in which they are involved develop a permanent authoritarian behavior.

THEOREM VI. It is impossible to disagree overtly with one's superior's opinions. Consequently, dissimulation is to be valued and should be considered a necessary skill to be mastered by someone wanting to live peacefully in Ruanda.

THEOREM VII. The verbal behavior toward a superior expresses dependence rather than truth.

THEOREM VIII. Dependent attitudes in hierarchical relationships extend to all social relations a utilitarian usage of language.[6]

These theorems, deduced from the premise of inequality, have been tested by the usual anthropological techniques of observation and interviewing. It has been found out that in fact Ruanda people behave as they are expected to.

What is to be concluded from this positive indirect verification? It is that the whole construct postulated by the anthropologist (the inequality principle induced from facts and its theorems deduced from the premise) is a useful logical tool. Another theory would perhaps be better, that is to say, synthesize more facts, have a deeper explanatory value and a broader predictive capacity. It is very likely that such a theory would not strip the inequality construct from its limited value but would rather include it in a larger frame.

If I have given so many details on the philosophical construct drawn from the Ruanda material, it is because this material provides us with an example of deductive anthropology and the characteristics appearing in that example are illustrative, I think, of the deductive stage of anthropology. Indeed, up to now, we have seen that (1) the study of a cultural philosophy (as any other anthropological study of a division of a culture, such as political institutions or family structure) is at the descriptive stage of anthropology, and (2) when we want to compare different cultural philosophies, we have to use theoretical constructs characteristic of the deductive stage of anthropology. We have seen also that (3) when an anthropologist wants to construct an implicit philosophy, he is immediately in the deductive stage of anthropology.

We are thus entitled to consider that the epistemological problems raised by the study of the philosophical aspect of cultures are not different from those concerning the epistemological value of descriptive or deductive anthropology in general.

Is Deductive Anthropology a Science?

This question should be raised, as it cannot be assumed that deductive method is synonymous with science. Professor Northrop has shown that the theoretical method—"a hypothesis proposed a priori, verified in part at least indirectly through its experimentally checked deductive consequences"—is characteristic of Western knowledge. And he includes in Western knowledge the doctrinal content of philosophy and religion as well as science.[7] This clearly indicates that the deductive method is not restricted to science *sensu stricto*.

If we consider the kind of reasoning used in the induction from the observed behavior to the principle of inequality, and in the deduction from the premise of inequality to the theorems, it appears to be "loose" in the sense that inferences and deductions are not strictly drawn, are not logically necessary. These relationships manifest only a certain logical coherence: they indicate some possibilities and exclude others; they explain what happened and predict what will probably happen. The word *premise* should not be thought to imply that the relationships between the cultural principle and its cultural consequences obey the strictest laws of rational logic. This relationship may be said to be logical only in a very broad sense. Or, more accurately, we must clearly distinguish between *logical* and *rational*. There are relationships which are meaningful, although they express a sequence which is emotional or "psychological" or even unconscious rather than rational. Such relationships, however, may be said to be logical in the sense in which we speak of a logic of sentiments or emotions. This simply means that we expect them, "understand" them.[8]

The above characterization of a "coherent but not logically necessary sequence" is far from being entirely satisfactory. However, it seems to me that this is the crux of the matter. If the propositions deduced from a premise could be different from what they are, it means that the anthropologist has a choice. The theorem "The use of language in all social relations is utilitarian" follows neither necessarily nor immediately from the proposition "Men are fundamentally unequal." In a hierarchical society, it could happen that the superior stratum imposes on the other a very strict discipline, punishing so severely any act of dissimulation that a utilitarian use of language would not develop; it could happen also that a very strong ethical tradition, stressing the obligation to speak the truth, may effectively counteract the utilitarian conception of language. Thus the anthropologist, in "deducing" the theorem of the utilitarian language rather than other equally coherent consequences, has been led by considerations other than a strict logical reasoning; he has been influenced by his global knowledge of that society. Now, if the intuition of the observer has such bearing on anthropological deduction, it means that the subjective component in anthropological knowledge plays a very important role.

For that reason, it seems that anthropology, even in its deductive form, does not realize one of the characteristics of scientific knowledge: independence of the observer's subjectivity. It should not be concluded from this that anthropology as a body of knowledge has no validity. Its type of validity should be compared to that of history, in which a large place is also left to the interpretative ability of the historian in his reconstruction of the past. Literary criticism and art history are other disciplines which reach valid but not scientific results.

This affirmation that anthropology is a knowledge but not a science—in the sense that physics is a science—is hard to admit for anthropologists. To preserve the scientific character of anthropology, it could be maintained that if the observer's subjectivity plays an important part in the formulation of hypotheses, scientific objectivity reappears in the verification of these hypotheses. Is it not that the usual anthropological research techniques are such that, if used by different anthropologists, the results would be the same, thus independent of observers' personal biases?

I do not think that a general answer could be given to that question. On certain points it is surely possible for different observers to reach an agreement based on the objectivity of the research techniques. If an anthropologist postulates, for some theoretical reason, that in a certain society cross-cousin marriage should exist, it is possible for several anthropologists to agree, after having done independent research, that in fact some cases of cross-cousin marriage have been reported in this society. It is less likely that they will independently agree on the frequency of cross-cousin marriage. And how could several anthropologists critically establish the "fact" that "a utilitarian use of language is extended to all social relations"?

We must admit that in the sphere of world views, it is particularly difficult to reach independently the same factual statement. The often discussed problem of the translation of qualitative into quantifiable data is relevant to our problem. However, we are not going to raise it here. Only, it should be remembered that whatever are the theoretical possibilities of treating mathematically and statistically cultural phenomena, such treatment has very rarely been attempted by anthropologists, and then, principally in the religious, artistic, and philosophical aspects of a culture. Consequently, "facts" in these fields are very rarely established by mathematical and statistical methods on which contemporary sciences base their objectivity.

To sum up: In its present stage, comparative anthropology, using inductive and deductive logical processes and controlling by observation the deduced hypotheses, produces a knowledge belonging epistemologically to the sphere of the humanistic disciplines rather than to the sphere of the physicomathematical sciences.

A Priori Categories of Comparison

When setting up an explanatory theory, the anthropologist finds his factual starting point in observations usually made in a single culture. Later on, the verification of the postulated hypotheses again refers the anthropologist to phenomena of the same culture. If the empirical consequences of his hypotheses are contrary to the data observed in the same society, the theory has to be discarded. This indicates that the bare facts keep the supremacy in anthropology and that they usually belong to the same culture.

A consequence of this is a very close relation between the data collected in a culture and the theory made to order, so to speak, around these data. This does not make easy the comparison between the different theoretical constructs; a need for broader categories is felt. Such categories are to be found, for instance, in Ruth Benedict's dichotomy of Dionysian as opposed to Apollonian configurations; in Professor Sorokin's distinction of sensate, idealistic, and ideational cultures; and in Father Tempels' metaphysical duality of being and becoming.[9]

Such categories are a priori in the sense that they are founded on a very general human experience to which the first logical principles have been applied. They encompass all the logically possible cases. For instance, Professor Sorokin's three concepts are meant to cover all the possible philosophical positions concerning the ultimate nature of reality: (1) Either reality is what men can reach through their sense organs and is thus material (sensate premise); or (2) the universe of our senses is illusory and the true reality is beyond what we can perceive with them (ideational premise); or (3) it is partly perceptible and partly suprasensory (idealistic premise). The epistemological possibles of Professor Northrop—radical empiricism, naive realism, and logical realism —are also categories which can be used to classify cultures.

Two general problems are to be tackled with reference to these classifications of cultures: (a) Can entire cultures be characterized by their philosophies, rather than by other cultural phenomena? (b) Is it advisable to use a priori large categories whose total range should cover all the logical possibilities?

Philosophical Characterization of Cultures

It does not seem possible somewhat to elucidate the first problem without assessing the role of philosophy within a culture, that is to say, with reference to the other aspects of a culture, such as the economic system, political organization, religion, and so on. In fact, such an assessment itself depends on a general theory of culture. Anthropologists with a Platonic bent will certainly be inclined to assert that cultures should be characterized by their philosophical conceptions, as ideas appear to them to have a predominant place in reality. Materialistically minded anthropologists, on the contrary, will not be prone to classify cultures under philosophical headings, as this seems to grant ideas an undue importance.

Here is not the place to propose a general theory of culture, but it appears necessary to outline some points which are relevant to the question discussed here.

A cultural philosophy expresses, on the intellectual level, experiences lived by the members of a society in their dealings with one another, with people of different groups, and with their physical environment. Through what can be called, approximately, a process of generalization or abstraction, these various experiences are translated from their concrete occurrences into general views, which, by being general, seem to be explanatory and perhaps, on another level, diminish anxiety. A band of hunters maintains its livelihood by collecting and hunting, adapting itself to the forest, following the clues of vegetal and animal life, thus getting what is necessary for individual and collective survival. This existential experience of "cooperation" with the forest will be translated into a world view in which nature is a protective reality, a mother, and not an enemy to be mastered. Incidentally, this intellectual transposition of an existential experience may be what is meant by the Aristotelian principle that there are no ideas in the intellect which are not first in the senses.

This conception of a cultural philosophy as an intellectual reflection of the existential conditions met by the life of a group should not be understood as a rigid determinism. First, no society elaborates its world view from a philosophical *tabula rasa*. Each society has a history; consequently, it has been through different existential experiences, every one of which resulted in a specific intellectual transposition. This means that the world view of a society results not only from the contemporary experiences of the group, but also from the preceding world views. Because of this historical accretion, the philosophical compartment of the culture may, in literate and complex societies, manifest a considerable independence from the social conditions and give the impression of an autonomous development. The situation is not so extreme in a nonliterate society, but the past philosophical ideas certainly play an important part in the creation of new ones.

Second, there are direct external influences on the intellectual level. For instance, elements of a political philosophy may be imported even if they do not reflect the political institutions of the importing society. Again, these borrowings are particularly intense in literate societies, but they also take place in others even if they are less rapid and visible.

The action of past and external ideas in the building of a cultural philosophy has been briefly mentioned here because it permits us to assess more precisely how existential conditions influence world views. These conditions set limits to the range of possible ideas in the same way as, say, the technical substructure limits the range of possible political institutions. A society whose technical means do not permit the production of any surplus could not support a centralized government with a staff of specialized civil servants, dignitaries, and so on. In the same way, a society with an authoritarian and hierarchical political organization could not produce or even adopt a philosophy of individual freedom and personal responsibility. A direct intervention of political authorities may promote some ideas and prohibit others, but, even without censorship, only the political conceptions pertaining to the situation will be accepted. The political experience of the members of a society limits thus the range of their possible political conceptions.

If the theory proposed here is accepted, a cultural philosophy expresses the choice made by a particular society among the systems of ideas compatible with its experience. It is an intellectual vision of what it means for the people concerned to live in a particular society at a certain time. To that reflection of an existential situation are added ideas inherited from the past and lagging behind their determinant situation and ideas borrowed from other groups.

A cultural philosophy is thus an image, somewhat distorted, of the whole culture. In spite of these distortions and because of their imagelike character, philosophies may be used in order to compare cultures. However, one should never forget that world views are not primary but secondary cultural realities. Consequently, such comparisons do not bear directly on the elements which, in a culture, are fundamental and leading.

Another point should also be stressed. As indicated earlier, not all nonliterate societies have an expressed philosophy. All that has been said here is applicable only to cultures with an expressed philosophy. Philosophical constructs, although called implicit philosophies, cannot be said to be images of man and reality produced by the existential experience of a society. A characterization of the cultures by their philosophies could not cover all the known cultures, as some are aphilosophical, not expressing a world view.

But philosophies are not to be considered only as reflections of cultures. They may be regarded just as philosophies and compared as such in the same way political institutions or economic systems are studied and compared.

Classification by Philosophical Categories

These qualifications made, we may turn now to the other problem. In a comparative study of cultural philosophies, should we adopt a classification of a priori categories covering all logical possibilities?

Such classification has the advantage of being logically satisfactory and of responding to the requirements of the student of philosophy who has chosen it. If Professor Sorokin has chosen to classify philosophies from the point of view of their metaphysical assertions on the ultimate nature of reality, it is because this question was crucial from the point of view adopted in his *Social and Cultural Dynamics*. If Professor Northrop's classification is centered on the relations between knowledge and objects, it is because epistemological problems are at the focus of his research. It is, of course, perfectly legitimate for the student of a certain class of phenomena to use the conceptual tools he wants and to distribute the phenomena in the categories suitable for his purposes.

The philosopher then asks, so to speak, the question on which he focuses his research concerning the different cultural philosophies. Some cultural philosophies are focused on the same point and consequently fit perfectly well in the student's scheme; others, without being centered on the same point, have however explicitly considered the problem; still others have not included in their scope that question which is the main criterion of the classification.

The last case may often occur in nonwritten philosophies, or even in written ones which are not Western. It seems to me that the Ruanda philosophy is an idealistic one, but I do not think that the nature of the ultimate reality has ever been considered, by the Ruanda people, in the Sorokinian terms of material versus nonmaterial reality. Epistemological problems have been still more rarely, it seems to me, explicitly mentioned in the expressed philosophies of nonliterate societies. In such cases, the student of philosophy has to answer himself the crucial question of his classification on the basis of what he knows of the cultural philosophy of the society concerned.

Again, this does not question the value of the classifications we are considering now, but indicates, I think, a difference of points of view between philosophers and anthropologists. Broad logical a priori categories are best suited to investigations oriented toward the elucidation of philosophical problems.

Now, what would be the alternative approach used by anthropologists for the comparison of cultural philosophies? The starting point would be the cultural philosophies of a few societies considered as data; from these data, the categories necessary for a classification would be inferred. It is a process of postulating concepts and building theories which is very similar to the one we have discussed in connection with deductive anthropology. Fundamentally, it is not different from what has just been called the philosophical approach. The only difference lies in the distance from the data. Philosophical categories are implied from a general experience—which claims to be simply "human"—whereas anthropological data are inferred from more specific data. It can be said that it is only a difference of degree of generalization or abstraction, but it is a very significant one.

In conclusion, let us sum up the results we have reached in this section. To characterize cultures by their philosophies is a difficult enterprise: World views reflect imperfectly and with some lag in time the complete cultures of which they are a part. Comparisons and syntheses of cultural philosophies are made by a logical process of induction and deduction, but philosophically oriented researches use rather large a priori categories covering all the logical possibilities, whereas anthropologically oriented studies prefer to utilize concepts immediately inferred from the cultural philosophies considered.

FOOTNOTE REFERENCES

1. Maquet, Jacques J., *The Premise of Inequality in Ruanda*, International African Institute, Oxford, London, 1961, p. 160.
2. Maquet, Jacques J., "The Kingdom of Ruanda," in Daryll Forde (ed.), *African Worlds*, International African Institute, Oxford, London, 1954, p. 164.
3. *Ibid.*, pp. 166–167.
4. Northrop, F. S. C., *The Meeting of East and West*, Macmillan, New York, 1946, p. 297.
5. *Ibid.*, p. 294.
6. Maquet, Jacques J., *op. cit.*, note 1, pp. 165–170.
7. Northrop, F. S. C., *op. cit.*, note 4, pp. 294–295.
8. Maquet, Jacques J., *The Sociology of Knowledge*, Beacon, Boston, 1951, p. 165.
9. Benedict, Ruth, *Patterns of Culture* (1st ed., 1934), Penguin, New York, 1946; Sorokin, P. A., *Social and Cultural Dynamics*, vols. I–IV, American Book, New York, 1937–1941; Tempels, P., *La philosophie bantoue* (1st ed., 1945–1946), Présence Africaine, Paris, 1959.

One

Philosophy in the Cultures of
Ancient Mexico MIGUEL LEÓN-PORTILLA

3

Introduction

Superior institutions of culture flourished in ancient Mexico for at least two millennia before the arrival of the Spaniards in 1519. A long process of cultural evolution with ups and downs had occurred in pre-Hispanic Mexico. Ceramics and sculpture; architecture and mural painting; writing and calendars; intricate religious doctrines and systems of education; different political, religious, and social organizations were some of the creations in that long cultural sequence.

These creations, especially the traceable history of ideas in pre-Columbian Mexico, offer the philosopher of culture a unique field of research: the opportunity of contemplating man, basically isolated from the old civilizations of Asia and Europe, creating institutions, doctrines, and forms of life in a different natural and cultural setting. The patient work of some of the surviving native wise men and a handful of humanistic missionaries immediately after the Conquest and of contemporary archaeologists, philologists, and historians have rescued for all time the cultural legacy, particularly the native documents so essential for the study of the civilization of ancient Mexico. This rich documentation makes possible an approach to what might be called the philosophy of the cultures of ancient Mexico.

The Sources

Limiting ourselves in this chapter to the cultures that flourished in Mexico's central plateau, it is possible to distinguish a triple documentary legacy. The first consists of about nine codices, or books of pictures, dating back to pre-Hispanic times, which are still preserved in American and European libraries. In addition to these there are about thirty other codices, which are copies made during the sixteenth century of the pre-Hispanic codices that had disappeared. Many of these books of pictures, written principally in ideographs but also in their partially phonetic representation of Náhuatl, the language of the Aztecs and Toltecs, are indispensable documents in the study of their philosophy.

The second source consists of the hundreds of folios written by some of the natives in the Náhuatl language, using the Latin alphabet they had learned, by which means they preserved the poems, songs, chronicles, and traditions they had been made to learn by rote in their schools during the era prior to the Conquest. It is certain that some of the humanistic friars had a hand in the editing of these documents, such as Sahagún, for example, who asked the Indians acting as his informants to write from memory what they knew about their ancient civilization. It is no exaggeration to say that these hundreds of folios constitute the richest record we have as a source for study. These texts have received more serious attention in the last two decades.[1]

Archaeological findings with their inscriptions and their representations of the gods which become richer day by day make up the third source for penetrating their religious and philosophical ideas. To all these sources can be added the various histories and chronicles written during the sixteenth century by missionaries and authorities of the Crown, also based upon information supplied by the Indians. If these works often interpret Náhuatl thinking in terms of their own, they nevertheless allow us a glimpse into the first reaction of the Europeans to the multiple evidences of the superior civilization of the ancient Mexicans.

Formation of the Náhuatl *Weltanschauung*

It is essential to caution the reader, who might be unfamiliar with the nature of the pre-Hispanic Mexican cultures, against the often mistaken notion that the Aztecs are singularly representative of this region of America. In reality, the Aztecs with all their military and political greatness constituted only one branch of the great tree of Náhuatl peoples. Having arrived in the Valley of Mexico at about the middle of the thirteenth century, the important role they played was confined to the last century prior to the Conquest. Around 1428, they embarked upon an extraordinary social and religious reform, and, in accordance with their notion of being the Sun's chosen people, they adapted several of the cultural institutions of more ancient peoples to their warlike ends. Archaeology places the origin of civilization in ancient Mexico between the second and third millennia before Christ, in the light of which the duration of Aztec power, coming at the end, is brief indeed.

In this study of ancient Mexican philosophy, we will take as our point of departure what is called the *classical* period, which began more or less at the start of the Christian era. In the central plateau at that time, there arose the imposing religious center of Teotihuacán, "the city of the gods," which is mentioned in the earliest written documents. The oldest traditions which relate the sacred sites to various myths concerning the cosmic and human origins appear to go back to this time.

In agreement with ancient Náhuatl lore, there appears to have occurred a definite fusion of peoples in the central plateau where, prior to the Christian era, the already established agriculturists and worshipers of an "old god" Huehuetéotl came into contact with peoples migrating from the northeast, namely, from the direction of the Pánuco River on the Gulf Coast. These migrants are described as a people with a high degree of culture, possessing books of pictures, music, and song, and as followers of a supreme god whom they designated "Master of the Everywhere, who is like the night and the wind" (*Tloque, Nahuaque, Yohualli, Ehécatl*).

Continuing their march, the migrants arrived at Teotihuacán, which is some twenty-eight miles northeast of the present city of

Mexico. There, as one text states, "they established themselves and the wise men became the rulers." After the decline of Teotihuacán, another people, the Toltecs, took up these beliefs. They were descendants, at least in part, of Náhuatl-speaking peoples who had come down from the northern plains and created Tula around the ninth century A.D. (Tula is approximately forty miles north of Mexico City.) Their ideas probably constitute the most ancient roots of a philosophy which was to spread, later, throughout the entire central highlands of ancient Mexico.

The Toltec Heritage

The value which the later Nahuas-Texcocans, Aztecs, Huexotzincas, and Tlaxcallans placed on everything of Toltec origin is demonstrated by the fact that their supreme ideals in art, education, thought, and way of life came to be identified with their concept, historical or legendary, of Toltec creation in these fields. The word *toltécatl* became synonymous with "artist."

The origin of *Toltecáyotl* (Toltecdom), the Toltec creations taken as a whole, was attributed by the Nahuas to Quetzalcóatl who, according to some Indian documents, lived around the ninth century A.D. in Tula. Quetzalcóatl built in the Toltec metropolis marvelous palaces oriented toward the four directions of the universe. There he discovered, for the benefit of his people, metals and precious stones, the cultivation of cotton and many other plants of inestimable value. He taught them their many arts: how to cure the sick; the technique of farming to produce a greater yield from the land; how to find precious metals and how to work them; the making of tapestries and plumed headdresses of colored feathers; the arts of song, painting, sculpture, and architecture. And in addition to all this, as the most precious fruit of his long hours of meditation, he gave them an aesthetic image of divinity, conceived under various names, as a supreme dual being with a male and a female countenance, who, creating and conceiving in perfect unity, produced the cosmic forces, the universe, man, and everything that exists. This supreme divinity, who was a single god with two faces, *Ometéotl*, the Dual God, "demanded nothing," as one text expressly says, "but serpents and butterflies which all men should offer him, which all men should sacrifice to him."[2]

The great priest Quetzalcóatl was born around A.D. 845. As culture hero of the Toltecs he appears as the creator of their various institutions, arts, and religious doctrines. The text quoted below, which is taken from an ancient compilation made in Cuauhtitlan, a town to the northwest of Mexico City, describes the penances done by Quetzalcóatl, his discovery of the supreme divinity, and his creation of the arts:

> Our prince Quetzalcóatl:
> Four were his houses,
> in which he resided:
> his house of turquoise-colored beams,
> his house of coral,
> his house of shells,
> his house of quetzal feathers.
>
> There he prayed,
> did penance and fasted.
> And very late at night,
> he descended to the waters,
> there in the so-called palace of water,
> the tin-colored place,
> and there he placed his thorns for self-sacrifice,
> on top of Mount Xicócotl,
> in Huitzco and in Tzincoc,
> and on the mountain of the Nonohualcas.
> And he made his thorns
> out of precious stones,
> and his offerings of fir branches
> out of quetzal plumage.
> When he offered fire,
> he offered real turquoises, jade, and coral.
> And his offering consisted of serpents, birds, and
> butterflies, which he sacrificed.
>
> And it is related, it is said,
> that he prayed to his god,
> to someone who is deep within the sky;
> to "She of the starry skirt,"
> to "He who makes the things to shine";
> Lady of our flesh,
> Lord of our flesh;
> She who is dressed in black,

He who is dressed in red;
She who lends support to the earth,
He who covers it with cotton.*
And there did he direct his words,
so it was known,
toward Omeyocan, the Place of the Duality,
the place of the nine beams
of which heaven consists.
And as they saw,
those who lived there,
Quetzalcóatl directed his supplications,
offered his prayers,
with great humility and repentance.

And in his time, Quetzalcóatl discovered great riches,
the precious stones, the genuine turquoises,
gold and silver,
coral and shells,
feathers of quetzal and of the turquoise-colored bird,
yellow plumage of the Zacuan bird,
and flame-colored feathers.
And he also discovered
different kinds of cacao,
different kinds of cotton.
He was a very great artist
in all his works . . .[3]

It is asserted that Quetzalcóatl, in his meditation mo-teotia, "searched for a god for himself," endeavoring, for his own sake, to get close to the supreme mystery of divinity. In this way, he went on discovering new attributes of the ancient Dual God, the master of two distinct faces. Among many others, he invoked him with the following pairs of designations, an example of what might be called impressionistic aesthetic images: She of the starry skirt, He who makes the things to shine; Lady of our flesh, Lord of our flesh; She who is dressed in black, He who is dressed in red; She who lends support to the earth, He who covers it with cotton.

That Quetzalcóatl the priest took his name from Quetzalcóatl the god, symbol of the wisdom of the supreme dual deity, is made plain in an ancient Toltec hymn:

* These are the different titles in litany form which were first used in Toltec times to invoke the Dual God, Ómetéotl, Lord and Lady of our flesh . . . who lives in the supreme Place of the Duality: Omeyocan.

Only one god did they have,
and they held him as the only god,
they invoked him,
they supplicated him;
his name was Quetzalcóatl.

The supreme guardian of their god,
his priest,
his name was also Quetzalcóatl. . . .
He told them, he preached to them:
"This one god,
his name is Quetzalcóatl.
Nothing does he exact
but serpents, but butterflies,
that thou shouldst offer him,
that thou shouldst sacrifice to him."[4]

The Toltec Concept of the World

The god Quetzalcóatl, symbol of the wisdom of the ancient dual deity, had given origin and form to the world in which we live. This world, drenched in symbols, in which man attempts to draw closer to the deity through sacrifice and meditation, takes on a definite shape in the Toltec mind. The surface of the earth is a great disk situated in the center of the universe, which extends horizontally and vertically. Around the earth is the vast water which causes the world to be "entirely encircled by the water" (cemanáhuac). The earth, and its vast ring of water, are divided into four great quadrants or sectors which, opening out from the center of the world, extend to where the water joins the heavens and receives the name "the heavenly waters." The four great parts of the world swarm with symbols. The east, where the sun rises, is the region of light and fertility symbolized by the color white; the north is the region of death, the black sector of the universe; the west is the dwelling place of the sun, the region of the color red; and, lastly, to the left of the sun's course is the south, the place of thorns and of the color blue.

Vertically above and below this water-encircled earth are nine celestial tiers and nine regions associated with the world of the dead. The heavens, together with the water which completely encircles the earth, form a kind of vault furrowed with courses separated from each other by the great celestial beams. In the first five tiers are the courses of the moon, the stars, the sun, the evening star, and the comets. Above them are the heavens of the different colors and, finally, the region of the gods. Over all is the Omeyocan (the Place of the Duality) where the Dual God, the Giver of Life and Guardian of the Universe, exists.

Because he is in all places, the supreme god is designated as the "Master of the Everywhere" (*Tloque-Nahuaque*). From beyond the clouds he rules the movement of the moon and the stars, which are "the skirt which covers his feminine aspect," and by giving the sun the power to illuminate the day, he reveals his masculine characteristic of creator, endowed with a marvelous life-giving power. The other gods, popularly considered as the sons of the Dual God, form the multiple extensions which make possible his omnipresence. First they were the four forces, the four *Tezcat-lipocas*, each being equivalent to one of the four elements: earth, air, fire, and water (an interesting parallel with classic Greek and Hindustani philosophy). They took action from the four sections of the universe in each of the four prior ages, or "cosmic suns," introducing into the world all conflict, cataclysms, and evolution of things. With a dialectic rhythm, which in vain attempts to harmonize the dynamism of opposing forces, the various ages or "suns" of the world consecutively appeared and vanished.

Centuries later the Aztecs would conceive an ambitious project, that of impeding or at least postponing the cataclysm which was to put an end to their Sun, the fifth of the series. This idea became an obsession which stimulated and made them powerful, ultimately transforming them into

. . . a people with a mission. A chosen people who believed their mission was to side with the sun in the cosmic struggle, to side with goodness to ascertain its triumph over evil, and to give all of humanity the benefits of the victory of the forces of light over the dark powers of night.[5]

But this idea of collaborating with and preserving the life of the Sun, which no doubt was to constitute the cornerstone of the Aztec world view, should not lead us away from its strictly philosophical origin. If the Aztecs drew such a mystico-religious concept from the ancient Toltec doctrine of the Suns or ages, the doctrine in itself surrenders an explanation for the nature and the becoming of the world.

The Toltec image of the world, the concept of the supreme dual god, the arts, calendar, and social organization of the followers of the priest Quetzalcóatl, became three centuries later a cultural heritage of many other peoples. About the twelfth century the Toltecs, overrun by hordes arriving from the north, had to abandon their city. Descending into the Valley of Mexico and intermarrying there with people of other groups, the ancient inhabitants of Tula gave birth, or at least new life, to several city-states of Náhuatl language and culture. Among the new centers of culture were Culhuacan, Azcapotzalco, and Texcoco. There the Toltec heritage was preserved and even enriched until the arrival of the Aztecs about the thirteenth century.

The Aztec Mystico-Martial World View

According to their traditions, the Aztecs, who were the last of the Náhuatl-speaking peoples, came to the Valley of Mexico from the mythical "place of the seven caves" (*Chicomóztoc*). There, in ancient times, their tutelary numen, *Huitzilopochtli*, had spoken to them, ordering them to move on in search of a kind of "promised land." The place in which they finally were to settle was to be marked by the presence of an eagle sitting on some cactus and devouring a serpent.

The prolonged wandering of the Aztecs was fraught with difficulties, and the vicissitudes which they suffered are described in several of their ancient codices. Their presence in the valley awakened suspicion and provoked persecution on the part of those ancient peoples who were the heirs of the Toltec culture. Barely a century after having made their appearance in the Valley of Mexico did they arrive at the site designated by their god, and, in 1325, the will of the gods being made manifest, they finally became established on the little island where they found an eagle devouring a serpent.

However, another hundred years were to pass before the Aztecs would initiate the period of their real greatness, which, in 1428, was given its impetus by their victory over their neighbors, the people of Azcapotzalco, who, until that time, had been masters of the island on which was erected the city of Mexico-Tenochtitlan. The result of their victory was a rapid change in all phases of Aztec life. An extraordinary Aztec figure by the name of Tlacaélel was to be responsible for the cultural and ideological transformation of his nation.

Determined to augment the grandeur of the Aztecs, not merely by titles and lands, Tlacaélel resolved to furnish his people with a new rendering of their history, for he felt that the ancient hieroglyphic books did not give either the Aztecs or their god Huitzilopochtli sufficient importance. Hence, he set out to burn the old codices "because they preserved many falsehoods and, in them, many have been falsely held as gods. . . ."[6] As is evident, this new perspective on Aztec history resulted from the desire to exalt a hitherto persecuted people, and his action provided a firm foundation for the subsequent grandeur and world view of the Aztecs.

The ancient Toltecs had believed that there had been several ages or suns prior to the fifth age in which they were living. Previous ages always ended in cataclysms. With these ancient myths as a basis, the Aztecs formulated a mystico-martial concept of the universe for the purpose of preventing the disintegration or death of this fifth Sun, called "The Age of Motion."

From an ancient myth speaking of the sacrifice of the gods, who, by means of their death and their blood gave life to the sun, the Aztecs concluded that the sun and the universe required a certain vital energy in order to exist, which, as the gods had established, was the blood—the miraculous substance which kept human beings alive. Therefore, the offering of human victims to the sun was vital because their blood would provide the sustenance that would prevent its death. "The Florid Wars," or ritual wars, were organized for capturing prisoners to be offered up to the sun Huitzilopochtli. Combining the idea of war and the conquest of peoples with their prime mission of preserving the life of the sun and of this fifth age, the Aztecs aptly fused their drive for martial superiority with the supreme—almost mystic—religious image of themselves as the chosen people and cosmic collaborators of the deity.

Closely related to their mystico-martial philosophy was the Aztec belief that all those who fell in the Florid Wars became the attendants of the sun. Transformed into exquisite birds, the warriors became part of the entourage which accompanied the sun as it moved across the sky illuminating the day. Similarly, women who died in childbirth, with a prisoner in the womb, also became the attendants of the sun.

Now dedicated to war, this once unknown people reorganized its armies and persevered in its conquests until its empire extended from one ocean to the other and reached as far south as what today is Guatemala. The ancient calendar, inherited from the Toltecs, set the yearly cycle of the sacrifices to the gods. In this way was established what might be called a perpetual drama in which the human victims, before being sacrificed, were actors playing the roles of the gods, and, hence, reliving in these rites the ancient acts of the gods who also died that their blood might make possible the life of the Sun and consequently of all that exists.

The Aztec celebrations and sacrifices, held in honor of their gods throughout the year, rooted in the mystico-martial ideals, kept alive their own interpretation of the ancient myths. The priests of the innumerable temples, erected in all of central Mexico, had in their charge the cult of the various deities who, in great part, were nothing more than the diverse names and representations of the supreme Dual God and of his first children Quetzalcóatl and the Tezcatlipocas. Thus the faith of the People of the Sun was kept vital and vigorous.

However, the native texts that speak of the mystico-martial splendor of the Aztecs also give testimony to other modes of thought current during the same period, which, in a certain way, were diametrically opposed to the martial ideal. These were developed by several princes and wise men of various Náhuatl cities.

The Doubts of the Wise Men

That there were men with a radically different philosophy from the mystico-martial one of the People of the Sun indicates that in pre-Hispanic Mexico there was a serious weighing of ideas. Several of the figures responsible for this new philosophical approach are known to us by name: Nezahualcóyotl, King of Texcoco; Tecayehuatzin, Prince of Huexotzinco; Ayocuan of Tecamachalco, among others. In a most interesting and enlightening text, Sahagún's informants describe the ideal *tlamatinime*, knowers-of-things, and in the margin of this text Sahagún, in his own hand, notes, "wise men or philosophers."

> The *tlamatini*: He who knows,
> a light, a torch, a stout torch that does not smoke . . .
> From him emanate the books of pictures,
> he is the embodiment of writing and knowledge.
>
> He is the way, the true guide of others . . .
> teacher of the truth, he never stops reproving.
> He makes other faces wise,
> he makes others take on a countenance,
> he makes them develop it . . .
> He holds a mirror before others,
> he makes them mindful and judicious.
>
> He shines his light on the world,
> he inquires into the region of the gods above,
> and into the region of the dead below. . . .[7]

It was one of the same *tlamatinime* who first expressed his doubts about the validity of the Aztec conquests by war, through the figure of the fifteenth-century King Itzcóatl, who, with his counsellor Tlacaélel, initiated the idea of the People of the Sun. It is true, he says, that Itzcóatl effected great conquests, but, despite everything, he too disappeared into the region of mystery:

> To this song goes the march
> to the region of mystery!
> You are celebrated, O Itzcóatl,
> exquisite were the words you spoke,
> but you are dead! . . .
>
> Hence, when I remember Itzcóatl,
> a sadness invades my heart,
> Is it that he was finally weary?
> Or that indolence overcame the master of the house?
> The Giver of Life makes no one endure . . .
> Thus, the cortege continues:
> it is the common march![8]

Reflections such as the above, which emphasize the futility of conquest by war, appear frequently in the ancient native manuscripts. One of the Náhuatl wise men, probably thinking about the ancient benevolent god of the Toltecs who had been obscured, to some extent, by the ever-increasing dominance of the Aztec warrior god, Huitzilopochtli, formulated the following questions: Why has the God who lives beyond the heavens, as they say, hidden himself? Is he, perhaps, weary, or is it that we can know nothing at all about him?

> You are in the innermost regions of the heavens,
> giving origin to your word . . .
> You, who are God.
> What is it that you determine there?
> Is it that for us on earth
> you have been overcome by weariness?
> Must you hide from us your glory and your splendor?
> What is it that you determine on this earth?[9]

Then, relating this long-forgotten god whose fame and glory are hidden from the earth to the meaning of man and his fate, the Náhuatl wise man asks himself:

> What are we to you, O God?
> Thus we live,
> thus, in this place of oblivion
> we go on losing ourselves.
> We mortals,
> where are we to go?
>
> Hence, I weep,
> for you are weary,
> O God.
> Jade shatters,
> the quetzal feather tears apart.
> O God, you mock us.
> Perhaps we really do not exist.
> Perchance we are nothing to you?[10]

In order to provide an answer to these questions, an assertion is made which, to some extent, appears fatalistic, but in reality aims at a possible explanation of the meaning of man in the eyes of the deity:

> Our Lord,
> Master of the Everywhere,
> thinks as he pleases,
> he determines, he amuses himself.

As he wishes, so it is.
He holds us in the cup of his hand,
moving us about at his whim.
Like marbles we roll around.
He shifts us about aimlessly.
We are the object of his diversion,
He laughs at us.[11]

This is a very different answer to the problem of man in relation to the deity from the Aztec's warlike mysticism. However, while man appears to be merely an object of diversion for god, the Náhuatl wise men were not, as might logically be expected, driven into a philosophy of pessimism. On the contrary, the native texts repeatedly maintain that man "in spite of everything, is free to make his countenance wise and his heart firm." Another ancient exhortation which might, at first glance, appear to be a Náhuatl version of Stoicism, confirms this belief:

Our god has given man
laughter, sleep, the sustenances of life,
his strength, his vigor
and, finally, the sexual act
by which he sows his seed.
All these give a rapture to life on earth,
that man not always weeps.
But even were it so,
were it true that man lives only to suffer,
were this the way things are on earth,
must man, then, always live in fear?
Must he drown himself in tears?

Man lives on this earth!
Here, there are lords, there is power, there is nobility.
Who goes about always moaning
that thus it is on earth?
Who tries to put an end to himself?
There is ardor, there is life, there is struggle,
the search for a woman, the search for a man.[12]

This type of profoundly human reflection was not the ultimate, however, to which the native wise men attained, for when they had justified man's existence on earth, they pushed their thinking still further. In the face of Aztec religious doctrines and practices is the assertion that possibly even the sacrifices to the gods cannot open the way to truth. Religion, particularly the religion of the People of the Sun, might help realize great conquests, but not resolve the great enigmas of the universe:

> Even if emeralds, even if fine unguents,
> we offer the Sun, Giver of Life,
> even if he is invoked with necklaces,
> and with the might of the eagle and the tiger,
> it is still possible
> that no one speaks the truth on earth.
> How many can say whether there is truth here?
> O god, Giver of Life,
> You are truly inexorable![13]

Leaving sacrifices to the religious cult of the people, the wise knowers-of-things propounded a series of questions quite similar to those posed by the thinkers in other times and other civilizations. Thus, they asked themselves: What is the root (in Náhuatl this signifies "the truth") inherent in this world? Their questions phrased in images are significant and expressive:

> Perchance, it is true that one lives on earth?
> Not forever on earth: only a little while here.
> Be it jade, it shatters,
> be it gold, it breaks,
> be it quetzal feather, it tears apart.
> Not forever on earth: only a little while here.[14]

If everything is transitory, if the world in which we live is fated to end in a cataclysm as the ages preceding ours have, then it is inevitable to ask oneself if life is a kind of dream, if it is unreal, if we can be certain of knowing anything:

> Perchance we speak some truth on earth?
> We merely dream, we merely arise from our dreams.
> It is just a dream . . .
> And here no one speaks the truth. . . .[15]

Further, if existence on earth appears to be a dream, the problem of the root, or truth of things, also becomes pressing with regard to man himself. There arises, then, in Náhuatl philosophy the direct question as to the reality of man:

> Man is real, perchance?
> If not, then our song is no longer real.

What is to happen?
What is it that can be achieved?[16]

Such questions as these urged the Náhuatl thinkers into a search for a solution, and the paths they followed to find the answers were numerous and varied. One characteristic example, among many that could be cited, resulted from a gathering of the wise men, around the end of the fifteenth century, in the house of Tecayehuatzin, King of Huexotzinco, where, more than merely a solution, an extremely original position was reached for framing the problems. The subject under discussion at this gathering was the meaning of poetry, art, and symbolism. Making use of a metaphor indigenous to the Náhuatl language, these pre-Hispanic thinkers gave a name to their supreme creations by joining two words. For them, poetry, art, and symbolism were "flower and song." In their own words, the purpose of the gathering was to clarify "flower and song" in its deepest sense.

The opinions of those present at the gathering were diverse. For some, "flower and song" provided a means for drawing closer to the deity; for others, it only signified that thing which makes friendship and understanding possible among human beings. For King Ayocuan, "flower and song" was the only thing of value that man could leave, as a remembrance, on earth; for another *tlamatini*, it was the maximum consolation for princes and wise men.

Finally, King Tecayehuatzin spoke. He saw poetry, art, and symbolism as the only means for speaking true words on earth, words capable of bringing the truth to man in a world which is like a dream, in which everything is transitory and, like a quetzal feather, tears apart. These are King Tecayehuatzin's words:

. . . The chirruping bird
winging and singing,
offers flowers, offers songs . . .
Flower and song:
The only truth, perhaps, there is on earth.[17]

This answer, implying as it does the principle of an aesthetical, radically empirical view of the world, to use F. S. C. Northrop's terminology, engendered many repercussions which are manifest in numerous Náhuatl texts, not just in the field of philosophical speculation, but also, more particularly, in art. Wise men and artists are transformed into questors after "flower and song." As

Robin A. Drews

is stated repeatedly, "flower and song" are present only in the soul of those who have learned "to converse with their own hearts." The result of this inner dialogue is a kind of deification of the innermost self which should impel the "deified heart" to undertake "the deification of things," that is, the introduction of "flower and song" into all that exists.

The native wise men were aware that whoever introduced "flower and song" into himself and even into inert matter was, in a way, creating a fiction. Referring to their potters, they said that by mixing symbols with clay they were "teaching it to lie," that is, making it take on infinite guises. They believed that, invention or not, the symbol in combination with matter or with the ego has a message and a truth for man.

In this way the *tlamatinime*, the knowers-of-things, discovered the hidden poetic potentialities of thought. Through the medium of "flower and song," as the texts show, they inquired into such problems as free will, time, immortality, and new concepts concerning the deity. Instead of taking the path of pure logic, the Náhuatl philosophers followed the way of poetic symbolism, so that in the face of human suffering and the universal evanescence of things, they could build a spiritual home for themselves in which "flower and song" made possible the incursion into, and the rooting of, the truth on earth.

Conclusion

Only the central themes in the evolution of the philosophical thinking in ancient Mexico have been discussed here. Investigators of Asian and European cultures will probably find several parallelisms with the thinking of the ancient Mexicans. The belief in a supreme dual principle, mother and father of the gods and of man, as well as a concept of the world with the four corners of the universe, their characteristic colors, the four elements, the heavenly tiers, and the nether world of the dead are undoubtedly analogous to some concepts in the civilizations of India, China, and Tibet. Are these simply parallelisms, or did there exist in ancient times some kind of cultural dissemination?

As yet, we believe that a definitive answer cannot be formulated. Those who are inclined toward the idea of cultural dissemination should remember the inexplicable absence of such cultural elements as the practical use of the wheel, the concept of weight, and the development of balance scales, among other things, in pre-Columbian Mexico. Besides, it cannot be ignored that many parallelisms in material or intellectual culture can also be explained as the independent result of the innate capacities of all human beings which make them apply relatively similar solutions to similar problems which crop up in different latitudes and times. It seems at least unquestionable that the peoples of ancient Mexico reached the climax of their culture radically isolated from the civilization of the ancient world. From this point of view, they offer a unique opportunity for the study of man, as the creator of a culture with a history and a specific philosophy.

FOOTNOTE REFERENCES

1. Garibay K., Angel Ma., *Epica Náhuatl* (Náhuatl Epics), Biblioteca del Estudiante Universitario, National University of Mexico Press, Mexico City, 1945; *Historia de la Literatura Náhuatl* (A History of Náhuatl Literature), Editorial Porrúa, Mexico, 1953–1954, 2 vols. (a fundamental work on the literary creations of the various Náhuatl-speaking groups of ancient Mexico); León-Portilla, Miguel, *La Filosofia Náhuatl, Estudiada en Sus Fuentes* (Náhuatl Philosophy, Studied at Its Sources), Ediciones Especiales del Instituto Indigenista Interamericano, Mexico, 1956 (2nd ed., National University of Mexico Press, 1959); *Aztec Thought and Culture* (English ed.), University of Oklahoma Press, Norman, 1963; "A Náhuatl Conception of Art," *Evergreen Review*, vol. 2, Spring 1959, pp. 157–164.
2. Codex Matritensis of the Royal Spanish Academy of History, f. 173 r.
3. The Annals of Cuauhtitlan, preserved in the Library of the National Museum of Mexico. See the paleography of this Náhuatl text apud Walter Lehmann, *Die Geschichte der Königreiche von Culhuacan und Mexico*, Stuttgart, 1938, pp. 75–78.
4. Codex Matritensis, loc. cit.
5. Caso, Alfonso, "El Aguila y el Nopal," in *Memorias de la Academia Mexicana de la Historia*, vol. V, 2, Mexico, 1946, p. 103.
6. Codex Matritensis, f. 192 v.
7. Ibid., f. 118 r.

8. *Manuscript of Mexican Songs,* preserved at the National Library of Mexico, f. 29 v.
9. *Ibid.,* f. 13 v.
10. *Ibid.,* f. 12 v.
11. Sahagún, Fray Bernardino de, *Florentine Codex, General History of the Things of New Spain,* book VI (unpublished). Preserved at the Laurentian Library in Florence, f. 43 v.
12. *Ibid.,* f. 44 r.
13. *Manuscript of Mexican Songs, op. cit.,* note 8, f. 26 r and f. 62 r.
14. *Ibid.,* f. 17 r.
15. *Ibid.,* f. 13 r.
16. *Ibid.,* f. 10 v.
17. *Ibid.,* f. 9 v.

BIBLIOGRAPHY

As already mentioned in this study, there are preserved in American and European libraries some pre-Hispanic Codices or "Books of Pictures" dealing with the religion and philosophy of ancient Mexico. There are also other manuscripts written in Náhuatl containing old Indian chronicles, hymns, and songs concerned with their world view and philosophy. Among them are: the *Colección de Cantares Mexicanos,* preserved at the National Library of Mexico; the *Madrid Códices* of the Royal Palace and of the Spanish Royal Academy of History; the various collections of *Huehuetlatolli* or "Discourses of the Elders"; the *Vatican Codex A;* a Collection of pre-Columbian Songs entitled *Romances de los Señores de Nueva España,* at the Latin American Collection of the University of Texas, etc.

Following are some bibliographical references concerning works of particular interest. Those wishing to consult a larger bibliography in this field are referred to the "Bibliography on Náhuatl Culture, 1950–1958," included in *Estudios de Cultura Náhuatl,* Institute of History, National University of Mexico Press, 1959, pp. 125–166.

Annals of Cuauhtitlan, preserved in the Library of the National Museum of Mexico.

Caso, Alfonso, "El Aguila y el Nopal," in *Memorias de la Academia Mexicana de la Historia,* vol. V, 2, Mexico, 1946.

Caso, Alfonso, *The Aztecs: People of the Sun,* University of Oklahoma Press, Norman, 1958.

Garibay K., Angel Ma., *Historia de la Literatura Náhuatl* (A History of Náhuatl Literature), Editorial Porrúa, Mexico, 1953–1954, 2 vols.

Garibay K., Angel Ma., *Veinte Himnos Sacros de los Nahuas* (Twenty Sacred Hymns of the Nahuas), Fuentes Indígenas de la Cultura Náhuatl. Informantes Indígenas de Sahagún, 2. Introducción, paleografía, versión y comentarios de . . . México: Seminario de Cultura Náhuatl, Instituto de Historia, National University of Mexico Press, Mexico, 1958.

León-Portilla, Miguel, *La Filosofía Náhuatl, Estudiada en Sus Fuentes* (Náhuatl Philosophy, Studied at Its Sources), Prólogo de Angel Ma. Garibay K., Ediciones Especiales del Instituto Indigenista Interamericano, National University of Mexico Press, Mexico, 1956; 2nd ed., Mexico, 1959. *Aztec Thought and Culture* (English ed.), University of Oklahoma Press, Norman, 1963.

León-Portilla, Miguel, *Ritos, Sacredotes y atavios de los dioses* (Rituals, Priests and Vestments of the Gods), Fuentes Indigenas de la Cultura Náhuatl. Informantes Indigenas de Sahagún, 1. Introducción, paleografía, versión y notas de . . . México: Seminario de Cultura Náhuatl, Instituto de Historia, National University of Mexico Press, Mexico, 1958.

Robertson, Donald, *Mexican Manuscript Painting of the Early Colonial Period*, Yale Historical Publications, Yale, New Haven, 1959.

Sahagún, Fray Bernardino de, *Florentine Codex, General History of the Things of New Spain*, books I–V, VII, VIII, IX, X, and XII, trans. from Aztec into English by Arthur J. O. Anderson and Charles E. Dibble, School of American Research and the University of Utah, Sante Fé, New Mexico, 1950–1961.

Séjourné, Laurette, *Burning Water: Thought and Religion in Ancient Mexico*, Vanguard, New York, 1956.

Seler, Eduard, *Gesammelte Abhandlungen zur Amerikanisched Sprach- und Altertumskund*, 5 vols., Ascher und Co.; Behrend und Co., Berlin, 1902–1923.

Vaillant, George C., *The Aztecs of Mexico; Origin, Rise and Fall of the Aztec Nation*, Penguin, Harmondsworth, England, 1953.

Value Conceptions
in Sub-Saharan Africa JANHEINZ JAHN

4

Introduction

An effort to describe the value conceptions of a culture "attempting to pass beyond detail and to achieve some simpler, broader,
and deeper characterization of a way of life . . . need not be one
which the members of the community would themselves overtly
make, but it is supposed to be empirical, in the sense that it is
distilled from ethnographic detail, and operational, in that it can
yield predictions of behavior subject to observational check."[1]
The system presented here for describing the value conceptions
in Sub-Saharan Africa is empirical insofar as it is built on facts
about the ways of behavior of African communities. It is operational in that it predicts ways of behavior which can be observed.
The terminology of this system uses key words taken from
African languages. Thus very complex conceptions are covered
by terms which are adequate to the subject matter and therefore
are simple. The terminology is general, such as could be used to
describe cultural structures outside Africa, but to do this it would
have to be modified. It permits within its frame limited comparisons with other cultures. In the first instance, however, it is designed, even as a construct developed from outside, to give a
nearly complete inside explanation of African cultural behavior.
The world view to be described is one often called "animism."
This term is purposely avoided, since it tends to connote the be-

stowing of souls on natural phenomena, thus improperly introducing this Western notion.

NTU

In African thinking, the universe consists of a network of living
forces. The universe is a field of forces. Man and woman, dog and
stone, even yesterday and east, beauty and laughter—all these are
forces related to each other and in continuous interaction. The
universe is a unity, in which each part depends on the others, and
no part is changeless. If you take possession of a part of a thing,
you thereby participate in its life force. If you tear a leaf from a
tree, not only does the tree quiver, but the whole universe is
affected, since nothing stands alone. For Europeans, force is an
attribute: A being *has* force. In African thinking, force *is* being,
being *is* force, a physical-spiritual energy and potency. The totality
of all these living forces is NTU, *Being* (*das Sein* in Heidegger's
sense), which, however, is never conceived of as separable from
its manifestations. In NTU, the cosmic universal force, all single
forces are tied together. The individual forces fall into four groups,
within each of which there is a hierarchical ordering: *Muntu,
Kintu, Hantu,* and *Kuntu.*

Muntu (plural: Bantu)

The Muntu group includes those forces which can think; more
precisely, those beings which are forces having command over
Nommo (the magic word). In the hierarchy of Muntu-forces, the
lowest rank consists of living men; above them are deceased men,
then deified men, then spirits, then minor deities, then major
deities, and, at the top, the creator-god. All these terms have over-
tones of reference to European ways of thinking, or to Greek
mythology, which are inappropriate and incorrect here. Therefore,
it is better to supply a different set of terms free from such con-
notations. We shall call "living man" *muzima* (plural: *bazima*),
"deceased man" *muzimu* (plural: *bazimu*), deified men, spirits,
and gods *orishas,* and the creator-god *Olorun.* Within the pyramid
of Muntu-forces, their Nommo-potency increases step by step from
bottom to top.

Death is the transition from muzima to muzimu; through appropriate rites, it increases Nommo-force. The deceased (bazimu) are more powerful than the living (bazima), but the living are "happier." Through sacrifices of Kintu-forces that have been charged with Nommo, the deceased can be elevated and intensified to the status of Orisha, but no further. A muzimu, like an orisha, can act favorably or unfavorably upon a muzima by means of his Nommo-force, yet remain dependent on the muzima's sacrifices. The dependence is reciprocal.

A child becomes a muzima not at birth, but by the act of being named and thus being *designated* as a person. The name may be that of a muzimu, who is hereby in a peculiar sense reborn. A child who dies before being named is not treated as human, but as a thing (Kintu). A single muzimu may be reborn in different grandchildren or great-grandchildren at the same time. An ancestor, as an aggregate of *magara* (life-force) can transmit to many different infants the small portions of magara that the latter need to start their lives. In contrast to Pythagorean and Buddhist theory, there is no reincarnation of individual souls, but only the handing down of portions of force.

The image of man in African sculpture seeks to represent a muntu as a unity of muzima and muzimu. Masks, however, split these two forms of muntu apart, because a masked dancer can represent only the one or the other. A muzima-mask (relatively rare) is, therefore, as naturalistic as possible; while a muzimu-mask avoids anthropomorphism.

Through their command of Nommo, Muntu-forces dominate all others. The African world view is quite anthropocentric.

Kintu (plural: Bintu)

This group includes those visible forces that cannot act of themselves but only by the command (Nommo) of a muntu. Here belong plants, animals, minerals, tools, furnishings, and so on. Highest ranking in this hierarchy are those objects that have been magically imbued with life-force, as, for example, amulets and medicines which by Muntu-action have become the recipients of a Nommo. Bintu are "congealed" forces (*forces figées*); they wait for the command of the magic word of a muntu. They can do nothing of themselves. They have no will of their own; at the utmost—as, for example, among animals—an instinct, by order of Olorun. Even a poison is not an effective substance in its own right, but merely a force that remains innocuous until set to work by a muntu. Only through the command of a muntu does a poison become a poison; by the order of a muntu, it can again become innocuous.

The relations among Muntu-forces, with or without the help of Kintu-forces, conform to a precise code of laws (the *Magara* principle):

1. Every muntu can directly strengthen or weaken every other muntu.

2. Every Muntu-force can directly influence any lower force (Kintu).

3. A muntu can influence another muntu indirectly, by acting on an intervening Kintu-force and causing it to act on the other muntu. This influence must necessarily work, except under the following conditions:

a. The other Muntu-force is stronger in its own right.
b. The other Muntu-force is strengthened by some third and stronger Muntu-force.
c. The other Muntu-force protects himself with Kintu-forces which are stronger than those evoked by the first.

The use of amulets, talismans, charm objects, sacrificial objects, votive pictures, masks, and so on, is all based on this third law. This is brought about by the use of Nommo.

Hantu

This group includes localizing forces, place-time (not space-time) as a unity. Since everything is force, everything is in all-pervasive and continual motion. Hantu includes those forces that localize our motions in place-time. Time in this context is not a continuum to be measured by a chronometer, but concrete, localized, living time. A man on a sick bed experiences an hour very different from an hour spent in the arms of his sweetheart. If to terms of time (such as an hour) we add terms of place (sick in bed or in arms of sweetheart), an hour does not remain an hour: one is long—even endless—the other far too short. Nor are places independent of time, since, if our man spends no time in a place, there is consequently no experienceable life, no activity. Thus in African thinking, only localized time, only temporalized place exist.

Each Hantu-force, each spatiotemporal there-and-then obeys a muntu because it is up to him so to behave that each there-and-then is full and brief rather than dull and long. The active experiencing of a place "shortens" the time. The intensity of experiencing of a man is proportional to the rank of his Hantu-forces.

Kuntu

Stemming originally from terms of spatial relationship (together, near, separating), the Kuntu group contains all the forces of relationship, of acting on and of manipulating, of way and manner of acting. They answer questions about the *how* of a culture—that is, about its *style*. Kuntu-forces are function-forces (*forces-modalité*). Since in the world of forces nothing is static, Kuntu-forces regulate the *how* of the continually necessary reestablishment of order among all relationships. As one looks at African behavior from outside, one can sort out different relationships, such as cult behavior (muzima-muzimu-orisha relations), social behavior (muzima-muzima-buzima relations), dealings with objects (muzima-kintu relations), the experiencing of environment (muzima-hantu relations), and so on. But all imaginable relations are, in the African world view, regulated by a single set of principles, the same Kuntu-forces, and therefore are not to be thus sorted out.

In the hierarchy of Kuntu-forces, Nommo holds the highest place, being the magic word, the word of command, word and seed together. Even procreation is not brought about merely by sperm, but by sperm and word. A being which is to be distinguished from animals and which is to find its place among Muntu-forces is not established in that status by the act of birth, but by being *designated* by a word that is also seed. By designation (*Ernennung, dénomination*), a tooth becomes an amulet, a carved piece of wood becomes an efficacious image, a string of empty speech sounds becomes a verse, a muzimu becomes an orisha.

Not all Muntu-beings have the same degree of Nommo-power. The Nommo of an orisha is more powerful than that of a muzimu, and the latter more powerful than that of a muzima. The degree of Nommo-power of a muntu specifies his position in the Muntu hierarchy.

All sorcery is word sorcery, evocation and banishment, blessing and cursing. Since the word has such power, everything one says is binding; there is no "harmless" or casual word. Every word has consequences. Therefore the word binds the muntu, and the muntu is responsible for his words.

What from the Western view (thus from an alien view) appear variously as religion, medicine, poetry, art, law, the natural and moral sciences, and social relations are, in the African view, all Kuntu-forces and hence are bound into an inseparable whole of multiple-related dependencies which are governed, influenced, and ordered by Muntu-forces using Nommo.

Applications

The elementary terms of the NTU system have meanings that are not alien to other cultures. The system pinpoints the *values* and gives us a key with which we can interpret from inside the behavior of members of Sub-Saharan African culture. As seen from outside, the behavior of Africans does not necessarily appear any different from that of members of other cultures. But what is quite similar, viewed from the outside, requires very different interpretations when seen from the inside.

For example: Two groups of farmers, one in Italy, one in Dahomey, are sowing their crops and singing. For the observer (from outside) their behavior is identical—both groups are doing two things at once, (a) sowing and (b) singing. But the two activities do not have the same values for both groups. For the Italians, the sowing is crucial, the singing an optional addition, which at most helps to make the work of sowing lighter. For the group in Dahomey, the seeds are Kintu-forces, which can do nothing by themselves, but await being called by a muntu to become active. The singing is the Nommo command that brings about growth, so that the singing is indispensable; but the activity of sowing is merely an addition, necessary only because the bazima are the lowest forces in the Muntu hierarchy. Even the bazimu have such a degree of control by Nommo that they can force their will on

Kintu-forces by word alone. This can be seen in numerous African tales. Thus the NTU system explains the relationship of the African to labor.

These two interpretations (of the Italian and the African activities of sowing) are from the inside view provable and irrefutable as, from the outside view, they are unprovable and refutable. As proof that Nommo can activate Kintu-forces without physical labor, the Dahomey can show one the virgin forest, which was simply commanded to grow by orishas, using no physical labor. If the Italians demonstrate that their seed will grow without the singing, the Dahomeyans can refute this "proof" by saying that the Italians sang silently to themselves, or that they have higher Muntu-forces helping them.

Even the conclusions of natural science experiments do not necessarily overthrow the value interpretations of the NTU system, because they also can be interpreted from this inside view—as, indeed, sometimes happens. A chemical formula is nothing but the correct Nommo for transforming kintu A into kintu B; an airplane is a proof that every muntu, using the correct Nommo, is able to fly; electricity is a Kintu-force which through correct commands is put into human service; nuclear physics is the proof that matter does not exist, but that all is energy—or force "as our ancestors have always said."

Religion

Cults reflect the architecture of thought. At the top of the religious hierarchy there is Olorun (with different names in the various languages), the personified representative of NTU, the world-creator, the sum of all orishas (which are the personifications of partial forces). Since, in the cults, each word of a muzima, being Nommo, will effect changes, therefore, it is only to an orisha (and to the proper one for the circumstances) that prayers, requests, and sacrifices can be directed for the real needs of the muzima. The woman who desires a child will turn to the orisha "Potency" (*Shango*); the fisherman prays for a rich catch to Yemaya, the Mother of the Seas. Prayers to Olorun make no sense. They would be meaningful only if one wished to bring about a change in the laws of nature (which are Olorun's Nommo), as, for example, if a woman wanted to arrange for men to do the childbearing. A prayer to Olorun would, therefore, be a criticism of the world order, and hence sacrilege.

The lower ranks of orishas (bazimu and spirits who are not forces of nature) can, by an act of designation, be enthroned or dethroned by bazima. Their activity depends on the quantity of Nommo invested in them by bazima. Through Nommo, a muzima —even a kintu—can be elevated to the rank of orisha. Here is an example, intentionally taken from European culture. A piece of colored cloth can, through designation, become a flag, which, as a symbol, is proportionately stronger and more taboo the greater the number of people who swear allegiance to it. If the symbol becomes dethroned—as people forswear it, saying, "You mean nothing to me any more"—then the flag becomes a piece of cloth and can be used to dust a floor or polish a car. This example shows why it is wrong to use the term *fetish* in the African context. A fetish is an object which in its own right has supernatural powers. In Africa, no kintu has any force in its own right. As Frobenius has said, "Ich habe in keinem Teil Negerafrikas die Fetischanschauung bei Negern gefunden."[2] The process of designation of an orisha is completely in awareness in Africa. In the Yoruba language, the expression for "worship" is *she orisha,* which is literally to "make" an orisha. On each occasion for worship, the orisha must be made anew by being redesignated—a radical empirical notion.

Bazima indeed occupy the lowest rank in the Muntu hierarchy, but the whole universe of forces is centered in them, as all other Muntu-forces can only continue acting on the world by means of bazima. This applies even to deities. Their activity is either a past one, the effects of which continue, or, in the case of personified natural forces, is constant and unchangeable in direction. The muzima evokes them with due regard for the specific sphere of each. He does not follow their orders, but orders them. In cultic ecstasy, he draws them into himself, makes them "ride" himself, incarnates them, identifies himself with them, and designates them to be the tools of his will. Religious activity is not adoration, but evocation.

In many of the areas influenced by Christian missionaries, the Muntu hierarchy has survived. In Catholic areas (principally Haiti and Brazil), the "Bon Dieu" is identified as Olorun and is not worshiped; the orishas are identified with the saints, who alone are worshiped. In Protestant areas, often each newly introduced "Jesus" or "Lord" brought in by a new missionary sect becomes an additional orisha. That several of these additional orishas may have the same name is quite irrelevant.

Medicine

As only Muntu-forces can think, only they can move the universe of forces. If a man is sick or dies, if he has sorrow or worry or a misfortune or pains—every disorder is an illness—some muntu, be it muzima or muzimu or orisha or the man himself, is responsible. The medicine man (physician) must discover either the responsible muntu or the charm (Nommo) used by him and must oppose a stronger "magic" in accordance with the Magara principle.[3] The patient is primarily interested in whether the physician knows the right Nommo word for getting rid of the disorder. Manipulations, medicines, and amulets are, like the work of the peasant in planting the field, mere paraphernalia, rendering the activity of the Nommo easier. No Kintu-force is of any use unless it is *spoken* to properly; its effectiveness rests wholly on the words. If the patient refuses to pay the physician after treatment, the latter by evocation withdraws the effectiveness (the Nommo) from the medicine and the patient again becomes sick. Of additional effectiveness, in the case of indirect malignant influences, is a reconciliation that the patient can force on the offended bazimu or orisha by redeeming heroic acts, such as inflicting pain, swallowing repugnant substances, and the like. Apart from a knowledge of medical herbs and of certain surgical procedures (the setting of broken bones, skull trepanation), African medicine rests on depth psychology and force of will therapy.

Law

Law is based on the Magara concept, which guarantees to every muntu an unextinguishable claim on magara, that is, on life, fulfillment, health, and happiness. Crucial for this is the conception of the interrelatedness and order of everything, from which it follows that the individual can only be happy if all those around him, including bazimu and orishas, are happy too. Legal procedure, as the means for reestablishing the harmonious order of everything, is thus a special branch of medicine, limited to muzima-muzima relations. The concept of punishment is totally lacking; what matters is the continually necessary reestablishment of harmony. Property rights do not exist; disputes which seem to involve material property are dealt with entirely in terms of personal rights. The spiritual injury to the plaintiff (his anger is a diminution of magara) is much more important than any injury to or loss of a material object. It is not sufficient to return a stolen chicken; the excitement and the anger of the victim must be restored to balance by giving him extra magara; often, in addition, offended bazimu and orishas must be consoled. The obligation of the offender is limited at that point to further claims which would reduce his own magara. The procedure is time-consuming and is intended to be so. The mutual abreaction of imputations is part of the reestablishment of harmony.

Poetry

Poetry is Nommo-force. The rhythmic words of the poet create images which, when strung together, become verse and prose. Reality offers "sleeping" forces as raw material which the words of the poet designate as images arranged as a guide to the future. The task of such poetry is not to describe what exists, but to produce visions of what should be, often using past deeds as paradigms. The poet and the "sorcerer"–medicine man are identical: existence is carried on properly by word commands (Nommo) and is, by the same means, pushed toward the cosmic order that must continuously be reestablished. Poetry is not indicative, but imperative.

Rhythm has the task of properly ordering being and life; it is "the architecture of being . . . the pure expression of the life force."[4] Against the basic rhythm, recurrent figures, such as alliteration, assonance, anaphora, metaphor, allusion, and leitmotiv, form secondary rhythms, which enforce the effectiveness of the whole, producing unity from variety. A poem is incomplete if it is not accompanied by at least one percussion instrument. Tension is achieved not by climax, but by repetition. From the multiplicity of recurrent and crosscutting rhythmic tensions emerge the desired evocative intensity—especially if the poem is sung and danced simultaneously. In the latter case, Nommo achieves its purest expression because it reflects the universe of forces.

The poet does not express his individual impressionistic experience; he speaks to and for the community. His task is a social one. Therefore he can remain anonymous.

Art

Like a poem, a carving is art only in use. Like any other kintu, it is *designated* into its function and can be dethroned and replaced by another. Its form is specified by the rhythm of its *determinants*[5] which express its meaning. The harmony of meaning and rhythm realizes itself in action: for a carving, in its function as a stimulus for the evocation of an orisha; for a mask, in the movement of the dance. Since art is also thought of as an effective force, it is manifested not in the art object (the *what*, Kintu), but in the art use (the *how*, Kuntu). African art is not objects but attitudes.

Culture Contact and Cross-Cultural Comparison

Since each culture is structured about its own value conceptions, its special achievements will be found at those points where the culture places the strongest evaluations. These may be constant or changing with history. The indigenous reinterpretation of practices introduced from outside is an effective barrier against disruption of the indigenous value system. Culture contact leads to cross-cultural comparison. Obvious gaps in one's own culture lead to the adoption of foreign features; but such foreign features will be evaluated according to one's own system. Such reevaluation renders possible the insertion of the alien into one's own culture, without disrupting the latter. Possibly the strength of a culture depends on the extent to which it can assimilate the alien without disruption.

In the vocabulary of the NTU system, and from its point of view, one can say that the achievements of African culture lie in the realm of Kuntu, while Kintu has been neglected; whereas the achievements of the West lie in the realm of Kintu, to the neglect of Kuntu. Thus has arisen a cultural exchange—in the realm of Kintu, Africa has been importing from Europe (technical equipment, pragmatic medicine, and so on); in the realm of Muntu, Europe has been importing from Africa (rhythms, artistic influences, possibly elements of psychotherapy, and possibly surrealism). The doubts expressed here reflect the fact that, while European exports to Africa are well known, influences in the other direction have not yet been thoroughly investigated.

In spite of their zeal for innovation, which seeks a speedy adherence to the modern world, African thinkers, poets, and politicians emphasize that they want to conserve the African value system. This may be expressed with such catchwords as "African personality" or "négritude" or may lead to a philosophical examination of traditions (as with Kagame)[6] or to cultural analysis (as with Senghor).[7] Whether these tendencies lead to an inverted racial arrogance and a cultural mystification (as with C. A. Diop)[8] or to a broadened humanism no longer centered on Europe (as with Césaire),[9] there is the common element that the African value system is not to remain merely in the form of leftover traces (as, according to Klausner's paper,[10] pre-Buddhistic traces can be detected in the current religious life of northeastern Thailand), but to stay as the core of any newly emerging orientation. Leading African thinkers even assign to their culture a broad influence on Western culture, expressing this most of all in neo-African poetry:

> Que nous répondions présents à la renaissance du Monde . . .
> Car qui apprendrait le rythme au monde défunt des machines
>   et des canons?
> Qui pousserait le cri de joie pour réveiller morts et orphelins
>   à l'aurore?
> Dites, qui rendrait la mémoire de vie à l'homme aux espoirs
>   éventrés?[11]

Critique

1. Unity. The unity of Sub-Saharan African culture, as hypothesized in the NTU system, is subject to challenge. But the system affords a basic frame of reference, which does not necessarily have to be present in complete and explicit form in every tribe

in order to serve for the comparing of values, or for the establishment of "goal hierarchies," to use MacKay's term.[12] The details from one tribe to another may differ, or even be contradictory, without any of them being in conflict with the basic value system. For example, whether twins are consecrated or killed, in either case they are afforded exceptional status.

2. Limitations. It has been charged that the NTU system is too general to distinguish African culture from others, such as Indian, Polynesian, or the like. This judgment is correct. The requisite comparisons have not yet been made.

In this connection, the statement by Professor León-Portilla[13] concerning Náhuatl thinking about "flower and song," poetry, art, and symbolism is interesting to compare with possible NTU equivalents:

"Flower and Song" is:

Náhuatl	NTU
1. "a means for drawing closer to the deity."	1. a means for drawing the deity closer to man.
2. "that thing which makes friendship and understanding possible among human beings."	2. Yes, but as a secondary result of other, more important functions.
3. "the only thing of value that man could leave, as a remembrance, on earth."	3. No, being only efficient in action "flower and song" (Nommo) has to be continually recreated; a man's word may be remembered thus, but it is not the only means of a muzima to remain effective to his offspring.
4. "the maximum consolation for princes and wise men."	4. Nommo acts on all, not only on a class; consolation is only a part of magara.
5. "the only means for speaking true words on earth."	5. Yes, full agreement.

Such comparisons, systematically developed and continued, may in the end lead to clearer definitions. But the major difficulties still are caused by the lack of good basic information on these subjects. Research on African thinking has only just begun.

FOOTNOTE REFERENCES

1. Hockett, Charles F., "Scheduling," in F. S. C. Northrop, and Helen H. Livingston (eds.), *Cross-Cultural Understanding*, Harper & Row, New York, 1964, p. 141.
2. Frobenius, Leo, *Kulturgeschichte Afrikas*, Phaidon, Zürich, 1954, p. 13.
3. See p. 58 above.
4. Senghor, Léopold Sédar, "L'esprit de la civilisation ou les lois de la culture négro-africaine," *Présence Africaine*, vol. VIII–X, Paris, 1956, p. 60.
5. For determinants, see Jahn, Janheinz, *Muntu, An Outline of the New African Culture*, Grove Press, New York, 1961, pp. 157–163.
6. Kagame, Alexis, *La philosophie băntu-rwandaise de l'Être*, Académie Royale des Sciences Coloniales, Bruxelles, 1956.
7. Senghor, Léopold Sédar, *op. cit.*, note 4.
8. Diop, C. A., *Nations nègres et culture*, Présence Africaine, Paris, 1954.
9. Césaire, Aimé, *Cahier d'un retour au pays natal* (3rd ed.), Présence Africaine, Paris, 1956, pp. 70–77.
10. Klausner, William J., "Popular Buddhism in Northeast Thailand," in F. S. C. Northrop, and Helen H. Livingston, *op. cit.*, note 1, ch. 5.
11. Senghor, Léopold Sédar, *Chants d'Ombre*, Editions du Seuil, Paris, 1945, p. 29.
12. MacKay, Donald M., "Communication and Meaning—A Functional Approach," in F. S. C. Northrop, and Helen H. Livingston (eds.), *op. cit.*, note 1, p. 170.
13. León-Portilla, Miguel, "Philosophy in the Cultures of Ancient Mexico," in F. S. C. Northrop, and Helen H. Livingston (eds.), *op. cit.*, note 1, pp. 50–51.

BIBLIOGRAPHY

Greenberg, Joseph H., *Studies in African Linguistic Classification*, Compass, New Haven, 1955.

Griaule, Marcel, *Dieu d'Eau*, du Chêne, Paris, 1948.

Jahn, Janheinz, *Muntu, Umrisse der neoafrikanischen Kultur*, Diederichs, Düsseldorf, 1958; English ed., *Muntu, An Outline of Neo-African Culture*, Faber & Faber, London, 1961; American ed.,

Muntu, An Outline of the New African Culture, Grove, New York, 1961; French ed., *Muntu, l'Homme Africain et la Culture Néo-Africaine*, Editions du Seuil, Paris, 1961; Italian ed., *Muntu, la civiltà africana moderna*, Einaudi, Torino, 1961; Swedish ed., *Muntu, neoafrikansk kultur i vardande*, Rabén & Sjögren, Stockholm, 1960; in preparation, Mexican ed., *Muntu, Fondo de Cultura Economica*, Mexico; in preparation, Dutch ed., *Muntu, Moussault's Uitgeverij*, Amsterdam.

Murdock, George Peter, *Africa, Its Peoples and Their Cultural History*, McGraw-Hill, New York, 1959.

Rachewiltz, Boris de, *Incontro con l'arte africana*, Martello, Milano, 1959.

Tempels, Placied, *Bantoe-Filosofie*, de Sikkel, Antwerpen, 1946.

Popular Buddhism
in Northeast Thailand WILLIAM J. KLAUSNER

5

Introduction

Although there is no lack of critical written material on various aspects of the Buddhist religion, little attention has been given to a description of Buddhism as it is actually conceived and lived by the rural masses throughout Asia. From a largely theoretical viewpoint, the extensive probing of the philosophical nuances of Buddhism is both stimulating and enlightening. However, the village populations, and the rural priests themselves, often think and act in ways that diverge quite markedly from the theoretical ideal as proclaimed in the Buddhist texts. The distinction between the theoretical principles of the Buddhist texts and the religion as it is practiced at the rural level can be compared to the distinction in the field of law between statute law and living or customary law. In order to identify the patterns of behavior operative in rural society and the influences on such behavior careful distinctions must be made between statutes and texts on the one hand and actual customs and behavior on the other.[1] There is no particular merit in pointing up the divergencies between the Buddhist ideal and practice at the rural level. There is a value, however, in examining the vital role the Buddhist religion plays in the life of the village people. An understanding of this pervasive force in village life will aid immeasurably in gaining an insight into rural modes of thought and action. This paper will deal solely with the Hinayana or Theravada sect prevalent in Thailand and specifically with the northeastern region of Thailand where I have been engaged in rural programming for the past few years.

Religion plays a dominant part in the lives of the northeastern Thai villagers. They are noted for their deep attachment to Buddhism, albeit a Buddhism conceived, interpreted, and lived by them in their particular environment. A description of Buddhism in the northeast area can to a certain extent be generalized throughout Thailand, but there are marked differences of degree which cannot be overlooked.

In the northeastern area of Thailand, the *wat*, or temple compound, is and has been for generations the focal point of the village. The wat is, at one and the same time, the religious, social, cultural, and artistic center of the village. In former days, it was also the educational and, to some extent, the political center as well. Today, these two latter functions have been largely removed, though, to a certain extent, vestiges of these roles still persist. Most villages have a wat with *bhikkhus* and novices in attendance.* Those few villages that do not have a wat consider themselves as belonging to the wat in a neighboring village.

Entrance into the Monkhood

Initial insights into popular Buddhism can be gained by examining the reasons why northeastern village boys follow the injunction of Theravada Buddhism to become novices and later bhikkhus, if only for a token period. It must be understood that Theravada Buddhism does not compel one to remain a bhikkhu indefinitely, nor are there any customary social sanctions requiring the bhikkhu to do so. In the greater number of cases, it is expected that he will only serve for the traditional three-month "Buddhist Lent" period. However, in the northeastern villages there is a tendency to remain beyond this token period. The village youth will usually remain in the monkhood upward of a year or two and in novicehood even longer.

The village boys enter novicehood and monkhood for a variety

* I have used the Pali term *bhikkhu* in this paper because neither priest nor monk accurately describes the Buddhist bhikkhu. It has been necessary, however, to use the term *monkhood*, as *bhikkhuhood* is unwieldy and not used in common parlance.

of reasons, but it is only very rarely that the principal reason centers about a search for the end to craving and the attainment of Nirvana. The reasons behind this traditional practice often do not even relate to the young man himself. For example, probably the most pressing motivation for taking the yellow robes is that by this action merit is accumulated, a good portion of which goes to the bhikkhu's parents. Although merit accrues from entrance into both the monkhood and novicehood, the monkhood stores up greater merit. Therefore even if a boy has become a novice, his parents expect him to become a bhikkhu after he reaches his twentieth birthday. The village youth realize that taking the robes is expected of them, and the boy himself has no serious reservations, as he respects his parents and has been brought up to revere and respect the bhikkhus into whose society he is entering. This act of "sending merit" to one's parents is conceived of as repayment to them for childhood care and upbringing.

Closely connected with the above view is the social imperative that a boy enter the monkhood before marriage. It is felt, among other reasons, that since the boy is to leave his parents' home and start a new family some token of respect and thanks are due to those who cared for and counseled him as a child. Such a view takes on added meaning considering that it is the traditional northeast custom for the boy, on marriage, to go to live with his wife's family.

Parents feel their life is incomplete unless they have received merit in this indirect fashion. It is not surprising, therefore, that the principal reason given for preferring sons to daughters is the fact the boys can and will enter the monkhood and thus accumulate merit for their parents.

Entrance into the monkhood cannot be explained solely in terms of obligation to one's parents, however. There is an obligation to the village society as well. Living under the rules of discipline of the Buddhist order and under the moral guidance of the elder bhikkhus is viewed by the villagers as the minimum training necessary for maturity and thus for being considered of social value to the community. The bhikkhus have the ideal pattern of moral behavior indelibly impressed on their minds and bodies. The villagers will often remark of one who has not been in the monkhood that he is "ignorant." The retort "He didn't go through the monkhood" is sufficient to explain immature actions on the part of a villager. At the same time, if a child acts improperly, the blame is often shifted to his or her parents, with the remark "The father never went through the monkhood" offered as explanation for the child's misbehavior. It thus becomes obvious that the villagers feel all male youth must enter the monkhood in order to pass over the threshold into manhood and gain a true understanding of morality and thus "an education" in village terms.

The entrance into the monkhood can be conceived of as the *rite de passage* for the young boys of the community. One is not considered a fully matured man until one has fulfilled this rite. In this context of morality and maturity, the distinction between novicehood and monkhood is important. The novice upholds but a few rules of discipline, the bhikkhus a great many. Thus, for the northeasterner, even though a boy may enter novicehood, he must either remain a novice until he is twenty and then become a bhikkhu or leave the novicehood and reenter when twenty, if he is to be considered fully matured, moral, and educated. It is not surprising that a girl will shy away from marrying one who has not yet been a bhikkhu and is thus immature and not yet a full man.

Because of the various distinctions made between bhikkhus and novices that I have noted above, it is common, in contrast to some other areas of Thailand, to find more bhikkhus than novices in northeastern rural wats.

The idea that entrance into the monkhood is a transition rite is further substantiated by the conferring of new names on entrance and special titles which remain with one even after leaving the monkhood. There is a gradation in the titles, depending principally on how long one has been in the monkhood and the educational progress made.

Of course, entrance into novicehood or monkhood is viewed in personal terms by the boy concerned. The young novice or bhikkhu may well view his yellow robes as a passport to a good education in village terms. He sees the years in the wat as an opportunity to learn certain subjects and trades that will be useful for him both during his monkhood years and in lay life when and if he disrobes.

Today, although the monks have largely been replaced by government teachers in the schools, the former still play an important educational role in teaching certain trades as well as in giving advanced language instruction. In many cases, four grades of formal schooling is the extent of the villager's education. However, provision is made for the boys to get further "schooling" during novicehood and monkhood. Although to some degree this schooling involves the reading and writing of Pali and modern and ancient Thai scripts, it also includes training in practical trades. In a northeastern village, the abbot and some of the elder bhikkhus are usually expert in one or more of the following: architecture, carpentry, sculpture, painting and decorative art, bronze casting, tile, brick and cement making, and medicine. When a boy enters the monkhood he must study certain subjects, such as Pali, the rules of discipline, Buddha's teachings, and Buddhist history. Specialized training in the trades mentioned above is in the form of "electives" in which the individual novice or bhikkhu may or may not interest himself. The bhikkhus in the northeastern villages get actual experience in these fields, as they are always working on some project involving the use of these trade skills.

Thus, the educational aspect of the wat experience is an important factor in motivating a young man's taking of the yellow robes. The educational motivation has still wider implication if one considers those bhikkhus who leave the village to get formal training in the bhikkhu schools at the District and Provincial Centers and even in the capital. Such schooling may continue up to and through the university level. The education is for the most part free, and many of these village bhikkhus can get such advanced schooling only through monkhood channels, as in lay life the difficulties involved might be insurmountable.

In personal terms, one's residence in the monkhood and the merit one accrues by such an act has a positive effect in overcoming one's previous sins, and, it is hoped, will tip the balance in favor of an abundance of merit. This will in turn bode well for one's future both in this life and in existences to come. The injunction to enter the monkhood before marriage can also be seen in this context. It is believed that the family's well-being will depend to a certain degree on the father's karmic status, and the monkhood service certainly helps to assure that, all things being equal, the family will not have undue hardships.

The Bhikkhus' Involvement in Secular
Village Affairs

The vast majority of the rural bhikkhus of the northeast are both concerned with and involved in the everyday life and problems of their followers.

The villager's religious conceptions, and those of the bhikkhus themselves, are the result of reinterpretation and adaptation of theoretical Buddhist doctrine and practice to the particular conditions and needs of the village. This adaptation can be seen very markedly in the bhikkhus' and novices' actions in the secular sphere as well as in the villagers' view of how those wearing the yellow robes should act.

The northeastern bhikkhus are generally very active in aiding the villagers solve their everyday lay problems. In the northeastern villages, the bhikkhus and novices can be seen helping in the construction of a village well, the building of a bridge or small dam, the laying of a new village road, or the erection of a village meeting hall or school. Such community activities are in addition to similar work the bhikkhus and novices may carry out in the wat compound, such as the building of bhikkhu quarters, a meeting and sermon hall, latrines, and wells. The bhikkhus do not confine their activities to within the wat boundaries and in the community-oriented activities mentioned above; they move outside the wat area both intellectually and physically.

In such activities, the bhikkhus' help may be manifested in a variety of ways. In almost all cases, the bhikkhus will have been consulted and their views and agreement concerning a particular village project solicited before work begins. Community projects in the northeast must have, at the very least, the bhikkhus' sanction if they are to have a chance of success.

If a project requires financial contributions, the temple often assumes the responsibility for the collection. A trusted lay assistant to the abbot is in official charge of the collection. In this way, the funds given acquire a "merit-making" label, and there is consequently less resistance to part with scarce funds. In some cases, such as the building of schools, the bhikkhus may offer land belonging to the wat in addition to other help given.

The bhikkhus do not confine themselves to mere approval of a project or solicitation of funds. They work at the project site as well. Both novices and bhikkhus take active part, and, to some degree, there is a natural division of functions due to the differences in their status, knowledge, and degree of adherence to the rules of discipline. In some cases, the bhikkhus limit their activities to directing the work in question. They tell the villager to dig here, lay a cement ring in just this way, put a beam in a certain position. This foreman role usually is shared to a certain extent with other official and nonofficial lay leaders of the community, but the most revered bhikkhu or bhikkhus of the village will more often than not take the lead. The bhikkhus' very presence and words at the work site encourage the villagers to work steadily and carry the project to its "meritorious" conclusion. In the case of buildings, the bhikkhus usually are the architects and lay out the plan for the building.

The bhikkhus often do not rest content with their foreman role. In some cases, they will actually help by contributing manual labor. This may involve sawing an already felled tree for the building of a school, or the making of tiles, bricks, or cement for a community hall. In other cases, the bhikkhus might lay the cement ring in a well or hammer boards into place on a new bridge being built. Less frequently, such physical work might involve the use of a spade or rake in a village road project. Of course, where the novices can do the physical work required, they, rather than the bhikkhus, carry it out. However, the bhikkhus themselves do not avoid physical labor where it is necessary either in terms of knowledge, manpower, or the creation of a working esprit on the part of the villagers.

Many of the village bhikkhus in the northeast have taken an active and leading role in governmental community development projects now in operation. The bhikkhus give aid and comfort in secular terms in a variety of other ways. In some instances, the bhikkhus still teach in the government schools. This practice, however, is becoming less and less frequent as the Ministry of Education builds up a cadre of trained lay civil servants in the teaching profession.

The bhikkhus, in many parts of the northeast area, give free medical diagnosis and treatment. Usually, one or more of the bhikkhus in a village wat will be particularly adept at mixing vil-

lage herb medicines and diagnosing village ailments. As the government health services spread out, some encroachment is naturally
being made on the influence of the village doctor, whether he be
a bhikkhu or a layman, but, as yet, the prestige of the village
herbalist is still high.

The abbot and other elder bhikkhus often act as arbitrators in
personal quarrels. Their arbitration role is unofficial, and they are
sought out by relatives or by those who particularly respect their
judgment in such matters. The bhikkhus endeavor to have the
contending parties agree to an equitable solution and above all to
"cool their hot hearts." Such quarrels as come before the bhikkhus
usually involve disputes over land boundaries, misrepresentation
in trade dealings, and the like. Such issues may be taken before
the village headman and commune head for consideration as well,
but taking such a step is considered to be more formal and official.
Family problems are often placed before the bhikkhus for consideration and arbitration, especially if the bhikkhu is a relative.
Such problems may involve husband and wife quarrels or misunderstandings between relatives. The bhikkhus' advice may even
be asked as to whether a certain boy or girl is suitable for marriage
into a family.

In many of the northeastern villages the bhikkhus fulfill a
"banking" role, though such a role is not in line with a strict
interpretation of the rules of discipline. If the villagers have any
large sums of money, they seek to place their funds in the care
of the abbot for safekeeping. The villagers in time of emergency
may also borrow cash from the bhikkhus, as the abbot or elder
bhikkhus may well have accumulated a good sum of money
through "merit" contributions. No interest is figured. Both the
depositing of money and borrowing from the bhikkhus are not
publicized, but the villagers consider such activity to be a part of
the village bhikkhus' functions in the community.

Aside from the functions mentioned above, the bhikkhus perform a most vital and important role in their efforts to preserve
the peace and social stability of the village society. Not only by
their counsel, but also by their example and the aura of quiet and
serenity that surrounds them, the bhikkhus throw a symbolic
mantle of gentleness over the community. This mantle is not
easily thrown off.

In some sections of the northeast, the bhikkhus assume the roles of fortune teller, astrologer, and purveyor of charms and amulets. Generally, however, the bhikkhus are not concerned with these activities except for that of astrology.

The wat serves as the village social welfare center as well. A few young lay boys can always be found living there. Sometimes these youth are orphans. Just as often, however, they may be from extremely poor families, be a bit "backward," or be so misbehaved as to warrant the parents' sending them to the wat for "correction." In this latter connection, the bhikkhus pride themselves on their ability to reform delinquents either by counsel, taking them into the wat as lay disciples, or having them take the robes and become novices or bhikkhus. Those children who are delivered into the care of the wat, for whatever reasons, become the lay helpers about the wat, are given food, a place to stay, and receive moral training and what formal instruction the bhikkhus may give them in addition to the ordinary four grades of primary school training.

Private aid is sometimes given by bhikkhus but is restricted to help to parents and very close relatives, and it is definitely regarded as an exception to the bhikkhus' accepted behavior. Today, such aid usually concerns help in housebuilding; e.g., sawing wood, design, laying foundations, and hammering. In former times, such private help even extended to helping with the harvesting of rice, though today such action would be regarded as improper.

From the description of bhikkhus' activities noted above, one realizes that the bhikkhus do not divorce themselves from the everyday life of their followers. On the contrary, they involve themselves in the community's life and use their knowledge and prestige to alleviate problems that are of the very fabric of village secular life.

Reasons Underlying Bhikkhu Secular Involvement

If a strict interpretation of the texts is followed, such secular involvement as described above will appear as contrary to the initial teachings and emphasis of southern Buddhism. And yet, throughout the villages of the northeast, the bhikkhus have for generations engaged in such work with no misgivings and no qualms of conscience. Rural bhikkhu leaders, if asked, can often justify their actions in terms of a more liberal interpretation of the texts. Some have pointed out that the attitudes of the rural bhikkhus in this matter of secular involvement may differ from those of their city brethren because of sectarian differences, the rural bhikkhus being largely of the less strict Mahanikaya sect.

Such explanations as noted above are on an intellectual plane that is far removed from the actualities of rural life. To explain fully the actions of the bhikkhus, one must go to the village and see the bhikkhus in their traditional setting.

The bhikkhus' response is a practical answer, on the one hand, to a vacuum of knowledge in certain fields on the part of the ordinary villagers and, on the other hand, to a relative vacuum of what today might be considered minimal government services: schools, medical facilities, a police and court system, banking institutions, social welfare services, and community development programming. As the villagers' scope of knowledge increases and as the government extends its services, both of which are happening slowly but surely, the bhikkhus are bound to lose some of their influence. In some cases, however, the bhikkhus have taken a creative part in new government programs, such as those of community development, and thus have maintained their strong leadership position. In historical perspective we can view the bhikkhus' secular involvement as a necessary utilization of specialized knowledge that was not to be found elsewhere. The villagers still appreciate this point today, noting that the bhikkhus have a certain expertise and knowledge that they do not have. The villagers query, "If the bhikkhus do not help us, who will?"

Not only do the bhikkhus have specialized knowledge, but, in the villagers' eyes, they have "free time" also. A certain amount of that free time, according to the silent opinion of the villagers, can and should be devoted to the community's welfare. The villagers have their field work to do. It is not "unreasonable" to expect the bhikkhus to do the work necessary to carry out a community project.

Despite the bhikkhus' expert knowledge in certain spheres and their "spare time," they would not necessarily be involved in the secular side of the villagers' life if it were not for the villagers' strong conviction that the bhikkhus should be so involved. The villagers living in a basically subsistence economy feel that every-

one, including the bhikkhus, must be a part of the cooperative
pattern of work that is such an important factor in maintaining the
social and economic stability of the village. The villagers do not
feel that the bhikkhus should be exempted from this exchange of
services context. The villagers and bhikkhus are living in the same
community. Although not expressed overtly, the villagers feel that
by virtue of this close and intimate relationship the bhikkhus
should not divorce themselves from the everyday life of the village.

Thus, the villagers do not view their merit offerings to the
bhikkhus in solely religious terms. They feel, though this feeling
is not overtly expressed, that they help the bhikkhus in giving
them food, so it is only right that the bhikkhus should help them.
Food offerings are made, following Buddhist doctrine, for the
merit that the giver obtains; but, while the villagers are principally
motivated in this merit context, they also realize that the bhikkhus
are dependent on them. The bhikkhus and villagers are interdependent. The villagers realize they could not live without the
bhikkhus, who carry out both religious and secular functions so
necessary to the villagers' spiritual and physical well-being.

The villagers would be critical of village bhikkhus who remained
aloof from the everyday affairs of the village. Such bhikkhus would
be thought of as selfish. In a similar vein, the villagers feel the
bhikkhus have been given an opportunity to study and improve
themselves intellectually. The resulting knowledge should not be
hoarded but put to use for the welfare of the community, which
supports the bhikkhus. Among other criteria, respect in village
terms is measured by willingness to help others and share burdens.
If the bhikkhus did not help the villagers, it would be tantamount
to their acting as if they did not respect the villagers. In turn, the
villagers would naturally feel less respect for the bhikkhus. The
villagers respect the bhikkhus as leaders in the secular as well as
religious sphere of life. If the bhikkhus were to forfeit their leadership in the secular sphere, they would naturally forfeit a good deal
of the villagers' respect.

Although such feelings as those noted above are never voiced
openly, they nevertheless form a vital part of the subconscious
communal psychology of the village people. While the above
views held by the villagers are in many instances contrary to the
textual teachings of Buddhism, they nonetheless represent the
actual village attitudes.

The bhikkhus themselves, for personal reasons, feel impelled to become involved in secular village affairs. The bhikkhus of any particular village have most likely been born there or in a neighboring one. They lived the arduous life of a rural farm community before becoming bhikkhus. They know and have experienced the day-to-day problems and hardships of village life. The bhikkhus continually come into close contact with the vicissitudes of village life, whether it be a shortage of water, sickness, an impassable bridge, or an inadequate and difficult-to-travel road system. They are bound to feel these problems emotionally. Insofar as these vicissitudes affect the food supply of the village, the bhikkhus are very obviously involved in a physical sense as well.

But they are also concerned for other reasons. The bhikkhus come into daily face-to-face contact with the villagers. Unlike the city bhikkhus, they are in the intimate physical and social presence of their followers day after day. Thus, they inevitably become a part of the villagers' lives and problems. Being related by blood to many of those within the village draws them even closer to the secular problems of village life. The wat and the bhikkhus have become so intimately tied into the whole fabric of village life that the wat itself is the naturally chosen physical site for village activities of a widely divergent nature. If a political election is to be held, the polling booths may well be set up in the wat grounds. If a movie is to be shown or lecture given, the wat compound is the likely site to stage the evening's activity. Many of the government schools with lay teachers are still using wat buildings. Village festivals, Buddhist or otherwise in nature, naturally center in the confines of the wat with preparations, actual entertainment, and group flirting, all under the bhikkhus' watchful eyes.

In summary, the bhikkhus play a secular role both defined for them and by them. Thus, there is agreement on the advisability of the bhikkhus' actively participating in certain secular aspects of village life.

Villagers' Conceptions of the Bhikkhus' Religious Role and Daily Behavior

The major role of the village bhikkhus naturally is in the sphere of their religious activities. In a religious sense, the villagers desperately need the bhikkhus. Popular Buddhism as practiced in the villages would have little meaning if there were no bhikkhu community to stand as a religious model of ideal behavior, to perform the necessary religious ceremonies, and to receive the care and offerings of the lay people so necessary to the latters' merit accumulation and consequent well-being.

The bhikkhus have an indispensable role to perform in the inevitable crisis ceremonies of family life. The bhikkhus are necessary for the successful completion of these ceremonies, whether it be a ceremony of marriage, housewarming, sickness, death, or protection against ill omens. The bhikkhus give their religious blessings as they carry out the necessary chants and rituals. Actually, participation in such ceremonies is more custom than "religious duty" if viewed in terms of textual Buddhism. However, in popular terms, such ceremonial attendance is conceived of as one of the principal religious duties of the bhikkhus. In the same vein, the sprinkling of holy water and words of blessing and protection are thought of as integral spokes in the religious wheel turned by the bhikkhus in their ceremonial activities.

In village festivals, the bhikkhus play a major role in the preparation and carrying out of the festival in question. The wat is the focal point for all activity, and the bhikkhus are the essential organizers of the festival. Most of the festivals are Buddhistic in nature and origin, and even those of Brahmanical or animist significance often have Buddhist elements mixed in.

Whether it be a family ceremony or a village festival, the protective aura of the bhikkhus' attendance is desired and needed by the village people. The same is true of any ceremony to inaugurate a community activity: the opening of a school or village resthouse and meeting hall, village dam or irrigation tank, or a new village road. It is quite obvious to the most casual village observer that the villagers would not conceive of life without their bhikkhus.

The bhikkhus also teach the Dhamma. Every day there is a reading of the texts in the late afternoon. Usually only a few of the elders attend these readings. However, a much larger audience attends the Sabbath-day readings and a still larger one those readings which are chanted during the religious festivals.

Thus the villagers consider their bhikkhus to be intimately involved in both the secular and religious spheres. The villagers' attitude toward the bhikkhus depends on the situation, and, in certain instances, the villagers view the bhikkhus as a separate group isolated from the ordinary laymen. For example, where an issue involving morality is concerned, the bhikkhus are considered as exemplars of ideal moral conduct and their actions judged against a theoretical ideal that does not apply to laymen. This line of reasoning applies to the bhikkhus' daily living habits in general. In this context, one can understand the seemingly incongruous fact that certain sanitary practices are followed by the bhikkhus but do not reach beyond the wat confines. Despite the bhikkhus' influence, the respect accorded them, and their leadership role in community welfare programs, the villagers do not naturally accept such sanitary reforms merely because the bhikkhus practice them. The villagers feel that such practices as boiling water, using a filter, wearing shoes, and using latrines are reserved for the bhikkhus and identified with their way of life. There is little consideration that such practices might apply to them. The villagers do not see the health factors underlying these practices and associate such acts as part of the Dhamma and rules of discipline of the bhikkhus. The villagers also note with a touch of rural realism that the bhikkhus, by the nature of their life, can afford to take the pains to carry out such practices as the wearing of shoes and the boiling of water, but the villagers would find it inconvenient to do the same.

The bhikkhus themselves are often not fully aware of the scientific reasons behind their sanitary practices, and, thus, relatively few bhikkhus have encouraged the villagers to adapt such scientifically accepted practices. The view that the bhikkhus' way of living is removed and on a higher plane from that of the villagers militates against the extension of the former's personal living habits to beyond the wat borders.

Thus, it can be seen that the villagers can and do intellectually shuffle the bhikkhus back and forth between those areas in which the bhikkhus are considered as leaders and coworkers and those areas where the bhikkhus are placed on an isolated pedestal. It is necessary to define these respective areas in order to fully understand popular Buddhism at the rural level.

In the spheres of morality and the living habits of the bhikkhus both the villagers and the bhikkhus view the rules of discipline strictly. For example, the money bhikkhus receive should be and is largely used for their basic needs and for the upkeep and improvement of the temple. If it is felt money is being hoarded by the wat, there may be an accounting called for, though this will be done in a very informal and roundabout fashion. This is especially true if village labor or money contributions are called for at a time when the villagers are busy with their own work or have had a bad year with their crops.

Although strict observance of rules regarding moral behavior is required, if and when a breach occurs, no sanctions other than disrobing will be enforced. Breaches of the rules in this sphere, when they occur at all, almost exclusively involve improper behavior with village girls. This rarely happens, but, over the years, such infractions of the rules of discipline do occur. In the village histories there will usually be a few such remembered lapses in bhikkhu virtue. This is not a topic that is considered proper to discuss. The cases on record most often involve a bhikkhu and a village girl either having sexual relations or at least being known to have been alone in the dark. More often than not the offender is a bhikkhu in his early twenties or a novice in his late teens.

Sometimes, however, such cases will involve bhikkhus who have been married but have left their families to enter the monkhood. In the villagers' minds, these latter bhikkhus are thought of as a special group. They refer to them by a special title, *Hua Paw,* "Father's Head," which is not used in face-to-face contact with these bhikkhus. The villagers seem naturally to expect that these bhikkhus who have left their families will have a more difficult time in keeping the strict rules of bhikkhu discipline. There are many folk stories in village lore dealing with *Hua Paw,* and most of them are of quite unabashed ribaldry. These stories dwell on the moral peccadilloes or near-peccadilloes of the bhikkhus, their preoccupation with the satisfaction of their sexual and other appetites, and their involvement with their family concerns. It must be realized that the villagers do not tell these stories in any sense of disrespect. Such folk tales are many-sided. They are, of course, entertaining, but they also stand as a reminder of what is proper behavior and thus as a lesson to bhikkhus to walk the straight and narrow path. And, yet, these tales seem to infer that the villagers appreciate the difficulties of mortal men, especially family men, in renouncing craving and worldly ways and living under strict discipline.

Villagers' Understanding of Buddhist Doctrine
and Its Influence on Rural Life

To understand popular Buddhism in its entirety one must analyze the villagers' intellectual conception of Buddhist principles and doctrine and specify to just what extent Buddhism motivates their daily actions. For the average villager, such a concept as Nirvana, the philosophical intricacies of the Dhamma teachings, or the involved meditation forms have little meaning. The villagers' intellectual conception of the Buddhist religion centers about the relatively easily understood concepts of Karma, Rebirth, Merit, and Sin. The villager understands these concepts in simple terms. He believes in them, and, therefore, they affect his life. The villager is certain his present existence is the result of accumulated actions, both good and evil, in both former existences and the present one. In this life and the next, he will reap as he sows. Thus, his present actions are directed toward bettering his merit position so as to achieve a better life both now and in future existences. The fact that the villagers believe actions in this life do affect one's position in the present life should be stressed. In these terms the label of fatalism often attached to Buddhism is a misnomer. A "better life" is defined by the villager in worldly terms which have little relevance to the Buddhist ideal of extinction of desire and craving. For the villagers a better life in the future, both in this existence and the next, means one of riches, power, prestige, perfect health, beauty, and very little physical labor. It is in expectation of such a life that merit is made. If sin outbalances merit in one's karmic scale, then a life of poverty and hardship would necessarily follow. Religious doctrines are thus translated into terms the villagers understand and which are a part of their everyday life. Although it is true that the villagers think in terms of accumulating merit for their own future wellbeing, this does not necessarily mean they are self-centered or selfish, as one of the ways of gaining merit is through selfless acts of charity and community help.

In terms of relative importance of acts of merit, the villagers would thus view the protection, care, and feeding of the bhikkhus as of primary importance. Of similar importance would be the repairing or beautifying of the temple and the participation in and working for the success of the various merit festivals throughout the year. As noted above, entrance into the monkhood is very high on the scale of meritorious acts, both for the boy and his parents. However, one may also accumulate merit by following the teachings of the Buddha in one's everyday life. The keeping of the commandmants against the taking of life, lying, stealing, adultery, and drinking intoxicants aids one's merit position.

The villagers consider, but with lessened emphasis, that one's actions vis-à-vis society also are important in establishing a credit or debit in the merit accounts. One's meritorious acts in connection with the bhikkhus and temple can be partially canceled by selfish, ungenerous, and unkind acts in the social sphere. Thus, one gains merit by giving food, comfort, or money to one's parents, elders, the blind, the poverty-stricken, or the orphaned. Any such help is translated into merit terms.

Community development and village welfare activities, though farther down on the scale of importance as ways to achieve merit, are still construed in this context. The village well and resthouse are traditional merit activities. However, roads, bridges, and schools are more and more being thought of in similar terms.

A wide variety of everyday actions are explained and rationalized in terms of merit and its antithesis, sin. Since merit accumulation is the focal point of their religious thought, a good portion of the villager's actions are bound to be justified and criticized in a merit and sin context. As the villagers are ever-anxious to build up their store of merit, it is quite natural that they would strive to tie the merit label to every act possible. In addition to the more ritualistic and accepted acts of merit mentioned above, certain other behavior patterns should be noted which, though observably less obviously connected to the merit context, may still be so explained by the villagers.

There is a very strong emphasis in village social life on overt calmness and serenity in human relationships. To express open anger, dislike, and annoyance is considered improper. Those who avoid such antisocial behavior are considered to be following the teachings of Buddha and thus living meritoriously. It is certainly true that Buddhist teachings emphasize the propriety of preserving harmonious personal relationships and also the sinful nature of showing hatred, anger, and even displeasure. But likewise, of course, the teachings state or imply that it is similarly sinful to harbor such thoughts or express them in a roundabout fashion. However, the villagers are unable to avoid these latter two more indirect expressions of their feelings. Thus, they credit themselves on the merit scale if they avoid open social conflict while entries on the debit side will, for the most part, only be made if there is open and direct expression of antisocial feelings.

The anthropologist might place more emphasis on a social rather than religious explanation of such behavior. In a largely subsistence economy, such as the villagers have, there has evolved a pattern of cooperation and exchange of services to meet the needs of the community. If overtly expressed feuds were commonplace, co-operation and mutual aid in such a closed community would be almost impossible to maintain. Thus, the avoidance of overtly ex-pressed antagonisms can be seen as an intelligent social response to the necessities of village life. However, Buddhism gives such behavior the aura of religious respectability and righteousness and hence strengthens this particular mode of behavior. In general, the strong injunction to be tolerant of others' opinions can be viewed similarly in both social and religious contexts.

In the village, if someone does an illegal or immoral act, the one who is injured will more often than not fail to retaliate. In social terms, one will be afraid of both bringing into the open an uncomfortable hostile situation and of, perhaps, leading the wrong-doer to further harmful action. The villager allows himself to be bullied whether it be a case of a boundary dispute, theft, or pay-ment of a loan. The villager will rationalize his action or lack of it by stating that the wrongdoer will reap what he has sown. Harm and misfortune will befall the latter because of the sinful action.

Brahmanist and Animist Elements in Buddhism

Buddhism at the popular level accommodates to the social, eco-nomic, intellectual, and psychological realities of its environment. In popular Buddhism's relationship to Brahmanism and animism one finds a similar accommodation.

It has been noted that Buddhism, especially that of the rural areas, is permeated with Brahmanical and animistic concepts. To

some extent this is true. For example, the villagers are very careful
not to joke about entry into the monkhood, as malevolent spirits,
hearing such banter, might strike one down before the safety of
the monkhood could be reached. There is a general taboo against
women entering into areas reserved for certain types of religious
work.

There is a taboo against pregnant women being present at the
time of ordination. There are also Brahmanical vestiges connected
with the ordination ceremony, such as initiates' assumption of the
name of a mythological creature, the Naga, and the binding of
the initiate's spirit or "vital living essence" to his body with sacred
thread.

The world of spirits and magic is never far away. Buddha images
in the minds of the villagers have a magical potency. If such an
image is mishandled, stolen, or melted down, dire harm will befall the culprit. If one finds a Buddha image and presents it to
the temple, good luck will follow. In some cases, certain "charmed"
miniature Buddha images are kept as talismans to keep one from
harm that might arise in the form of accidents, theft, bullet
wounds, and the like. Actually, protection against such harm is
more often accomplished by the use of sacred symbols tatooed
on one's body or engraved on small copper plates rolled up and
worn about one's neck. For the most part, the villagers in the
northeast do not wear charmed Buddha images, but rather keep
them in their homes if they possess them at all. The actual wearing of such images is more prevalent in the towns. If such a potent
charm is either worn or kept in the house, one must be careful to
follow certain rules, or misfortune and harm will redound to the
owner. For example, the image must be taken off or placed in
one's mouth when one enters the bathroom. On sabbath days,
proper rites of respect must be performed with variations peculiar
to the image in question. If such rules are broken, then not only
may ordinary vicissitudes befall the owner, but, in certain instances, he may be turned into the dreaded spirit of the northeastern area, the phi pawb.

The villagers believe that a few special Buddha images reposing
in certain temples have magical powers and if properly importuned
will answer one's wishes. Requests to these images may concern
the curing of sickness or the satisfaction of a desire for children,
riches, and the like. Such special Buddha images are rare and are

located almost exclusively in famous temples in the larger towns.

It is true that the villagers may in certain instances pray to the Buddha images in their temple for a calmness of spirit, health, wealth, and the like. However, in general, the villagers conceive of the Buddha not as a god, but as a great teacher; not as an all-seeing, all-powerful being who can give immediate help, but as a religious sage who reached Perfection. In this context, the Buddha image would be viewed as a symbol of Buddha's teaching.

The small charmed images mentioned above are not viewed as symbols of Buddha's life and teaching, but as talismans whose power is due to the sacred formula chanted and placed inside the image. It is the magic formula, not the image per se that has the supernatural power protecting one from theft, bullets, accidents, and so on.

In numerous other instances, Brahmanism, and—reaching further back—animism, find expression in the popular Buddhism of the villagers. In Buddhist ceremonies performed by the bhikkhus, whether it be at a marriage, housewarming, sickness, or death, there are certain elements which are non-Buddhist in origin. There is the ubiquitous sacred thread which can be traced certainly to a Brahmanical source and perhaps much further back in time. This thread is believed to act as a boundary cord carrying the words of the bhikkhus wherever the cord extends and also concentrating the power of the words chanted within the confines of the boundary thread, thus consecrating, protecting, and blessing the people and site therein. Before the bhikkhus partake of the food presented by the villagers, miniature dishes of rice and "with rice" delicacies are placed next to the Buddha image in a ceremony that recalls animistic rituals from time immemorial. The sprinkling of sacred water not only reaches beyond Buddhism for its origins, but even the leaf used for such sprinkling is connected through the last syllable of its name to the King of Death, whom the evil spirits fear.[2]

While certain animistic and Brahmanical survivals have become a living part of Buddhism as popularly conceived, the Buddhist monkhood and the villagers have, in certain cases, actively sought to involve the bhikkhus in certain festivals which are animistic and/or Brahmanical in origin. One of the most notable examples of this is the famous *Bun Bang Fai*, or Skyrocket Festival of the northeast. Although the actual history of the origins of this particular festival is unknown or only vaguely understood by the villagers, they explain the shooting of the rockets as an expression of reverence to the rain god, which they refer to as the rain god of the Brahman religion. The villagers are quite aware that a god with such powers is outside the scope of Buddhism, and yet the Buddhist bhikkhus have come to play a very active role in this festival. The skyrockets are prepared in the wat under the bhikkhus' watchful eyes. The bhikkhus are responsible for the rockets' efficiency, and the success or failure of the rocket shooting has a definite effect on the bhikkhus' prestige. The rockets are paraded around the wat, and the bhikkhus supervise the firing.

The desire for rain and the desire for the general well-being of the community require that the villagers involve the village guardian spirit as well as the bhikkhus in this festival. Thus, the skyrockets are taken out and, along with village "moonshine," presented to the guardian spirit before being shot off. If the festival is not held, the guardian spirit must be told, and the spirit's permission obtained before postponement.

The bhikkhus are involved in supplication for rain in another ceremony where they chant special charmed stanzas to bring rainfall. On this particular occasion, the bhikkhus sit in a circle surrounding small clay and wax figures molded into a wide variety of sexually suggestive poses, again a potent reminder of the ever-present animist influences in village society.

The reasons for the inclusion of what might be considered alien Brahmanical and animist elements in Buddhist doctrine and ritual can partially be found in the Buddha's own approach to the establishment of Buddhism. The Buddha, in formulating his doctrine, took much from the Brahmanical world about him. In addition, he did not specifically deny the existing gods, angels, and spirits, although he did say they were mortal, as is all in the universe, and one should not look to them for help. Most commentators feel the Buddha well realized that he could not fully deny the prevalent gods and spirits and still maintain the interest of the masses in his religious teaching.[3]

The Buddha noted that there are many levels of teaching and of acceptance depending on the intellectual and spiritual capacity of the individual. Such an approach certainly would tend to open the way for accommodation to folk beliefs. However, higher metaphysical teachings were not neglected, being reserved for those few bhikkhus and laymen who were capable of responding to them.

Buddhist teaching left many unanswered questions as the Buddha considered that the focus of attention and speculation should be concentrated only on the central issue of man's suffering, its causes, and its removal. This approach likewise left room for incorporation of ideas from other sources to fill the gaps left by unanswered questions.

As the religion spread out, it was predictable that further such accretions would occur. Wherever Buddhism spread, those responsible for its dissemination to the rural masses realized that the religion could not be cut off from the life and beliefs, the hopes and fears, of the people.

Even though Buddhism accommodated itself to various folk beliefs and religions by incorporating to a certain degree such concepts into the religion, the merging had its limits. In many more cases, Buddhism adopted an attitude of polite tolerance to the rural beliefs which enabled these beliefs to live side by side but not within Buddhism. Buddhism as a popular religion took cognizance of the fact that if the religion itself does not help the rural masses to control the forces of nature and serve their material preoccupations, it, at least, must not openly negate those methods and beliefs that do serve such functions. Thus, there grew up and still exists in the rural areas today, especially in the northeast, an effective coexistence between Buddhism, Brahmanism, and animism. To date this fact of coexistence has been much less emphasized than the fact of various Brahman and animist facets within popular Buddhism. There are obviously non-Buddhist elements within Buddhism, but the powerful forces of Buddhism, Brahmanism, and animism in the community also operate independently, each one serving a specific function and each reserved to its special sphere, not conflicting with the others. Not only do Buddhism, Brahmanism, and animism not conflict, they often reinforce each other, as noted above in the various ceremonies connected with the asking for rainfall. Sometimes when ill omens have to be warded off or sickness cured there will be successive Buddhist and non-Buddhist ceremonies. In the village one is married in separate Buddhist and Brahmanical ritualistic ceremonies.

What to a Westerner may seem like a conflict between these forces or logical inconsistencies do not appear so to the villager.

In accepting Buddhism, no irrevocable choice was put before the villager, nor is such a choice implicit today. The rural masses have maintained their other beliefs. They see no inconsistencies, nor do the bhikkhus emphasize any. The villagers are able, without resorting to any mental gymnastics, to worship Buddhism, Brahmanism, and animism, each in its own right, each with full respect. What appear as contradictions to the outside observer are not viewed as such by the villager.

The world of spirits, magic, good luck, and ill omens has for the most part remained in the separate sphere of Brahmanism and animism, though in some instances this world has permeated the theory and ritual of popular Buddhism. However, Buddhism largely has its importance and function elsewhere.

Conclusion

It is to be hoped that this chapter will shed some light on the neglected subject of popular Buddhism and encourage additional studies in this field. I have placed special emphasis on the sharp differentiation between textual injunctions and the actual behavior patterns at the rural level, whether one is considering entrance into the monkhood; secular involvement of the bhikkhus; religious role, doctrine, and practice; or the merger of Buddhism, Brahmanism, and animism. Village studies should also give attention to identifying conflicts and correspondences between government statutory law and village customary behavior.

FOOTNOTE REFERENCES

1. This thesis has been developed in great detail by Professor F. S. C. Northrop both in lectures and published materials.
2. Anuman Rajadhon, Phya, "Popular Buddhism in Thailand," in *Life and Ritual in Old Siam*, Human Relations Area Files, New Haven, 1961, p. 91.
3. Conze, Edward, *Buddhism, Its Essence and Development*, B. Cassirer, Oxford, 1951, pp. 70–88.

Recent Studies on the
Japanese National Character TATSURO YAMAMOTO

6

The main purpose of this chapter is to offer some data, selected from recent studies on the national character of the Japanese people, as raw materials to be used for the formulation or verification of theories of comparative cultural anthropology.

History of the Study

Any study of the "national character" in Japan usually includes "the way of thinking." This interest first appeared in connection with the rise of national consciousness in the late nineteenth century, when the attention of the people was directed both to the national tradition and to the outside world. The catchword of the time was "Japanese spirit, Western talent" (wa-kon yō-sai), corresponding approximately to the expression "Chinese substance, Western utility" (chung-t'i hsi-yung) of the same period in dynastic China. The observation and evaluation of Japanese culture by Westerners became the direct concern of the people, and Western writings on Japan attracted the attention of intellectuals. This is to be explained not only in terms of curiosity or necessity, but also of the sensitiveness of the Japanese to outside standards. Added to this was the belief that a foreigner's observation is different and that they know better in many respects. Lafcadio Hearn became the most popular writer on things Japanese, and his works are still in wide circulation, along with the writings of Bruno Taut. During the subsequent rise of ultranationalism, from around the beginning of the twentieth century, the national character was studied rather systematically but with much stress upon the merits of the people. This strong nationalism came into collision with the opposing power of democracy, became weaker in the twenties, and regained power in the thirties. It was closely connected with imperialism, supported by the growing military and economic power and, ideologically, by the family-state hierarchy, combined with the Tennō worship, sanctioned by mythology, which claimed that the supreme authority came down from heaven through the unbroken linear descent of the imperial family. The spirit of the time continued till the end of World War II. This atmosphere could be symbolized by the frequently debated word *kokka* (*koku-ka*, the state), which means literally "state–family." Studies on the sensibility and traditional morals were carried out by scholars of Japanese literature and history. The well-documented results are still very useful in spite of the egocentric bias and preaching connotation.

The end of World War II drew the demarcation line for further studies on national character. The over-all change of the social system and ideology caused by the defeat, and the inflow of "democracy," stimulated learned interest from different angles. The backwardness of Japanese mentality, remnants of the feudal regime, and so on, were put in contrast with the idealized types of Western thought and history. The general atmosphere was that of self-depreciation. Emancipated from the military state authority, critical studies on traditional Japan developed rapidly in various branches of the humanities and social sciences. Just at this time Ruth Benedict's *The Chrysanthemum and the Sword* was introduced and translated into Japanese. It fitted exactly into the learned atmosphere of the time, and the impact of this book was very strong and wide both on the scholarly world and the general public. In spite of the critical opinions from various angles, it stimulated a great deal of further study on culture and personality, and new research methods in the behavioral sciences were adopted. Analyses of traditional literary works, newspaper columns, and popular songs were made along with the socialization of children and overseas Japanese.

Rorschach tests, thematic apperception tests, and problem situation tests became widely used. The technical immaturity of the beginning stage was ameliorated by the increase of trained specialists and international collaboration, mainly with the United States.

Interdisciplinary collaboration programs were also organized. The Human Relations Research Group (*Ningen-Kankei Sōgō Kenkyū Dan*), headed by Tsuneo Muramatsu, Professor of Psychiatry of Nagoya University, consisted of thirty-four members representing psychiatry, psychology, sociology, cultural anthropology, with the participation of historians, economists, statisticians, social workers, and specialists on religion. Samples of 250 individuals were obtained from three selected rural settlements, mountain, fishing, and lowland rice-farming communities, and a sample of over 2000 individuals was collected in the cities of Okayama and Nagoya. This study also includes the data of some follow-up studies of children for nine years.[1] Another group, directed by Seiichi Izumi of Tokyo University, was also interdisciplinary and has been engaged in the larger regional differences of culture and personality. The Research Committee of Japanese National Character of the National Institute of Statistical Mathematics carried out nationwide surveys extensively in 1953 and 1958. The object was to study the ways of thinking. The data covering 3000 persons were collected, and the direction of change at an interval of five years is being investigated. All boroughs, cities, towns, and villages were stratified according to metropolitan, urban, and rural divisions, to population size, to district, and so on, and from each stratum one individual was selected by means of random sampling, the probability of selection being proportionate to the size of population.[2] Another research group, headed by Yoshitomo Ushijima of Kyūshū University, performed cross-cultural comparative studies on personality formation in West Europe and Japan, with the collaboration of scholars of the United Kingdom, West Germany, and France. The result has shown a great difference and rapid change in the Japanese younger generation. Considerable progress was made by the recent studies, but by and large systematic interpretation has not been well developed.

Several Results of Recent Studies

Among numerous publications concerning the Japanese national character, thirty-seven books were selected and analyzed recently.[3]

The following is a list of traits rearranged and paraphrased by the writer:

1. Delicacy, fondness, beautification of life, harmony with nature, sensitiveness to seasonal change, love of small-scaled completion and simplicity, *tampaku* (unemotional, frankness, indifference), love of purity, cleanliness, attachment to the past.

2. Politeness, courteousness, respectfulness, delicacy and sensitiveness to interpersonal feeling, fulfillment of promises, sycophancy, well-intentioned lie, dislike of flat confrontation.

3. Nonextremism, moderation, harmony, gentleness, tolerance, compromise, mediation-system.

4. Diligence, sincerity, patience, self-control, self-sacrifice, perseverance, sanguine temperament, blowing hot—blowing cold.

5. Love of peace, but bravery in war, martial spirit, and if the opponent is found to be stronger in a fair and square fight, frankness in surrendering at discretion.

6. Imitativeness, lack of creativeness and originality, ability to assimilate, receptiveness, adaptability, utilitarianism, pragmatism, progressiveness, sensitiveness to the external world, reliance upon external standards and help, quick response to the outer impact, inferiority complex in facing foreign civilization.

7. Order, discipline, and self-sacrifice in the family, utmost importance of filial piety, nonestablishment of individual's place in the family, tradition of benevolent housefather, higher position of mother than wife, indulgence to infants, high estimation of family name and family honor, adoption of son for the continuation of household, *inkyo* (abdication of the headship of a family), ancestor worship, veneration of *kami* (god) together with the worship of ancestors, family suicide (including children).

8. Prominence of national interest, the nation as a disguised family, the religion of Tennō worship, mythological sanction of the position of the ruler, sympathetic relations between the imperial family and the people.

9. Thinking much of prestige, dignity, and honor, fear of being mocked, maintenance of dignity, attitude of protection from disdain, aggressive when insulted or blamed, virtuously vengeful when insulted.

10. Paternalistic benevolence in social contacts, boss-and-follower relations fictitiously identified with father and son, submis-

sion and nonresistance to authority, devoted service to lord annihilating private concerns—sometimes connected with the ascetic practice of Zen Buddhism, self-immolation on the death of the lord.

11. Having proper place in the graded social system, importance of honorifics and self-abasing expressions in the language, weakness of class consciousness, underdevelopment of public morality, indifference to politics, shame at being involved in political affairs.

12. Placing more importance upon limited human relations than universal ethics or religious belief, less importance on individuality than particular human groups, social tie of *on* (favor flowing down) and *giri* (sense of obligation created by *on*), conflict between humanity and *giri* obligation, endurance of the feeling of gratitude.

13. Immediate perception, intuitive and realistic thinking, actualism, empiricism, worldliness, love of practicality, nonmeditativeness, nonmetaphysicality, dislike of abstract thinking, not giving recognition without concrete evidence, stressing *koto* (things, happenings) more than *ri* (reason, fundamental principle), vulgar materialism, acceptance of existing reality, stressing the particular more than the universal.

14. Nontheoretical irrational thinking, underdevelopment of scientific spirit, ambiguous consciousness of subject and predicate in the expressive form of judgment, lack of imagination and criticism, classification by simplified categories, biased attachment to theory detached from actuality, general conclusion based upon one fact.

15. Dislike of religious commandments, more reliance upon humanity and sympathy than law, weak consciousness of the superexistence over human groups, observance of social norms irrespective of one's thoughts in mind, changing principle of behavior according to time and place, inconsistency, opportunism.

16. Little care about life beyond the grave, no god of preeminence distinct from human being, double belief in Shintoism and Buddhism with no contradiction, no cruel treatment of infidels, belief in the divine favor in this world, subordination of religion to ancestors, parents, lord, and nation, suicide normal and not a sin, *shinjū* (lovers' suicide).

17. Belief in the uncertainty of life, fatalism, quick resignation, little consciousness of guilt, lack of profound hatred of sin, nonchalant optimism, *oharai* (expulsion of sin and impurity by means of Shinto ritual).

This list of national traits is a somewhat arbitrary mixture of heterogeneous writings; nevertheless, taken as a whole, it shows a general tendency from the observation of diverse authors and leads us into the philosophy of culture and epistemology. As the above-stated history shows, these traits are contrasted, by and large, to Western ones.

Hajime Nakamura, Professor of Indian Philosophy, doing research on the Japanese ways of thinking, particularly in connection with the process of accepting Buddhism, stressed the tendency to emphasize a particular social nexus, the irrationalistic disposition, the acceptance of actuality.[4] Studies on Japanese *langue* and *parole* by Haruhiko Kindaichi clarified the nature of thinking based upon diversified sources. The tendency not to speak out, the love of the briefest expressions, indifference to difficulty of understanding, reflection of social norms, and so on, were revealed. For illustration of the language, the writer cites two examples: one from the kabuki theatre (A),[5] the other from the *haiku* poetry of Bashō (1644–1694) (B).

A. People used different words and expressions, according to their social status, consolidating the status itself. This case concerns the different types of verb possible in the sentence "When did you come to Edo?"

When	Edo	to	came	
Itsu	Edo	e	oide nasare mashita	head of a merchant family
Itsu	Edo	e	okoshi de gozai mashita	woman of warrior class, wife of a merchant
Itsu	Edo	e	gozatta	father
Itsu	Edo	e	gozarashatta	mother
Itsu	Edo	e	mairareta	warrior
Itsu	Edo	e	kiyashan shita	prostitute
Itsu	Edo	e	gozan shita	senior girl of gay quarters
Itsu	Edo	e	kinasan shita	geisha girl
Itsu	Edo	e	gozari mashita	Buddhist priest, physician
Itsu	Edo	e	oidenasē mashita	craftsman, fireman
Itsu	Edo	e	gozarasshari mashita	housemaid

B. This briefest form of poetry shows several characteristics of the language.

ta	ichi-mai	uete	tachisaru	yanagi	kana
paddy field	one piece	planted	go away	willow	tree

One piece of paddy field planted, I leave the willow tree.

The poet started from the foot of the willow tree, after having enjoyed the scenery for some time, during which a farmer finished the work of planting rice in a piece of paddy field (surrounded by a footpath). The season was early summer, and perhaps the poet had been sitting at the foot of the tree.

The tradition of the ways of thinking lives in present-day Japan. In his psychological analysis, Hiroshi Minami pointed out the ambiguous and misty atmosphere encircling individuals, the lack of their clear-cut human relations and definite confrontations, and so on. A few examples will be cited from the above-mentioned study of the Institute of Statistical Mathematics.[6] (See following charts 1958 and 1953.)

1. (Show picture.) Imagine this situation. Mr. M was orphaned at an early age and was brought up by Mr. A, a neighbor. The As gave him a good education, sent him to a university, and now Mr. M has become the president of a company. One day he gets a telegram to say that Mr. A, who brought him up, is seriously ill and would he come at once. This comes just at the moment when he is going to an important meeting which will decide whether his firm is to go bankrupt or to survive. (Show card here.) Which of the things written on this card do you think he should do?

    a. Leave everything and go back home.

    b. However worried he might be about Mr. A, he should go to the meeting.

2. The last question supposed that Mr. A had taken him in as an orphan in his youth and brought him up. Suppose that it had been his real father who was on his deathbed: Which would have been your answer then?

	(a)	(b)	Others	D.K.	Total
Mr. A (1958)	50	39	2	9	100
(1953)	54	41	1	4	100

| Father | (1958) | 50 | 41 | 2 | 7 | 100 |
| | (1953) | 49 | 48 | 1 | 2 | 100 |

3. (Show picture.) Suppose that someone who has been good to you in the past has a son who applies for entrance to a firm. Someone from the firm comes to ask you what kind of person the son is. You happen to know that the son is not very reliable. What would you say to the representative of the firm?

	(a) Commend him	(b) Reply vaguely	(c) Say he is not reliable	Others	D.K.	Total
1958	20	18	50	2	10	100
1953	23	19	48	2	8	100

4. (Only for those who gave answers (a), (b), or (c) to the former question.) If people get to know what you have done, what do you think they would think of you?

	Would approve	Would say I had no choice	Would disapprove	Others	D.K.	Total
(a) 1958	27	33	22	4	14	100 (468)
1953	27	41	14	7	11	100 (433)
(b) 1958	10	42	26	4	18	100 (421)
1953	14	49	12	10	15	100 (309)
(c) 1958	14	24	44	8	10	100 (1,191)
1953	21	31	31	10	7	100 (898)

5. (Only for those who say "no choice" or "would disapprove" in answer to last question.) Would it worry you that people thought that way?

	Would be worried	Would not be worried	Others	D.K.	Total
No choice	27	67	2	4	100
Disapprove	35	62	1	2	100

6. (Show card.) Suppose you are working in a firm. There are two types of department chiefs. Which of these two would you prefer to work under?

     a. A man who always sticks to the work rules and never demands any unreasonable work, but, on the other hand,

never does anything for you personally in matters not connected with the work.

   b. A man who sometimes demands extra work in contraven-
tion of the work rules, but, on the other hand, looks after
you personally in matters not connected with the work.

	(a)	(b)	Others	D.K.	Total
1958	14	77	2	7	100
1953	12	85	1	2	100

7. If you have no children, do you think it necessary to adopt
a child in order to continue the family line, even if there is no
blood relationship? Or do you not think this is important?

	Yes	Would not bother	Depend on circumstances	Others	D.K.	Total
1958	63	21	8	1	7	100
1953	73	16	7	1	3	100

8. What would you think about adopting the child of a relative?

	Would	Would not	Depend on circumstances	Others	D.K.	Total
1953	38	35	18	2	7	100 (597)
1953*	83	9	5	1	2	100 (2,254)

9. Some Prime Ministers, when they take office, pay a visit to
the Imperial Shrine at Ise. What do you think about this practice?

	Should go	Better to go	Can please himself	Better not to go	Should not go	Others	D.K.	Total
1958	5	33	27	12	5	2	16	100 (1,449)
1953	7	50	23	6	2	2	10	100 (2,254)

Considerable data have been collected, but the methodological
considerations on over-all analysis and general characterization are
still to be developed. Explanations heretofore accepted are now
being reexamined. To cite an example, George de Vos recently
argued against the widely held view that Japanese culture is best

* It is assumed that those who would adopt an unrelated child would also
adopt a relative's child.

characterized as a "shame" culture in the frame of the guilt-shame dichotomy, and he pointed out the undercurrent of guilt in terms of the family relations, especially that of children to their mother. The Japanese mother, without conscious intent, has perfected techniques of inducing guilt in her children by such means as quiet suffering. She takes the burden of responsibility for their behavior and, as also with bad conduct on the part of her husband, will often manifest self-reproach if her children conduct themselves badly or in any way fail to meet the standards of success set for the community. If one fails to meet social expectations, one thereby hurts one's mother, and also hurts other family members; as a result, one suffers unhappiness and feelings of guilt.[7] This analysis might also be extended to clans, regional groups and lord-vassal relations, consolidated by *on-giri* ties—"sloping favor-obligation relations," as the writer calls it—accompanied by the feeling of guilt which could be regarded as "internal" both of individuals and of social groups. Theoretical problems presented to this symposium are of extreme importance, and when we apply the epistemological criteria of Professor Northrop, naive realism, radical empiricism, and logical realism, the traditional Japanese ways of thinking fit nicely in the second.

Studies are being made on historical vicissitudes as well as regional differences, and synchronic-diachronic treatments of materials are differentiated. Generalization is always important for the study of enduring philosophy and core values, but some aspects of radical change in history are to be noted. Each period of ancient imperial rule, middle and modern feudalism, and post-Meiji regime has distinct features, but the most extreme change came after World War II. The days of "mental collapse" following the defeat marked the demarcation line. In the name of democratization a far-reaching upheaval occurred, and change continues at present with rapidity in many aspects of culture and personality. On the above-cited table, the difference of figures which appeared at the interval of five years is 10 percent at 7 and 17 percent at 9. Might these not be regarded as indicative of a fundamental historical change? If so, the direction of the change is away from the traditional mentality of the family line and the atmosphere of a state religion. Seventeen percent have considerable probability. These statistics cover individuals of 20 years and over, but a more radical change is now on the way among the younger generation. Ushijima's recent study of comparative personality formation shows us the amazingly rapid change of Japanese youth.[8] During infancy there was found no great difference between the English and the Japanese except for a slightly more aggressive attitude among the latter. But a marked divergence appears in childhood concerning religious attitudes, which is obviously strong in Western Europe. In adolescence, Japanese youth become much more progressive, radical, and pacifist than their counterparts of Western Europe. The weakest points of Japanese youth are the underdevelopment of individuality and religious attitudes. The radical change of national character is inseparably connected with the problem of epistemology. Now we can notice that logical realism is grow-

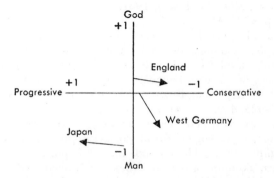

ing in many respects. It is quite obvious that the law of contract is prevailing in daily life side by side with modern science, creating new ways of thinking. The development of a unilinear notion of time is also to be noted. In this respect, the earlier influence of Spencer and the later influence of Marx is important, with their ideas of evolution and developmental stages. We have to analyze in this connection the word feudal (hōken) which is in common use in daily life, meaning those traditional things which are taken as obstacles to progress oriented to one direction in the future.

In general the epistemological change is now going from the radical empirical to the logical realistic. Are the criteria applicable universally?

The writer's anticipation is affirmative. The writer's expectation, as a historian of comparative cultural anthropology, is to work out general theories and criteria, constantly applicable to any given culture at any stage of its historical development, to clarify fundamental typological differences, to identify irreversible directions and forces of change, and to illuminate the dynamic process of historical reality.

FOOTNOTE REFERENCES

1. Muramatsu, Tsuneo (ed.), *Nihonjin; Bunka to personality no jisshō-teki kenkyū* (The Japanese; Studies in culture and personality), Reimei-shobō, Nagoya, 1962.
2. Tōkei Sūri Kenkyūjo, Kokuminsei Chōsa Iinkai (The Institute of Statistical Mathematics, Research Committee of Japanese National Character), *Nihonjin no Kokuminsei* (A Study of Japanese National Character), Shiseidō, Tokyo, 1961.
3. *Ibid.*, pp. 530–541.
4. Nakamura, Hajime, *The Ways of Thinking of Eastern Peoples*, Japanese National Commission for UNESCO, 1960.
5. Kindaichi, Haruhiko, *Nihongo no Seiri to Shinri* (Physiology and Psychology of Japanese Language), Shibundō, Tokyo, 1962, p. 151.
6. Tōkei Sūri Kenkyūjo, Kokuminsei Chōsa Iinkai, *op. cit.*, note 2, pp. 423–425, 429, 421, 415.
7. Norbeck, Edward, and George de Vos, "Japan," in Francis L. K. Hsu (ed.), *Psychological Anthropology; Approaches to Culture and Personality*, Dorsey, Homewood, Ill., 1961, pp. 26, 27.
8. Ushijima, Yoshitomo, *Seiō to Nihon no Ningen-keisei* (Formation of Personality in West Europe and Japan), Kaneko-shobō, Tokyo, 1961, pp. 356–372.

BIBLIOGRAPHY

Balandier, George, "Réflexion sur une anthropologie dynamique et critique," *Shakai-gaku Hyōron (Japanese Sociological Review)*, vol. XII, nos. 3–4, 1962.

Kindaichi, Haruhiko, *Nihongo* (Japanese Language), Iwanami-shoten, Tokyo, 1957.

Minami, Hiroshi, *Nihonjin no Shinri* (Psychology of the Japanese), Iwanami-shoten, Tokyo, 1953.

The Common Elements in the Philosophy of Matrilineal Societies in India U. R. EHRENFELS

7

An attempt will here be made to arrive at some common denominator in the value patterns of various matrilineal societies in India. The sets of people under study are the tribal Khasi and Garo of Assam in the northeastern corner of India, several tribal groups in the highlands of Kerala, as well as caste groups in the lowlands of the country on the southwestern coast of the peninsula.

Each of the matrilineal clusters stands out against quite different traditional backgrounds. While a simple to fairly specialized kind of shifting cultivation characterizes the economy of the preliterate tribal groups in both Assam and Kerala, there are also in the South stratified social classes with a complex heritage of literary traditions, including close contacts with Brahmanism, Sanskrit, and other elements of ancient civilizations. Among all these peoples, acculturative influences were felt in quite different ways and times. If, in spite of these stressed differences, there are common sets of values significantly characteristic for the groups under consideration, and if, in addition, these values are crystallized into a *Gestalt*—a holistic entity of attitudes—we are then justified in considering this entity as an adequate and meaningful expression of a common underlying philosophy.

The Sources

This paper is based mainly on three kinds of sources. There are, first, the reports of early travelers, mostly Arab and Portuguese, particularly that of Barbosa; second, numerous references in the Reports of the Census of India and the series of monographs on castes and tribes compiled at the beginning of this century.[1] Partly akin in approach and time of compilation, partly of an altogether different nature, are numerous scattered articles and bigger works, discussing isolated aspects in the life of matrilineal societies in India. A remark should be made on this latter source of information to caution the reader, unfamiliar with the ethnology of South India, against the impression he could get from this scattered material that "the Nayars" are the isolated and only instance of matrilineal societies in India. In reality, the Nayars are not only one among many other, though less populous, such societies in Kerala, as we shall see later, but their general culture has also much in common with that of numerous other social classes in South India outside Kerala. This resemblance to, and relationship with, other now patrilineal societies among the Dravidian-speaking Indians need not, for the purpose of this paper, be considered, though it holds the key to the understanding of common South Indian problems.

Finally, there are the author's own observations, made during five field trips to Khasi and Garo Hills in Assam and extensive field work conducted over a period of fifteen years in Kerala.[2] The findings largely corroborated an earlier and theoretical work,[3] still a product of armchair anthropology, though methods and results of this first work had to be thoroughly revised and partly altered.

Background Picture

The Austro-Asiatic-speaking Khasi (and Lyngngam), as well as the Tibeto-Burmese-speaking Garo of Central Assam are both Mongoloid highland tribes and were shifting cultivators. They remained politically independent until, for the first time in their history, they were conquered by the British during the second half of the nineteenth century. Traditional Khasi crafts, such as iron smelting and blacksmithery, types of tools and house construction, and much of their poetry and religious lore show little trace of precolonial contacts with the Hindu-Buddhist or Muslim centers in the lowlands of Assam, Burma, and Bengal. Only one among the numerous Khasi *siem* (independent rulers) shifted his residence every winter from Jowei in the eastern Khasi Hills to Durgapur in the plains, now of East Pakistan, thus introducing some Hindu elements in his state.

The Garo were traditionally less specialized in technical skill and governmental organization than their eastern neighbors, the Khasi. They knew neither iron smelting nor institutionalized dynastic organization. Garo social structure is quite different from that of the Khasi, though their tradition has it that matrilineal succession and matrilocality have been taken over from them.

By contrast, the preliterate, shifting cultivators in Kerala, the Kannikkar, Muduvar, Kuruchar, Virpat Malayalar, and others, are not culturally isolated from their matrilineal neighbors in the plains of South India. Traditionally they even consider themselves, and are considered by others, to be *Malai Nayar*, Hill Nayars, or Forest Tiyyas. The designation *Nayar* covers a large social stratum with a history of feudal rulership and land owning, comprising warriors, temple servants, cultivators, and the presently emerging middle-class élite of Kerala. Closely akin to these lowland Nayars are other Hindu caste groups with an old literary tradition, such as the Menon, Pillai, Samantham, Nambiar, Nambisan, Ambalavasi, Poduval, and also the North Malabar Mapillais, the Key, and others who are Malayalam-speaking Muslims. Against this background of cultural and historical diversity, certain similarities stand out which may be seen as part of these peoples' philosophy of life and which in turn shape their value systems.

Common Elements in Matrilineal Societies

Attitude Toward the Male

No logically clear-cut separation of attitudes toward the sexes can be distilled from any social system, as these attitudes are everywhere complex and, to a certain extent, reciprocal. However, in matrilineal societies, such as those of India, the differentiation between attitudes is further enhanced by the double role in which the average man finds himself if he has a married sister and is married himself. Toward his sister's (or sisters') children he acts in the role of a maternal uncle with special obligations and rights, while toward his wife's (or wives') children his obligations are more of an emotional, less formal character. A similar dichotomy does not exist for women in their roles as mothers or aunts, though the attitude of any woman to her brother is generally closer in matrilineal social systems than it is in patrilineal ones.

Thus the position held by the maternal uncle in matrilineal societies of India, as indeed the world over, is significant. The legal position assigned to this relative finds expression in the respect, but also somewhat formal awe, shown to him by his family. He is treated, in Assam and Kerala alike, as the managing head of the family property. However, if the maternal uncle of Kerala, the *karanavan*, holds a position similar to that of the u *kni*, the maternal uncle in Khasi society, there is, on the other hand, a significant difference.

Through the very close and frequently marital ties between women of the matrilineal classes and Nambudri Brahman men, the example-setting behavior of the latter added consistently to doubts about the advantages and merits of matriliny in the eyes of those among its followers who had adopted Brahman values and oriented their attitudes accordingly. Thus the rule of the *karanavan* is, or was, in the matrilineally extended family of Kerala approximately that of the head in a Brahman patrilineal family. The u *kni* of the Khasi in Assam, though scarcely less important, was not quite as powerful and dominating as his counterpart in Kerala.

As for attitudes taken toward male members of the family in the role of a husband, they also conform to a common pattern among most matrilineal societies in India. There prevails generally the attitude to the husband as an emotionally important, but legally somewhat marginal, family member, with less stress on economic and legal ties between husband and wife than in the case of patrilineal societies.

An interesting but somewhat atypical feature exists among the Garo. At marriage a man shifts to his wife's house to become the manager, almost virtual owner of the property. But he stays as a sort of adopted member in his wife's clan. To protect him against possible injustice on the part of that clan, the *nokrom* (generally his nephew) acts as the advocate of his clan relative in an institutionalized position. Traditionally the husband retains his place in his wife's clan even in the case of her death, when her clan procures a substitute. In the case of his mother-in-law's widowhood, he would marry her as a cowife of her daughter.

More typical, and also more instructive for our purpose, is the situation among the Khasi and both tribal and socioeconomically higher classes in Kerala. In all those groups the husband shares his influence in one form or the other with his wife's brother, that is to say, the important maternal uncle as seen from the children's point of view. This in itself inculcates a plural distribution of family authority and with it a characteristic feature—communal cooperation. One might here think in terms of democratic, as against monarchic or totalitarian, forms of government if one wishes to illustrate matters with slogans taken from political conceptualizations of the day. If this mode of comparison contains some misleading features, it also brings out the basic fact that there are fundamental attitudes at work in the shaping of the matrilineal, as against the patrilineal, family system. In the latter, the predominance of the paterfamilias tended to lead to a monolithic situation based on a more or less absolute source of power.

Differences between attitudes toward the male in Kerala and Assam can best be brought out by looking into the propaganda against the matrilineal system and the response to it. Characteristically criticism against the traditional matrilineal family runs along different lines in different areas.

Active propaganda began, though at different times, with the appearance of European missionaries, government administrators, and less formal contacts. It has been recently intensified by the ever-increasing number of newcomers from other patrilineal areas in India. Individuals within the matrilineal societies who responded to the various forms of propaganda, assimilation, and enculturation pointed out that the matrilineal family head was behaving autocratically and without due consideration of his matrilineal family members. The main complaint here was that he often favored his wife and children in the role as husband and as father. In contradistinction to this, the Khasi in Assam responded less easily to adverse criticism and antimother-right propaganda and, if they expressed anything at all, it was the need to conform to patrilineal neighbors and, above all, to the powerful European example. Among the Khasi, the disadvantages of the matrilineal system are mainly verbalized by pointing to the case of a wife's early death. If the husband then marries into another group, the children are taken over by the mother's family, possibly their maternal uncle, the u *kni,* and altogether separated from their father.

We are obliged to limit ourselves to the discussion of attitudes toward the male in his double role as the maternal uncle and husband. Other sides of this complex will best be brought out by contrasting them with the actual position of women in society.

Attitude Toward the Female

The impression an observer gets from the daily life in one of the traditional matrilineal families in the plains of Kerala is indeed one of general conformity with Brahman patterns. Women live in separate quarters; they often serve men at meals; they show the somewhat formal respect to important male members, including their own husbands, by which Brahman etiquette is characterized. For instance, they customarily stand in the presence of elder seated males and generally talk to them only if spoken to.

However here, as in other matrilineal societies, women hold a central position, especially in the role of mothers, approximating that of a family head. Significantly, criticism may be directed against an assuming *karanavan.* But the chances to hear much criticism directed against a tyrannical woman in an authoritative position are scanty. Further, if an exacting wife or an overbearing mother-in-law are familiar features in patrilineal, "patriarchal," societies, this does not seem characteristic, much less typical, of family squabbles in matrilineal societies, though inheritance laws and succession assign important functions to women. Thus the key position which they legally occupy does not imply that they play the role of the family boss. The closest approximation to a "matriarch" is the Ka *Iawbei,* the oldest leading woman in a traditional Khasi extended family. Even there, however, the u *kni* and the husband are by no means henpecked.

The point to be made clear is that it is the *female principle* in society, rather than the assumption of dominant roles by individual women, which is strengthened through the customary inheritance and name succession in the female line. This is a subtle, but important, point. It changes, among other things, the nature of the brother-sister relationship and, above all, that of parents to their daughters.

The strengthening of the female principle has such an impact on the general mentality that every facet of daily life is affected. Also new socioeconomic opportunities in acculturation to Western values are perceived, and made use of, in a characteristic fashion. We have only to compare achievements of women in matrilineal societies with those of their sisters in corresponding patrilineal ones. Girls of matrilineal groups in Kerala were the first women in India to take up university education at the close of the nineteenth century. Khasi girls are outstanding among all the Highland peoples of Assam as independent workers or career girls, such as nurses, doctors, secretaries, journalists, and even politicians.

The inheritance through the female, especially if linked with matrilocality, places the daughter of a family in an advantageous position. As it is through the daughter that the family continues, girls are welcome. When taking a village census at Maw Syn Jri in the Central Khasi Plateau, I came to a house which was described by neighbors as going to die out because there were only two sons and no daughters in this family. A similar situation would also arise in one of the matrilineal communities of Kerala, though it would be of lesser importance because house names lost much of their functional importance during the last half century.

But if girls are welcome, boys are nowhere in matrilineal societies customarily neglected in the way girls very often are to a greater or lesser extent in patrilineal societies. I never came across sons being condescendingly treated just because of their being "mere boys."

The importance of daughters for the continuation of a family finds expression in the ritualistic celebration of the first menstruation. In South India it is one of the big family feasts, connecting the reproductive capacity of the girl with the prosperity of the family, and it is conducted on a grand scale, especially among the Nayars in Kerala. It is popularly hinted at as advertising the girl (for marriage), though it has, as we see, a still deeper meaning in the matrilineal family context. Earlier reports compared the role taken by an eldest daughter in a Nayar *taravad* to that of a prime minister in the traditional family republic. The importance of girls in a Khasi house is much the same, except for the emphasis placed on the youngest instead of the oldest.

The Khasi preference for the ka khun kaddu, the youngest daughter, is indeed interesting. She acts as an indispensable assistant in religious ritual. It is she who arranges the leaves of the sacred Khasi oak for family feasts, and it is she who carries the bones after cremation of a relative to the stone receptacle of the family. Her functions resemble those of the first-born son in many patriarchal societies.

The preference for the youngest child emphasizes a general feature of mother-right. This feature is the provision of certain preferential rights to the "weaker sex," the natural course of events bringing more power to the stronger. A cultural reversion of the natural order is here manifest, even though most matrilineal people in India would not verbalize the philosophy of their social organization in this way. Rather, they say that it is natural for a child to belong primarily to his mother because there are no doubts about motherhood.

The conflicting opinions about what is more "natural" may be quite futile from the anthropological point of view. Yet their study leads toward grasping the internal mechanisms by which elements are linked in the philosophy of a culture.

Simplicity and Color in Daily Life

The prominence of puberty rites for girls, especially as we have seen, among the higher classes of Kerala, illustrates a widespread trait in matrilineal societies: the ready acceptance of the biological facts of life, specifically those connected with the reproductive qualities of the female body. This attitude entails a frame of mind inclined to frankness and averse to the ideology of hiding, hushing up, or, so to say, driving these facts underground. This attitude also goes along with a more realistic approach to womanhood as well as individual women.

Traditionally, education has been provided for girls of the higher matrilineal castes in Kerala. The kalaris, or gymnasia, are institutions which used to impart both theoretical and physical education. Teaching was dispensed in book knowledge, art, religious lore, sport and fighting, and promoting physical prowess. The comparison with the Greek gymnasium suggests more than a merely formal similarity.

This kind of instruction for Hindu girls is traditionally unique, at least in the post-Buddhist period, when it continued to subsist only among the matrilineal classes in India. It is among them that swimming is, or at least was, generally known and practiced. Three times a day baths were taken in the temple tank, and diving, swimming, and water games of various kinds were part of traditional daily routine or feasting in Kerala.

It fits into this general picture that hygiene, cleanliness, and a seminudity, of at least the upper part of the body, are important features. Traditionally men and women refrained from colored and sewn garments. The white *mundu*, or loin cloth, which they alone wore was meticulously clean. The cleanliness of the peoples of Kerala and their white dresses were, and are even now, well known all over India. The simple but exquisite beauty of the human body, revealed by this traditional dress, has been captured in stone, bronze, ivory, and paint.

Thus, the temperament of simplicity and cleanliness, which had been characteristic for the classical Buddhist and the post-Buddhist periods all over India, was typically preserved in Kerala for generations after it had disappeared elsewhere in India under the growing influence of foreign elements and examples. Almost all representations of Indian men or women show them in the same style: a free upper part of the body, a simple, unsewn dress, but rich ornaments of precious metals or stones. The exceptions were a few stray cases of figures, depicting foreigners or Indians wearing foreign dress at special occasions. In Kerala, even today, one can see at times aristocratic elderly ladies who continue to wear the old traditional form of dress, and this not only in their spacious country houses, but also, for instance, in first-class compartments on the railway.

The attitude of mind here expressed in style of daily life cannot be claimed as an exclusive product of mother-right. Dress, sports, games, and entertainments are much the same among both matrilineal and patrilineal tribal highlanders of Assam and Kerala. Dancing, archery, competitions, and so on, have been preserved in tribal areas and are generally practiced today. What is of significance is that a way of life, most congenial to the philosophy of mother-right, is last given up in the present acculturation trend by matrilineal peoples.

Religious Conceptualization

Except for the small group of Mapillais in North Malabar, the matrilineal peoples of Kerala, both in the plains and in the hills, are Hindus. As such they have for centuries intimately participated in the life and growth of Hindu philosophy. By contrast, the Khasi and Garo of Assam have evolved their own tribal religious traditions outside the pale of Hinduism.

While there are in Kerala strong Christian communities, established during the early days of Christianity, these Christians have abandoned their traditional social systems and consider themselves socially separated from their parent communities. The situation is basically different in Assam, where it is only recently that Christian converts have been made in increasing numbers. They contribute more than their numerical share to the present growing tribal intelligentsia. They retain, however, their matrilineal system of social organization, and their general outlook is that of the other members in their respective tribes. Conversion to Christianity here is not tantamount to the abandonment of the traditional matrilineal background nor to disintegration of tribal unity.

Thus, the socioreligious configurations of the various matrilineal groups in India are quite different indeed. Considering these wide differences, one could expect to find equally fundamental contrasts in the philosophies of life among the groups concerned, for religion is both a reflection of communal attitudes and also the shaper of these very attitudes.

A comparative study of the folk religions among matrilineal societies in India is in one way more instructive than the abstract and theoretical contents of these religions. It reveals, as we are going to see, a number of basically common elements.

Religion in Kerala

Hinduism, the recognized religion of highlanders and lowlanders in Kerala, is a very complex thing. Its formal and folk aspects allow more shades of differentiation than Buddhism, for instance, where the canon of the official religion is more clearly defined. It is certainly not the same in the little accessible shifting cultivator hamlets in the hills and in the stately temples of the plains, but, everywhere, mother–goddess worship and a strong bias toward Shivaism are present.

Shivaism and Vaishnavism are well differentiated in the Tamil-speaking eastern part of South India. They are much less clearly distinguished in Kerala and least of all among the matrilineal classes. Krishna as an *avatara* of Vishnu is an object of great devotion and religious affection. He is often seen in the role of the divine child as the *Bhakti* tradition depicts him.

The influence of the *Bhakti* cult with its strong ties to Shivaism has been particularly emphasized in the plains ever since Chaitanya's days and his preachings, centered around the devotion to divine love. There is one element in this *Bhakti* cult which serves as a link between the tribal religion and village Hinduism. It is precisely this element which links up with traditional mother–goddess worship and which has its parallels in Assam, parallels which go much further than a few mere isolated points of similarity, such as the cock sacrifice and the importance of rites connected with agricultural works, fertility, and *rites de passage*.

The goddess worship in Kerala takes many and varied forms, some of them being peculiar to the area, as, for instance, the representation of the goddess in colored powder, over which the *vellichapad*, a kind of shaman priest, dances. She is worshiped in small village shrines represented by crude unhewn stones; she is seen also as the victor over the demons, as the bloodthirsty goddess Durga, for instance, in the famous shrine of Cranganore, with its bloody cock sacrifice and the exuberant songs, sung by pilgrims and devotees, or, in a more philosophically abstract sense, as the active energy, the Shakti of Shiva.

Though the worship of Shakti, the female energy or "consort" of Shiva, is common to Hinduism all over India, it is particularly emphasized in the South, more than anywhere else in the subcontinent, with the possible exception of Bengal and—to a lesser extent—also Assam among the Hindus in the plains.

A peculiar representation of the female aspect is *Ardhanarishvara*. The right half of this figure is male—Shiva—and the left side is female—Parvati, his Shakti. The legend explaining this unusual

representation is equally remarkable. It centers on Bringi, an exclusively male-oriented saint, devoted to Shiva alone as his lord.
He had no consideration for the God's female aspect, for Parvati
as his Shakti. When Shiva tried to teach him better and appeared
to him with Parvati, the devoted Bringi circumambulated Shiva,
passing between the Lord and his Shakti, thus refusing to show
devotion to the female deity. On seeing this, Shiva united his
form with that of Parvati and hence appeared as Ardhanarishvara,
male and female in one body.

Though only one among many legends, woven like garlands
around the pictures of South Indian deities, this explanation brings
out an essential trend in the religious coloration and, with it, in
the life philosophy of matrilineal people in southwestern India:
The female aspect is not necessarily the dominating counterpart
of the male deity in purely patriarchal societies. But it is an essential and indispensable part of the divine.

Religion Among Khasi and Garo

Khasi and Garo religions are, as we have seen, independent entities with scarcely any traditionally acculturated elements from
either Hindu mythology or Hindu philosophy. Khasi religious
concepts include a number of lesser spirits and local tutelary deities with a paramount God, Blei, the creator. This great god is
nowadays generally seen as masculine, like the popular representations of God in most other religions with which the Khasi have
recently come into close contact, i.e., Christianity, Hinduism, and
Islam. There is, however, evidence that this deity was traditionally
felt to be comprised of both sexes. The definite articles, the
masculine U and the feminine Ka, are both applied to the same
substantive, Blei. There are prayers and exclamations to one and
the same deity: U Blei–Ka Blei. In an old prayer recited before
preparing the fields, both aspects of the divine, the male as well
as the female, are invoked:

I bow, I kneel down to your golden and silver feet [O] Father God,
Creator [Nongthaw] and planner [Nongbuh]. Now I stand to hoe, to
cut, to work, to touch [ka trei ka ktah]. As thou hast created, planned
me the seed [or "core"] of mankind to work, to touch. Thou wilt
forgive and have mercy on the commissions and omissions of myself.
Hear, O Mother Ramew [Mei Ramew] above [hajrong], O Mother

Ramew below [*Tbian*, i.e., on the earth, or ground], now that I will stand to cut on thee [*halor jong phi*]. You will have mercy on the omissions and commissions of myself, the seed [or "core"] of mankind. the care [*ka ri*], the carrying [*ka bah*], the keeping on the lap [*ka thum*] [and] the suckling [*ka aibuin aithiang*] are thine alone. To complete me, the seed [or "core"] of mankind, as it was created [by] Father God, [*Pa Blei*]—that has been laid on your shoulders [is your responsibility].

Though two divine forms are no doubt discernible in this prayer, the parallelism in addressing them, and the similarities of feeling toward them, are also strong.

In another exclamation, the female aspect alone is invoked:

> Ka Blei ka wa buh ka wa shna ka wa buh
> mynsen wa buh mynsngaid
> (Goddess who creates, who shapes, who puts;
> Spirit who gives the essence of life)

This double sex aspect of the deity is neither confined to matrilineal social systems nor can it be claimed to be exclusively their product. Still, in conjunction with other aspects of their *weltanschauung*, this trait adds a unique feature to the over-all picture.

Many of the poetic Khasi fairy tales depict the sun as a Queen of Heaven. In one of these stories we find humankind in the simile of a peacock and the divine in that of the celestial queen. He, as her admirer, flies into the open sky until he is admitted to the radiant crystal palace of the sun goddess. In heavenly happiness she takes him as her lover. One day, however, the peacock sees from the sky, on one of the steep slopes on earth, a field laid out in the shape of a woman. He falls in love with the distant figure and flies back to earth. But as the sun goddess sees his mistake, she cries over her lost lover and the drops of her tears fell on him, forming the oval ornaments which can still be seen on the peacock's beautifully colored tail.

By tradition the Garo believe, as we have seen, that they took over the matrilineal order from the Khasi, but they preserved their own form of religion. This is comprised of a pantheon of gods, both male and female, and resembles the religious pattern of other tribes who, like the Garo, but unlike the Austric-speaking Khasi, belong linguistically to the Tibeto-Burmese group. The importance of the cock, the cock sacrifice, and the egg oracle which are so characteristic of Khasi belief are absent in Garo religion.

Abstractions

Individualized matrilineal groups in India stand out as unmistakably defined cultural units. In spite of their differences they have, however, a number of traits in common, and the matrilineal family situation could be schematized as follows.

Normally every man has a sister with children and is also married to a wife with children. He plays an important role in both these women's lives: his sister's and his wife's. Consequently, each family contains (seen from the point of view of the children in any one mother's household), three important family members: (1) the mother, (2) her brother, the maternal uncle, and (3) the mother's husband, the father. This situation is different from the monolithic, almost exclusive position of the powerful father in the traditional patrilineal family. It is therefore necessary for the children, and indeed all the members of the family, to work with, and adjust to, this plural authority, as against the one, and more or less, absolute source of power to which patrilineal systems generally tend.

Seen in the context of plural authority, the matrilineal family could be visualized as revolving around a focal point. This hinges on the female principle, which is represented by either an actual woman or at least a male relative on the mother's side, the maternal uncle. The emphasis on the female principle does not assign to a single woman the indisputably leading position of the eldest male member in many patrilineal systems. In this sense it is true that matriliny does not imply gynecocracy.

Without going into a discussion of the reasons, concomitances, or prime causes for social patterns, we have yet to take cognizance of existing situations. The matrilineal-extended family, and by implication also the abstract concept of mother-right, can be seen as a self-contained system, revolving introvertedly around the maternal focus or female principle. The patrilineal family, on the other hand, tending to concentrate power and authority upon one person, and generally also to externalize energy, may be compared to a lineal arrangement with the eldest male at its head.

The externalization of energy finds expression in all sorts of ways, including marriage customs. Characteristically marriage with close relatives and village endogamy are prohibited among most patrilineal Hindus in northern India. A Rajput village, for instance, has been found to be connected with not less than four hundred others through exogamous marriage ties of its inhabitants.

An opposite situation characterizes rural life in South India, which has been determined by matrilineal organizational features. By tradition the most desirable form of marriage for Hindus is that between cross-cousins, i.e., children of brothers and sisters, and often within the same village, even neighborhood. The present distribution of these marriage patterns does not coincide with the present distribution of matriliny and patriliny, but it is quite likely that it delimits their prevous fields of influence in India.

Culture Change and Legislation

The topic of matrilineal survivals brings up the question of culture change and legislation in this context. Though it is not possible to go into details within the frame of the present discussion, the matter is of such extreme importance that it may here be treated in the way of an appendix.

The tradition of mother-right in India goes way back into the past and perhaps even as far as the antique civilizations of the Fertile Crescent.[4] It has been on the retreat for at least two thousand years in South India outside Kerala, though it has left, as proof of its cultural and religious vitality, a lasting mark on the Indian world picture, the *weltanschauung*, of the subcontinent.

Inside Kerala Hindu-Brahman patterns of thought did change the working and the significance of the matrilineal system, but they did not lead to its disintegration. The last step in its abolishment has been taken indirectly through general legislation aiming at a unification of succession, marriage, and family regulations among Hindus. Following the old patrilineal Hindu system, daughters had a right to a dowry but none to inherited property. The Hindu Succession Act of June, 1956, which, as its name indicates, applies to Hindus all over India, rules among other things that daughters and sons have equal claims to inherited property and that women may divorce and remarry. This law certainly brings, at least theoretically, improvements for the large majority of women in patrilineal societies, but it entails at the same time a loss of status and privileges for women in the matrilineal communities.

Women of these societies have always had, unlike most of their patrilineal counterparts, the right to get a divorce on their own decision and to remarry after divorce or in the case of widowhood. The practice of child-marriage for girls, too, was not generally followed and the marriage ceremonies were simple, free from the heavy economic burden which marriage expenses, in many patrilineal societies of the country, place on the father of daughters—a situation reflected by the added discrimination between the religiously desired sons and the economically dreaded daughters. Matrilineal women were, at least in theory, transmittors of property inheritance and name succession, though their property rights have been, during the last few generations, increasingly curtailed by the powers of the *karanavan*.

The newly proclaimed law does not mean so much a loss for individual women as one for the status of womanhood. Women are no more the medium for transmitting inherited property. Moreover, they lose by the imitation of Western naming patterns and the simultaneous neglect of the matrilineal house names. The loss of status is further enhanced by the adoption of the dowry system and prestige expenses at marriage. These new customs are spreading from richer to even middle-class families. The "dowry" does not go to the young couple, but to family members of the bridegroom, and the demand for dowries increases as marriageable girls outnumber marriageable boys more and more. The surplus was about seven percent in January, 1960. Thus the daughter, formerly occupying a privileged position, now becomes an expensive burden for the entire family.

All these changes are being adopted with a feeling of eagerness to imitate and conform: "Why should we be different from others?" seems to be the simplest and most popular expression of this eagerness. Seeing only the apparent and immediate advantages, the women of the affected groups do not seem to mind losing their sovereign position, as this loss goes by the name of equality before the law. In fact we saw that this equality is fictitious. *Marumakkattayam*, the matrilineal order, is not seen generally as something inherently primitive or bad, such as it had been judged by early travelers or missionaries, but it is believed to be no longer suitable in the new way of life. Few people realize that it is not the necessities of the changing world but their own changed minds which inaugurated the abolition of matriliny.

The Hindu Succession Act does not apply to the Khasi and Garo who are not Hindus. It has been pointed out that most missionary Christian churches did not openly take a stand against the matrilineal order and that tribal unity has not been completely disintegrated through conversion. The Khasi and Garo generally retain their tribal consciousness and are proud of belonging to an old tradition of which their mother-right is an essential part. The comparatively very few tribal members who are critical of the matrilineal system object to it on a frankly antifeminist ground: "Why should our women have more privileges than those of our tribal neighbors?"

The argument of conformism is used by those tribal women, or more often by descendants of mixed marriages, who are ideologically alienated not only from their traditional matrilineal system, but from the tribal in-group consciousness as well.

Conclusions

The plurality of historical, economic, social, and, above all, religious backgrounds, against which each of the matrilineal groups in India stands out, is reflected by individualized life-patterns of these groups.

The study of these specific cultural norms, however, reveals an inherent structural oneness—much as markedly differentiated folk cultures or national groups have within the orbit of any great religion. There are obvious differences and yet also a common *weltanschauung* among, say, Ethiopian, Alpine, or American Christians, or among Siamese, Ceylonese, and Japanese Buddhists, or again among Turkish, Pakistani, and Indonesian Muslims.

The common structural basis discernible in the life of various matrilineal societies can best be defined as a culture *Gestalt*, a holistic unit. It exercises its influence without being consciously perceived in the way religious systems no doubt are. Still it "exists" as a living and palpable force, if not in the conscious mind, yet in the behavior patterns of human individuals and in the societies which they form. It is this which has to be perceived in order to understand the underlying philosophy of mother-right.

FOOTNOTE REFERENCES

1. Thurston, E., and K. Rangachari, Castes and Tribes of South India, Government Press, Madras, 1909, 7 vols.; Iyer, L. K. Ananthakrishna, The Cochin Tribes and Castes, Government of Cochin Publication, Eruakulam, 1909.
2. Ehrenfels, U. R., "Traces of a Matriarchal Civilization among the Kolli Malayalees," Journal of the Royal Asiatic Society of Bengal, vol. IX, n.s., 1943, pp. 29–83; "The Double Sex Character of the Khasi Great Deity," Journal of the Madras University, vol. XXII, no. 1, 1950, pp. 26–39; "Khasi Kinship Terms in Four Dialects," Anthropos, vol. 48, 1953, pp. 396–412: "A Malayalar Mock Fight," Jubiläums Band zum 25 jährigen Bestehen des Institut der Völkerkunde an der Universität, Wien (Festschrift), Verlag Herold, Vienna, 1956, pp. 291–307.
3. Ehrenfels, U. R., Mother-right in India, Oxford University Press, Bombay-Hyderabad, 1941.
4. Ibid., esp. pp. 179 seq., 185 seq., 202 seq.

BIBLIOGRAPHY

As already mentioned, relevant material, mostly in article form, is scattered over a large body of literature. Only a short selection can be given here.

The items marked with an asterisk (*) contain additional bibliographical references.

Altekar, A. S., The Position of Women in Hindu Civilization, Hindu University Press, Benares, 1938.*
Bachmann, Hedwig, Von der Seele der indischen Frau, Tipografia Rangel, Pastora, 1941.
Banerjea, J. N., The Development of Hindu Iconography, University of Calcutta Press, Calcutta, 1941.*
Barbosa, Duarte, The Book of, issued by The Hakluyt Society, London, 1918, vol. I.

Bechert, H., "Mutterrecht und Thronfolge in Malabar und Ceylon," *Paideuma*, vol. VIII, No. 4/6, 1960.*

Cantlie, Sir Keith, *Notes on Khasi Law*, H. Munro, Aberdeen, 1934.

Chandra, Moti, "The History of Indian Costume," *Journal of the Indian Society of Oriental Art*, vol. XII, 1944.

Chattopadhyaya, Deviprasad, *Lokāyata: A Study in Ancient Indian Materialism*, Peoples, New Delhi, 1959.*

Dasgupta, Shashibhusan, *Obscure Religious Cults as Background of Bengali Literature*, University of Calcutta Press, Calcutta, 1946.

Ehrenfels, U. R., *Mother-right in India*, Oxford University Press, Bombay-Hyderabad, 1941.*

Ehrenfels, U. R., "Matrilineal Family Background in South India," *Journal of Educational Sociology*, vol. XXVI, 1953, pp. 356–361.*

Ehrenfels, U. R., "The Comparative Study of Matrilineal Civilizations in India," *Journal of the University of Gauhati*, vol. IV, 1953.*

Ehrenfels, U. R., "The Matrilineal Background," *Status of Women in South Asia*, Longmans, Calcutta, 1954.

Ehrenfels, U. R., "Three Matrilineal Groups in Assam," *American Anthropologist*, vol. 57, no. 2, 1955, pp. 306–321.*

Ehrenfels, U. R., "The Culturological Approach to Non-Alignment," *Indian Year Book of International Affairs*, vol. IV, University of Madras, Madras, 1955, pp. 124–136.

Ehrenfels, U. R., "A Malayalar Mock Fight," *Jubiläums Band zum 25 jährigen Bestehen des Institut der Völkerkunde an der Universität Wien*, (Festschrift), Verlag Herold, Vienna, 1956, pp. 291–307.*

Ehrenfels, U. R., and P. V. Velayudhan, "Legislation against Matriliny," *The Anthropologist*, vol. III, no. 1–2, 1956, pp. 35–67.*

Elmore, W. T., *Dravidian Gods in Modern Hinduism*, The University Studies of the University of Nebraska, vol. XV, January, 1915, Lincoln, Nebr., pp. 1–145.

Fawcett, F., "Nayars of Malabar," *Government Museum Bulletin*, vol. III, no. 3, Madras, 1901, pp. 1–322.

Gopalakrishnan, M. S., *The Mothergoddess*, dissertation, University of Madras, Madras, 1953.*

Gurdon, P. R. T., *The Khasis*, Nutt, London, 1907.*

Hutton, J. H., *Caste in India*, Cambridge, London, 1946.*

Kakati, Banikanta, *The Mothergoddess Kamakhya*, University of Gauhati, Gauhati, 1949.

Karve, Iravatti, "The Culture Process in India," *Man*, no. 232, 1951.

Logan, William, *Manual of the Malabar District*, Government of Madras, Madras, 1906.*

Pillai, Elamkulam P. N. Kunjan, *Some Unknown Aspects of Kerala History* (in Malayalam language), University of Trivandrum, Trivandrum, 1957.

Playfair, A., *The Garos*, Nutt, London, 1909.*

Tambiah, H. W., *The Laws and Customs of the Tamils of Ceylon*, Government of Ceylon, Colombo, 1953.*

Tambiah, H. W., *The Laws and Customs of the Tamils of Jaffna*, Government of Ceylon, Colombo, 1956.*

Scheduling CHARLES F. HOCKETT

8

This paper extends to ethnography certain assumptions and procedures of linguistics.

I

An observation is a function of two variables, the observed and the observer. In physics, the theory of relativity seeks to lay bare those properties of the observed that are invariant from one observer (actual or imaginable) to another, and only such properties are ascribed to physical reality. In ethnography, a similar search yields different results, for we find two equally objective views that can be taken towards the life of any human community.

One is the outside view, whose frame of reference is that of physics. An ethnographer speaks from this view when he locates a tribe by latitude and longitude, or estimates its population, or describes its habitat. A linguist speaks from this view when he describes the speech sounds of a language in terms of articulatory motions. In aim, if not always in actuality, any properly trained observer—including one who belongs to the community under examination—would agree with such reports.

The other is the inside view. This does not arise in physics because stars and electrons are not observers. The members of a community are, and they perceive and react to things in certain ways. An ethnographer speaks from this view when he locates a tribe in a valley at the center of the world, surrounded successively by mountains, a river, and a sea of fire. A linguist speaks from this view when he describes a phonemic system. The inside view is subjective for the members of the community, but for the investigator it is just as objective as the outside view.

Both of these views are necessary for ethnography. Conjointly, they are sufficient. Other approaches are approximations or mistakes. Such terms as "religion," "property," or "schizophrenia" are only dubiously to be ascribed to the frame of reference for the outside view, and until a particular community has been studied one cannot know if they are relevant for the inside view of that community. Hence, a proposal to investigate the religion of some largely unstudied community constitutes a projection from one inside view—that of Western culture—into another. Such cross-cultural projections are inevitable as an ethnographer begins his work; the work is not complete until they have been eliminated.

For the outside view, the ethnographer can solicit help from a vast array of fellow scientists. For the inside view, he stands alone, except, of course, for the members of the community he is studying, and he must often extrapolate from what they teach him in ways in which they would not. (For example, people speak within a phonemic system they cannot ordinarily describe.) The inside view is thus the special province of the ethnographer, and is our concern in this paper.

II

The ethnographer's task is to discover and describe the ways of life of a human community. The discovery is achieved at best by participant-observation, though no technique is taboo unless it is inhumane. Up to a point, what the ethnographer does as a participant-observer parallels what a member of the community does by growing up within it. One obvious difference is that the ethnographer is pledged to report what he learns, while the community member is not. This suggests an approach to ethnographic theory. We ask: How can an ethnographer, back from the field, process his findings to yield a report of maximum accuracy and clarity? Is there an optimal format into which he can cast his data? If so, can advance knowledge of the format guide him in the field and obviate some gaps and uncertainties in the ultimate report?

Such questions emphasize the role of the ethnographer as a link between the community he studies and the anthropological profession. Accuracy and clarity are not independent. The most accurate understanding of a community might be achieved by an ethnographer who went native and published nothing. The clearest exposition could perhaps be written by an imaginative novelist who did no field work. But private accuracy is abortive, and factitious clarity is fraudulent.

The linguist in the field is an ethnographer with a restricted assignment: just the language of the community, not its whole way of life. (It is almost certain that "language" is a valid term in the outside view, so that the restricted assignment is legitimate.) There is an established format for the linguist's report. It will appear as a grammar and dictionary.

A dictionary is a serial list of linguistic elements of a certain sort. Such elements occur from time to time as the language is spoken. There are constraints on the circumstances in which each element is apt to occur. The constraints are of two kinds, grammatical and semantic. The former are limitations on the ways in which linguistic elements combine with one another; thus, in English, we do not commonly say 'the men is'. The dictionary subsumes constraints of this sort by cross-reference to the grammar. Semantic constraints have to do with the non-speech context of speech. These are described in the dictionary itself.

A grammar covers three matters. It sets forth the grammatical constraints on the elements listed in the dictionary. It describes the phonemic system of the language. And it specifies the habits by which lexical elements—the dictionary entries—are mapped into sequences of phonemes.

A form that recurs, or may recur, as a language is spoken does not necessarily belong in the dictionary. It must be listed only if its occurrence and the circumstances attendant thereon cannot be inferred from the rest of the information in the dictionary and grammar. Thus, English 'boy' requires listing; 'boys and girls' does not; 'time heals all wounds' does.

A language is an open system: its speakers often say things that have not been said before, usually with no disruption of communication. This property of a language is matched by the linguist's report in the following way. To the extent that a dictionary and grammar are complete, one can interpret a newly observed utterance in the language. If the whole utterance is not in the dictionary, then its parts are, and the patterns by which the parts have been put together are in the grammar. To the extent that the dictionary and grammar are accurate, one can draw information from them and generate a new utterance that will pass the test of casual acceptance by the speakers of the language. Thus the linguist's report parallels the language skills that the speakers carry inside their heads. There is, of course, neither need nor reason to assume that the spatial organization of these skills in a speaker's central nervous system conforms to the distribution of data that the linguist finds convenient in his report.

A language is also a changing system. The mechanism of change that works most rapidly is that forms are spoken in circumstances that are in one way or another unusual, thus giving rise to new lexical items. A fixed dictionary and grammar cannot reflect this property of a language. It is possible, however, to observe the patterns that are most favored in the formation of new lexical items and to report this in the grammar. It would also be possible to prepare a dictionary and grammar in loose-leaf form and revise as the language changes, but the result would not be what is usually wanted, which is a portrayal of the workings of the language as of a specified date.

There is another sort of variation in language habits, however, that an account must cover. No community is homogeneous. Different members and subgroups behave in different ways, in speech as in other respects. The active vocabulary of a fisherman is not that of a woodworker. A chief may be permitted turns of phrase forbidden to a commoner. Such differences reflect, and constitute part of, the social structure of the community. It would be incorrect, not merely uneconomical, to prepare a separate grammar and dictionary for each social dialect, since this would obscure the extent of their overlap. The fisherman can learn the technical terms of woodworking; the commoner can understand, if he may not imitate, the chief. The proper description presents the common core of all dialects and then describes the departures from it.

III

We now introduce the terminology of scheduling.

We recall a point made above: that a linguistic element is something that occurs from time to time in the speech behavior of the community. From the outside view, a word exists as, and only as, it is occurring. Between occurrences it does not exist, though records of it exist in the central nervous systems of the speakers (if nowhere else). These internal records are such that the word is recognized when it does occur, and also such that the word is expected to occur under certain conditions and not, or only with lower probability, under others. We paraphrase by saying that in the expectations of the speakers the word is *scheduled* to occur under certain conditions. The grammar and dictionary prepared by a linguist are a statement of such schedulings.

To say that a word is recognized when it occurs is to say that, when a word occurs, users of the language can tell what word it is. Recognizability is not absolute but differential. It turns on the contrast between, first, a word and a non-word and, second, one word and any other word. If the users of a language can identify an event as an occurrence of a certain word rather than of any other word or of any non-word, it is because they are attuned to certain sensable physical properties of the word, or of its immediate setting, that differ from those of any other word or of any non-word. These are the *distinctive* properties of the word. An occurrence of a word typically has also sensable properties that are not distinctive: e.g., English words sound differently from male and from female speakers, but are the same words none the less. What has just been said is the principle of *contrast*. It lies at the heart of ethnography. To realize its importance one need only imagine trying to play bridge with a blank deck.

All that is said above about a word applies without modification to such a social phenomenon as, say, American presidential inauguration. This is scheduled to occur every four years, on a certain day, at a certain place, with certain participants identified by role, and with a prescribed sequence of constituent actions. Some variation is permissible, but there is a distinctive core that cannot be violated: if the departures are too great, the event is not recognized, and not accepted, as a presidential inauguration. The ceremony exists only as it is held. Between occurrences, all that exists is records. The records constitute the scheduling of the phenomenon and are the basis of the recognizability of the ceremony when it does occur.

I shall use the term *trait* for any lexical element in a language and for any such social phenomenon as American presidential inauguration. A trait, then, is a thing that recurs, or may recur, in the life of a community; that exists only as it occurs; the occurrences of which are scheduled in one way or another in the expectations of the members of the community; and an occurrence of which is recognizable by them by virtue of specifiable distinctive properties. As with language, so also in the general case, a potentially recurrent phenomenon is not a trait if it is built out of smaller elements and if its occurrence and the attendant circumstances are subsumed by an adequate description of the latter and their schedulings. 'Boys and girls' is not a lexical unit, hence not a trait; a dinner of several courses in a customary sequence is not a trait. 'Boy' and a soup course are traits. 'Time heals all wounds' and American presidential inauguration are traits despite their internal complexity; that is, although they include smaller traits, they are not, as wholes, predictable purely in terms of those smaller traits and their schedulings.

Some schedulings are tighter than others, but all are contingent and probabilistic rather than absolute or determinate. A linguist cannot predict the exact time and place of a use by a speaker of English of the word 'are', nor can the speaker predict this with certainty even of his own speech. Both know, however, that if a sentence begins with 'the boys' (contingency), the next word is more likely to be 'are' than 'is' (probability). We are most apt to hear 'Good morning!' in the morning. An American dinner could start with pie and end with soup, but this would clearly be deviant.

IV

I propose the following answer to the questions about ethnographic theory posed at the beginning of II above. The ethnographer's report of the inside view should appear as a tabulation of the traits of the community, of the distinctive properties of each, and of their schedulings. There is nothing to be said of a community's way of life that cannot be said in this fashion, and no format can yield greater accuracy and clarity.

These assertions constitute the theory of scheduling. Certain kinds of ethnographic data fit the specified format almost effortlessly, and we shall discuss these first. But ethnographers also indulge in generalizations that are perhaps true and profound but that would seem to be more resistant to the scheduling format. Resistant they may be—the claim of accuracy and clarity does not imply ease of application.* I shall try to show that the theory allows for such more profound inferences provided they are meaningful (Section X).

The theory of scheduling is not supposed to apply to the outside view. Yet that view is indispensable for the application of the theory, in that it must be evoked in describing the distinctive properties of traits. The vowel system of a language is an inside-view matter; its description requires reference to tongue and lip positions, which is outside view. Similarly, the preferential manufacture of axe handles from the wood of a certain tree is inside view; the taxonomic identification of the tree is outside view.

For the inside view, it is not at all the ethnographer's responsibility to report his observations, though there are two good reasons why he may. One is to afford concrete examples of how schedulings "actualize" in behavior in the community. The other is that the reader may check on the ethnographer's inferences and perhaps add his own. When a linguist appends a sample text to a grammar, the purposes are these. Neither purpose justifies the presentation of raw data as a substitute for the description of inferred patterns.

V

Many traits in any community have an obvious scheduling in terms of natural cycles: the year, the (lunar) month, the day, the life cycle, the menstrual cycle, the recurrent increase and release of pressure in the seminal vesicles, and others. These natural cycles

* In any case, this article is not concerned with practical difficulties. Note that all the strictures of II, as to what a description of a language can and cannot do, apply equally to the whole of culture and its description.

are given by the outside view. They vary with geography and, to some extent, with genetic constitution. Many communities have also man-made periods such as the week. All scheduling relative to such natural and pseudo-natural cycles will be called *calendrical*.

It is standing practice to report really tight calendrical schedulings. No account of a Cree band would ignore the seasonal cycle of dispersion in small hunting groups for part of the year and collection at a central point for the rest. If a ceremony is performed with the first spring thunderstorm, or before sunrise each day, or when a boy reaches puberty, this is mentioned.

In fact, however, every trait is scheduled calendrically. The correlation between the occurrences of a certain trait and, say, time of year may be zero. But zero correlation must be distinguished from the case in which the investigator does not discover what the correlation is.

The scheduled activities of a community move its members about along scheduled routes. What they see as they move depends on what they are trained to look for and on the physicogeographical environment, including in the latter the modifications, such as houses, trails, and garbage dumps, that they have imposed on it. This spatial aspect of scheduling is the *dwelling pattern*. Farmers who live on the land they work have very different dwelling patterns from those who live clustered in villages and travel out to their land. All traits work into the dwelling pattern of a community, in the same sense in which all have some kind of calendrical scheduling.

Differences of scheduled activities from one individual or subgroup of a community to another generate a pseudo-spatial distribution of people commonly called social structure. The outside view affords two dimensions of social structure, sex and age, the former inoperative only in a monastic community, the latter universal. Every community elaborates these two in its own way (American society has "sex-grading" as well as age-grading) and adds others. If any of these others is universal, that is a fact awaiting empirical proof. Every trait is scheduled relative to social structure.

Personality and social structure are conjugate variables. Personality is the idiosyncratic way in which a particular individual plays his roles in the community. But an individual's roles are just his position in social structure. To change the way in which roles are played is to change the roles, hence also the social structure. It is a mere matter of convenience that we use both concepts. The facts to be described can be subsumed wholly under either.

Artifacts are modified parts of the physico-geographical environment. They are not traits, but their manufacture, manipulation, and ultimate disposal are scheduled activities composed of traits. But an artifact is also a record. Some of the skill necessary for the use of a hammer is stored in the user; some is stored in the hammer. If this were not so, archeology would be futile.

VI

Calendrical scheduling and the dwelling pattern are *external* constraints on the occurrences of traits; the schedulings of traits relative to other traits are *internal* constraints. A set of traits constitutes a *cultural system* (or just a *system*) if the constraints on their occurrences require to be sorted out in this binary way. The aggregate of all traits of a community is thus a system. Language is a system: the semantic constraints are external (even when they are internal to the whole culture), the grammatical ones internal.

One cultural system may be wholly included in another; we may then say that the first is a system of a lower "level" than the second. The language of a community is part of its total way of life; the language consists, in turn, of two non-overlapping smaller systems, the grammatico-lexical and the phonemic. (Two systems are non-overlapping if no trait belongs to both.) Hunting, housebuilding, courting, and many other activities for which English supplies labels are doubtless systems in various communities, but the ways in which these overlap with, include, and are included in others vary and are difficult to discover. In general, it is easier to demonstrate that traits belong to the same or to different systems at some level than it is to discern the exact total arrangement of systems. It is easy to list traits that certainly do not belong to the same low-level system: e.g., the word 'boy', trumping one's partner's ace, and striking a nail with a hammer. More important is a basic test: if two traits can be acted out by the same person at the same time, they must belong, at some level, to different systems. We intone as we utter English words: intonation and words belong to different subsystems, though both are included within the language. We can clap our hands and shout 'Encore!' simultaneously: the former is gestural, the latter linguistic, and these do not overlap each other, though both overlap with concert-going.

'Time heals all wounds' and American presidential inauguration are both *complex* traits, in that they incorporate smaller traits but cannot be wholly accounted for in terms of the latter. Every trait, simple or complex, belongs to at least one system. 'Time heals all wounds' belongs to a system to which its smaller included traits also belong: the language. American presidential inauguration, on the other hand, involves smaller traits of many different systems, of which perhaps none is a system to which the complex itself belongs. We must thus distinguish between *one-system* and *cross-system* complex traits.

In language, a form larger than any one lexical element (simple or complex) is *composite*. Composite forms are built from lexical units by grammatical patterns called *constructions*. By eliminating the specific reference to language, we can use these terms for any cultural system.

The structure of a composite form is typically hierarchical. That is, the whole form consists of smaller forms some of which are also composite; those in turn of still smaller forms some of which may be composite; and so on until one reaches the ultimate constituent traits. 'The books on the bottom shelf are all blue' consists of the immediate constituents 'the books on the bottom shelf' and 'are all blue', put together by a construction called predication. The same construction appears in 'psycholinguistics appears to be a strange field', though with different constituents. 'The books on the bottom shelf' consists, in turn, of 'the books' and 'on the bottom shelf', involving another construction; the second of these consists of 'on' and 'the bottom shelf', with still another construction; and so on. Similarly, the eating of a dinner has, as its immediate constituents, the eating of each successive course; the eating of a single course consists, perhaps, of the successive bites and sips. The particular set of constructions that are manifested in 'the books on the bottom shelf are all blue' are manifested also in an indefinite number of other sentences; in the same way, if one starts with chopped liver instead of herring, and continues with noodle soup instead of consomme, lamb instead of beef, apple strudel instead of seven-layer cake, tea instead of coffee, the result is still the eating of a dinner. A construction is a frame into each slot of which any of a set of interchangeable forms (simple or composite) can be inserted. The forms also fit various slots in other frames; two composite forms can share no trait and yet involve the same frame.

A complex trait typically consists of simple traits put together by familiar constructions. This is the case with 'time heals all wounds,' which has subject 'time' and predicate 'heals all wounds'. It is a complex trait, rather than merely a composite form, because it is remembered as a whole and recited from memory rather than being built anew upon each occurrence. Similarly, if a family forms the habit of a fixed menu for Sunday dinner, then Sunday dinner is a complex trait despite the fact that it consists of compatible courses as does any other dinner. A description of dinners in general, no matter how detailed, could not subsume the Sunday fixation, just as a description of English predication, no matter how accurate, could not subsume the idiomatic quality of 'time heals all wounds'.

Composite forms, like complex traits, can be one-system or cross-system. This means that there are cross-system constructions as well as intra-system constructions. Various styles of nodding the head and various intonations are compatible with each other and with saying 'yes', but some gestures are not: shaking the head while saying 'yes' is an incongruity in our culture just as is saying 'the men is'.

Activities conducted simultaneously need not stand in clear-cut cross-system constructions to build complex traits or composite forms of some more inclusive cultural system. Sometimes they are merely compatible. One can carry on a conversation while driving a car, or eat a sandwich while watching television, or plait sennet while gossiping. Yet mere compatibility is itself a fact of scheduling, and the absence of any cross-system connection should not be hastily inferred. Samoan men commonly plait sennet as they sit and rest after a meal, a time also appropriate for gossip.

There is no outer limit to the length of a composite form or the complexity of the constructions by which it is built. A lecture is typically much longer than a single sentence, but it has a hierarchical structure. The annual cycle is a construction for the whole way of life of a community. The life cycle is a construction for any one individual. Even the great ground swells of growth and decline over many generations, suspected by some scholars, may conform to constructions, though in this case the constructions probably escape the inside view of any single community (save via hindsight).

There are traits that cannot be acted out by a single individual. We take these to be complex by definition. The contributory actions of any one participant stand in cross-personal constructions with those of the others. Cross-personal constructions also generate multi-personal composite forms of varying degrees of complexity— in the end, the whole history of the community.* Differences of expected role in multi-personal activities yield social structure, which we have already discussed.

VII

Apart from the cultural systems to which they individually belong, constructions fall into a number of types based on formal properties.

A construction is centered to the extent that the choice of one constituent imposes more widely ranging constraints on surrounding choices (within the same system) than does the choice of the other or others. In 'the books on the bottom shelf', 'the books' is the center or nucleus, and 'on the bottom shelf' is a satellite; in 'the books', the nucleus is 'books'. Thus, if we replace 'books' by 'book', the predicate given earlier ('are all blue') is rendered unsuitable: 'are' must at the same time be replaced by 'is'. If 'the' is replaced by 'these' or 'those', there are no such reverberations, nor are there if we replace 'on the bottom shelf' by 'in my study' or 'that he has written so far'. A housewife planning the menu for a dinner party usually settles on the entree first and then decides what other courses are suitable; this suggests that the entree of a dinner is the nucleus. The intonations we use while speaking seem in general to constitute running commentaries on, and hence satellites to, the words.

Not all constructions are centered in this simple sense. Some seem to have two or more coordinate centers: the phrase 'men and women' is not built about 'men' as center any more than it is

* Except that traits and schedulings change.

about 'women'; in ballet, one could argue whether the music accompanies the dancing or vice versa, which probably means that they are coordinate. Some seem rather to be *uncentered*: the subject and predicate of 'the books on the bottom shelf are all blue' show some congruences but are forms of diverse sorts, whereas 'men' and 'women' in 'men and women' are highly similar forms. There are problems here that have not been solved even for the simple case of language. Whether the coordinate and the uncentered types can be distinguished outside of language is not clear.

Experiencing a long composite form, in any cultural system, is something like crossing over a range of mountains. Insofar as the form is built by centered constructions, the successive nuclei are like the successive ridges, some higher than others. The intervening valleys find their analog too, and the point at which successive constituents abut is often signaled by a trait specialized for that function. In English phonemics, there are as many intonation phrases in an utterance as there are primary stresses, and between any two successive primary stresses there is one and only one terminal contour. English primary stress, or any other trait the occurrences of which mark nuclei or climaxes, is a *culminator*. An English terminal contour, or any other trait that marks the boundary between successive constituents of some larger form, is a *demarcator*.* At the end of an interview with a student, the professor's voice increases slightly in volume: this is a demarcator. In music, the pauses between the movements of a symphony are demarcators; cadences within a movement are demarcators of a lower order. Beethoven used dissonance for culminative effect against a backdrop of consonance; Hindemith reversed this. Not all peaks and boundaries are marked by culminators and demarcators, but it is important that some traits are specialized for these functions.

VIII

We view an individual, or a group engaged in a multi-personal activity during which they are validly to be segregated from the rest of the community, at the momentary interstice between suc-

* The terms are adapted from Trubetzkoy.

cessive acts of a single cultural system. The individual or group is the *actor*. The actor is in a *state*.

Suppose someone has just said 'That man over there is my —'; at this point we stop the camera to survey the possibilities. With only this much information, about all we can say relates to the grammatical constraints of English. The next word may be a noun such as 'father', 'son', 'friend', or an adjective like 'good', 'worst' (due to be followed in turn by some noun), and so on. The linguistic possibilities for the next word are finite because there are only a finite number of words in the language. There might not be any next word—the speaker might stop, or be shot—but this we treat linguistically as a single additional possibility. If we know more of the attendant circumstances, we shall be able to narrow our prediction. Let the speaker be young and the man pointed to old. We shall not then expect the next word to be 'son'.

The more we know, the more precisely we can predict. Does this mean that, at the limit, to know all the attendant circumstances (from the outside view as well as the inside) would enable us to predict exactly what the next act will be? The question is meaningless because it is impossible to reach the limit. From any vantage point, including that of the actor, only some of the contributing factors can be discerned. This yields a range of indeterminacy.

We wish to characterize the actor's state from the vantage point of the actor himself, not from that of any outside-view observer. States differ from one another at least in these four ways: (1) predictability; (2) freedom of choice; (3) urgency; (4) anxiety.

The predictability from a state varies inversely with the indeterminacy of the state; the latter is a function of the number of alternatives available for the next act and of the relative probabilities of each. We shall speak of the *alternative array*. The actor need not be consciously aware of all the alternatives actually available.

There is some correlation between the degree of indeterminacy of a state and the point the actor has reached in the hierarchical structure of a composite form. Indeterminacy is higher (and predictability lower) at the end of some large form than at the end of its constituents: higher at the end of a sentence than at the end of its subject; higher at the end of a dinner than after a non-final course; higher as one is about to graduate from college than when one has just completed the junior year and is planning the senior year's work. It is lower in the middle of what may become a complex trait than in the middle of an equally complicated composite form: after 'Hell hath no fury like a woman —' we are quite surprised if the next word is anything but 'scorned', but after 'I went to town yesterday afternoon and bought —' there are numerous unsurprising possibilities.

Predictability can be precisely quantified: see the Appendix to this chapter.

Freedom of choice and predictability are independent. Suppose we observe that a certain man invariably wears a blue necktie, and infer that his state each morning, as he selects his necktie, has high predictability. Discreet detective work then reveals that he has ties of many colors in his wardrobe and that, in his own opinion, he freely chooses the color he prefers each time. This does not materially alter our estimate of the predictability. The information bears on a different parameter: an actor has as much freedom of choice, in any state, as he believes he has.

A person is an actor as he speaks, and also as he listens to someone else speak. In the former case, predictability and freedom of choice are often both high; in the latter, both are often low. However, predictability is high and freedom of choice low for a ceremonial participant; predictability is low and freedom of choice high for the contemporary painter who applies pigment to canvas with anything from a blue necktie to a shotgun.

The urgency of a state is the inverse of the amount of time available for the selection of the next act. Whenever urgency is sufficiently low, there is time for tentative trial-and-error "editing" (itself scheduled) before the definitive selection of next act is made.[1] A young man drafting a sonnet for his beloved experiences no great urgency, though if there is a deadline the urgency may increase as it is approached. When urgency is high, the actor must exercise his freedom of choice quickly or outside factors change the state. Waiting for the doctor to choose between whole blood and plasma, the patient dies.

Urgency is obviously quantifiable.

Anxiety has to do with the actor's concern about the consequences of the next act: what new state it will establish, what subsequent acts and states it will render more or less probable.

An actual experience can be painful. Anxiety is not pain but the expectation of probabilistically scheduled pain.

A state can be characterized by a profile of four numbers, of which the first relates to predictability, the second to freedom of choice, the third to urgency, and the fourth to anxiety. Using "H" for relatively high numerical values, "M" for intermediate ones, "L" for relatively low ones, and "V" for variable, indeterminate, or irrelevant, we can describe the typical states encountered in certain familiar cultural systems:

sitting in the dentist's chair:	HLHH
sitting in the barber's chair:	HLHL
watching a football game:	MLVV
playing in a football game:	MMVM (or MMVH)
listening to a favorite familiar piece of music:	HLHL
encountering a truck in one's lane as one reaches the top of a hill:	MLHH
selecting proper therapy for a slow but deadly disease:	MMLH
selecting proper emergency treatment for a bad accident case:	MMHH
sleeping:	HLLL.

A ritual is a scheduled sequence of events during which the states are predominantly of type HLVL. This does not exclude the case in which a designated participant (say, one due to go under the sacrificial knife) experiences states HLVH. Games are characterized by MMVL: for onlookers the second index is lower, and for active players the fourth may be higher, but if anxiety is too high the activity loses its game character. Adventure is LHVL; an exciting episode in an adventure is LMHM.

IX

The ethnographer's initial contact with a community, like that of any other outsider, is characterized by the presence of two different sets of expectations: those of the community and his own. The extent of the difference between the expectations of any two individuals or groups defines the amount of *code noise* that characterizes their joint activities. We cannot expect code noise to be completely absent in any transaction between humans or human groups, even when they belong to the same community. The noisiness of cross-personal activities tends to diminish as the activities are repeated (if they are), since the expectations of each participant are modified by the actual behavior of the others. For example, tribelets that speak mutually unintelligible languages often conduct their wars according to shared conventions that have arisen through past contact. Clearly, code noise plays a vital role in culture change.

The term "community," accepted uncritically so far in this paper, need not remain undefined. A community is any cluster of people in social structure—that is, any group whose activities are tied together by cross-personal constructions and thus marked by some degree of freedom from noise. We may at will apply the term "community" either to a village, or to a single family within a village, or to a functioning group of villages. This freedom of scope is not license: we cannot dissect entirely to suit our own fancy, but must follow the joints.

X

When an ethnographer speaks of the themes of a culture, or of its values, or of national character, modal personality, or philosophy, he is attempting to pass beyond detail and to achieve some simpler, broader, and deeper characterization of a way of life. The generalization need not be one which the members of the community would themselves overtly make, but it is supposed to be empirical, in the sense that it is distilled from ethnographic detail, and operational, in that it can yield predictions of behavior subject to observational check.

Generalizations of this sort find their place within the scheduling framework. We shall see that it is no accident that terms used in portraying "national character" or "philosophy" tend to be those used in describing the character or personality of individuals.

Suppose a culture repeatedly subjects participants to states in which freedom of choice is low and anxiety high. The participant learns this pattern, and comes to interpret all sorts of states as though they involved little freedom and much anxiety. This is a change of personality; hence, because of the conjugate nature of personality and social structure, it is also a change in social structure. The habits acquired by a newcomer to the community depend on where in social structure he enters the community. Newcomers (children) can be exposed in increasing numbers to the VLVH pattern. In due time the whole community may be marked by fatalism and anxiety. Alternatively, such a combination as fatalism and anxiety might become widespread for certain cultural systems only, other systems having different properties.

The degree of ritualization of a way of life is the extent to which states in various cultural systems are characterized by the HLVL pattern. It has been suggested that if a way of life involves great anxiety in certain contexts, it compensates for this by ritualization in others. The Japanese live on seismically unstable islands, where a major disaster may come at any moment without warning. The Japanese play baseball by American rules, but with differences of style: if a Japanese batter is called out, he bows politely to the umpire and returns to the dugout.* Ritualization reduces noise, but it also cuts down on the rate at which information flows. It is not surprising that the uncertainty and anxiety of dealings between nations should be accompanied by a high degree of ritualization of diplomatic transactions.

Shame and guilt are different properties of cross-personal constructions, reflected in the relation of predictability to freedom of choice and to anxiety.

Hostility, tolerance, and love have to do with scheduled ways of dealing with noise in cross-personal and cross-group transactions.

Appendix

Predictability varies inversely with indeterminacy; it is the latter that we quantify.

In some cultural systems, including language, the alternative array for any state is discrete and finite. Suppose that the actor has just finished a word. Let the words of the language be w_1, w_2, ..., w_{n-1}, and let w_n be the "zero word" we shall say has occurred if the speaker does not continue with any actual word. With each w_i is associated a probability $p(i)$ that it will be the next word. No probability is less than zero, and the whole set sums to unity,

---

* The suggestion and illustration were proposed by W. F. Twaddell.

so that none is greater than unity. The degree of indeterminacy of the state can be measured by Shannon's entropy formula:[2]

$$H = - \sum_{i=1}^{n} p(i) \log_2 p(i) .$$

This is never negative, and is zero only if one of the alternatives has probability unity and all the others have probability zero.

The formula is applicable without change to any cultural system in which, as in language, alternative arrays are always discrete and finite. Some systems do not have this property. Suppose that someone is about to point. Neglecting elevation, he may point in any of a simple infinity of compass directions. Associate real numbers $0 \leq x < 1$ with directions, say by assigning 0 to north, .25 to west, and so on. Let $y = f(x)$ be the probability that the direction of pointing will not be greater than x. The function is defined for the closed unit interval. Clearly, $f(0) = 0$, $f(1) = 1$; and without loss of generality (because of the general case taken up below) we can assume $f(x)$ continuous, monotonic increasing, and differentiable throughout the interval. The probability that the pointing will be in a direction between x and $x + dx$ is then $dy = f'(x)dx$. We define

$$H = - \int_0^1 f'(x) \log_2 f'(x) \, dx$$

$$= - \frac{1}{\ln 2} \int_0^1 f'(x) \ln f'(x) \, dx .$$

By stipulating that $0 \cdot \ln 0 = 0$, we render the integrand continuous in the closed unit interval, so that the integral exists; from the conditions, it is positive.

Pointing up and down, as well as in compass directions, yields a double infinity of possibilities and requires a suitable double integral. Neither this nor any continuous case of higher dimensionality makes any difficulty in principle.

In the general case, an alternative array may consist of any (finite) number of subarrays, all discrete from one another, and at most one consisting of discrete single possibilities (since if there are more than one of the discrete type we can lump them together). Let S be the whole array; let S_1 be the subarray composed of discrete alternatives, so that $S_2, \ldots, S_n$ all contain continua of alternatives. $H(S_i)$ can be computed for each subarray separately, on the contingent assumption that the next act actually be chosen from that subarray (so that the probabilities of the alternatives within the subarray sum to unity). Let p_i be the probability that the next act will be chosen from subarray S_i. Then the total entropy of the state, $H(S)$, is the weighted sum $\Sigma p_i H(S_i)$.

An alternative is a trait. An alternative array has at most the cardinality of the continuum (if its cardinality is less, it is finite). The set of all traits of a community also has, at most, the cardinality of the continuum. The number of possible states is at most denumerable. Description in terms of a finite number of states is adequate, however, because traits and schedulings change too rapidly for the error involved in a finite approximation to have any effect.

We have provided for continuous arrays, but not for a continuous sequence of acts. The assumption is that, from the inside view, all sequences of acts are discrete.

We hypothesize that any actor computes the indeterminacy, hence the predictability, of any state, and that the result bears on his behavior. It is not implied that the actor understands the mathematics involved, except in the sense in which it might validly be claimed that electrons "understand" the equations of wave mechanics.

FOOTNOTE REFERENCES

1. Editing is discussed more fully in Hockett, Charles F., "Ethnolinguistic Implications of Studies in Linguistics and Psychiatry," in William M. Austin (ed.), *Report on the Ninth Annual Round Table Meeting on Linguistics and Language Study at Georgetown University*, Washington, D.C., 1960, pp. 175–193.
2. Shannon, Claude E., "The Mathematical Theory of Communication," in Claude E. Shannon, and Warren Weaver, *The Mathematical Theory of Communication*, University of Illinois Press, Urbana, Ill., 1949, pp. 3–91.

Two

Some Old Ideas About the Human Brain from a Recent Point of View VALENTINO BRAITENBERG

9

This chapter is concerned with the cybernetical character of the human nervous system. The topic raises two questions: whether the human brain has a cybernetical character, and what kind of a character it has, cybernetically speaking. Since the first question again offers two interpretations, depending on the wider or narrower use of the word cybernetics, we shall proceed in order.

Taking cybernetics, according to N. Wiener,[1] as the kind of discourse which is concerned with questions of control and communication in the animal and in the machine, and therefore implicitly, as the attitude characterized by the willingness to use the same terminology for the animal and for the hardware, our question can only be: Is the human brain sufficiently characterized by a cybernetical description, or will we miss something unless we introduce concepts which our work with hardware would never suggest? This question can be very rapidly dismissed in a context such as the present volume: I am professionally involved in discussing the brain as if it were a machine, and will do so here. The question of the sufficiency of my models is one that cannot be decided by me, unless I turn rapidly—and quite amateurishly—into a sociologist, for that is the level at which the decision has to be made. Since it is the level of this symposium, I will be spared the embarrassment of transcending my competence.

Taking "cybernetic" in a narrower sense (which I think is the dominant sense in America), "related to the activity of the steersman" and therefore "tending toward a goal" or "controlled by feedback," the question becomes: Can we say anything surprisingly new about the human nervous system if we adopt the language of feedback and of goal-directed behavior?

Within the blueprint of animal nervous systems so many circular arrays of causal connections have been discovered, both of the kind involving inhibition (negative feedback) and of the positive kind (to which belong McCulloch's "trapped universal" circuits), that we may doubt whether there are any connections not matched by the corresponding anticonnections. Intuitively we are satisfied by such a view: the structure of the brain laid down in sets of reciprocal action, each delicately balanced to insure a certain state of equilibrium and each individual state of equilibrium in turn balanced by higher order feedback connections. Ultimately, we may think of the "well-being" of the organism as the state of equilibrium toward which the highest order feedback tends, or to say it in a biological, not a medical, frame, the supreme scope of further existence of a physical realization of the logical blueprint which represents the animal.

The highest order feedback, which keeps animals the way they are and lets them even improve, justifies a methodological remark which may seem obvious once it is made, but which puts some of our cybernetical discussions about brains outside the code of rules of other branches of natural science. I mean that the very fact that organisms are controlled by feedback allows me to speak of them, and, therefore, of their brains, in teleological terms, to consider them as if they were faultlessly engineered for the purpose of their survival and, therefore, to adopt for their analysis the gimmick of identifying myself with the intentions of the nonexisting engineer. Teleology is again methodologically a clean term after Rosenblueth, Wiener, and Bigelow.[2] In a broad biophysical view it may be put as follows:

When we construct a physical theory, we postulate the existence of certain elementary entities (particles, forces, and so on) and rules of combination of these into higher order entities. By this process we generally arrive at statements about the probability of certain types of these higher order entities under given conditions. (Very often the theory will be phrased in such a way that the probability resulting from it will be 1 or 0.) These probabilities can then be compared under experimental conditions with the actual frequencies of objects (measurements) which we identify with the higher order entities of the theory. Quite the same should hold for biophysics. Here, however, we deal with objects characterized by the distinctive property of reproduction. The frequency of their occurrence (and of the occurrence of any detail of their structure) should be compared with the probabilities resulting from a theory which, in order to be complete, would have to contain the entire history of all the environmental conditions which ever influenced the probability of reproduction of that structure and of its ancestors. Darwinian selection will for some time to come enter our theory only in the form of the general supposition of a highest order feedback from the environment which tends to keep the organisms close to their optimal performance. Teleological statements are shorthand expressions of this general supposition.

In the following I shall improvise freely about some cybernetical (in the wider sense) aspects of animal brains.

Neural Optics

Traditional philosophy has to a large extent identified "messages" within the brain (as well as messages which reach the brain from the outside and messages emitted by the brain) with visual *images*, so much so that the Greek word for image (*eidos, edeia*) has become synonymous with message in the old philosophical approach to information handling. Accordingly we could describe the brain as an apparatus which receives images as input, operates on them according to certain rules, and again emits images. Somewhat facetiously we could call such a model of the brain an optical model. As in geometrical optics, we could study the rules of transformation of images within the apparatus either by following the course of individual rays throughout the apparatus or by observing the intermediate images in various planes. We shall see how far this model can take us.

At the receiving end of the brain we have sense organs, essentially collections of elements capable of producing nerve impulses in response to stimulation with some particular form of energy at the frequency to which they are tuned. These elements are, generally, rigidly arranged in a geometrical array, very often two-dimensional, sometimes one-dimensional, as in the lateral line of fish or in the cochlea. (I know of no three-dimensional case.)

Things outside the animal will project images such as shadows, patterns of shock waves or of mechanical vibration, chemical gradients, electrical potential fields, and so on, onto these arrays of sense cells, in some cases directly, in others through such complicated machinery as the "photographic camera" of the vertebrate eye, or after transformation of different frequencies in different places in the cochlea, and so on. What is conducted from the senses to the brain is very much the same for all senses: images consisting in patterns of active fibers in large bundles. Let us forget the intermediate stations for the time being, where various kinds of ancillary services are performed, such as to keep the image as stable as possible or to adapt the sensitivity of the receiving apparatus. The general pattern is that of "projection" and has been described with this very term in textbooks of neuroanatomy: systems of fibers carrying different sensory modalities fanning out from a narrow central core, the diencephalon, onto the large vault of the cerebral cortex, each ending in its own well-delimited region of projection. I hardly think any anatomist since Meynert, who was the first to introduce this planetarium-like description of the relationship of the senses and the cortex, has ever doubted that the images of the periphery are again neatly reproduced in the loci of their cortical "projection," as they called it. The calculus of ideas within the brain being, to many at least, a calculus of images, this projection may well have looked like the necessary first step. As we shall see later, besides the "optical" way of looking at a brain, there are other ways which would lead us to expect anything but a recomposition of the images of the periphery within the brain. Still, as physiological methods were used to follow up the anatomical conjectures, it was found that the geometry of each sensory array was again and again repeated in successive way stations within the brain. Most likely, if we had electrophysiological methods to show sparks on the surface of the cortex wherever a fiber becomes active, we could easily recognize, say, a fish outlined in sparks whenever the subject looks at a fish, and when someone listens to a run of thirds on the piano, the sparks on the cortex would show a picture quite similar to the appearance of the hammers in the piano when the run was played.

Similarly, on the output side we find regions of the brain in which the entire muscular apparatus is pictorially represented point for point, and, whatever an animal does with his muscles, we might be able to infer from the play of the sparks in the corresponding regions.

Let us see what kind of advantage this "optical" way of transmission of information offers to the brain. No doubt a large part of the things that matter in the life of an animal present themselves in the form of certain delimited characteristics of the environment in connected regions of space; in other words, as solid objects. An enemy is such an object, or a tree which I have to climb, or a path which I have to follow.

My action will be a consequence of a set of measurements which I take on the image of such an object, and since the kind of measurement which I will take and which may become decisive depends in a complicated fashion on other clues derived from other images in different senses, it pays to have the images ready as such, as some sort of geometrical representations, as close as possible to the site of supreme decision, in order to allow for the most flexible possible operations on this material.

What kind of measurements the brain can perform in the "planetarium" is a matter for interesting speculation. We have some indications from more peripheral sites, which may reflect some of the general principles. About the frog's eye it is known from Lettvin, Maturana, McCulloch, and Pitts[3] that it will extract from the visual image information about where highly contrasted borders between light and dark regions are located, where the outline of a shadow is most curved, and other similar items.

Hartline[4] has shown a simple mechanism in the eye of the horseshoe crab, based on destructive interference between fibers which is the more pronounced the closer two fibers are to each other. This mechanism will enhance contrast lines—a very useful function if we remember that what matters are frequently solid objects, and these give themselves away chiefly because of their continuous sharp contour. It will also furnish a measure of the "indentedness" of a contour, another useful function, if we have to deal with images of other biological organisms. It will also separate two points of light even if considerable smearing or defocusing has fused them into one in the original image (Reichardt[5]). But here, considering such mechanisms of interference, the paradigm of geometrical optics breaks down; even more so if we ask ourselves what kind of optics it takes to transform images of the input projection into such images in the output projection as will insure in each case the most favorable action. Here, too, in this mysterious central piece of the conduction through the brain it will be conduction along quite the same kind of "rays," i.e., individual nerve fibers, but there will be stages where our hypothetical experiments showing sparks for action potential will not reveal anything interpretable by sheer inspection. We have to revert to other kinds of models.

Logical Aspects

Ever since we began building machines, whose function is most appropriately described in terms of logic rather than of physics, we have become accustomed to speaking of "kinds of logic" in a manner which might have seemed (and still might seem) unorthodox to many traditional philosophers. Different logics (only recently the word acquired a plural) being the formal descriptions of different kinds of logical machines, the way is open to finding a machine for every logic and a logic for every machine. In connection with the human brain, there are two interesting aspects of this problem. The first question is: What kind of logic appears to be most useful as a tool for a formal description of the structure and function of animal brains? The other question is wider and has not even been clearly formulated as yet. Taking the various kinds of logic which have been formulated (but not formalized) by philosophers or psychologists as legitimate products of an introspective process, what kind of a machine must we postulate which would obey those rules? Both these questions constitute the central core of the cybernetical program. Both promise to produce results which will in turn be applicable to a more correct formulation of the questions themselves. Thus the search for the most appropriate logic for the description of available facts about the brain will, no doubt, lead to the observation of further facts about the brain. In turn, the search for mechanisms which would incorporate the informal descriptions of the thinking process will necessarily produce models which, being physical models, must be amenable to a precise formal description which will be a very likely candidate to supplant the older unformalized theory. Out of the workshop of cybernetics we shall produce some sketches without, unfortunately, being able to connect them into a coherent picture.

McCulloch and Pitts' Nerve Nets

I may limit myself to a few remarks, since Professor McCulloch's chapter will cover this subject.

When we looked at the brain as an optical apparatus, we were tacitly neglecting a very crucial property of the fibers which carry "images" from plane to plane, the so-called all-or-none characteristic of their function. What is meant is that such a fiber, given sufficient excitation at one end will become active and for less excitation will stay inactive; it will not become partially active or moderately active for insufficient excitation, nor will it become exaggeratedly active for more than sufficient excitation. The "firing" of a certain neuron (this terminology is from McCulloch and Pitts)[6] is then—like the presence or absence of a certain mark in an algebraic formula, where no intermediate reading is admitted —an unambiguous symbol ideally suited to cut the universe of all situations in two parts, the class of situations for which this neuron fires and, its complement, the class of situations for which it does not. We can easily see that a sufficiently large number of neurons variously connected with sensory cells will, so to say, cut the universe to any degree of parcellation, in the sense that their combined states will indicate a situation more and more specific the larger their number is.

Moreover, for any such situation of the universe, we can imagine a nerve net suitably constructed with realistic neurons, culminating with one neuron which will become active always and only when (or rather a short time after) this situation occurs. In the construction of such nerve nets we do not have to bend the facts to any strait jacket, since neurophysiology has provided, long before logic was applied to it, just exactly the kind of connections between neurons, involving the branching of one fiber toward many, the confluence of many branches toward one neuron, summation, excitation, inhibition, and threshold, which we would have to postulate on theoretical grounds. They provide exactly the operations of logical sum, logical product, complementation with which we may write logical formulas corresponding in structure to the nets in question.

These logical formulas may have two interpretations. On one hand we may think of sets of active sensory elements and sets of such sets and consider each neuron as the indicator of the particular set (or set of sets) of sensory elements whose activity will make it active. On the other hand, changing the interpretation but not the formalism, we may think of the elementary proposition describing the state of each sensory element, or if we wish, the proposition represented by each sensory element in its active state, such as "Sensory cell A perceives blue light," "Sensory cell B perceives pressure." Other neurons of the net will then represent more complex propositions involving the elementary propositions represented by the sensory cells. The rules of the calculus of propositions, which allow us to synthesize propositions from atomic propositions, will be isomorphic with the net of connections between neurons, where inhibition corresponds to negation, summation with a certain threshold corresponds to negation, summation with a certain threshold corresponds to logical sum and with another (higher) threshold to logical product.

The representation of propositions by neurons of a net offers some more interesting aspects if we ask ourselves what kind of a proposition is represented by a neuron which is part of a circle, i.e., of a chain of neurons leading back onto itself. Given suitable connections, the neurons of such a circle, once activated, will remain periodically active. The proposition represented by a neuron of a circle will be of the type "at some time in the past such and such a situation has occurred" (for a circle which is set in motion by that situation) or else "it has never occurred that . . ." (for a circle which would be stopped by the event in question) or again "up to now, always . . ." (for a circle which can remain active only under a particular condition). Propositions of this type belong to the predicate calculus, or calculus of quantifiers, a step beyond the calculus of propositions in the hierarchy of logical calculi. But to go into this would be most definitely transgressing into Professor McCulloch's territory.

Note that the variable which is quantified in the expression corresponding to a circle of neurons is time, in other words the propositions contain terms such as "at some time," "never," "at all times," but not "something," "nowhere" or "somewhere," and so on; quantification does not apply to space or object variables. The problem of how a brain will express quantified propositions in general shall detain us some more.

The Microcosm

We may ask ourselves what kind of a relationship between a brain, a set of objects, and another brain it is when brain A says to brain B "All featherless bipeds are humans" or "All red apples are sweet" or "Some green apples are sour" or other expressions involving statements about properties pertaining to the totality of a class of objects mentioned.

Brain B is irrelevant to our discussion, since we are not interested in language but in the function of brains and take it for granted that we correctly understand the linguistic expressions of A. The heart of the question, which becomes more poignant if we propose to construct a brain capable of such expressions, is: Must a brain (a piece of apparatus) contain in its archives a record of every single instance of the thing in question in order to be able to speak competently about "all featherless bipeds" or "all red apples," and so on, or is there a shortcut available?

A few remarks about universal quantification in symbolic logic will help us. There are two essentially different situations in which we prefix a proposition with a universal quantifier, meaning that the proposition is true for all substitutions of the variable in question. We do this on one hand when we postulate a certain relation between a predicate and a variable for reasons outside of the logical system, simply in the way of an assertion whose further consequences we want to investigate by means of the rules of the logic. On the other hand we may write a universal quantifier in front of any expression, which is tautologous according to the rules of the logical system, following the principle that a relation between predicates which *always holds* will hold no matter to what variables the predicates refer.

It is evident that in order to establish a tautologous relation between predicates a brain will not have to consult its archives at all, but only the rules according to which it operates on the predicates. Because of the obvious limitation in capacity of any physically realistic archives, let alone the limitation of individual experience, it is clear that it is only in this second sense that a brain can produce true universal propositions. It is easily seen in the case of the quite artificial situation of a brain producing propositions about mathematical objects, as it has often been said that mathematics is the art of producing tautologies. It is more problematic in the case of propositions about physical objects. We may save the principle however if we suppose that the things of the outside world are represented in a brain in such a way that if we take these representations as logical expressions (as we learned to do earlier in the McCulloch and Pitts' nerve nets) a composite expression which is tautologous reflects a generally valid correlation between the physical objects whose representations enter in this expression. Thus if we suppose that red apples are represented in the brain by the expression "sweet red apple," the proposition "all sweet red apples are sweet" earns its universal quantifier by virtue of the fact that it is tautologous.

There is an important difference between a brain containing in its archives all individual images of all apples, red, green, sweet, or sour, which it has ever perceived and one which contains only the images (expressions) "red sweet apple," "green sour apple" or whatever other kinds of apples it knows. In the former case, the process of inscription of the images into the brain is simple; the storage space however must be large, and the analysis of the images in terms of universal sentences is a fairly complicated process. In the other case, the burden of the "abstraction" lies on the process of inscription of the images; the storage space can be much reduced, and the production of universal sentences is a simple process. In neither case can the statements about external objects be more generally valid than the experience that went into the brain. But while in the first case the statement can only have the form of an hypothetical generalization of a limited experience, in the second case the brain can produce truly universal propositions, being propositions about relations between the representations (in a way, about the names) of the external things, not about the things themselves. In this second case, what is hypothetical is the correspondence of things and their names (internal representations).

I suppose this view of the brain repeating, or rather approximating, in its logical structure the correlational structure of the outside world is close to the philosophical vision of the microcosm, of man reflecting in his own internal order the order of the universe.

The Lullian Machine

In the preceding discussion we were assuming that a brain would have no difficulty in discovering whether a certain proposition involving internal states of the brain (which we have interpreted as representations of outside objects) is tautologous or not. On the grounds of symbolic logic, this supposition is no doubt justified, since the "decision problem" for the calculus of propositions, i.e., the problem of finding a test which will reveal whether a composite proposition is true by virtue of its own structure (independently from the truth of the constituent elementary propositions) reduces to the simple tabular method of Wittgenstein.[7] This consists in a display of all possible combinations of truth values of the constituent elementary propositions, coupled with a function which will give for each combination the corresponding truth value of the composite proposition. If this function will give the same value for all combinations, the corresponding proposition is a tautology (or a contradiction). It is quite easy to invent mechanisms built out of neuron-like elements which will incorporate the principle of Wittgenstein's tabular procedure whenever we deal with a small number of elementary propositions. For more complex propositions, the combinatorial procedure will soon become unwieldy, and it would be difficult to house the corresponding mechanism in a nerve net of natural dimensions. We may help ourselves in two ways. First, the different combinations, instead of being displayed together, may be produced in succession, in some cyclic order, for instance, or else at random; a sufficiently prolonged random succession will be to a brain sufficient guarantee of having explored all combinations. This will take time but save space. Second, the logically simple performance of the combinatorial display may be relegated to some primitive auxiliary organ which may become coupled with the brain just for the occasion. Both these extensions of the power of the brain as a combinatorial mechanism are familiar to us from the specifically human activity known as thinking. It takes time before a relation between objects, about which we are thinking, suddenly comes as a flash to our mind in the form of a universal, tautologous proposition. Also, we will systematically go through different cases of a problem by putting them into a one-to-one relation with our fingers, or we will sketch them on a piece of paper or draw geometrical figures to aid the process, and so on.

At first sight Raymond Lull's contraptions[8] would seem as far removed from our concept of a logical machine as his "ars magna" is from present-day symbolic logic. He used sets of concentric disks on the margin of each of which was written a number of different kinds of objects or attributes. Rotating the disks relative to each other in a stepwise fashion and reading for each position the resulting combinations of neighboring names on the different disks, the user of Lull's wheels could think about each of an exhaustive set of situations involving the objects of his interest. In conjunction with a thinking brain (i.e., with a brain which is able to discover tautologies) the Lullian machine could perform a logically trivial but cybernetically significant function. Symbolic logic finds no difficulties of principle when it has to deal with very large numbers of objects. On the contrary, in cybernetics, the economy of the number of parts is almost always the most serious consideration.

The Drumskin Analogies

We owe yet another explanation of a mechanism which was left open in the preceding constructions, the mechanism of memory which will incorporate information from the environment into the logical structure of the brain. We had assumed that if all red apples are also sweet, the internal representation of "red apple" will invariably have associated with it the representation of "sweet." This is *association*, still, as in the times of Hume (and of Aristotle), one of the most useful hypotheses on the function of the brain. Since we realize now more fully that the representations which will be associated have in turn grown into "concepts" by a similar associative process, and, since, reasoning in terms of internal representations of things, rather than in terms of the things themselves, we can formulate the laws of association more simply than Hume could (he lists resemblance, contiguity, and causality as the causes of association), we prefer to express the phenomenon in a more general way.

Consider the following model. On a finite number of elements, each capable of a finite number (say two) of states, connected together to form a brain, we can impose patterns of activity from the outside, specifying the state of each element for a certain period of time. If the same pattern of activity has been imposed a number of times, we suppose that by virtue of the connections of the elements this pattern may occur in its entirety even if it has been only partly specified from the outside. Thus, if this pattern contained the image *A* as well as the image *B*, it may be sufficient to impose *A* in order to produce also *B*. This is the prototype of a number of phenomena in experimental psychology, of which the conditioned reflex is perhaps the best known. It has been called the principle of reintegration of patterns.

If I had to construct such a brain, I would soon run into great difficulties. I might use counters of coincidences (including delayed coincidences) in order to establish for any two elements how much their states were correlated in time and so reconstruct ("reintegrate") a pattern from a partial specification in the most likely way on the basis of the data from these counters. But this would mean a very large number of counters and would still be insufficient, since besides coincidences between individual elements, the machine would also have to count coincidences of sets of elements. This would make the number of counters prohibitively large in any case, besides requiring a complete classification machine in the sense of Uttley,[9] (i.e., a classificatory neuron for each set of neurons) as a basis for counting. (Example: The phrase "from the . . . House, the President of the United States" is immediately reintegrated even if none of the individual words has a high correlation with the word *white*.)

Consider on the contrary the following model: a drumskin made of some material which is both elastic and plastic (deformable). I may excite it in different places with various frequencies, and I may stop it at different places; in other words, I may impose patterns of vibration by imposing locally bellies and nodes. Suppose that the tension of the drumskin relaxes in the places of the bellies and stays unchanged in the places of the nodes. Reasoning in terms of energy, it is plausible that the drumskin will tend to fall into patterns of vibration which it has previously experienced for some time, even if they are only partially imposed, and thus it may reintegrate some nodes and bellies of the original pattern. Though I know of no such experiments on learning drumskins, it is an undoubted fact among instrument makers and violinists that a new violin will learn (i.e., it will produce more and more easily) the imposed patterns of vibration by being played.

I do not believe that elastic-plastic membranes will make useful thinking machines. Over the relatively simple (neighborhood-coupled) structure of such membranes, the animal brain has the advantage of a fibrous structure which provides a very large number of very specific point-to-point connections. But these connections are not sufficient for interpretations such as our coincidence-counter model. Some principle related to that of the drumskin must be invoked to explain how a brain "self-organizes" itself, to use a fashionable word. Unfortunately, the mathematics of such models has not yet been provided.

FOOTNOTE REFERENCES

1. Wiener, Norbert, *Cybernetics*, Wiley, New York, 1948.
2. Rosenblueth, Arturo, Norbert Wiener, and Julian Bigelow, "Behavior, Purpose and Teleology," *Philosophy of Science*, vol. 10, 1943, pp. 18–24.
3. Lettvin, Jerome Y., H. R. Maturana, Warren S. McCulloch, and W. H. Pitts, "What the Frog's Eye Tells the Frog's Brain," *Proceedings of the Institute of Radio Engineers*, vol. 47, 1959, pp. 1940–1951; Maturana, H. R., Jerome Y. Lettvin, Warren S. McCulloch, and W. H. Pitts, "The Anatomy and Physiology of Vision in the Frog (*Rana pipiens*)," *Journal of General Physiology*, vol. 43, no. 6, supplement, 1960, pp. 129–175.
4. Hartline, Haldan K., and Floyd Ratliff, "Inhibitory Interaction of Receptor Units in the Eye of *Limulus*," *Journal of General Physiology*, vol. 40, 1957, pp. 357–376; "Spatial Summation of Inhibitory Influences in the Eye of *Limulus*, and the Mutual Interaction of Receptor Units," *ibid.*, vol. 41, 1958, pp. 1049–1066.
5. Reichardt, Werner, "Über das optische Auflösungsvermögen der Facettenaugen von *Limulus*," *Kybernetik*, vol. 1, 1961, pp. 57–69.
6. McCulloch, Warren S., and W. H. Pitts, "A Logical Calculus of the Ideas Immanent in Nervous Activity," *Bulletin of Mathemati-*

cal Biophysics, vol. 5, 1943, pp. 115–133; with H. D. Landahl, "A Statistical Consequence of the Logical Calculus of Nervous Nets," *ibid.*, pp. 135–137; Pitts, W. H., and Warren S. McCulloch, "How We Know Universals, the Perception of Auditory and Visual Forms," *ibid.*, vol. 9, 1947, pp. 127–147.

7. Wittgenstein, Ludwig, *Tractatus Logico-Philosophicus*, Routledge & Kegan Paul, London, 1922, pp. 93–105.

8. Gardner, Martin, *Logic Machines and Diagrams*, McGraw-Hill, New York, 1958.

9. Uttley, A. M., "Conditional Probability Machines and Conditioned Reflexes," in Claude E. Shannon, and J. McCarthy (eds.), *Automata Studies*, Princeton, Princeton, N.J., 1956; Uttley, A. M., "Temporal and Spatial Patterns in a Conditional Probability Machine," *ibid.*

A Functional Approach DONALD M. MacKAY

10

This chapter attempts to outline an approach to human behavior from the standpoint of communication science, which may serve as a link between the study of individual man and that of social groups. Since both the human organism and the human group are systems that "run on information," it may be of some interest to ask what informational mechanisms may embody the processes that anthropologists study.

Man as a mechanism is (as we have seen in other chapters in this symposium) a teleonomic, or goal-directed, system. In a general sense, we can say that information as to the current state of his environment (including results of his own activity) contributes to the ongoing selective process by which his behavior is organized.[1] The numerous goals and norms of the human system form a partially ordered hierarchy, such that many goal-settings are under the control of "superior" subsystems. The setting of such goals, in other words, constitutes a *means* to a (temporarily or permanently) dominant end. Thus for a solitary man the acquisition of a tool, or the turning of a control knob, may be a subgoal prescribed by superior normative calculations. Since the rank-ordering of subgoals generally depends on current information as to the state of the field of action, we need a term which covers both the current goal-settings and the "matrix of conditional probabilities" which determines what change *would* take place *if* such and such information were received. Let us refer to this as the "goal-complex" of the system.

When the environment includes other members of the same (or sufficiently similar) species, a new kind of possibility emerges. In addition to the ordinary methods of interaction, the individual has now the possibility of influencing his environment by way of another individual, by inducing changes in that individual's goal-complex. This latter is the process we call communication.[2] Clearly, it introduces the further possibility of back reaction from the second individual to the first, directed toward alteration in *his* goal-complex. Where this is the case (as normally in dialogue), it may become logically impossible to dissociate the two goal-complexes. The individuals have acquired a relationship in which their individualities have partly merged. They constitute for certain purposes a single goal-directed system. For these purposes, it becomes meaningful to refer to them as a social unit.

The Concept of Information

Human beings modify one another's goal-complexes in a variety of ways. We make indicative statements, ask questions, issue requests and commands. To summarize discussions presented elsewhere,[3] it seems possible to distinguish fairly clearly between the mechanical aspects of such processes by looking at their different effects on the goal-complexes involved.

Remembering that the goal-complex implicitly embodies a representation of "what is believed to be the case," as well as the hierarchy of goals being pursued, we may distinguish between two kinds of change which can be effected by an utterance—between two kinds of "target" which an individual's goal-complex presents to his interlocutor. The first target is the current "map," or representation of the state of affairs, implicit in his goal-complex. (This includes stored data on the past, including the subroutines or "tricks" found useful in the past.) The second is the current content and rank-order of the goal-hierarchy.

An *indicative* utterance is goal-directed toward the completion or alteration of the "map" implicit in the *recipient's* goal-complex

—i.e., it is uttered as a means of alerting his system to the situation indicated by the utterance; and any sign that it did not have the required effect on the recipient's "map" would normally evoke further corrective or adaptive action by the originator.

An *interrogative* utterance, on the other hand, is goal-directed toward the "up-dating" of the *originator's own* "map." The recipient becomes a link in the forward path of an action-under-feedback, whose goal is the filling up of an inadequacy in the originator's state of readiness. Of course, the utterance cannot help having an indicative aspect as well: It alerts the recipient to the inadequacy it reveals in the originator. That this is not normally its primary goal may be seen, however, by asking what would happen if the originator's inadequacy were remedied without the recipient's realizing its nature and extent.

The way in which analogous functional distinctions may be drawn between other types of utterance will now be obvious and need not here be labored. Imperative utterances, for example, have as their primary target the goal-structure rather than the orienting "map" of the recipient; and so forth.[4]

I have mentioned these technicalities only because I think a coherent account of semantics requires us to widen our view of the communicative process (so often discussed only in terms of source, channel, and sink) to include the whole pattern of goal-directed activities within which it plays a part. In ordinary subjective terms, to have one's "map" brought up to date is to receive "information." "Information-about-X" is that which *determines the form* of one's state of readiness for X. In objective terms exactly parallel statements can be made about the human mechanism, by replacing "one's" by "its." In short, to talk in terms of "information," "determination of form," "map," "goal," "state of readiness," and the like, provides us with a common conceptual language in which it is relatively easy to make connections between correlated subjective and objective data that concern us. Up to a point, we can even frame definitions that can be used interchangeably at the two levels.

The concept of information that emerges in these terms is essentially *relative*. I have elsewhere suggested that we define "information," in isolation, as "that which determines form." This definition has the advantage of applying equally well to what "flows" along artificial communication lines and what "passes" between human beings; but it still invites us to ask: "The form of what?" Conceptually our picture is incomplete unless we specify what information is *about*—what it represents or betokens. In other words, the concept of information (*pace* communication engineers, whose ideas are fitted into the picture below, in the section "The Mathematical Theory of Communication") is inseparable from that of *meaning*.

The Concept of Meaning

The purpose of communication being the modification of goal-complexes (in recipient and/or originator), it seems possible[5] to define the *meaning* of a communication as its *selective function* on the range of possible states of the goal-complex concerned. We could perhaps abbreviate this to its *"orienting function."*

Note first that this too is a *relative* concept, allowing essential distinctions to be drawn (in obvious ways) between, for instance, meaning-to-originator, standard meaning, and meaning-to-recipient and between indicative, interrogative, and imperative meaning.

We may note further the difference between this definition in terms of selective *function*, and attempts to define meaning as the *effect produced* in the recipient. The effect produced by a message may well *betoken* its meaning; but it would be absurdly restrictive to *equate* it with the meaning. It may be true that, for instance, if meaning is vague and ill-defined, the effect produced is also vague and ill-defined. In that sense many terms that qualify "meaning" can also qualify "effect produced"; but the conceptual reduction of "meaning" to "effect" represents in fact a confusion between a *function* and the result of its *exercise*.*

At the risk of oversimplification, we might liken the meaning of a message to the "opening power" of a key in relation to a given lock. To turn the key has the *effect* of opening the lock, but the opening (a change in the lock) merely *betokens* the opening power of the key and cannot be equated with it. Opening power

---

* The point here is related to the distinction made in mathematics between the concept of a (mathematical) function, and that of its numerical values— a distinction clarified only after much labor by d'Alembert and his successors.

is a property of the key (in relation to that lock) which could in principle be established by inspection of lock and key, even if the key were never used.

Similar objections can clearly be made to the dictum that "the meaning is the use." Its intention to be "operational" is laudable; but it fastens upon the wrong operation. In the case of our key, the operation required is to look inside the mechanism of the lock and see what would happen if the key were used. In the case of a human recipient, the corresponding operation may well be impracticable for good social and surgical reasons; but this is no excuse for Procrustean distortion of the conceptual picture. Not even the most hardened operationalist pretends that all his "operations" could be performed in practice: what matters is that they are possible in principle; and in principle (if our notions of the causal organization of behavior are at all valid) the orienting function of a message (qua potential input) could be determined just as readily by advance inspection of the brain, as the opening power of a key by advance inspection of the lock.

It may be only fair to point out that what the slogan "meaning is use" was meant to reject is equally strongly excluded by our present definition—namely, the idea that meaning could be defined solely in terms of the form of the message. While for many purposes we may discuss the meaning of utterances safely enough in terms of their orienting function for a "standard recipient," it would be philosophical folly to conclude from this that meaning was an absolute property of an utterance, definable without reference to any recipient. This would be like arguing that the "opening power" of a master key was an absolute property of the geometry of its wards, definable without reference to any lock.

Simply by asking what gives any physical event-sequence the status of a communication, we can detect the reference to specific goal-complexes implicit in even the most artificial "languages" of the logician. Thus, for example, it is not the rules that give meaning to the moves in a game of chess. What introduces the element of meaning is surely the _agreement of players_ to abide by those rules: that is, to adopt a standard pair of (sub-) goal-complexes. The moves can be said to have their chess meaning (selective function) only in relation to those goal-complexes. The movement of a black pawn may mean to the "white" player a threat, to the "black" player a relief, and to an ignorant onlooker the displacement of a piece of carved wood. Each reveals his goal-complex (artificial or natural) by the meaning he assigns. In each case, at the mechanical level, we may expect corresponding differences between the respective "states of readiness" upon which it impinges, to account for the diverse effects of the same physical stimulus.

One final point of great importance should be noted. Our definition of meaning places no restriction on the *levels* of the goal-complex upon which selective function may be exercised. Since many subgoals in the human system concern internal bodily states (e.g., visceral or hormonal) of which the agent himself may not be articulately conscious, it is impossible to regard the full meaning of an utterance to an individual as always coextensive with what he can (even in principle) say it means. To say what something means to one is to try to fabricate other verbal selective operators, with identical function; but if one's power of introspection is limited (as psychologists tell us it is) then this is only a crude and approximate performance at best. The selective function of an utterance for an individual may obviously be perfectly well-defined, although he can *say* nothing well-defined about it. It seems important to rid ourselves of the current dogma that only what can be expressed precisely in words has precise meaning. Once again, we may lack opportunity in *practice* to observe the selective functioning of an utterance on the mechanism embodying a human goal-complex; but simply to envisage it in principle should be enough to unsettle any dogmatic restriction of meaningfulness to what can be described in words.

Conversely, it is clear that from our present standpoint an utterance needs to be viewed as a physical whole if we are to make proper sense of its semantic function. Important though the phonemic aspects of the physical stimulus may be, its selective function for a given recipient has other determinants (such as intonation, rhythm, and context or background) which in some cases may completely dominate the operation on his goal-complex. Only our lack of a conventional notation for these other (equally potent) features of utterance can explain the extent to which they are ignored, as in our legal and social conceptions of truthtelling and lying, for example. Everybody knows at heart that for some purposes the phonemic reduction of an utterance can be as dangerously inept as a black-and-white photograph of a traffic light.

If the investigation of other people's ideas is ever to have the status
of an exact science, ways must be found to articulate and document
all the salient features of the communicative process. There would
seem to be no fundamental obstacle to our doing so eventually—
or at least doing better than at present—along lines suggested by
our present approach; but to say so is of course to sketch a program rather than a solution.

Failure of Communication

The same analysis that enables us to handle the concept of
meaning throws interesting light on the different ways in which
the communicative process can *break down*. As "failure of communication" must be one of the anthropologist's most common
sources of frustration, it may be well to sketch its formal features
explicitly from our present viewpoint.

Failure may be partial or total. In every case, it means that the
intended and actual selective functions differ significantly—i.e.,
sufficiently to transgress the originator's "criterion of mismatch."

Since the originator has the double task of envisaging the goal-
complex (the "lock") upon which he wants to operate, and of
designing and emitting a stimulus (the "key") with the required
orienting function, he can fail if either the "lock" or his "key" is
significantly different in fact from what he believes or intends it
to be. At the worst, his effort can be "meaningless."

Total meaninglessness can be defined simply as "absence of
orienting function" (relative to a given recipient). Clearly, we
must then distinguish between the meaninglessness of (a) undefined utterances (where no structure in the recipient's goal-complex has been preestablished to match the stimuli), and that of
(b) illegitimate utterances (where the established selective functions of different components of an utterance are incompatible).
Examples of each respectively might be (a) "the jolks preed,"
(b) "the milk is isosceles."

For the anthropologist, partial breakdown of communication
(distortion of meaning) may present the more subtle problem.
Clearly (in terms of our "lock and key" image) such distortion
of the intended orienting function can arise from ignorance of
the "lock" or faulty design and/or use of the "key." The problems

of design and use will not be further elaborated. Ignorance of the "lock," however, has two radically different aspects that merit discussion.

First (to drop the metaphor), the originator has to discover and understand the *goals and subgoals* of the recipient. Apart from certain major goals common to all human beings, this may present difficulty enough. Yet by far the biggest problem arises at the second step—the elucidation of the principles on which these goals and subgoals are hierarchically ordered to form the goal-complex.

I have elsewhere suggested[6] that the internal representation of the world of an organism may be thought of as a statistical model of the "pattern of demand" made by the world upon the organism. By the "pattern of demand" I mean not merely those features of the world (such as heat and cold) that bear upon and disturb the equilibrium of the inert organism, but all those that the active organism has to take into account when conducting goal-directed activity. The suggestion is that the organizing system developed to match this pattern of demand (to do the necessary "taking into account") can *itself* serve as the internal representation of the world.

It follows from this (if true) that the categories in terms of which the world is perceived and conceived will depend on the various ways in which it has been found to thwart, facilitate, and mold the pursuit of the organism's particular goals. Aspects of the world which call forth (or have received) no adaptive internal "matching response" will simply fail to be perceived or conceived.

The conceptual structure of the world so perceived will obviously be closely bound up with the structure of the organizing system. If, for example, a regular pattern appears in the sequence of demand, then the internal organizer that is evolved to "match" it adaptively will constitute an internal symbol for that pattern. Wherever that pattern recurs, whether in the input or in the internal traffic among the organizers themselves, it is likely to arouse this organizer. The concept which it represents will then be a constituent of the new situation as perceived.

Thus in general, complex situations will tend to find themselves "matched" (internally represented) by the best possible (hierarchic) combination of the basic organizers that previous experience of goal-pursuit has evolved in that individual. Conceptual innovation will not of course be impossible,[7] but in the absence of sufficient incentive and/or suitable training there are liable to be epistemological blind spots in conceptual areas to which no readily formed combination of organizers corresponds.*

Clearly, with a different pattern of past experience, or a different set of goal-priorities, it is possible for one human organism to have evolved a single complex organizer to represent a feature of the world almost (if not quite) beyond the conceptual grasp of another, whose organizing system could cope with it only at the cost of major dismantling and rebuilding operations. Since the same is likely to be true in reverse, we have here a most potent and subtle source of failure of human communication. The point I would stress is that in these situations mere ostensive definition and exposure to common stimuli offers no remedy. The two individuals simply do not have the same perceptual experience when confronted with the same stimuli, so that ostensive naming could only breed further confusion. Any approach, to be fruitful, must start further back, by probing the respective goal-hierarchies for the disparity of priorities which has made his conceptual framework of the world turn out so differently for each. The participants must not be surprised if beyond a certain point the process ceases to be academic and becomes (in today's jargon) "existential." For what we have been uncovering is one of the relations between human knowledge and human values. The goals pursued in life inevitably condition the terms in which it is perceived and understood. There can be a moral element in conceptual blindness.

What then of the implications for anthropology? Everyone knows the story of the medical missionaries in central Africa who discovered that to disclaim magical powers was equivalent to telling their tribespeople that they could not help them. But how effectively can we guard ourselves against the same kind of misunderstanding in reverse? Is it even possible in principle? To do so at all thoroughly, we should need to understand our own goal-complexes *from the outside*—and this smacks of "pulling oneself up by one's own bootstraps." Perhaps in the end the investigator's best hope is to enlist the aid of his subjects, in the endeavor to

---

* Mathematical readers may be reminded of similar limitations to the usefulness of, for example, Fourier series as descriptions of waveforms. Although in theory any waveform can be described as the sum of sine waves, in practice the method becomes infinitely cumbersome for impulse-type functions. The language of frequency-analysis has a "blind spot" for the concept of "sudden change."

track down his own blind spots. He must realize, of course, that no process of this sort can do more than change their shape and their location; but at least it should lead to the improvement of communication; and at best it may conceptually enrich one or both sides beyond their imagining.

Perhaps a fair illustration might be taken from the difficulty, even in his own civilization, that faces the nonreligious investigator of religious belief. However adequately he may feel that he has "tied up" religious practice in his own categories, he cannot readily ignore the assurances of his subjects that his analysis, whose accuracy they may not dispute, is missing the point. If genuine religious commitment (as distinct from mere acceptance of credal affirmations) involves the uprooting of a "self-centered" goal-structure and its gradual replacement by a new set of goal-priorities, then it is inevitable that, in pursuit of these, new categories and concepts become meaningful and relevant, even though (in the Christian religion, for example) they do not necessarily render the old meaningless.

The Mathematical Theory of Communication

Accepting the foregoing as a rough summary of the mechanical aspects of human communication, how can we quantify our thinking in this area? For several decades problems of this sort have troubled communication engineers, for good economic reasons. Their most general solution, which often goes by the name of Communication Theory, has found applications in a surprisingly wide range of disciplines; indeed at the present time it seems to many of us to have suffered a little from "overselling," so that some confusion exists about its purpose and its true value.

The communication engineer views himself as an *intermediary* between the originator and recipient whom we have been discussing. His job is to deputize for the originator in certain prescribed and restricted tasks. He can thus regard the problem of communication (for *him*) as one of *identifying* or *selecting* something (a task) from a finite set or range. He must, of course, at some time have had a "briefing session" when the range of possible tasks was defined and agreed code-numbers or other designations assigned to them; but thereafter, assuming that the tasks (such as

printing letters of the alphabet) can be mechanized, he can afford
to forget their significance to the recipient and simply concentrate
on making the selective process as economical as possible.

From this standpoint, what matters is normally the *size of the
range* from which selection is made. Since the simplest selective
step is to identify one out of two equally likely possibilities
(thereby *halving* the range from 2 to 1), it is convenient to measure the size of a selective operation by asking how many such
successive halvings would have been necessary to narrow the range
down to the same extent.

Clearly 1 out of 4 equally likely tasks can be identified in two
such steps; 1 out of 8, in three; 1 out of 16, in four; and so on. In
general, then, we can measure the size of a given selective operation by the *logarithm* (*base* 2) of the number of equally likely
possibilities it has reduced to 1.

Now if n possibilities are equally likely, the probability of each
is $p = 1/n$. Hence we can write our definition of the size of a
selective operation as $\log_2 n$ or $\log_2 (1/p)$. In the second form
(skipping some questions of mathematical rigor) we have a way
of measuring the size of any selective operation to which we can
assign a probability, without reference to the number and probabilities of its alternatives. It is this quantity that the communication engineer terms the "selective-information-content" of the
operation concerned. He is usually interested in the *average* value
of $\log (1/p)$ over a run of operations whose probabilities (or relative frequencies) may be $p_1, p_2, \ldots p_n$. This can be written as
the "weighted mean,"

$$p_1 \log_2 \left(\frac{1}{p_1}\right) + p_2 \log_2 \left(\frac{1}{p_2}\right) + p_n \log_2 \left(\frac{1}{p_n}\right), \quad \text{or}$$

$$\sum p_1 \log_2 \left(\frac{1}{p_1}\right)$$

The latter expression, often denoted by H, is (regrettably) often
called the "entropy" of the selective process.

What is the significance of all this? Since p_1 is a probability,
$1/p_1$ measures the *improbability* of the selection concerned.
$\log_2 (1/p_1)$ is therefore a logarithmic measure of improbability,
which we may term the (mathematical) *unexpectedness* of the
selection. $\Sigma p_1 \log_2 (1/p_1)$ is simply the *average unexpectedness*

per selection. To dress it up as a "definition of information," as some exponents do, seems a most unfortunate obscurantism. Unexpectedness is a measurable *property* or *attribute* of information —not a definition of it!

What makes this attribute important for the engineer is its relation to the number of code-signals necessary to prescribe the corresponding selective operation. The mean unexpectedness, H, represents the number of yes-or-no code-signals (selective instructions) that should be necessary and sufficient on the average to identify each successive task. It therefore provides an invaluable yardstick by which to judge the efficiency of alternative encoding systems and to stimulate and guide the invention of better ones. Furthermore, if the same sequence of instructions must be relayed in a number of successive stages, perhaps encoded in a variety of different forms (Morse radio signals, semaphore, teleprinter code), this basic measure enables the "channel capacity" required in each stage to be specified and economically "matched" to the job.

One implication of the mathematical form of H may be worth mentioning here. For a given number of possibilities, the mean unexpectedness is at a maximum if all are equally likely: i.e., if all probabilities p_i are equal. If the p_i are seriously unequal, then the mean unexpectedness drops, and the selective process is said to be "redundant." This means that in principle a code can be found which requires fewer selective operations to transmit the same total of instructions.

An alternative possibility emerges, however. If a sequence of selections is redundant, this means that a certain calculable proportion of errors or "noise" can in principle be tolerated in transmission. Our ability to spot and correct occasional misprints in English text is a good example. The development of natural languages may indeed be studied with much profit by observing the different ways in which redundancy has been introduced to aid intelligibility under difficult conditions, and how a balance has been struck in different cases between selective capacity and resistance to corruptive "noise."

Now although the measure H was found useful by engineers in their role as intermediaries, it is of course a perfectly general index of mean unexpectedness, which was in fact developed first by physicists to quantify their uncertainty of the distribution of gas molecules in a thermodynamic system. It is therefore open to us to apply it also to the selective process performed by a message on the goal-complex of a recipient. Formally, the expression for H is the same. The big difference lies in the significance of the probabilities p_i. Instead of being objectively observable frequencies, they become subjective probabilities. The term "mean unexpectedness" now takes on its full subjective significance; and it is intuitively obvious and reasonable that where the unexpectedness is zero, no "information" has been received, in the sense that no change in state-of-readiness (goal-complex) has been evoked.

Although along these lines it is possible formally to quantify the "amount of information" conveyed to the recipient of a message, it may often be more important to evaluate other features than the "unexpectedness" of a selective function. Two obvious

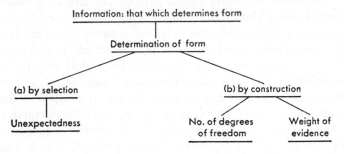

things to measure, for example, are the *number of degrees of freedom* specified and the *weight of evidence* represented. The technicalities need not concern us here.[8] What matters is that we should appreciate the "multiplicity" of the idea of "amount of information" and the dangers of confusion and fruitless debate if we try to make one measure do duty for several unrelated purposes. The diagram above may serve to summarize the distinctions between "information" and the various measures of "amount."

Social Groups as Information Systems

In this concluding section we must glance at the over-all significance of communicative processes within a social group. By way of introduction to the basic notions, imagine first two goal-seeking systems of equal power (two thermostatic air conditioners will do) with incompatible goal-settings and a common field of operation. In the ordinary way, each is bound to be driven by its feedback signal to run eventually "flat out" in opposition to the other—one heating, the other cooling—so that the temperature lies somewhere between their two goal-settings.

How could this absurd and wasteful situation be resolved or prevented from arising? In the absence of a third party, we must imagine one or both systems to possess some kind of additional effector system, capable of physical action upon the environment, to be brought in automatically when goal-conflict arises. The simplest might be a destructive weapon of some sort deployed (presumably by each "side") with the subgoal of cutting the power to the other or otherwise putting it out of action. Given a situation not too symmetrical, one system could then emerge triumphant, and its primary goal would be attainable.

Suppose, however, that by chance or by design, the physical activity of one (or both) succeeded in *altering the goal-setting* of the other. Displaced in one direction, it would of course make matters worse; but if instead the displacement brought the two goal-settings *together*, then we would have the beginnings of a wholly different kind of "resolution." Instead of being rivals, the two systems could evidently become *partners*, sharing the effort of furthering the common goal. The closer the approximation of their respective settings, the greater the economy of total effort.

We can now take up the thread dropped at the end of the first section. Consider first the case where one of two systems, A, keeps its goal-settings totally isolated from outside influence. Here the only mutually viable alternative to deadlock would be the common pursuit of A's goals. If, however, the other system, B, though not so isolated, has an inbuilt resistance to externally imposed goal-changes (i.e., evaluates them negatively for feedback purposes), then beyond a certain point B may "stick," and destructive tactics may again be the only way out of deadlock. A situation in which goal-adjustment is wholly one-way is not fully "social." The "adjusted" member is virtually an extension of the "adjusting" member.

Consider next, however, the case where the two systems A and B are on an equal footing. Each is open to goal-adjustment, though each evaluates externally imposed adjustment negatively for feedback purposes. Here a genuinely "social" situation can develop.

Each can pursue its goals only by taking into account the goals of the other, not only as facts about the world, but as potential members of its own goal-hierarchy. To the extent that B's goal-directed activity can alter the goals of A, and vice versa, it may become impossible to attribute certain goals to A or B alone. The social unit formed of A + B-in-interaction becomes a goal-seeking system in its own right.

Clearly, insofar as A and B retain any individuality within such a system, it becomes advantageous for each to acquire advance information on the goal-structure of the other. If the end result of interaction must be the mutual adjustment of goal-settings, then to prepare some adjustment in advance becomes a positively evaluated achievement, by contrast with the negatively evaluated status of externally enforced goal-change. The exchange of conventional representations of goal-structure becomes an important social activity. Increasing smoothness of relationship (avoidance of deadlock and goal-conflict) can result from increasing ability to "convey" (i.e., evoke states of readiness for) the outlines and details of the hierarchic structure of one another's organizing system. Hence, of course, the importance of congruence between A's and B's basic goal-priorities, noted above. Without this, the process of "touching up" the recipient's state of readiness to match the originator's may have to be desperately indirect and cumbersome, if not impossible.

Once certain basic goal-settings have been approximated and social goal-pursuit has commenced, each individual will attach positive value to anything that brings the organizing system of the other up to date, to match the current state of the field of activity. In short, one of the goals of each will be to share information with the other, bringing their respective "maps" into agreement. Another will be to share tricks or skills. This means inducing the development of similar organizing subroutines in the two goal-complexes. Such subroutines may simply organize external effector-action (as in tool using, climbing, and so on); or they may concern the internal processes of calculation-in-view-of-ends (as in solving mathematical problems). In either case the organizers of subroutines, once established, take their place among the "conceptual building bricks" in terms of which the individuals and the social unit form their images of the world.

When the number of members of a social unit increases beyond two, still another level of complexity opens up. If all could simultaneously adjust one another's goal-settings into conformity, no special problem would arise; but because of the serial nature of most communicative processes, what emerges is a self-organizing system with *internal delays*. Such systems are notoriously hard to keep stable. Even with only two members, the familiar example of two people trying to give way to one another on a narrow street shows the insidious power of a time lag to frustrate mutual adjustment. In a large social unit, complete symmetry is out of the question. However similar the members may initially be, the problems of organizing for goal-compatibility require some to take on different roles from others if the whole is to form a stable system. Hierarchic ordering (i.e., asymmetry in relationships to prevent vicious closed loops and deadlocks from forming) and the central coordination of at least some goal-priorities, seem inescapable.

In such a large group, then, we find ourselves confronted with topological problems of second order. We began by thinking of a goal-seeking system as a pattern or network of interactive elements, which had to evolve an organizing hierarchy in order to cope adequately with a world of hierarchically ordered complexity. Considering the interaction of two such systems, we have traced the necessity for communication channels to develop between them to prevent deadlock or mutual destruction. The result of this is the formation of a social unit, with goals assignable to it rather than specifically to any member. When a larger number of members are linked by communication channels in this way to form a goal-directed social network, we find ourselves in many senses back at stage 1, contemplating (ruefully?) once again the necessity for hierarchic organization.

There is, however, one fundamental difference. This time, the elements of the system are individuals capable of forming concepts of the system. The concepts they form, insofar as they affect their goal-complexes, are liable by the same token to affect the nature of the system—and so *to affect their own validity*.[9]

We cannot, of course, conclude from this that any generalization regarding a social unit can become true (or false) if enough members believe it—i.e., embody it in their goal-complexes. What we can affirm, however, is that a generalization of this sort cannot be promulgated without exchanging some of its scientific (*predictive*) status for an (implicitly or explicitly) *normative* one. Like the "predictions" of an apprehensive backseat driver ("You'll be in the ditch in a minute"), its semantic function is to inform, not future expectation, but present action.

We cannot pursue this topic here. I mention it only to warn against oversimple hopes of what scientific investigation can do to establish predictive "facts" in this area.

Conclusion

We have driven our way up from the level of primitive goal-conflict to that of politics and social organization, tracing along the way the mechanics of communicative processes as far as we could.

Have we done more than repeat in cumbrous terms the commonplaces of the psychologist and anthropologist, with which we have found ourselves making contact from time to time? I do not profess to know. I think the train of development of the present ideas has seemed at times to have a momentum of its own, suggesting that it might, if followed, lead to genuinely fresh insights into the nature of social organization; and I am solaced by the thought that this was a task laid down for me as appropriate to the present occasion.

But I must confess that it seems to me early days to encourage anthropologists to delve deeply into the theory of communication. It is the *approach* of the information theorist, rather than his theorems and jargon, that may conceivably at this stage have something to offer. My hope is that at least the "flavor" of this approach may emerge clearly enough from the present paper to initiate a fruitful discussion.

FOOTNOTE REFERENCES

1. Rosenblueth, Arturo, Norbert Wiener, and Julian Bigelow, "Behavior, Purpose and Teleology," *Journal of the Philosophy of Science*, vol. 10, 1943, pp. 18–24; MacKay, Donald M., "Towards an Information-Flow Model of Human Behaviour," *British Journal of Psychology*, vol. 47, 1956, pp. 30–43.
2. MacKay, Donald M., "The Place of 'Meaning' in the Theory of Information," in Colin Cherry (ed.), *Third London Symposium*

on *Information Theory*, Academic, New York, Butterworth, London, 1956, pp. 215–225; "The Informational Analysis of Questions and Commands," in Colin Cherry (ed.), *Fourth London Symposium on Information Theory*, Butterworth, London, 1960, pp. 469–476.

3. *Ibid.*

4. MacKay, Donald M., "The Informational Analysis of Questions and Commands," *op. cit.*, note 2.

5. MacKay, Donald M., *op. cit.*, note 2.

6. MacKay, Donald M., "Towards an Information-Flow Model of Human Behaviour," *op. cit.*, note 1.

7. MacKay, Donald M., "Operational Aspects of Intellect," *Proceedings National Physical Laboratory Conference on Mechanization of Thought Processes, November 1958*, Her Majesty's Stationery Office, 1959, pp. 37–52; "Information and Learning," in H. Billing (ed.), *Learning Automata*, Oldenbourg, Munich, 1961, pp. 40–49.

8. MacKay, Donald M., "The Informational Analysis of Questions and Commands," *op. cit.*, note 2; "Quantal Aspects of Scientific Information," *Proceedings of Information Theory Symposium*, London, September, 1950, lithoprinted 1953, American Institute of Radio Engineers; "Complementary Measures of Scientific Information Content," *Methodos*, vol. VII, 1955, pp. 63–89; Gabor, D., "Theory of Communication," *Journal of the Institution of Electrical Engineers* (London), vol. 93, part III, pp. 429–456.

9. MacKay, Donald M., "Information Theory and Human Information Systems," *Impact of Science on Society*, vol. 8, 1957, pp. 86–101; "On the Logical Indeterminacy of a Free Choice," *Mind*, vol. 69, 1960, pp. 31–40; "The Use of Behavioural Language to Refer to Mechanical Processes," *British Journal for the Philosophy of Science*, vol. XIII, 1962, pp. 89–103.

A Historical Introduction to the Postulational Foundations of Experimental Epistemology* WARREN S. McCULLOCH

11

I shall sketch a theory of knowledge compatible with our modern physiology of the knower. For all its appeal to epistemic correlates,[1] physiology has, from its beginning, been largely a hypothetical and deductive system in terms of postulated recognizables constructed to explain the causal relations of perceived events.

The Haemic Theory of Knowledge

In that beginning one finds several postulated entities called "mixtures." One, sometimes called by Aristotle the "conate pneuma," an airy blood, is postulated by the Hippocratic school to explain quickening five months before the first breath. The Atomists supposed pure air pumped from the lung directly to the foetus, at variance with anatomy; the Empiricists, that quickening only occurred at birth, at variance with both hearing and feeling! The second, or perfect, mixture was postulated to account for generation. This mixture specifies to the female the form of her progeny, thus conserving kind. Thus the perfect mixture is the natural cause of the conception, formation, and growth of the

* This work was supported in part by the National Institutes of Health (Grant NB–01865–05); in part by the U.S. Army, the Air Force Office of Scientific Research, and the Office of Naval Research; in part by the U.S. Air Force (ASD Contract AF33(616)–7783); in part by The Teagle Foundation, Inc.; and in part by Bell Telephone Laboratories, Inc.

progeny; its bound cause. Clearly it is the precursor of the shuffling of genes postulated by Mendel to explain frequency of occurrence of traits in phenotypes.

The postulation of the determinants of pure form to be embodied by a process of development, leading to the adult, and ultimately to its death by natural causes, gives us the law of the conservation of species, much as potential energy gives us a law of the conservation of energy. Because the bound cause is sharply distinguished from accidental, or casual, causes, it carries with it a value judgment, those things being good which are to the ends of the living thing and all else either indifferent or evil to it. The former promote health; the latter produce disease. To physiology the idea of the bound cause has contributed the notion of a function as the end in, and of, an operation. We return to it later.

The third mixture is postulated to explain knowledge. With much help from my most scholarly friends, I think I have begun to understand the origin of that postulate. In the continuum of sensation and perception, the world is this up to where it is that. Of this continuum Aristotle says "each this and that contains its end points." When a hand grasps an object, it conforms to the object, "the fulls of the one filling the hollows of the other," as the seal impresses the signet on the wax. In the form and proportions determined by the impression, the elements (earth, air, fire, and water) of the known mix with those of the knower. This mixture forms in the blood of the knower. The veins, anastomosing, mix the blood from various parts of the knower, and the final mixture takes place in the heart. Such was the cardiocentric theory of knowledge. The nerves were only reins to govern the muscles, and the brain a phlegm to cool the blood. The last time I heard this haemic theory taken seriously, except for hormones and immune reactions, was in the nineteen-twenties, when the neurosurgeon, Dandy, declared that he knew to his sorrow that consciousness was in the left anterior cerebral artery. Any psychiatrist, working with poor immigrants from backward rural areas, could tell you that to "think with one's blood" is still an ordinary notion. At its best, in the old days this notion yielded theories of contagion and infection, and so gave us quarantine and sanitation about two thousand years before Paracelsus postulated that a disease was a living thing, a virus that could be poisoned without killing the patient, thus laying the theoretical foundation for antibiotics. Pasteur was the first to see a pathogenic bacterium. Only in the last year has electron microscopy depicted what is thought to be the smallest virus.

Please note that the germ, the postulated bound cause of a disease, is a mixture of the second kind, prescribing a process leading to its own multiplication; whereas the reaction of the host, in forming specific agglutinin, and antibodies generally, makes the blood a mixture of the third kind, one that knows the antigen. Since the beginning of this theory, it has been postulated that the protein of the host, the antibody, is specifically shaped to grasp the antigen. No one has yet seen the shape, but we may expect it to be deduced rather soon, as we have the shape of the molecule of hemoglobin, which, with oxygen, forms the mixture of the first kind: the conate pneuma, the vital air.

The genetic structure of a cell is carried by deoxyribonucleic acid. It specifies ribonucleic acid, which, in turn, specifies the protein to be made. When a cell that makes antibodies to a given antigen first encounters it, within half an hour there is a great rise in ribonucleic acid, and the requisite protein synthesis is under way. That cell may live a matter of days before it divides and its daughter cells inherit the specification for making that antibody. In the case of the virus for smallpox, the immunity may last some seven years. Such is the memory in the savant mixture of the blood. Even more, the immunity can be conferred by inoculation with a strain of virus attenuated for that host. We use cowpox to protect ourselves from smallpox, and we made vaccination a legal requirement for entry into the U.S.A. while the virus and the antibody were still postulates, leading by deduction to hypotheses which checked with experience.

In various places in the Hippocratic corpus, and in a fragment of the words of Empedocles, there are two kinds of attraction to be noted. One is the attraction of likes for each other, as in our notion of gravity, which he calls "strife." It is to be seen when the rich come together on one side and the poor against them on the other. The second attraction is called "love," for it resembles that of opposite electrical charges. It is therefore love that begets knowledge, by mixing things which are in some way unlike. In the mixture that which is shared is a pure form or shape. In Pylus, the dry sand is soft and the water is soft, but close to the tideless sea the beach is hard where, by capillary attraction, the water fills the voids of the sand exactly. Thus the mixture, wet sand, has properties which are not proportioned between those of the components, as in the mixture of wine and water. This applies to all three kinds of mixture, and it led Aristotle to reject these entities because, he argued, there would then be small enough parts to be entirely the one or entirely the other of the components. Had he been an Atomist, he would have said the same for wine and water; nor would it have saved him had he imagined chemical combinations. The rejection of these mixtures left *idos* and *telos* without postulated things to embody them, so that they seem little more than rules of right speaking about living things. Hence his biology remains marvelous in description and classification, but useless in inquiring into the underlying mechanism and hence a poor basis for a physiological theory of knowing. Unfortunately, as Aristotle was the schoolmaster of the Western world, epistemology has been slow to become an experimental science.

The theory of the savant mixture, which served well for smell, taste, and feeling, began to fail for sight, in which a ray from the eye was supposed to touch the known, much as a blind man might with his cane. Democritus is believed to have said that all our senses were a kind of feeling. Without a theory of geometrical optics, which had to wait for Kepler, the alternative theory, that lighted things shed shells, some of which entered the eye, did not really work. It is here that a new approach was tried, some say first by Democritus' dissection of animals to learn the seat of madness. This ultimately transposed knowing from the blood to the brain. This may sound extreme; but, although on a careful rereading of the Hippocratic texts on epilepsy and on head injuries we see symptoms correctly attributed to loci in the brain, we still find the brain regarded only as an organ to cool the blood.

The Nervous Theory of Knowledge

There is a disease called sympathetic ophthalmia, in which infection in one eye leads to blindness of both. In 450 B.C., Alcmeon of Croton excised the human eye successfully. He held that the optic stalks carried vision from the eye to the brain. He thought that fire was intrinsic in the eye and water in it passed to the brain carrying the light with it, and thence the water came back to the eye. Moreover, he studied the optic chiasma and concluded correctly that it explained the fusion of the images of the two eyes and had something to do with their yoked motions. He said: "Things human are two," as black and white, and so on, and perhaps based his whole theory of opposites on similar operations, although Aristotle says that he threw them out at random. Finally I should add that, according to Theophrastus, Alcmeon thought that the seat of all sensations was in the brain "which somehow fitted them together." Here also, he thought, was the "governing faculty" and "intelligence," which is more than animals have in "perceiving by the senses." Either he or his followers seem to have traced hearing from the ear to the brain, and perhaps did the same for touch in the face.

But, be that as it may, dissection grew up slowly, culminating in a school in Alexandria which finally gave a good gross anatomy of the nervous system. When it died, the picture deteriorated so that even the ventricles were grossly distorted. This was corrected by Leonardo da Vinci.

Based on eight years of dissection of eyes and brains in Leiden, René Descartes postulated that (1) nerves were composed of parallel tubes too fine for him to see them individually even under his magnifying glass; (2) each tube was filled with liquid in which pulses of hydraulic pressure went from the brain and spinal marrow to muscles causing them to contract; and (3) each tube had a fine thread in it which, as the muscle contracted, signaled back to the central nervous system to close down the valve.

In the *Dioptrices*, Descartes, following Kepler, shows that the optical properties of the cornea, lens, and vitreous humor produce a picture of the world on the retina, and then he argued correctly that there were enough tubes from eye to brain to transmit the picture. Next he argued that thence to the master valve of his hydraulic system, the pineal gland, he did not believe there could be enough parallel tubes to convey the picture; he therefore postulated that it had to be conveyed by temporal sequences of pulses which need look no more like the picture than our word must resemble the thing we describe. This is the first great coding hypothesis of nervous activity based on the postulated nervous impulse. By it he gave his automata ideas, departing signally from the signet.

Recently, there has in fact been some evidence that a mechanical pulse is present in the nervous impulse. Galvani, however, turned attention in another direction by postulating animal electricity to explain nervous impulses and muscular contraction. In the last century, with the invention of the capillary electrometer, it became possible to detect activity in a peripheral nerve, and in 1875 Caton was able to demonstrate to the Royal Society of Medicine electrical waves of the brain. Only with the help of the vacuum tube amplifier could Forbes in 1924 and Adrian in 1926 see the postulated electrical nervous impulse in a single tubule. By "see" I mean deduce it and its temporal form from the temporal fluctuations of a record from a capillary electrometer driven by the electronic amplifier.

Long before that time the microscope had revealed tubules, and it had been found that when one excited a whole nerve electrically, after the exciting current reached a certain value, no greater pulse appeared in the nerve. This led to the postulation that the impulse in the single fiber was of a size independent of the current that evoked it. This is the so-called all-or-none law: that once the stimulus exceeded the threshold, the propagated impulse was determined in size and shape by local conditions—the tubule doing all that it could then do there.

Today much is known of the rate of propagation and form of the pulse, of its refractory periods, and of its sources of energy, but not enough yet of its physical and chemical basis. There are, in these tubules, fine threads of hyaluronic acid, whose function is not known, but it is certainly not that which Descartes proposed and which ultimately let his automata become purposeful.

Early in the nineteenth century Magendie defined the function postulated by Descartes for his threads as a reflex, supposing that when a process, such as the contraction of a muscle, occurred in some part of the body, impulses passed to the central nervous system, from which they were reflected to that part of the body where they arose, and there stopped or reversed the process that gave rise to them. By 1819, he had proved that these impulses always entered the spinal cord by the dorsal roots, or sensory roots, and emerged over the ventral roots. Hence evolved reflexology, beautifully clear in the writings of Sechenov, which, as a side line, produced the homeostasis of Cannon and Rosenblueth. A similar class of systems had grown up in the form of governors of prime movers, and in the controllers of telephonic relays. Once Julian

Bigelow noted that it did not matter how the information was carried, but only that the machine be informed of the outcome of its previous act, cybernetics was born, and teleology had its proper mechanistic base in engineering and in biology. The operation of such systems generally is such that the output decreases the input. When they act over a path that closes within the body, they regulate it; and when they act over paths closed by way of targets in the external world, they account for appetition. With the appearance of Wiener's cybernetics, the basic notions became rapidly popular. Russia woke up late, but now has five institutes of cybernetics, and may soon have three more. It will be taken for granted by their high school graduates in a few years. Its great importance for our present purposes is first that, by accounting for purposeful behavior in a general manner, it makes a sharp distinction between those things which are useful and useless to the built-in ends of the machine or animal; and, second, that it poses the question of how utility is mediated specifically in the physiology of particular anatomical structures.

Near the end of the last century Ramon y Cajal postulated (1) that all the nervous tubes were outgrowths of nerve cells, and (2) that it was only these cells and their processes that carried nervous impulses. The remaining cells, or glia, he thought served only metabolic or mechanical functions. His first postulation was proved by his own beautiful histology; and his second, confirmed by microelectrode techniques for neurons, is generally accepted, even if a few neurophysiologists suspect glia may have something to do with memory or may serve as passive conductors.

Following our direct line of descent in experimental epistemology, from Helmholtz, Rudolf Magnus, and Dusser de Barenne, my group decided to sharpen our hypotheses as much as possible, to adhere strictly to an electrical hypothesis of excitation and inhibition, and to see how far it would suffice to guide an experiment. Such a hypothesis requires that, from known anatomy and precise location of pick-up electrodes, one should be able to predict the outcome of an experiment. This postulate has worked well for us and led us to an understanding of the interaction of impulses afferent along separate fibers on their way to a terminal cell or cells. This possibility frees a real nervous system from the restriction to "threshold logic," from which imitations have suffered, and allows any cell to compute any logical function of the signals that approach it from any number of sources. This may seem trivial, for, with a neuron having only two inputs, all but two of the 16 logical functions (namely ⌐ . . . if and only if . . . ⌐ and the exclusive ⌐ . . . or . . . ⌐) are computable without interaction. But when one comes to functions of three arguments, only 104 out of the 256 functions can be had with threshold logic; and, for any reasonably large number of arguments, the fraction computable becomes negligible.

The importance of this interaction became obvious to us in our two-year experimental study of what the frog's eye tells the frog's brain. The known anatomy was sufficient for us to try to assign to each of the five kinds of ganglion cells in the retina the function it computes and of which it informs the brain. The connections between these five kinds of ganglion cells of the retina and the frog's brain are such that they map the four form functions in four discrete levels—one visual part of the frog's brain—and the four maps are in register. The fifth form is concerned with color and goes to another part. If the optic stalk is cut, the fibers regenerate, reconstituting the four maps in register.

I should mention two things. First, the frog's eye is built to detect things in motion and reports their presence for at most a short time once they stop. This is important for a beast who lives by catching insects. Second, the things that his ganglion cells do report, such as the radius of a spot, are obviously useful in this pursuit. My group of collaborators is inclined to agree with Whitehead's theory of percipient events, in this case the life of the frog, that perception requires cognizance of spots, be they large or small, by adjective; and cognizance, among spots, by relation, here preserved by the maps in register. In this instance, the frog's rods and cones, his transducers from light to nervous impulses, single out different wave lengths to respond to them; next, the bipolars single out certain patterns of signals from rods and cones; and finally, the ganglion cells single out still more elaborate patterns of their input from the bipolar cells. The frog's brain cannot see around, but only through, these channels. They yield his adjectives of the spots—in his case, moving spots. Small dark objects in motion in given directions are thus elementary constructs for him, and his four maps, preserving spatial relations, enable him to capture a fly. Let me say it this way: A fly in motion is one of the simplest things sensible to him. Literally he has no, and he needs no, cerebral cortex to generate the idea of a fly regardless of time, position, direction, and velocity of flight. Similarly, he has an "AAH" resonator built into his ears by which to find his mate.

When one studies the carnivore, all this changes. He can be shown to recognize a tune regardless of pitch and a square regardless of size. For these he requires his cerebral cortex, without which he can still distinguish sounds and somehow see enough to get about. Using the word "universal" in the sense of Aristotle, of the *Isagoge* of Porphyry, of the commentary on it by Boethius, and so in the sense of Peter Abélard, of Duns Scotus, and of William of Occam, which became formalized in the universal quantifier, $(x)\phi x$, Pitts and McCulloch showed how brains could embody these universals. Our article may have been wrong in any particular attribution of function to local anatomy or local physiology; but it cannot be wrong in its all-important proof that for a man to know such universals as shape regardless of size or chord regardless of key it would be sufficient for his brain to compute enough averages. Each average is an Nth of the sum, for all N transforms belonging to the group (say, dilations or translations), of the value attributed by some functional to each transform as a figure of excitation in the time and space of an appropriate matrix of relays. Thus the mechanism derives an invariant under that transformation, and so shape can be seen regardless of size and chord heard regardless of key.

So much new experimental evidence has been accumulating that in the next few years I expect a formulation to appear, new in almost every particular, but in no way that affects the sufficiency of our argument. So much for the perceived universals.

The Knowing Automaton

William of Occam, for all he would not have entities multiplied beyond necessity, stated bluntly that man thinks in two kinds of terms. The first, or natural, terms man shares with other animals. It is of these we have been speaking, even when the term was a natural universal, like a chord regardless of pitch. The second, or conventional, terms are enjoyed by man alone; and Occam somewhere adds that the greatest of these is number.

I think it was about 1929 that Gödel arithmetized logic, proving that the deduction of a proposition from a finite set of premises was precisely equivalent to computing a number. Within ten years Turing had shown that a finite machine with a finite number of states, working on a tape as long as need be, could compute any number that a man could compute.

In 1942, Pitts and McCulloch wrote "A Logical Calculus of the Ideas Immanent in Nervous Activity."[2] In it they considered a net of formal neurons with two inputs each, each neuron having a threshold that determined whether one input was sufficient or both were necessary to fire it and each neuron being liable to absolute inhibition. They showed that, with a proper circuit, a net of such neurons could compute any computable number, and hence could reach any conclusion given by a finite set of premises, or abstract any figure given in the excitation of the net. From the Turing machine have evolved our vast digital computers, and from the proposed logical calculus has sprung the deluge of automata studies.

To ask whether these computers can think is ambiguous. In the naive realistic sense of the term, it is people who think, and not either brains or machines. If, however, we permit ourselves the ellipsis of referring to the operations of the human brain as "thinking," then, of course, our computers "think," their primary language being that of number. Turing designed his machine for computation, which is deductive; but, because he made the value of the operand effective in determining the next operation, his machines are also capable of induction and are now so used.

What these machines lack by contrast with the human brain is the ability to operate in our natural terms. For this they require very special programing even to resemble simple perceptive automata. It is really an abuse of a Turing machine to compel it to "think" in our natural terms, but the very complexity of the programing required for such an abuse supplies a clue to the nature of the ordinary perceived universal.

The original Turing machine had no memory beyond the state it was in and its marks on the tape. The latter, or passive, storage had this great advantage, that what was stored, say, the Nth digit, was stored in the $(N + K)$th place; and its location was so related to it that one did not have to have a stored system of addresses to find it. Storage of this kind is often called associative, and has many advantages in long-term retention. W. Ross Ashby postulates it in his *Design for a Brain*,[3] which makes what is to be sought, and where it is to be sought, functions of the sequence of learning. It, and its invasions always deeper into the central nervous system, all too well known in the case of causalgia, brings us to the question of dynamic storage.

Before 1930, no spontaneous activity of neurons and no activity that was regenerative over a closed path were known. In 1930, Kubie[4] proposed both to account for thinking, which he did not believe required activity over a path through effectors and receptors. Within six weeks Ranson had proposed it for an entirely different reason. Next I proposed it, as occurring over a regenerative loop, to account for fits and certain kinds of facilitations. Lorente de Nó suggested it to account for a prolonged nystagmus following a single volley over the vestibular nerve. In both forms, within cells and among them, these representative neural activities are well known today. In the cat's somatic afferent system, a single volley sent into certain cells in the spinal cord produces a burst of eight or more impulses about one thousandth of a second apart. A similar performance is noted in the sensory cortex. Here the impulses are not necessarily equally spaced; and in the associative cortex it seems as if their patterns in time depend upon their place of origin in the cortex. This is in line with what MacKay and I proposed years ago, pointing out that by pulse interval modulation one could get far more information through a nervous junction than just one bit per pulse, as in my scheme with Pitts.

I have mentioned these things, and could mention many others which can only enrich the properties Walter Pitts and I attributed to our abstracted neurons. The ability of a single neuron with interaction of afferents to compute any logical function of its input is another example. But all of these are beside my point in the creation of a logical theory of nervous activity. Thanks to Gödel it is well known that, for a formalist logical theory, the only hardware one needs is the natural numbers. The only operations necessary are addition, subtraction, or division. It was for this reason that we abstracted from real neurons everything irrelevant. In a nervous system composed of such neurons, a closed regenerative path can sustain a sequence of impulses patterned after its input, provided only that the sequence in the input is of shorter duration than the time around the loops. A network composed of such elements can sort out and respond to any one figure in the sequence of impulses. The signal chasing itself around the loop represents an idea, presented once, but repeated at all subsequent times until the action is quenched. The process is a dynamic memory, making an invariant under translation in time, which issues in what Whitehead calls "Primary Recognition." What is more important is this: It is completely indifferent as to whether the signal embodies a perceived universal or a proposition concerning a postulated scientific object. Many men, working in automata studies, have put a sharp limit on what can, and cannot, be computed by such a closed reverberant path. They say that such circuits and subassemblies can compute the form of all definite, and no indefinite, events. Ten thousand ones is a definite sequence, a definite event; but one followed by any number of zeros followed by one is an indefinite event, although the sentence that describes it can be shown to be a definite event. Hence, we may put it this way: whatever may be defined by a finite sequence of symbols can be defined indefinitely by such a loop. Thus in finite loops, as long as they continue to reverberate, our brains "trap" any universal that can be defined in a finite and unambiguous manner. But when we get a bump on the head or go to sleep or simply switch our attention to something else entirely, the circuit ceases to reverberate, and the universal would be lost to us if the reverberation had not made some enduring alteration in the brain. Modern evidence indicates that all our acquired ideas, or learned generalizations and specifications, are carried on for nearly half an hour by regenerative activity, of which there is beginning to be some electrical evidence. If this activity is interrupted during that time, no memory remains. From the evidence to date it seems that if the process has not been interrupted, and if one looks at the appropriate neurons half an hour later, one finds that there is a great rise in ribonucleic acid, and protein synthesis is under way. So, while we do not yet know how or where this building material will be distributed, we may see nature using the same trick as in the immune reactions. Whatever the details of this process, it is clear that it must determine local changes in the electrical properties of neurons, which will fit together in some new fashion at some places. There is much of clinical interest which might be said here but it is beside the point. What matters is that universals, represented first by reverberating circuits whose activity persists for half an hour, may become embodied in anatomical structures and so fix future performance in accord with the learned idea.

The Prospect

Let us summarize the present state of experimental epistemology. It seems that, by postulation, we have created for ourselves the right kind of scientific objects to handle ideas and purposes in terms of circuit actions of oversimplified components in known relations. This has been done in terms of a most general notion of excitation and inhibition relating effects to locations or connections. It has served us well in the brain and spinal cord and in the frog's eye. If we are right, we have an algorithm to determine from anatomy those functions of its inputs that a given neuron can compute. These are sufficiently well substantiated for us to attribute one of the four shape functions, that we know are computed by ganglion cells in the frog's eye, to each of four kinds of ganglion cells. The projections to the brain preserve spatial relations. Whitehead's cognizance by adjective and cognizance by relation are thus anatomized. We have theories, perhaps wrong in details, to account for the perception of universals like squares and triangles as mediated by mammalian brains; and we have a general theory of reverberating activity that can account for the trapping of universals of any kind. There is evidence that if these activities persist for half an hour, the universals may become anatomically embodied.

In short, the central problem of experimental epistemology seems in principle to be soluble along lines sufficiently well verified to reduce every particular question of the physiology of knowledge, however intricate experimentally, to a strictly parochial problem.

FOOTNOTE REFERENCES

1. Northrop, F. S. C., "Toward a Deductively Formulated and Operationally Verifiable Comparative Cultural Anthropology," in F. S. C. Northrop, and Helen H. Livingston (eds.), Cross-Cultural Understanding, Harper & Row, New York, 1964, chap. 12.

2. McCulloch, Warren S., and Walter H. Pitts, "A Logical Calculus of the Ideas Immanent in Nervous Activity," *Bulletin of Mathematical Biophysics*, vol. 5, 1943, pp. 115–133.
3. Ashby, W. Ross, *Design for a Brain* (2nd ed.), Wiley, New York, 1960.
4. Thanks to Jerome Y. Lettvin we are able to trace the idea of circular paths a few years further back. For Kuhlenbeck wrote in 1957 as follows:

I am well aware of the objection, voiced by Rashevsky and others, that a single neuron cannot form a self-reexciting circuit because the excitation will fall within its own refractory phase. When, in 1927, I formulated the concept of a true self-reexciting circuit, such circuits were assumed to consist at least of two neurons. Nevertheless, since a great number of unknown variables may be involved, I do not consider Rashevsky's objection cogent, and I see no reason why, for theoretical purposes, single neuron self-reexciting circuits should not be assumed. Such arrangements might actually be realized in the central nervous system. The objection is furthermore immaterial, because it can easily be avoided by only slightly more complicated constructions, involving internuncials.

Kuhlenbeck, Hartwig, *Brain and Consciousness, Some Prolegomena to an Approach of the Problem*, Supplement to vol. 17, *Confinia Neurologica*, S. Karger, Basel and New York, 1957, pp. 242, note 40.

Toward a Deductively Formulated and Operationally Verifiable Comparative Cultural Anthropology F. S. C. NORTHROP

12

It is normal for any Western empirical science to pass through two stages. The first is appropriately called its natural history period; the second, that of deductively formulated theory with its correlated operational definitions. Is cultural anthropology at the transition point?

Its past procedure has been largely inductive, concerned primarily with the observation and description of the data. Its language has been that of the culture of the anthropologists, most of whom have been Westerners. Hence, non-Western as well as Occidental cultures have been described with the two-termed subject-predicate syntax of the Aryan languages. Many languages of other cultures have a different syntax. The mathematical language of deductively formulated physics has a many-termed relational structure. These considerations raise the question whether even the natural history data can be correctly described unless cultural anthropology passes to the more syntactically and semantically sophisticated stage of deductively formulated theory.

The Characteristics of a Mature Science

In its second stage, the natural history descriptive work continues, but a much more critical and linguistically less naive language and scientific method are introduced for analyzing and describing the natural history data. Also the aim is to find the minimum number of elementary theoretical concepts and propositional assumptions necessary and sufficient to account for all the observable data. Consequently, whereas in the natural history stage the emphasis is on field work, allowing its naive description of the facts in ordinary language to provide the theory, in the more mature stage, the emphasis is upon deduction with its unique syntactical, and more critical, semantic language, correlated with operational definitions and an indirect method of verification. As the careful student of scientific method, Professor Henry M. Sheffer, has indicated, in the natural history stage the quest is for maximal implicational consequents, i.e., the largest number of described empirical facts; in the stage of deductively formulated theory, the search is for the minimal theoretical antecedents.

How is this to be done? The answer is well known to creative theoretical mathematical physicists such as Einstein and to competent philosophers of this science. The transition has the following characteristics: (1) In its natural history stage there tend to be as many independent assumptions and propositions in a science as there are naively observed facts. An example is natural history biology, with its volumes of descriptive statements concerning all plants and animals. (2) In the stage of deductively formulated theory, however, all the inductively described natural history facts are first analyzed and then described in terms of the smallest possible number of primitive or undefined concepts and elementary or unproved propositions. The customary name for these elementary assumptions is "postulates." From the primitive concepts all the other concepts of the subject matter are derived by definition; from the postulates all the other propositions, called theorems, are deduced by logical implication.

Euclid's *Elements* was the first classic example. Newton's *Principia* is similar. Because such a theory is more trustworthy the fewer its assumptions, the principle called Occam's Razor governs. Thus, Newton's classic opens with eight technical definitions. Immediately following, Newton tells us that he has defined them in terms of the four undefined concepts of space, time, position, and motion. Then comes his well-known three "Axioms," or Laws of Motion. The remainder of the *Principia* consists of a formal logical or mathematical proof of all the remaining theorems of the volume in terms of their deduction from Newton's three laws and eight defined concepts. In addition, the theory has enabled one to predict countless previously unobserved phenomena which later observations confirmed. Except for an aberration in the motion of Mercury, not until 1885 did any experimental fact appear which was incompatible with the assumptions of Newton's theory. Notwithstanding its minimum elementary assumptions, deductively formulated theory has unique predictive power; whereas natural history science is verbose descriptively and negligible predictively.

Another remarkable characteristic of deductively formulated scientific theory is that as it includes more and more natural history data in additional branches of science, the fewer and the logically simpler become its theoretical assumptions. This is as it should be if Occam's methodological principle holds. In the advance of modern physics from Newton's Mechanics through Maxwell's Electromagnetics, Einstein's Special Theory of Relativity, the General Theory of Relativity, and Quantum Mechanics, the postulates and assumed concepts frequently become fewer, yet the older theories come out of the more general theory as a special case. In Einstein's General Theory of Relativity, for example, Newton's three laws of motion are replaced by merely one law.

Of even greater importance for cultural anthropology is its increased epistemological sophistication. One reason is that in natural science the elementary concepts and postulates of such theory do not get their meaning by direct observation. Instead, they are speculatively discovered and indirectly confirmed. Such recourse to unobservables becomes necessary when careful examination of the deliverances of one's senses shows that no sensed object, property, or relation is publicly the same for all knowers. Instead, it is relative to (1) where in nature one is standing when one observes, (2) the moment of observation, (3) one's sense organs, such as the rods and cones in one's eyeballs, and (4) even different sense organs of the same perceiver. This is what Einstein means when he tells us that "The belief in an external world independent of the perceiving subject is the basis of all natural science. Since, however, sense perception only gives information of this external world or of 'physical reality' indirectly, we can only grasp the latter by speculative means."[1]

The need for greater epistemological concern shows also when one notes that the ordinary language of natural history science is semantically ambiguous. Any of its words has several different epistemological kinds of meaning. This becomes evident when ordinary sentences such as the following appear: "Electrons are pink," "Sweetness is square," and "Consciousness is in the brain." All these examples are nonsensical. But why? The answer is that the subject term in each case refers to one epistemological world of discourse, the predicate term to a different one, and when two words referring to different worlds of discourse are put thus in the same sentence, the result is nonsense. Unfortunately, ordinary language does not have epistemological tags attached to its words. Neither does natural history science in its use of ordinary language.

The first step, therefore, toward mature common sense or science begins with the realization that every word of ordinary language is semantically ambiguous, having several species of epistemological meaning with rarely any sign of which is which. The second requirement then becomes evident. It distinguishes the several species of semantic or epistemological meanings of any ordinary word from one another. The species relevant for present purposes are (1) radical empiricism, (2) naive realism, and (3) logical realism. Their differentia will concern us in a moment.

When this is done another weakness in the ordinary language of natural history science appears. Only in (1) its radical empirical meaning does it correctly state what observation with nothing but the senses gives. But, as shown above, in epistemological meaning (1), it leaves meaningless the common-sense and scientific beliefs in external objects in a public spatiotemporal world. This is why, as Einstein noted, one has to resort to theoretical physicists with their speculatively discovered, deductively formulated theory and its indirect method of confirmation.

Even so, they are not sufficient. In addition, they must use a language different from ordinary language. For ordinary language which does not distort what the senses give, by leaving the relativity to the observer out of its statements, must be restricted to its radical empirical meaning (1). However, in this meaning there are no objects invariant for all knowers. Only the invariant language of the symbolic logic of relations and pure mathematics can give the latter kind of objectivity.

But such a language describes merely a possible world. To have any relevance for the actual world, some relation must be established between the speculatively discovered, deductively formulated assumptions and unique language of the theoretical scientist and the ordinary language of direct sense awareness in its nominalistic radical empirical meaning. What this relation is and the theoretically and nominalistically defined operations that accompany it must also be described.

We are now able to understand more fully the aforequoted statement by Einstein. It merits being repeated: "The reciprocal relation of epistemology and science is of noteworthy kind. They are dependent upon each other. Epistemology without contact with science becomes an empty scheme. Science without epistemology is—insofar as it is thinkable at all—primitive and muddled."[2] In fact, it is to escape the muddles due to the semantic ambiguities of ordinary language in the natural history stage of any empirical science that (1) epistemology and (2) the shift to speculatively discovered, deductively formulated scientific theory arise together and reinforce one another.

The experiences of mathematical physicists warn us also that it is wise for cultural anthropologists to make the shift in two parts, being content first to achieve a statics and leaving until later the attainment of a theoretical dynamics. Economic science confirms this judgment. As Professor Lionel Robbins in his classic *An Essay on the Nature and Significance of Economic Science,* and the writer in Chapter 13 of *The Logic of the Sciences and the Humanities* have shown, economics has a deductively formulated statics but not a dynamics. If the latter has not yet been achieved for merely the economic portion of a culture, it is hardly likely for the whole of any culture, to say nothing about a comparative theory of all cultures.

Nor is a theoretical dynamics indispensable. In the aforementioned Chapter 13 and in *Philosophical Anthropology and Practical Politics,* it has been shown that by watching certain empirical factors to see if they remain constant, considerable predictive power is possible by means of merely a theoretical statics, even with respect to future events. In fact, greater predictive power is achieved with such a methodologically understood theoretical statics than has been obtained by the "historical determinists," who claim they know with absolute certainty what cultural evolution will be. In any event, we shall restrict ourselves to a deductively formulated, culturally anthropological statics. The aim, however, will be a generality within which any present culture will fall as one or another special case.

To this end, the differences between a deductively formulated statics and dynamics are important. Common to both is the set of undefined concepts and primitive propositions or postulates, together with the derived concepts and theorems of a deductive theory. Common to both also is the state function and its independent variables. Given also are correlated operational definitions which specify how one experimentally, or observationally, determines the empirical values of the independent variables of the state function of the system in question at any present moment of time. When the deductively formulated theory has achieved merely a statics, the deduced theorems of the theory then enable one to determine, without further observation, what other empirical characteristics the system will have at that particular moment of time. When, on the other hand, the postulates of the theory are such that having, via the epistemically correlated operations, determined the empirical values of the independent variables in the state of the system at a particular moment of time t^1, the assumptions of the theory enable one to logically deduce, or, in other words, mathematically calculate, the empirical values of the system at any past or future moments of time, then one has a theoretical dynamics.

This assumes, of course, that the system is an isolated one. Operationally speaking, this means that external influences upon it are either eliminated or kept constant in the experiment in question so that they may be treated as negligible.

In the theoretical dynamics, defined just above, the strongest possible mechanical causality holds. Stated in terms of chance and its probability, in such causality, the theoretical concept of probability enters neither into the temporal relation between the states of a system at different times nor into the state function itself. Probability is present only under the name of "the theory of errors," on the epistemically correlated operational side. Theoretically, the concept of probability does not appear in either the postulates or deduced theorems of the deductively formulated theory.

The latter consideration enables us, by way of contrast, to understand Quantum Mechanics. It is a theoretical dynamics in which the concept of probability does not enter into the time relation between the states of the system. In this respect, it is like the strong causality of Einstein's Theory of Relativity and Newton's

Mechanics. What distinuishes Quantum Theory from traditional mechanically causal theories is that it introduces the concept of chance and its probability into the theoretical state function of the system. Thus Quantum Theory has chance in its deductively formulated statics, but not, one might say, in its deductively formulated dynamics, except as in the latter the state of the system at any time is defined not merely in terms of its independent variables, such as momentum and position, but also their accompanying probability numbers.

We see now why it is folly to talk about the changes of a cultural system with time until one has first achieved a deductively formulated, culturally anthropological statics. For without an unambiguous and clearly defined state function, there is no deductively formulated scientific theory of any kind.

The importance of the papers by Professors Valentino Braitenberg and Donald M. MacKay and Dr. Warren S. McCulloch should now be evident. They provide us with at least some of the theoretical ideas of recent mathematical physics, logically constructed neurophysiology, and communication science necessary for a deductively formulatable, operationally testable, cultural statics or dynamics. A few key points in their papers are relevant here.

First, within deductively formulated, naturalistic systems in which the time relation between states is mechanically causal in the sense of strict logical implication, there are two species: (1) nonteleological, i.e., nongoal-guided mechanically causal systems, and (2) teleologically mechanical causal systems. One of the reasons why traditional modern natural science, humanistic philosophy, and cultural anthropology had to throw purposeful evaluating man out of nature is that the major mechanically causal systems studied initially were of the nonteleologically mechanical species. It is this that led to the Kantian distinction between the *Naturwissenschaften* and the *Geistenwissenschaften* and to the similar gulf between natural science and the humanities that still persists generally, as the recent incident at the University of Cambridge shows. It also had the result with Kant of providing no meaning for human purpose in either his natural science or his moral and legal philosophy. Otherwise, he would not have thought it necessary, after completing his analysis of both descriptive and evaluative statements, to write his *Critique of Teleological Judgement,* in which he found it to be a mere *als ob*. Second, the papers by Braitenberg, MacKay, and McCulloch suggest that the nervous systems of human beings are teleological or goal-guided mechanisms. This puts goal-guided man back in nature. Third, such naturalistic human beings have the capacity to trap formal representatives of the stimuli that fire their sensory end organs and then store these representatives and permute them in the association areas of their cortices. This makes both fanciful novels and speculatively discovered scientific theory possible. This enables us to understand ideational goal-guided man in terms of natural man. By means of these representatives of past stimuli, the Whiteheadian recognition of the same adjectives in a present event that one has seen in a past one becomes possible, and one has the standpoint necessary to make at least a beginning at a correct understanding of information theory.

The important thing to note, however, in connection with the inquiry of the present paper is that all these ideas are deductively formulated concepts, falling within systematic contemporary mathematical physics. Moreover, they are imageless, logically constructed concepts. This is why it was not sufficient, for example, for Dr. McCulloch to have merely an intuitive imageful idea of cortically trapped universals. It had to be logically relationally constructed by symbolic logicians such as Pitts, Kleene, and others. These logical constructs are not without their importance for comparative cultural anthropology, as Chapters 14 and 15, by Professors S. Sambursky and Joseph C. Smith, indicate.

The concept of probability in the definition of the state of any system in Quantum Mechanics may provide an analogical tie to the state of a cultural system as described by Professor E. A. Hoebel in his comparative anthropological study *The Laws of Primitive Man*. This book made two things clear: First, in the description of the normative legal statics of seven different so-called primitive societies he had to use a deductive method to state his natural history descriptive findings. This occurs when he gives seven postulate sets which specify the customary legal norms of the steady state of his seven primitive societies. Second, when the cultural anthropologist so describes the norms of a culture, he is not affirming that every person in the society believes in or behaves according to these norms. In the language of McCulloch, every person in the community does not share this set of trapped universals for ordering social behavior normatively and adjudicating disputes in the case of deviants. Instead, the cultural anthropologist is affirming a concept of the state function of a culture which is (1) in part *universally qualitative* in the sense that these postulates specify the norms by which all are judged, and (2) in part *quantitatively statistical* in the sense that only a majority believe in and practice these norms spontaneously; otherwise there could be no deviants. In short, in even the most homogeneous culture, the concept of probability enters into its statical definition of state.

Radin and Kluckhohn independently confirmed the qualitative factor. They found that in order to describe correctly even the natural history data of a particular people and culture, one cannot use the unconsciously assumed descriptive concepts and elementary assumptions of the anthropologist's own culture. To this it needs to be added that neither can one use the concepts of some Western school of social science or psychiatry. Instead, if one is not to falsify the empirical natural history data in the very act of describing them, one must think about and describe everything that one sees and hears in terms of the way the people in that culture think about it and describe it.

Professor Maquet, in Chapter 2, has given reasons for believing, in the case at least of illiterate cultures, that neither Kluckhohn's nor present anthropological methods do this, nor do they provide logically constructed postulates for their subject matter and logically deduced theorems, correlated with operational procedures, thereby gaining the objectivity characterizing the more epistemologically complex method of mathematical physics. May not these two things be connected? Should such be the case, Kluckhohn's universal conclusion might stand were anthropology to use the epistemological analysis and method suggested here.

In any event, when Radin and Kluckhohn proceeded to determine the way primitive people think about their cultural artifacts and behavior, these two anthropologists believed themselves to be confronted with a very subtle and complex native cultural philosophy involving normative humanistic and naturalistic beliefs that were essentially connected. One should not be surprised, since the word "philosophy" is but the name for the elemental concepts and assumptions in terms of which any subject matter is thought of, described, and understood.

This is why a culture is nonetheless philosophical, and fundamentally and leadingly so, should its particular people take "the distribution of goods and services" as elementary and then attempt to semilogically define or infer all the facts of nature and all the artifacts of culture from its causal effects.

Kluckhohn noted also that in the case of most people, especially if their culture is an old one, their cultural philosophy is subconscious and covert to an extent such that they may think they have no philosophy. The latter phenomenon also should hardly surprise us. Only, as with the creation of the American legal and political system by scientifically and philosophically erudite minds such as Jefferson and Franklin or in the case of the Bolshevik Revolution in Russia during World War I, when a new cultural philosophy is being introduced are the leaders likely to be overtly conscious of the elemental ideas and assumptions they are using to reform the old culture and create the new.

Two cautions are to be noted. The first is methodological; the second, linguistic, having to do with the two stages of any empirical science.

The methodological caution has been made evident by Professor Maquet. How can one be sure, when either Radin or Kluckhohn infers the philosophy of a particular culture by giving a postulate set for that culture, that the result is the people's own philosophy rather than a mere *als ob* philosophy of the observing cultural anthropologist?

The linguistic caution and question are even more serious. Is the ordinary English or any other Aryan language, which many cultural anthropologists use to state the specific philosophy of a non-Aryan people, trustworthy as a linguistic scientific instrument? That the latter question must be taken seriously becomes evident when one realizes that any word in ordinary language, especially if it be of the Aryan linguistic type, has at the very least three different possible epistemological meanings. Professor Maquet reminds us, in Chapter 2, that there is also the Kantian idealistic epistemological species of meaning of Sorokin's idealistic cultures. The use, therefore, of Western ordinary language to describe the philosophical mentality of people in a non-Western culture tells us little about the mentality of the latter unless the anthropologist goes on to specify theoretically the various possible epistemological meanings his ordinary language may have and then uses operational tests in the field, epistemically correlated with these different meanings of any ordinary word, to determine which epistemological way of thinking is that of the people in the culture in question. In the latter connection, Professor Campbell's cross-cultural perception tests described in Chapter 18 become most important.

Another methodological caution supports this conclusion. This caution is that the use of a postulate set in the sense of Professor Hoebel, or Radin and Kluckhohn, is not to be confused with the achievement of a cultural anthropology that has arrived at the stage of logically realistic, deductively formulated theory. This becomes evident when one notes that all three of these anthropologists were merely attempting to observe and describe the natural history data of their science by means of ordinary language. The task of finding the minimum set of elemental theoretical concepts, within which the natural history postulate sets for all the different cultures fall as special cases, begins after the natural history descriptive task has been completed. It begins, moreover, only when (i) one realizes that the ordinary language used in the natural history postulate set for describing a particular culture is epistemologically ambiguous and often "objectively" misleading to the point of producing what Einstein calls "muddles," and (ii) one then proceeds to introduce the epistemologically more precise language and scientific method necessary to prevent the natural history scientists from misrepresenting the observed facts in the very act of stating what they are.

The crucial question, therefore, arises: What is the linguistic difference between the language of an empirical science in the mature stage of deductively formulated theory and ordinary linguistic postulate sets of the natural history stage? The differences are threefold: (1) syntactical, (2) semantic, and (3) interconnective. (1) Syntactically, the language of deductively formulated theory is imageless and many-termed relational, whereas that of the natural history stage, especially for all scientists of Aryan linguistic cultures, is sensuously imageful with a two-termed subject-predicate grammar. (2) Semantically, ordinary language, as noted above, is ambiguous. The language of deductively formulated theory is, on the other hand, an epistemic correlation of (a) ordinary language in one of its three possible semantic meanings with (b) the many-termed relational syntactic language of the symbolic logic of relations and pure mathematics. (3) Interconnectively, the "deductions" from the postulates in the case of the ordinary language of natural history science are usually, as Professor Maquet has shown for cultural anthropology, more emotive and intuitive; whereas, in the mathematical or symbolic logical language, the deduction of theorems and predicted observable data is more mathematically and logically rigorous. Any mature theoretical statics or dynamics also describes a disjunctively related set of all formally possible worlds within which the empirical subject matter of the science in question falls as one species.

The task of the empirical cultural anthropologist, therefore, who would take his subject matter, from the natural history stage of its description with ordinary language, to the mature stage of deductively formulated theory, consists in finding the minimal set of theoretical possibles (corresponding to the possible worlds of the pure mathematician) *within which the ambiguous ordinary linguistically described postulate set for the philosophical mentality of the people of a particular culture falls as one, or a compound of several, of the possibles.* Is there any clue as to what the elemental theoretical possibles of the cultural anthropologist might be?

The aforementioned semantic ambiguities in ordinary language suggest the answer. Since what any person can mean by the ideas in his mind or the symbols of communication in his culture is, of necessity, a function of where he thinks all ideas and symbols get their meaning, it follows that we will have the elemental theoretical possibles of cultural anthropology if we distinguish the major species of epistemologically meaningful ideas. This amounts to the thesis that whereas in the natural sciences it is the symbolic logic of many-termed relations and pure mathematics that defines the theoretical possibles, in the cultural sciences it is epistemology.

To this end, four things must be specified: (1) The major possible sources and types of meaning which any symbol of ordinary language may have. (2) The source and type of meaning which the imageless, many-termed relational symbols of mature, deductively formulated knowledge in natural science possess. (3) Operational tests to be used in the field which will enable the cultural anthropologist to determine whether the people in question think with symbols of one species of epistemological meaning or another or with combinations of two or more kinds of epistemological meaning. (4) Analysis within any epistemological species of culture to determine which factors, given in that mode of knowing, are taken as elementary or primitive by the people in question, and which are derivative, either rigorously or emotively, as the case may be. This permits countless different cultural philosophies within cultures of the same epistemological species.

The Epistemological Possibles

What is epistemology? It is the science that investigates the sources and methods of obtaining knowledge. The important thing to note about knowledge is that it is capable of being in error. This entails that science involves more than facts, since facts merely are and are neither true nor false, good nor bad. In short, facts cannot be in error. Only a proposition about facts, or human behavior which is the causal effect of belief in a proposition which may be empirically confirmed to be true or false, can be meaningfully said to be in error.

Propositions are composed of (a) their terms, (b) the syntax by means of which the terms are related and given their syntactical, as distinct from their semantic, meanings, and (c) their semantic references. The epistemological possibles become evident, therefore, when the different possible ways in which ideas or symbols get their meaning are specified. It will suffice for our present purposes if we concentrate our attention on the three major, but not the only, species of meaning which any word may have. We have called these three species (1) the radical empirical, (2) the naive realistic, and (3) the logically realistic meaning of any word.

Radical empiricism is the thesis that for any word or symbol to be meaningful, rather than a mere noise or mark on paper, it refers for its entire meaning to directly observable or immediately experienced data. Naive realism is the epistemological thesis that such naive, i.e., direct, observation or immediate experience gives us at least some determinate objects of knowledge which are independent of their relations to the percipient and are, therefore, the same for all knowers, the scientific defining properties of which are directly sensed or introspected. Logical realism is the epistemological thesis that directly observed or immediately experienced determinate items of knowledge are (a) relative to the observer, his physical frame of reference, his respective sense organs, and the moment of observation, and that, therefore, (b) objects the same for all knowers are possible only by means of speculatively discovered, imageless, syntactically constructed, deductively formulated theory which is tested as to its truth or falsity through its deductive consequences by "epistemic correlation" with radically empirically known and relativistic data. Logical realism, therefore, is an epistemic correlation of (1) the words of ordinary language in their nominalistic, radically empirical meaning with (3) the imageless many-termed relational constructs which the writer elsewhere has called "concepts by postulation which are concepts by intellection"[3] and which hereafter for short will be called "concepts by intellection."

The epistemic correlations are of crucial importance. The discovery of them is probably the greatest achievement of recent philosophy of science. Their importance derives from the fact that they prevent one from corrupting the data of concrete experience in the act of describing it by thinking of the many-termed relational sensed qualities which one directly observes as the persisting predicates of supposed directly sensed or introspected substances that exist, purportedly, objectively independent of their relation to the perceiver. Linguistically this means that they prevent the two-termed subject-predicate syntax of natural history science and the ordinary language of all Aryan cultures from being confused with the nature of things. That such confusion is serious becomes evident when one examines one's concrete experience afresh to note with Whitehead that sense objects, such as an immediately observed "red," ingress into nature in many-termed relations. More specifically, epistemic correlations force one to realize that descriptive sentences such as "The barn is red" or "The water in the ocean is blue" or "The go sign on the traffic light is blue"* are elliptical sentences containing several implicit unstated phrases referring to many other factors (such as "the sun's shining," where one is standing, the rods and cones in one's eyeballs) and are not the complete and explicit sentences the naive realistic natural history scientist takes them to be. In short, these correlations prevent words referring to epistemologically different worlds of discourse from being predicated of one another

* Such is the case for the writer.

as if they had the same semantic reference. Thereby one escapes the body-mind and other pseudoproblems and many other muddles which ordinary Aryan language and naive realistic "observing" and "describing" generate.[4]

Recent theoretical physicists and philosophers of science have given these relations various names. Reichenbach in his *Philosophie der Raum-Zeit-Lehre* referred to them as "Zuordnungsdefinitionen." Professor Henry Margenau in his *The Nature of Physical Reality* and others prefer to call them "rules of correspondence." The writer uses the name "epistemic correlations" for two reasons. First, their two terms cannot be defined, the one in terms of the other; hence to call them "definitions" is misleading. Furthermore, they are epistemological relations. In other words, they are two-termed relations, one of whose terms refers to (3) the logically realistic world of discourse and the other to (1) the nominalistic, radically empirical world of discourse. The adjective "epistemic" makes this unequivocally clear, whereas the expression "rules of correspondence" does not, since the correspondences might be, as with a map, between entities in the same epistemological world of discourse. The name however is not of the essence. On what is meant by our respectively different names, Reichenbach, Professor Margenau, and the writer agree.

More completely stated, epistemic correlations relate (3) *logically realistic* directly unobservable, speculatively discovered, and theoretically designated public scientific objects in invariant space-time as designated by deductively and logically constructed imageless many-termed relational concepts by intellection to (1) *radically empirical*, immediately experienced or directly sensed many-termed relational data. (1) is described best by the more nonsyntactical, largely pointing, and pictographic languages of non-Aryan cultures, and second best by ordinary Aryan language in its purely nominalistic, radically empirical semantic reference, with the muddled distortions of its subject-predicate syntax, as far as possible, eliminated.

Whitehead's attempt at such a reformed English prose shows this elimination not to be easy. The difficulties are so great that the ordinary language description of non-Western cultures, whose language and thinking is non-Aryan, by Western anthropologists and "experts" in Area Studies are likely to be misleading. At the 1939 East-West Philosophers' Conference in Honolulu, the writer discovered that translations into English of Asian classics whose epistemology is radically empirical are similarly misleading because the Western translators lack the epistemological training necessary to prevent the result from being nonsense due to the linguist's own Aryan prose and his naive realistic philosophical mentality. This is why the presence in this symposium of scholars born in or epistemologically sophisticated with respect to the cultures of Burma, Thailand, China, Japan, India, and Africa is a necessity.

Even so, they, like the rest of us, also must learn to think about ideas and symbols in terms of the possible species of epistemological reference and meaning they may have. For non-Aryan cultures have their naive realists also. In fact, there are reasons for believing that most of the cultures which anthropologists from both non-Aryan and Aryan cultures have studied are those of people who think radically empirically or naive realistically or in a manner that is a combination of both.

Anyone, however, who understands (i) Western mathematical physics, as conceived either by the ancient Greek Democriteans, Platonists, and Stoics or by modern scientists since the time of Galileo, Descartes, and Newton, and (ii) Western law of Contract, knows that Western culture in its law and theology, as well as its natural science, simply cannot be understood unless one realizes that it contains imageless, logically realistic concepts. The papers by Professors Sambursky and Smith in this symposium make this unequivocally clear.

The major event of the contemporary world is that so-called primitive peoples and the very sophisticated Far Eastern Confucian, Buddhist, Shinto, and nondualistic Vedantic Hindu Asians are appealing to the cosmopolitan, liberal democratic, contractual legal, and political ideals of this logically realistic West to warrant the rejection of foreign imperialists and the domestic demand of the right to build their legal and political institutions on Western contractual legal and political models rather than those of their pre-Western kinship anthropological Maharajas, Emperors, or tribal chieftains. These models require for their understanding and their validity logically realistic thinking. They are not justified by either (1) radical empirical or (2) naive realistic thinking even though, as will be shown later, radical empirical thinking is not merely compatible with them but also essential for their confirmation or disconfirmation. The same thing is true of the scientific technology which the Far East and Africa are importing from the modern Occident. As the writer has shown in his article in *Man's Role in Changing the Face of the Earth* (ed. William L. Thomas, Jr.) it is different from the world's previous tools. The latter derive from radically empirical aesthetic naive realistically conceived naturalistic materials. Contemporary technology is impossible without the logical realistic ideas of concept by intellection mathematics and its physics.

Hence, if comparative anthropology is to (a) correctly describe the world's traditional and present cultures, (b) correctly diagnose the schizophrenic personal and social conflicts which arise when incompatible naive realistic and logical realistic universals and their respective cultural values are trapped in the same person's brain, and (c) make the scientific contribution to the resolution of these conflicts which an epistemologically informed comparative cultural anthropology is capable of making, three things are necessary. Its scientists must become clear on the differences between (1) the radical empirical, (2) the naive realistic, and (3) the logically realistic meanings of any idea or symbol. Let us begin by defining the epistemological word *realism*.

Realism is the thesis that one knows objects of knowledge that are the same for all knowers and which exist independently of their relation to the observer. The belief, therefore, in external objects in a public spatiotemporal world, the same for all knowers, instances a realistic theory of knowledge. Naive realism is the thesis that such knowledge is given by the senses alone in direct observation.

Radical empiricism and logical realism deny this thesis, maintaining that every determinate item of knowledge given through the senses, be it an entity, a property, or a relation, is relative to the perceiver, to different sense organs of the same perceiver, and to where he is standing and when he is looking. Thus radical empiricism denies that there is any *determinate* knowledge that is the same for all knowers. It does, however, admit an indeterminate factor in immediate experience that is identical for all experience. It will concern us in the sequel.

Logical realism, on the other hand, affirms that we do have knowledge of external scientific objects in a public spatiotemporal world even though such knowledge is not given by naive observation to a single or the several senses. Instead, such realistic objective knowledge is possible only by imageless logically or mathematically constructed many-termed relational, speculatively discovered theory which is indirectly confirmed empirically via its deduced theorems as epistemically correlated with the relativistic, directly sensed data of the nominalistic radical empiricists.

It is to such logically realistic theory that Einstein referred in the first quotation in this chapter when he said that physics, like common sense, rests on the belief in an external world and we only know such a world by speculative means. For a more detailed description of this way of knowing, see the writer's chapter entitled "Einstein's Conception of Science" and the latter's comment thereon in the Einstein volume of the Library of Living Philosophers.

Practically the belief in logically realistic concepts by intellection has the following important consequence. This becomes evident when one compares the ideas in the intellect of the physics, metaphysics, and theology of Aristotle and St. Thomas with those of Democritus, the Platonists, the Stoics, and modern mathematical physicists. Both Aristotle and St. Thomas, at least in their articulate epistemology, were naive realists. This shows when they affirm, as does John Locke in his *Essay Concerning Human Understanding*, that there are no ideas in the intellect which are not first in the senses. Logical realism, on the other hand, entails that there are ideas in the intellect which are not given first in the senses.

It does this, moreover, for very good reasons: First, the concepts of the mathematics of Western mathematical physics cannot be defined in terms of sense data. Second, common-sense and mathematical physical scientific beliefs in external objects the same for all knowers in a public spatiotemporal world would be left meaningless. For were the logical realist to define his external objects in public space-time in terms of ideas given through the senses, he would automatically fall into the "muddles" which characterize naive realistic thinking. In other words, he would purport to define scientific objects, and the space-time which makes them external and the same for all knowers, in terms of entities, properties, and relations all of which are relative to the percipient. To do this is to affirm the self-contradictory. It follows that the naive realistic thinking of natural history science, which any ordinary language of the Aryan type encourages, is not a species of meaning which ordinary language may have as one of its possible meanings; instead, it is self-contradictory nonsense if taken as nonelliptical. This is the fundamental reason why any empirical science, once its scientists become epistemologically critical and informed about the sources of the meaning of the words they use, leaves naive realistic, natural history description for logically realistic, deductively formulated theory. But if the logical realist is not to fall into the same nonsense, then the ideas he uses to define his external objects and public realistic spatiotemporal world cannot be ideas which derive from the senses. In short, there must be ideas in the intellect that are not first in the senses.

How such concepts by intellection take on specific meaning remains to be made clear. The epistemological problem is this: Since realistic scientific objects, space and time, are not given in observation through the senses and cannot therefore be defined in terms of ideas that derive their meaning entirely from the senses, and because everything given to the senses is imageful, it is necessary to strip the idea of a realistic epistemological entity, property, or relation of all images. This result is the discovery of what symbolic logicians and pure mathematicians today call "the variable," where by a variable one means "any one." There are, then, two variables —the entity variables, which are the terms or relata in the relation, and the relational variables. The usual nomenclature is to use the symbols x, y, z . . . to designate the former and R to denote the latter. This is what Whitehead meant when, in the early 1920s he said to me that the first of the two greatest achievements of the Western mind was the discovery of the variable. He then added that the second was Eudoxus' use, in what we now know as Definition 5, Book V, of Euclid, of the universally quantified variables m, n within a given relation R to define the meaning of what the Greeks called "similar mathematicals," whether the magnitudes of the mathematicals were arithmetically incommensurable or not and where the variables m and n have as their range the natural whole numbers.

Whitehead's second observation reminds us that entity variables may be quantified universally for all values of the variable or existentially for at least one value of the variable. The symbols (p) or (x) expressed the universal quantification; $\exists p$ or $\exists x$ the existential quantification.

Even so we still know nothing about the properties of either the entity or the relation. How in logically realistic thinking are we to assign properties to the entities and their relations without using any qualities given through the senses? The logically realistic ancient Greeks discovered the way. It consisted in assigning no properties to the scientific events or objects, i.e., the x, y, z . . . , except as they are given to the entity variables by the imageless formal properties that are postulated syntactically for the relational variable R. We give a contemporary elementary example:

Postulate I   (x, y) x ≠ y: either (x R y) or (y R x).
Postulate II   (x): not (x R x).
Postulate III (x, y): if (x R y) then not (y R x).
Postulate IV   (x, y, z): if (x R y) and (y R z) then (x R z).

Postulate I affirms that for any two distinct entities, x, y, in the field of R in the subject matter of the deductively formulated science in question, x and y are related by R. A relation with this formal property is called "connective." Postulate II affirms that the relation R is inreflexive, i.e., it is meaningless to relate any entity to that entity itself by R. Postulate III adds that for any two entities in the field of R if R relates x to y, then its formal properties are such that it does not relate y to x. Such a relation is called "insymmetrical." Postulate IV assigns to R the imageless formal property such that for any three entities in the field of R, if R relates x to y and y to z, then R holds between x and z. This relation is called "transitive."

It might be thought that these four postulates which assign imageless formal properties to the relational variable R would not *ipso facto* entail very important properties for the entity variables x, y, z . . . making up the relata, or field, of R. Such a conclusion is, however, quite erroneous. What the relation R with the four formal properties of Postulates I–IV does to the entities in its field, be they finite or infinite in number, is to turn them into serially ordered entities. In fact, Postulates I–IV define what a logically realistic, as distinct from a radically empirical or naive realistic, mathematician means by serial order.

It is to be noted that these postulates assign no properties whatever directly to the scientific objects of the deductively constituted theory. Instead, its entity variables comprising the field of R derive all their theoretical properties from the imageless formal properties assigned to the relation R by the postulates. This is why in his

The Meeting of East and West and *The Logic of the Sciences and the Humanities* the writer called these logically realistic concepts "concepts by postulation," making it clear also for careful readers, of which there are a few, that in this expression the word "postulate" is being used in its specific sense and not in its generic meaning of the assumption of any scientific or philosophical theory whatever—be its concepts radical empirical or naive realistic. It is the derivation of all the essential properties of the scientific objects or events from the imageless formal properties laid, so to speak, on R by the specific logically realistic postulates which entails tautologically, as Professor Braitenberg notes in Chapter 9, that the formal properties of R hold for all instances of its entity variables. Consequently, to be an individual person, object, or event in this logically realistic meaning of individuality is to instance a universally quantified law. This property of logically realistic individuals has several important implications.

First, applied to descriptive science it means that no mature scientist supposes that his scientific job is done when an observer in the field or a laboratory reports a naively observed and described fact, f^1. In addition, three things must be done: (a) A theoretical scientist must speculatively discover and postulationally specify, after the manner above, the universally quantified logically realistic law R of which the fact f^1 is an instance. (b) From the specific postulates, theorems must be rigorously deduced together with their epistemically correlated operational definitions which predict the existence of unexpected previously unobserved facts f^2, f^3, f^4. Finally (c) an experimental scientist, skilled in the operations of (b) must confirm the deduced and epistemically correlated predictions. It is in connection with (b) and (c) that the papers in this symposium by Professors Campbell and Hockett are of special significance.

Second, such logically realistic, deductively formulated theory makes it possible to affirm tautologically true scientific statements about an infinite number of entities in the subject matter of the science in question. Thus Cantor's theory of the different classes of infinites arises and Peano's Fifth Postulate for arithmetic is found to be a tautologically true analytic proposition, rather than either a synthetic a priori proposition, as Kant's idealistic epistemology inferred, or an empirically true or false synthetic proposition, as previous radically empirical or naive realistic students of mathematics had supposed. Moreover, when these logically realistic tautologically true propositions of pure mathematics are epistemically correlated with radically empirically interpreted ordinary linguistic data and operational definitions, thereby turning these tautologically true analytic descriptive sentences into synthetic empirical statements, of which it is meaningful to say that they are empirically true or false, it is then possible by the methods (a), (b), and (c) above to affirm, providing the crucial experiments (c) confirm the deduced predictions, that the statements about an infinite number of entities in the field of R are empirically the case for our actual world.

Logically realistic concepts have a third unique implication. Only by means of them can the problem of empirical, mathematical, or moral and legal induction be solved. This problem has to do with how, after one has radically empirically sensed or naively observed merely some instances of the variables in a universal proposition, one is able to state that the law holds universally for an infinite number of values of its variables. Without this assumption, as Peano showed, even the most elementary rule in primary school arithmetic cannot be proved or justified. Also, as the writer pointed out first in *The Complexity of Legal and Ethical Experience*, this problem of induction appears in law when one asks what moral or legal obligation there is for one who disapproves of the majority-approved statutes of the legislature to be judged by those statutes. Yet any legal and political system would break down instantly if the defendant could make the plea that the court had no jurisdiction because he dissents from the majority-approved statute which makes the killing he committed a crime. No radical empirical or naive realistic theory of the meaning of ethical and legal language can answer the question of how one passes from the legal obligation of the majority to be judged by the statutes which they approve to the legal obligation of everyone else to be so judged. Only a logically realistic theory in which to be an individual citizen means to instance the formal properties of a logically realistic relation R that is universally quantified tautologically can do so. Even then certain restrictions are indispensable. A specification of these restrictions is of considerable anthropological importance.

Some Anthropological Examples

As the Greek and Roman Stoic natural and normative scientists Zeno, Chrysippus, the Scaevolas, Scipio, Cicero, and Epictetus noted, this logically realistic concept of the individual entails the thesis that (a) morally good, (b) legally and politically just, and (c) religiously virtuous man or woman is any one p, standing equally with any other person in nature before a common freely assented to, contractually constructed, logically realistic law. In Stoic language, moral and just man is "cosmopolitan man."

Stated with contemporary analytic logically realistic precision, this gives the following criterion of when any person's behavior or any political system's statutes are good and just:

(1) (p) (x) :. x is intrinsically just : = : x is an instance of a syntactically constructed logically realistic relation R such that:

(i) (p) R,

and (ii) (p) s of R, where x is the behavior of p or the object of any moral or legal judgment and s is the substantive content of R.

Expressed in ordinary language, interpreted logically realistically, this analytic expression is:

For any one person p and any one object of moral and legal judgment x, to say that x is intrinsically good and just is equivalent to saying that x instances a law R which is such that (i) R is universally quantified tautologically for all persons and (ii) the substantive content of R is also universally quantified for all persons.

Item (ii) is very important. It means that for any constitutional or legislative statute to be just, it is not enough, or even necessary, for it to be approved by the majority. Instead, justice means that if the statute in its substantive content assigns certain rights or obligations to one person p, or one class of people A, in the legal system, then any one must be substitutable for that person p, or the class of people A, with respect to those rights and duties. Although defined completely formally without any reference to sensed properties, this logical realistic theory of cosmopolitan morals, law, and religion is by no means empty. In fact, it is the only theory, of which the writer's extensive reading has made him aware, that warrants the unanimous decisions of the justices of the Supreme Court of the United States in the desegregation cases when, as is the case, there is no majority-approved Federal Congressional statute making it a crime for any political state to have its segregated cultural customs and their corresponding positive segregative legislative educational statutes.

Contrast this logical realistic theory of the meaning of moral, legal, and religious normative words with that of any kinship culture. This contrast has been described very clearly by Sir Henry Maine in his *Ancient Law*. Although he does not use kinship language, he makes it clear that in such a culture a person's rights and duties are determined at birth by his naively realistically sensed sex, primogeniture, or lack of it, of birth, and color of skin racial ancestry of breeding in the ancestral joint family and in the tribe. In short, morally and legally just man and religiously virtuous man or woman is naive realistically conceived natural history biological man. Such a kinship anthropological culture Sir Henry calls a law of Status society where by Status, as his use of the capital S indicates, he means not status in the generic sense present in any society whatever, but Status in the specific sense of being determined by naive realistically conceived, natural history biological properties fixed by one's genealogical table at one's birth. A society, however, in which these biological considerations have nothing to do with one's moral, legal, or religious worth and in which instead the moral and legal person is neither the ancestral joint family nor the tribe but the logically realistic any one *p* individual, Sir Henry calls a law of Contract society, where again by Contract, as the capital C indicates, he does not mean contract in the generic sense, such as occurs when a patriarchal God of the tribe enters into an agreement with a prophet of the tribe, but means instead what the Stoics called "cosmopolitan man" and which is clearly defined in its ideal by Principle (1) above.

Sir Henry was well aware also that what he described as "the movement from Status to Contract" arose due to the impact of Stoic Roman scientific and philosophical thinking upon Roman law which was originally, as the studies of Fustel de Coulanges and Westrup show, of the naive realistic patriarchal kinship anthropological law of Status type. These considerations show that to shift in one's epistemology and science from a naive realistic to a logically realistic theory of knowledge and scientific method is as important for the humanities and cultural sciences as it is for the natural sciences.

Confucian, Buddhist, and Hindu Asian empirical scientists and epistemologists discovered before the ancient Greeks and Romans that naive realism is a self-contradictory theory of knowledge, and hence it and its kinship morality is either a false or a second-best law, morals, and religion. They did not discover logical realistic concepts by intellection. Hence, with them the shift was not from Status to Contract, but from Status to the mediation of a perfectly consistent radical empirical theory of knowledge. The result in classical Asia was the Confucian teaching that the superior person does not indulge in litigation, there being no meaning to realistic, determinate common law having the same content for all persons. Similarly in Buddhist Asia there arose the ethics of mediation and its middle path. This ethics, law, and politics is impractical beyond the local village level. To attain national political unity it was necessary, therefore, to retain naive realistic first joint-family kinship thinking at the federal level. Shintoism provided this factor for Japan. The various dynasties did it for China. The importation of the Hindu Aryan epics, law, and Raj did it for Buddhist countries before the advent of Western law of Contract. For a further account of these matters, see the writer's 1960 Cornell Law Quarterly article, "The Comparative Philosophy of Comparative Law."

The ways in which time is observed and conceived by people who think (a) radically empirically, (b) naive realistically, and (c) logically realistically is especially interesting. Postulates I–IV above give the pure mathematicians' concept of serial order. When, as with Newton, one of the xs in this infinite linear series is epistemically correlated with Greenwich observatory, operationally inspected, and calculated nowness, one has the logical realist's concept of time as a sequence of nature-embracing nows extending linearly from the infinite past to the infinite future. Also, by making and then synchronizing clocks and watches, people in such a culture can arrange and keep punctilious social engagements to a degree which is undreamed of by people in radically empirical or naive realistic cultures. Even more remarkable, this way of thinking about time has become that of the most untutored villager or backwoodsman in any contemporary modern Western nation.

The concept of time for people who think radically empirically or naive realistically is quite different from this. For them, as for the naive realistic Aristotle, time is cyclical. The reason is obvious. Radical empirically or naively observed time is the sensed succession of sensuous qualities, and this sequence is cyclical. The most obvious is that of the sensed all-embracing continuum of darkness followed by brightness repeating over and over again. Within the former dark continuum called night there is, after some thirty daily cycles, the cycle of two-dimensional golden patches of crescent, one-quarter, semicircle, three-quarter, and full circular shapes, followed by the reverse sequence month after month. Also, there is the sequence of points on the horizon at dawn when the differentiated darkness fades out into the oncoming brightness with its reversal at dusk. The sequence of sensed points on the horizon and their repetition gives the yearly cycle.

Every dawn and dusk at Benares any anthropologist who wants to observe Hindu Indian culture can see some thirty thousand top-caste Hindus radically empirically experiencing this cyclical sequence in which the daily cycle and the yearly cycle become one in the undifferentiated continuum at the transition point which is neither darkness nor light. This transition point being undifferentiated is an eternal now timelessness; of this, more later. Interesting however are two considerations: Because the transition point which is dawn and that which is dusk are both undifferentiated, they are per se indistinguishable. The linguist Max Müller tells us in his Introduction to the Vedas that the original Sanskrit word for dawn and that for dusk is identical.

Within the all-embracing differentiated continuum of brightness called daytime, over the yearly cycle of daytimes, there is another directly sensed cycle of differentiated colors and odors—the light greens and sweet fragrances called spring, the darker greens, reds, and rich yellows called summer, the dull browns and fading yellows called fall, and the blacks or whites and grays called winter. Finally, over the cyclical sequences of the years there is the longer cycle from birth through the springtime, prime, and decline of human life to death, over and over again in every human generation.

Because for them determinate time is sensed time imagefully differentiated, the radical empiricist and the naive realist have no alternative but to affirm that differentiated time is a cyclical sequence of qualitative, sensuously imageful perishing particulars, coming again and again, and over which, with one important exception, man has no control. The Hindu calls these uncontrollable cyclical sequences karma. This is the radical empiricist's and the naive realist's concept of causality. Note again its remarkable descriptive power and also its incapacity to predict anything novel. Obviously this is something quite different from the deductively formulated, theoretical dynamics in either its weaker or stronger forms which is the logical realist's concept of causality.

The radical empiricist has a second way of thinking about time which the one-hundred-percent naive realist's way of knowing leaves meaningless. Because the latter, reinforced in Aryan India and the West by the subject-predicate syntax of an Aryan language, thinks of all the facts of his experience in terms of particular substances and their directly sensed defining properties, he has no concept of the undifferentiated except as it is an abstraction from a particular differentiated substance.

For the radical empiricist, however, as Hume showed and the Confucian, Buddhist, and Vedantic Hindu Asians observed eons before him, the concept of substance is not given to either the inner or the outer senses and is, therefore, radically empirically meaningless. This freed the Asian empiricists and epistemologists from the distortions of any subject-predicate language such as the Aryan Hindu's Sanskrit and enabled even the latter to apprehend direct experience. The result was the following conclusion. One's immediate experience is an emotively felt, cosmically all-embracing continuum out of which one's differentiated consciousness, including its subjective sensing and its relativistic sensed objects, arise at birth and to which they return at death. In short, radical empirical experience antecedent to all thought about or linguistic description of it is (i) a timeless *undifferentiated* cosmic field consciousness within which (ii) transitory sensuous impressionistically aesthetic perishing particulars temporally succeed one another cyclically. (ii) gives the radical empiricist the cyclical theory of differentiated time which he shares with the naive realist. (i) gives the radical empiricist his unique concept of both time and his own self as an eternally now, undifferentiated and hence unlimited and therefore completely satisfying immediate experience.

This radically empirical undifferentiated cosmic consciousness the Vedic and Upanishadic Hindu calls "the Atman-that-is-Brahman-without-differences." The Aryan Hindu is, therefore, a naive realist with respect to law of Status joint-family and caste norms during the Householder stage of the four stages of the Hindu's life and a radical empiricist with respect to the other facts of human experience and the other three stages of the Hindu's life. The Buddhist calls (i) Nirvana. Because both the Hindu and the Buddhist language mean little to Westerners, the writer, in order to help the Westerner to find (i) in his radical empirical continuum of experience, chose the words "the undifferentiated aesthetic continuum," where "aesthetic" is used (a) radically empirically in the sense of recent Western impressionistic art, and neither (b) naive realistically nor (c) logically realistically in the sense of the Euclidean three-dimensional proportional concept of the beautiful and its later two-dimensional images foreshortened as guided by the logically realistic laws of perspective discovered by the Muslim mathematical physicist, Al-Hazen.

The undifferentiated eternally now cosmic consciousness of (i) combined with (ii) its cyclically sequential differentiations appears in Buddhist aesthetics as the timeless pool and its lotus upon which the emotively blissful Buddha sits with equanimity, as with non-attachment he inspects (ii) his transitory determinate self and its relativistic sensed perishing particulars succeeding one another cyclically. The American psychologist and radical empirical epistemologist William James came to a similar conclusion when he observed that radical empirical experience is differentiated only at the focus of attention and is undifferentiated at its periphery.

It has been noted that people in Asian cultures think both (a) radically empirically and (b) naively realistically. It appears that (b) applies only to the Status legal norms within the particular ancestral joint family and to the first joint family that gave political unity to the nation. Elsewhere their thinking is radically empirical.

That pre-Muslim Indonesian, Polynesian, and African joint-familial or tribal folk have the naive realistic Status norms of (b) is obvious. The interesting question arises whether they also have the radical empirical, eternally now undifferentiated cosmical concept of the self and its timelessness of (i) just above. Javanese graduate students in my seminars have faced this question. They report that in their pre-Muslim Adat positive law and cultural customs, still persisting in themselves and their native villages, one never thinks of oneself as a spectator looking from outside at nature as something unaesthetic, unconscious, and unemotive to be exploited. Such an attitude would be regarded as both false empirically and immoral normatively. Instead, they think of themselves as immersed within nature and as deriving their own emotive aesthetic qualities and moral worth from a proper relation to nature. This suggests something very close to (i) above. The light which the experts on African cultures can throw on this question will be of interest. I suspect that the voluntaristic Shakti aspect of (i) in Hindu culture as described by Sir John Woodroffe in his classic *Shakti and Shakta* finds its counterpart in the music and dance of the Africans.

FOOTNOTE REFERENCES

1. Einstein, Albert, *The World as I See It*, Covici Friede, New York, 1934, p. 60.
2. Einstein, Albert, in Paul A. Schlipp (ed.), *Albert Einstein: Philosopher-Scientist*, The Library of Living Philosophers, Evanston, Ill., 1949, pp. 683–684.
3. Northrop, F. S. C., *The Logic of the Sciences and the Humanities*, Macmillan, New York, 1947, chap. 5.
4. Northrop, F. S. C., *Philosophical Anthropology and Practical Politics*, Macmillan, New York, 1960, chaps. 3 and 4.

The Burmese Language:
An Epistemological Analysis KHIN MAUNG WIN

13

As U Wun, a noted scholar of the Burmese language, has said: "The Burmese language belongs to the Tibeto-Burman group of the Tibeto-Chinese language; but unlike Chinese, it is not ideographic. That is, it does not have characters which originated as pictures, but an alphabet, of eleven vowels and thirty consonants, derived from the Pahlavi script of India."[1] To understand the mind of the Burmese people, it is necessary to subject this language to a more detailed philosophical analysis.

I

One of the philosophically important features of Burmese is that it is a tenseless language. That is to say, tenses—past, present, and future—are not so important in the Burmese language as they are, for example, in English. The main function of the Burmese language is to talk about actions regardless of the time that they take place, will take place, or took place.

If we pick up a contemporary Burmese novel at random, we find that sentences in it contain verbs in the present tense. When a Burmese novelist wants to specify time, he always makes it explicit by using such phrases as "two weeks ago," "two months ago," "two centuries ago," and so on. After giving a specific time, he again comes back to the present and describes the actions in the present tense. This is also true when he writes a novel about things to come. This way of writing shows that the past and future find their reality only in the present.

Let us take a simple Burmese sentence, "*U Pu thwa de.*" It contains a proper noun and a verb. *U Pu* is a proper noun meaning "man"; *thwa de* is a verb which means either "go" or "went," depending on the context in which it is used. In English, the word *go* is in the present tense, meaning "move on" or "proceed"; its past tense is *went*. But in the Burmese language, both *go* and *went* are expressed by one word, *thwa de*. For example:

1. *Ma ne ga U Pu thwa de*

Ma ne ga means "yesterday"; *thwa de*, therefore, should be rendered *went* here, because it is preceded by the word *ma ne ga*, which means "yesterday." So, *ma ne ga U Pu thwa de* means "Yesterday U Pu went."

2. *Di nay U Pu thwa de*

Di nay means "today"; *thwa de*, therefore, should be translated here as "goes," because it comes after the word *di nay*, which means today. So, *di nay U Pu thwa de* means "Today U Pu goes."

But if the specific time, such as today or yesterday, is not mentioned, then *U Pu thwa de* can be translated into either "U Pu goes" or "U Pu went." It is thus that Burmese may be called tenseless.

What is philosophically important is that verbs in the Burmese language stand for immediately known actions. In other words, actions in the past and in the future are talked about as taking place in the immediately experienced present. In the case of verbs which express the future, a little change is made. Instead of saying *thwa de*, the Burmese says *thwa me*. But here also the future is not clearly stated; it only tells us that the action is not yet definite.

This analysis of the language shows that the Burmese people live temporally in immediately experienced present events. Therefore, generally speaking, most Burmese are not so happy if they have to make very exact temporal appointments with other people. For the Burmese, determinate time is subjective; their conception of it is sometimes referred to as *ba-ma-na-yi*, meaning the Burmese time. The Burmese very commonly use such expressions as *hta-min-ta-lon-chat*, which means the time of cooking a pot of rice or nay-win-yo-yi, meaning the time the sun is about to set. But these show that time is not definite and objective; time is relative and subjective. It is very difficult to say how long cooking a pot of rice will take. It depends on the size of the pot and the power of heat applied to cooking. We have also to think of the kind of rice that is cooked. The expression *the time the sun is about to set* is also equally relative and subjective. Clearly, the "time" referred to is impressionistic sensed time; it is not mathematically constructed, quantitatively measured and exact time.

II

Besides, in the Burmese language verbs are the most important concepts. For a Burmese the action is more important than the actor. This also is revealed by the language. In English a verb by itself does not make a sentence, unless as in a sentence like "Stop!" where all know that You is omitted. But in spoken Burmese a verb by itself can become a complete sentence without it being known exactly who is the actor for whom the verb stands. The actor can be "I" or "You" or "They" or "He" or "We." Who performs the action can be determined only by the context.

Thwa de is a perfect sentence in spoken Burmese. It means "go." But it can mean "I go" or "You go" or "They go" or "He goes" or "We go," depending on the context in which it is used. And since verbs are also tenseless, *thwa de* can mean "I went" or "You went" or "They went" or "He went" or "We went," also depending upon the context. Thus, if the person who is making this statement is referring to himself, the sentence *thwa de* means "I went" or "I go," depending on the time the action is supposed to take place.

Let us take two Burmese, A and B. A wants to know whether B went somewhere the other day. A asks, *Ma ne ga thwa tha la*.

Ma ne ga means yesterday; *thwa* in this connection should be translated as "went" or "did go"; *tha la* makes the sentence interrogative. So, A asks, "Did (you) go yesterday?" (Note that "you" is not mentioned in the original Burmese.)

B replies, *thwa de*, which we shall translate here as "(I) went." Again, in Burmese "I" is omitted, but in translation we insert "I" rather than "We" or "They," because we know that the speaker is referring to himself.

So, in the context, if the speaker is referring to himself we add "I" in the translation, but if he is referring to a group of people of whom he is one, we insert "We." If the speaker is referring to a group of people and if he is not one of them, we insert "They" in the English translation. In the same way, if the speaker is referring to a third person we insert "He"; if he refers to a second person or persons, we add "You"; if he is referring to one inanimate object, we insert "It"; if to several objects, we add "They."

But the fact that these pronouns are not usually mentioned shows that for Burmese the action is much more important than the actor. A sentence which expresses an action without referring to the actor who performs it is considered in ordinary daily Burmese to be complete. Such a sentence is entirely meaningful. Thus, all that is real is action; all is in flux. There is no such thing as substance, physical or mental, which serves as an unchanging substratum of changing phenomena. Only that which is given in purely immediate experience is real. Therefore, in the Burmese language all concepts are *radical empirical concepts*, to use Northrop's term.

III

The fact that the Burmese people live in a radically empirical world is revealed also by the structure of the Burmese language. In spoken Burmese, if there are five separate actions, there are five separate sentences to describe them. For example, in English the following five actions are expressed in one sentence: "I went downtown, bought a chicken, came back home, cooked it, and served it to my father."

Here the five actions performed by me in the past are expressed together in one sentence. But in ordinary Burmese, this sentence has to be broken up into five parts, since it consists of five separate actions: "Go downtown. After go downtown, buy chicken. After buy chicken, come back home. After come back home, cook. After cook, serve my father." (Note that there is no "I" and that the verbs are in the present tense.)

The absence of the "I" suggests that the person is conceived not as a realistic ontological substance, but as the sequence of immediately experienced events. What is philosophically important here also is that since each sentence talks *primarily* about one action, that sentence refers primarily to the action that takes place in the immediately felt present. An action is real only at a particular moment. When two actions are connected, they are connected by the expression "after . . . ," but both actions are expressed by verbs in the present tense. Therefore, for a Burmese, time is nothing but a series of these immediately felt actions. Time is relative to the particular occasion; so also is space.

The subjectivity of space is revealed by the nature of the Burmese name. Let us take a man named *Ba*. This person Ba is not thought of as in objective space. A person who is older than Ba calls him *Maung Ba*. Ba is called *Ko Ba* by those who are of the same age. Those who are younger call him *U Ba*. Thus, the name Ba is temporally relative to each percipient. As the name Ba is relative to these persons, the person named Ba himself is relative to these persons. Moreover, he has different obligations to these people, which are to be expressed by different actions, physical, mental, or vocal. But the person named Ba is nothing but a collection of these actions and similar actions. Thus *the person named Ba is radical empirical in character.* What is true of Ba also is true of all other things in space. Hence space is subjective.

But this theory of the subjectivity, or the relativity to each occasion, of space and time is held not by the Burmese alone. It is shared by all other Buddhists. With regard to the Buddhist conception of time, Professor Takakusu says: "People are accustomed to regard time as progressing in a straight line from the infinite past through present to infinite future. Buddhism, however, regards time as a circle with no beginning or end. Time is relative."[2]

Not only is time subjective; time and space are not separate entities but correlative. Professor Takakusu again says:

But it is to be particularly noted that time has never been considered to exist separately from space. That is to say, every being or thing has time of its own. Space and time are always correlative. Men have an average wave length, or life time, of fifty years. But a crane is said to live for a thousand years. And with the heavenly beings, their one day and night is said to be as long as the whole fifty years of the earthly men. A day fly and a morning glory, on the other hand, live a short wave length of only one day.[3]

The Burmese language, therefore, reveals nothing more than the Buddhist conception of space and time. If these are correlative and subjective, the reader may now wonder how the Burmese could conceive of objects which are not actions. For example, a chicken is a physical object, and it is mentioned in the sentences above, which are literally translated from the Burmese.

In order to answer this question we have to keep in mind the distinction between the radical empirical, the naive realistic, and the modern Western scientific epistemological conceptions of an object. We shall use Professor Northrop's classification of some different types of conceptual meaning.

The essence of naive realism is that the existence of a physical object, such as a chicken, is known directly by perception; at the same time it is conceived as a thing which exists in the external world independently of the perceiver. This kind of epistemology poses a problem: "How can a thing whose existence is known only by direct perception in terms of images that are relative to each percipient and occasion be said to exist in the external world independently of the perceiver and the occasion?" If an object's existence is known only by images that are different from one perceiver to the next and from moment to moment, then since the images perish, so does the object; also, since the images vary, there is no meaning for an object independent of its relation to the particular percipients and occasions. Therefore, to say that the existence of an object is known directly by perception and also that it is a thing which exists in the external world independently of the perceiver involves a contradiction.

Because of the foregoing consideration, Buddhists deny the existence of an object in the external world, independent of the perceiver. All objects exist only relative to, and vary with, the percipient and even the occasion. "To be" means "to be perceived"; *esse est percipi*. Also, the perceiver is relative to the content of his immediate consciousness; he is as relative to the perceptions as the perceptions are to him. The Buddha himself stated the non-realistic nature of all objects in the *Surangama Sutra*:

Suppose, Ananda, that you and I are again sitting in the Jeta grove, looking over the gardens, even to the sun and moon, and seeing all the multitudinous objects, and no such thing as perception of sight can be pointed out to us. But, Ananda, among all these multitudinous phenomena, can you show me anything which does not belong to the perception of sight?

Ananda replied: Noble Lord! True, I see every part of the Jeta grove but see nothing which does not belong to perception and sight. And why? Because if the trees in the grove do not belong to the perception of sight, we could not call them trees. But if the trees belong to the perception of sight, why do we still call them trees? It is the same with space. If it does not belong to the perception of sight, we could not see space, and if it does belong to the perception of sight, why should we still call it space? I am convinced now that all objects whatsoever, be they little or big, wherever they are manifestations and appearances, all belong to the perception of sight.[4]

Clearly one assumption underlies these observations. It is that anything not given in immediate experience simply does not exist. But positively, this means that the Buddha is affirming a radical empirical concept of all objects.

In this kind of epistemological philosophy, all the concepts are what Professor Northrop calls *concepts by intuition*, which he defines as those "which denote, and the complete meaning of which is given by, something which is immediately apprehended."[5] Therefore, for a Burmese or a Buddhist the idea of chicken is a concept by intuition. The object, chicken, is nothing more than an agglomeration of the qualities of an object which is named chicken. Not only are all these qualities given in immediate experience, but each varies from percipient to percipient and from one here-now event to another. Hence, the Burmese indicative sentence is composed largely of verbs.

But according to modern Western scientific epistemological theory, the object, such as chicken, is more than an agglomeration of immediately given qualities. The chicken exists in the external world independently of the perceiver's mind. But, unlike naive realism, this view does not hold that the whole of the object is given in immediate experience; there are other aspects of a chicken which are known only theoretically, by means of indirectly confirmed postulates. Since part of the meaning of the concept of a chicken is of the latter type, it can be called, to use Professor Northrop's terminology, a *concept by postulation*. This he defines as one "the meaning of which in whole or part is designated by the postulates of the deductive theory in which it occurs."[6]

The essential thing to note about this definition of a concept by postulation is that implicitly and explicitly it requires a formally constructed set of postulates of a deductive theory to be present in the scientific or philosophical bases of any culture, if the people of that culture conceive of the data of their experience in terms of concepts by postulation as well as concepts by intuition. The inclusion of the words *in whole or part* in the definition permits some concepts to have other sources of meaning than formally constructed theories and still remain concepts by postulation. These concepts by postulation are divided by Professor Northrop into at least four different species.

When a concept's meaning is given *completely* by formal axiomatic or syntactic construction it is a concept by postulation—which is a concept by intellection. An axiomatically constructed theory of contemporary mathematical physics, for which there is no sensed or imagined model, is an instance. The three other species of concepts by postulation noted by Professor Northrop are: logical concepts by inspection, concepts by imagination, and concepts by perception. Each of these three subclasses gets part of its meaning by formal syntactical construction and another part by reference to either the senses or the imagination. Thus, according to Professor Northrop's definition, all concepts by postulation are in part at least concepts by intellection; but that species which he calls a concept by intellection is completely so.

In our present concern with a Buddhist culture and its linguistic symbols one question arises: Does the Burmese language contain any symbols that are concepts by perception?

Professor Northrop defines concepts by perception as axiomatically constructed "concepts by postulation designating factors which are in part sensed and in part imagined."[7] Then he gives two examples:

1. Monistic: e.g., The public space of daily life.
2. Pluralistic: e.g., Other persons, tables, chairs, and the spherical moon with its back side which we do not see as well as its presented side which we do see.[8]

It has been shown that for Burmese, like other Buddhists, space is not public but sensed as relative to each percipient and occasion.

So it is clear that their concept of space is not a monistic concept by perception. But Professor Northrop also lists other things—such as persons, tables, chairs, and the spherical moon—as pluralistic concepts by perception. The Burmese, like other people, also see such images. The question thus arises, "What, then, is the difference between the Burmese conception of, say, the moon and the moon as conceived by a modern Western scientist?"

The moon to a Burmese is a radical empirical object. In Burmese villages, for example, the children play with the moon. In a village called Padu, near Mandalay, children play in the open air at night whenever the moon is in the sky. Since there are no electric lights in the village, at other times they have to retire earlier in the evening. But when they see the moon, they are happy. This village is so designed that there are three or four houses in a big compound, facing one another. At the center of the compound is a large space where the children play. When the moon shines in their playground, they jump up and down and make all kinds of noises while looking at it. Then they ask the moon to give them rice on a golden plate. They consider the moon their friend. They tell the moon all their secrets and wishes. They call the moon *ma-tha-le-ta-tha-le-ta san-da-la*, meaning "the moon —the one which we always desire whether it shines or not."

The elderly people also believe that the moon has some sort of power to stop a child crying. When a young child cries, his mother takes him to a place where the child can see the moon and sings this song:

> A hare is sitting in the golden moon;
> There is also an old man polishing rice.
> Look at the moon, child!
> The moon god shows himself to stop you crying.

Therefore, the moon is something which can stop a child crying. It is something which can be a friend of the children. In short, the moon is something as immediately present to any child as are his playmates. It is right here in the playground, not faraway off in the sky. Furthermore, the moon is laden with emotive content. It is not thought of as an unemotive, unconscious spherical material moon, with its back side which we do not see as well as its presented side which we do see. Consequently, the moon is not conceived by a Burmese as an object of scientific study; instead it is an immediately felt object of love and admiration. It is bright and beautiful. Thus the concept "moon" is not at all a concept by postulation which is a concept by perception. Its whole meaning is given in immediate experience. Hence all concepts in the Burmese language are concepts by intuition. There are no concepts by postulation in it.*

The Buddhist concept of the self is no exception. Buddhism is not only a religion but also a philosophy. However, this does not mean that the Buddhist philosophy is one thing and the Buddhist religion is another. The difference is only in approach.

If we study Buddhism as a religion, we have to emphasize the practical aspect. Here one would have to get a set of rules for meditation from a master and practice in seclusion in order to attain liberation, i.e., the "True Self." This means to get out of "the wheel of lives," or, in other words, to escape from the sequence of perishing determinate experiences of the cyclic theory of time. Time is cyclical for the Burmese because it is derived from what is immediately sensed, and sensation exhibits the cycles of darkness and light, spring, summer, fall, and winter, and birth, youth, maturity, old age, and death. Since this cyclical consequence entails suffering, to escape from suffering is to escape from the cyclical sequence. This escape is called liberation. Positively, liberation is the attainment of the True Self, which is the timeless consciousness.

But Buddhism is also a philosophy. Hence one can attain the meaning of liberation and find the philosophical concept of the True Self by philosophical methods.

The philosophical approach to the Buddhist theory of the self begins with the common-sense beliefs of ordinary experience. Due to this belief people suppose that they directly sense (1) a substantial external object possessing the properties one directly perceives, and (2) a substantial determinate self.

From this naive realistic belief in substantial selves and objects, the Buddhist philosophical method proceeds by a series of negations. Its first negation gives the realistic Hinayana school of Buddhist philosophy. This school negates the doctrine of a determinate substantial self. But this school is still called realistic Hinayana

* The foregoing is reprinted here from *Main Currents*, Vol. 16, No. 5, May, 1960, pp. 112–114, with the kind permission of its editor.

because it retains the naive realist's belief in determinate external objects.

Anyone who is well acquainted with Buddhism knows that it has three cornerstones. They are: *Anisa*, *Dukkha*, and *Anata*. *Anisa* means that everything determinate is always changing. *Dukkha* means that life in this world is full of suffering. *Anata* means that there is no determinate self. These three philosophical ideas are accepted by all Buddhists, regardless of the particular philosophical school to which they belong.

Meditation is the most important factor in Buddhism in Burma. It exemplifies radical empiricism also.

According to the teachings of the Buddha neither reasoning nor the knowledge of Buddhist scriptures can lead one to the final realization of Nirvana, which is the aim of all Buddhists. In order to realize Nirvana one has to meditate. This is one of the reasons why there are so many meditation centers in Burma. One that is well known is called the Sonlun Meditation Center, which was founded by a Buddhist monk named Sonlun Sayadaw. This Buddhist monk has many disciples. As a result there are many branches of this Sonlun Meditation Center all over the country. The Sonlun method demands great efforts from the meditator, though it is considered to be the most effective method.

To carry out this method one has to sit cross-legged and breathe in and breathe out *very deeply*. While doing so it is necessary to fix one's mind always on the tip of one's nose; such a fixation of one's mind on a part of one's body is important. After meditating this way about three or four hours a day for two or three days, one has painful feelings in all big joints of the body. It is important not to be frightened and stop there; one must continue to meditate. Then these painful feelings are over and one comes to have pleasant feelings instead. This is the starting point of different meditative experiences.

I have interviewed quite a few meditators who had gone through these meditative experiences. One of them was a lecturer in mathematics in the University of Rangoon who did his graduate work at Harvard University. He told me that he experienced painful feelings in all the large joints of his body after two or three days of meditation. But he continued to meditate, and one day, while he was meditating, he saw a snake going out of one of his feet. After that all painful feelings were gone, as if the snake were the cause of all these unpleasant feelings. According to him this snake was as real as any other snake we can see in our daily life.

He then continued his meditation and again one day he saw the Buddha (the real Buddha in flesh and blood and not the image) sitting cross-legged on the top of a small hill, and at the foot of that hill was a lake. The scene was so real that he felt that he himself was there. He told me that he had never seen such a beautiful scene in all his life, and it gave him a very pleasant feeling which was inexplicable.

In fact, such experiences are not uncommon to any serious meditator. He will have them sooner or later. Some meditators saw higher beings who are called "nats," or beings who are to be worshiped. No devout Buddhist takes these experiences as the projections of one's mind. Some present events have merely been succeeded by these remarkable present events. The latter are as real as the former, and they are revealed, so to say, to the meditator because his mind is now becoming purer and purer day by day. Some even claim to have seen events that had taken place in the remote past. Some claim to have seen events that will take place in the future. The past and future are here and now radically empirically in the present. Such meditative experiences are called "visions," and in them we see the past and future events. Some people make their decisions—business or political—depending on these visions. But a really serious meditator must not cling to these visions; he must continue to meditate till he attains the experience of Nirvana, which is the ultimate goal of all Buddhists.

No one has, so far, claimed to have had the experience of Nirvana in Burma. In fact, even though someone might have experienced it, the Buddhists believe that this knowledge is incommunicable. In the lower stages of meditation one sees two-dimensional objects, as mentioned above. These two-dimensional objects, which are considered to be more real than ordinary objects because they are revealed in meditative experience, are the denotative reference of what Professor Northrop calls concepts by intuition. He defines a concept by intuition, let it be recalled, as "one which denotes, and the complete meaning of which is given by, something which is immediately apprehended."[9] But to be more precise, these concepts are what he calls concepts of the differentiations of the immediately experienced aesthetic continuum. These objects have forms. For example, the Buddha has his human form; the hill has its form; the lake has its form; and the nats also have their forms. We can differentiate one from the other because they have forms. In other words, they are what Professor Northrop calls *differentiations*. But if one continues to meditate one will gradually be free from these differentiations and at last will have the aesthetic continuum with no differentiations in it. This is Nirvana.

As no one has openly claimed to have had the experience of Nirvana, no one can tell us the nature of it with certainty. Many Buddhist monks, however, have tried to convey its nature by using analogies, though here again these analogies cannot be taken very far. Ledi Sayadaw, one of the greatest authorities on Buddhism in Burma, wrote a book called *Nibbana Dipani,* or *Nirvana Explained.* In this book he compares Nirvana with health. According to Buddhism all of us are living in the world of suffering, and the realization of the Nirvana means the elimination of the differentiations called suffering from the continuum of immediacy. So we, whose continuum of immediacy is differentiated by suffering, are like a man who has pains all over his body. We can count these pains as one pain, two pains, and so on. But when we realize Nirvana, we are like a man who has perfect health. Though pains can be counted, we cannot count health. Though we can point out and show the location of each and every pain on our bodies, we cannot point out and show health and say, "Well, this is health." Health is something we immediately experience, and it has no differentiations, as we cannot count it. Although we ordinarily say "We have (good) health," in fact, we should say "We are (good) health." So also, although we say "We have the undifferentiated experience of Nirvana," in fact, we should say, "We are Nirvana." There are not different Nirvanas for different people; we all experience, or become, the same Nirvana. In Nirvana there is no John or Jones. All differentiations disappear. Such is Nirvana, and one who has realized it is free from all suffering and change. He has become Eternity. Such Eternity is called *Ah-thin-ka-ta-dut* in Burmese Buddhist literature. In the Northropian terminology this Eternity is none other than the undifferentiated aesthetic continuum, or, in other words, radically empirical immediacy with all differentiations eliminated.

FOOTNOTE REFERENCES

1. Wun, U, "The Burmese Language," *The Atlantic*, February, 1958, p. 153.
2. Takakusu, J., *The Essentials of Buddhist Philosophy*, Univ. of Hawaii, Honolulu, 1947, p. 31.
3. *Ibid.*, p. 53.
4. Lin Yutang (ed.), *The Wisdom of China and India*, Modern Library, New York, 1955, p. 530.
5. Northrop, F. S. C., *The Logic of the Sciences and the Humanities*, Macmillan, New York, 1947, p. 82.
6. *Ibid.*, p. 83.
7. *Ibid.*, p. 94.
8. *Ibid.*
9. *Ibid.*, p. 82.

Structural and Dynamic Elements in the Greek Conception of Physical Reality S. SAMBURSKY

14

The fundamental significance of Greek science for the understanding of our contemporary civilization, based on science and technology, stems from two facts. One is that the Greeks were the first to discover the scientific method and to inaugurate the rational approach to reality. Many of the great achievements of their classical period, such as epic literature and art, have counterparts in several ancient cultures all over the world, but the emergence of a logical mode of thought out of mythology in the comparatively short stretch of two hundred years is a unique phenomenon of fateful significance for all subsequent developments. There can be no doubt as to the Greek parentage of modern civilization in all that concerns its mode of scientific cognition and its striving toward an objectivization of reality.

The second fact of significance for our problem is that the Greeks, in the four hundred years from the Milesian philosophers of nature until the Alexandrian period, have to their credit hardly any technical achievements comparable to the enormous strides they made in science. European civilization, on the other hand, has in a shorter span of time seen the rise of a technology not less imposing and formidable than the parallel advances in the field of the sciences. Our civilization is characterized by an intertwining and integration of science and technology, a factor decisive for the rapid development of both components, whereas the Greeks were fundamentally interested only in understanding the physical world and felt no need to conquer it or to change it. The basic difference in attitude toward nature, the contemplative and the aggressive, which is also expressed in the fact that the ancient Greeks, with few exceptions, did not practice any systematic experimentation, has an important bearing on the problem of the specific character of their mode of cognition. While being logically realistic, like ours, it was essentially governed by a structural conception, by an approach largely defined in terms of harmony, proportion, and symmetry. As we shall see there were some notable exceptions to this, showing the beginnings of a dynamic conception of reality, but they remained rudimentary as compared with the structural one. It was only from the times of Galileo and Newton that the logic of scientific thought and discovery was determined by the dynamic conception and that man began to think in terms of change and forces instead of harmony and structures.

Establishment of a Deductive System of Reasoning

The greatest creation of Greek science, geometry, clearly demonstrates the predilection of the Greeks for a structural mode of thought. Straight lines and circles, regular polygons, regular bodies such as the five Platonic bodies, are objects of this discipline, exhibiting by themselves, or in combination with each other, in a most striking way the traits of regularity, symmetry, and harmony. The starting point for mathematics had been the Pythagorean theory of numbers and arithmetic, but this soon led to difficulties when it was discovered that, in the theory of proportions, not every ratio of quantities can be expressed in terms of integers. For instance, the quantity x in the simple proportion $1 : x = x : 2$ cannot be expressed as a "rational" number, i.e., a ratio of two integers. This discovery of the irrational numbers was a shock which to a large extent was responsible for the relatively poor advance of algebra in Greek antiquity, another retarding factor being the lack of a suitable notation. In geometry it was different; here line segments of a length irrational with regard to other segments could easily be constructed and dealt with exactly as any other line. Such was the case for the diagonal of the square or for the two unequal parts into which a segment could be divided by an elegant construction yielding the famous "golden section," or for innumerable incommensurable line segments.

Geometry could deal with all magnitudes, whether commensurable or incommensurable, or whether of one- or two- or three-dimensional extension, in the framework of a single deductive science which was finally developed into the first coherent and consistent body of systematic thought, comprehended in Euclid's *Elements*. The logical architecture of this system became the prototype of all subsequent attempts to represent the sum total of various disciplines of knowledge and thought *more geometrico*, i.e., to start with definitions, to proceed by simple statements taken as postulates or axioms and to continue with theorems which can be proved rigorously by basic assumptions or by theorems already proved before.

It is well known that it was Plato who assigned to geometry an exalted place among the sciences. In the *Gorgias* (508a), for instance, Socrates reproaches Callicles and says that he seems never to have observed that geometrical equality is mighty among both gods and men. Plato alludes here to equality expressed in geometrical proportions which for the Greek mind symbolized harmony and order by which heaven and earth are bound together forming an ordered whole, the cosmos. From the context it is clear, moreover, that Plato saw in geometrical proportion also a symbol of justice, in a more general way even than this is expressed and illustrated in our days by the scales of justice. It was a conception which lasted throughout antiquity and lived on in the tradition of the celebrated lines believed to have been written above the entrance of Plato's academy:

> Nobody ignorant of geometry should enter my roof,
> That is, no unjust person should pass these portals,
> Because geometry is equality and justice.[1]

If one finally remembers the great importance of the theory of proportions and of the concept of symmetry for Greek art, one will realize the singular significance held by geometry as a link between art, science, and ethics. There is another aspect to this problem, most revealing of the Greek attitude to geometry, and to mathematics in general. All fundamental mathematical constructs, like numbers, lines, and shapes, had their origin in empirical beings and were parts of material entities. Arithmetic developed from the Pythagorean practice of representing numbers by a row of pebbles, and the beginnings of geometry went back to geodesy applied by the Egyptians to practical ends, whereby points were represented by stones or holes and lines by furrows or other material patterns. It thus seemed quite natural to regard mathematics, and geometry in particular, as perceptible things seen in abstraction from their material qualities. This was indeed the gist of Aristotle's philosophy of mathematics, whose view was that the objects of mathematics are abstractions of material entities. According to him the difference between a snub nose and a concave line is "that snub is a combination of matter and form, whereas concavity is independent of perceptible matter."[2]

The Aristotelian conception, however, was rejected by the long Platonic tradition which prevailed for about 900 years, from Plato until the last Neoplatonists, and which was the essential moving spirit behind the spectacular development of geometry. Plato assigned to mathematics an autonomous position as a separate entity in the intermediate region between the intelligible world of pure forms and the material world of perceptible things. Mathematics is thus both eternal and permanent in essence and accessible to the human mind. Proclus in the introduction to his commentary on Euclid's *Elements* (5th century) again and again emphasizes that to assume the subsistence of mathematical forms by material abstraction would mean in fact a dependence of the soul on material shapes, debasing her below the level of matter. On the contrary, the cogency of mathematical reasoning and the beauty and exactitude of mathematical forms are clear evidence of the fact that mathematics has its primary subsistence in the soul, which is the creator of all mathematical species.

The Application of Mathematics to the Physical World

The Platonic conception of the intermediate place held by mathematics between the permanent realm of the intelligible world and the changing world of physical phenomena formed the basis for the firm belief of its adherers in mathematics as a language suitable for the description and explanation of physical reality. Its roots go back to the first great success of applied mathematics—the Pythagorean theory of musical harmony. In the century preceding Plato it was discovered that simple musical consonances, like the octave, the fifth, or the fourth, are related to simple numerical proportions exhibited by the relative length of the sounding strings or, generally, the relative dimensions of sounding bodies. The respective proportions 1:2, 2:3, 3:4 became the starting point for a rich and ramified theory of harmony as well as for further developments in arithmetic which led to the definition of the three means, the arithmetic, geometric, and harmonic, and the three corresponding proportions.

But still more important from the viewpoint of the history of ideas was the Pythagorean attempt—so typical of a scientific train of thought—to extend the successful application of mathematics to other realms of the physical world. By a bold association of ideas, acoustics and music, based on the periodic phenomena of vibration, were connected with the revolutions of the planets and their periods, and thus gave rise to the idea of the harmony of the spheres and led to a systematic search after regularities in celestial motions, expressible in terms of mathematics. Mathematical astronomy, which evolved from this, was the second great creation of Greek science. It was a strictly geometrical discipline, beginning under Plato's influence in the middle of the 4th century B.C. and rising to the heights of the Ptolemaic system five hundred years later. Greek astronomy is the most striking example for the structural approach of the Greeks to reality, and more shall be said about it in the following section. However, it is worthwhile quoting here a later source, the Neoplatonic philosopher Iamblichus (A.D. 300) in order to show how these developments were connected in retrospect with the Pythagoreans, who had been the first to apply mathematics to physics: "The Pythagoreans found out what is possible and impossible in the structure of the universe from what is possible and impossible in mathematics, and they derived the celestial revolutions from causal rules according to commensurable numbers, by defining the measures of heaven by certain mathematical laws and, generally, by establishing the prognostic science of nature through mathematics and by making mathematics a principle for all that can be observed in the cosmos."[3]

Iamblichus, as a Neoplatonist, was of course prone to stress the importance of the Pythagoreans and to overlook later developments in the field of applied mathematics. Among these mention must be made of geometrical optics and of the mechanical treatises of Archimedes, by far the most important scientific achievements of Greek antiquity. But it should be emphasized again that the famous law of the levers, for instance, to be found in the treatise on the *Equilibrium of Planes*, is a purely statical law, expressed in terms of proportions like the Pythagorean laws of musical harmony. The laws of dynamics which we use to associate with the foundations of classical mechanics of the seventeenth and eighteenth centuries, stem from that dynamical approach to reality which only began to prevail after the Renaissance. One could perhaps see an exception in Aristotle's law of motion, stated in his *Physics*, but on closer inspection one has to admit that this is true only in a very limited sense. In his law, Aristotle constructs a relation between the distance over which a load (e.g., a ship) is moved, the size of the moving force (e.g., the number of ship haulers), the time during which the force is applied, and the bulk of the load. He arrives at the conclusion that the distance is in direct proportion to the force and the time and in inverse proportion to the load—a result which, by the way, is not correct. Insofar as Aristotle's formula deals with a kinematic event and includes a driving force, one can attribute to it a dynamic character. However, one has to remember that in the modern sense dynamics is concerned with changes in time, which means that time in this case is an independent variable entering the description of phenomena in an indirect way, in the form of velocity or acceleration. But one will look in vain for a strict definition of even the elementary concept of velocity in the whole of ancient literature; this was given in a rigorous sense only by Newton after the invention of the calculus.

Still, the successful application of mathematics in the field of statics and in astronomy was for the Platonists a sufficient indication of the immense potentialities of mathematics as a language for the description of reality and for the deciphering of the laws of nature. Already Theophrastus, a disciple of Plato and Aristotle, had an inkling of it, which he expressed in a very impressive way at the beginning of his *Metaphysics*: "The first question is whether there is a connection and a kind of interaction between mental concepts and natural phenomena; or whether there is none, but somehow both, while remaining separate, work together towards the elucidation of reality. It is obviously more rational to assume

that there is some connection and that the universe is not in-
coherent. . . ."⁴ But Theophrastus, despite this splendid formulation of the problem, still has his doubts: "If mental concepts
belong solely to mathematics, as some say, the connection with
the senses is not very clear nor does it seem capable of actually
performing anything. For mathematics would seem to be constructed by us who put figures, shapes and ratios into things which
in themselves do not exist in nature and therefore cannot unite
natural objects so as to produce life and movement in them. . . ."⁵

It was only at the close of antiquity that the Neoplatonists,
with an insight matured by the perspective of six centuries and
more, arrived at a clear understanding of the function of mathematics as the language of science. They realized that mathematical
constructs could be used symbolically for a rational description of
both celestial and terrestrial phenomena. In the last instance it
all derived from Plato's conceptions, as Iamblichus put it so aptly:
"The mathematical sciences . . . have to be imagined as something like the Ideas, and in them they have their foundation. They
are not to be conceived as abstractions of the perceptible things,
but being below the Ideas they derive from them their image-like
character by acquiring magnitude and appearing as extension."⁶
But another passage by Iamblichus which represents a most lucid
definition of the methods of mathematical physics, is more than
just a paraphrase of Plato. Here, in the typically repetitive language
of late antiquity, the many facets of the mathematization of an
empirical discipline are elaborately described as follows:

Sometimes, it is also the practice of mathematical science to attack
perceptible things which mathematical methods, such as the problem
of the four elements, with geometry or arithmetic or with the methods
of harmony, and similarly other problems. And because mathematics
is prior to nature, it constructs its laws as derived from prior causes.
This it does in several ways: either by *abstraction*, which means strip-
ping the form involved in matter from the consideration of matter;
or by *unification*, which means by introducing mathematical concepts
into physical objects and joining them together; or by *completion*,
which means by adding the missing part to the corporeal forms which
are not complete and thus making them complete; or by *representation*, which means looking at the equal and symmetrical things among
the changing objects from the point of view where they can be best
compared with mathematical forms; or by *participation*, which means
considering how concepts in other things participate in a certain way

in the pure concepts; or by *giving significance*, which means by becoming aware of a faint trace of a mathematical form taking shape in the realm of perceptible objects; or by *division*, which means considering the one and indivisible mathematical form as divided and plurified among individual things; or by *comparison*, which means looking at the pure forms of mathematics and those of perceptible objects and comparing them; or by *causal approach* from prior things, which means positing mathematical things as causes and examining together how the objects of the perceptible world arise from them. In this manner, I believe, we can attack mathematically everything in nature and in the world of change.[7]

What is described here by Iamblichus is a programatic statement which had to wait for its realization until the time of Newton and the theoretical physicists after him. Antiquity did not yet succeed in inventing the theoretical construct of a physical quantity such as velocity, mass, force, work, and so on, to translate this into a mathematical quantity, and to subject these quantities to a mathematical procedure leading to results which can be translated back into the language of perception. But the very fact that the Greeks did reach the programatic level on which modern developments are based makes them the spiritual ancestors of our own logically realistic culture. In this sense the words of Proclus' biographer and successor Marinos (c. A.D. 500): "O that every thing were mathematics!"[8] can be interpreted as an anticipation of Kant's celebrated statement that "in every department of the natural sciences, science proper is to be found only to that extent as it contains mathematics."[9]

The Structural Approach

In this section two illustrations will be given of what earlier in this paper was defined as the structural approach of the Greeks to reality. Let us first look at mathematical astronomy. The main driving force behind the gradual evolution of this discipline into a rational and self-consistent system was not so much pragmatism as religion, a kind of sublimation of star worship. The celestial motions were regarded as a "moving image of eternity," be it that of the Platonic world-soul or that of the pure form of Aristotelian actuality. The dichotomy between heaven and earth, established by the Pythagoreans and Plato and elaborated in Aristotle's cosmology, was founded on the belief that perfection prevails only in heaven and that the imperfect and uncertain events in the sub-lunar region are amenable to an ordered description only insofar as they are dependent on the regular phenomena of the celestial sphere. The geometrical pattern of perfection was the circle, represented by the circular movement of the "first heaven," the diurnal rotation of the sphere of the fixed stars. In the closed world of the ancient Greeks, the circle was the only regular shape allowing for a uniform and eternal movement, the analogy to the inertial motion along a straight line in the infinite universe of Newton. In the Greek cosmos, motion along a straight line had necessarily to come to an end at a finite distance or to continue in the opposite direction after coming to rest.

The fact that for the Greeks uniform and circular motion occupied the place of our inertial motion deserves some consideration. Already Plato in the *Timaeus* had given preference to rotatory, spinning motion over the translatory types of movement and had seen in it the motion "belonging to reason and intelligence" which, combining so to say movement and rest, is superior to all rectilinear motions. In this sense, one of Aristotle's definitions of nature was interpreted by later commentators. Aristotle, at the beginning of the second book of his *Physics*, states that "all things that exist by nature seem to have within themselves a principle of movement and rest."[10] Heaven, the supreme manifestation of nature, at first sight looks like an exception, because it never rests. However, as John Philoponus (6th century) remarks: "Rest is also found in all things. For the perpetually moving heavens partake in rest, because the very persistence of perpetual motion is rest."[11]

The conception of the perfect circular motion as rest has to be borne in mind when trying to understand the essence of Greek astronomy. On closer inspection it had become evident that the description of celestial motions as uniform and circular was in many respects a simplification. The only simple circular motion was that of the diurnal rotation of heaven from east to west in which all the stars partake, including the seven planets. Among these, three types of additional movements could be distinguished, superimposed on the diurnal rotation. One, the proper motion of the planets, from west to east, with a different period of revolution for each of them and in directions oblique to that diurnal circle; the second, peculiar only to Mercury and Venus, adding to their proper motion from west to east an oscillatory movement with the sun as a center, thus making them appear sometimes as morning stars and sometimes as evening stars; and similar oscillations, though not round the sun, peculiar to Mars, Jupiter, and Saturn: Each of them interrupts its journey from west to east after certain intervals and for a while performs a retrograde motion after which, by describing a loop, it continues its west-east motion.

The problem which confronted the astronomers from the fourth century B.C. on was how to explain away all these intricacies and how to restore divine circularity to all the celestial motions. The task was given a challenging formulation by Plato, who requested the astronomers "to save the phenomena of the planetary motion by hypotheses based on uniform, circular, and ordered motion."[12] The problem was further complicated by the discovery that there are considerable variations in the distances of the planets from the earth, which was supposed to be the common center of all the revolutions. It is not necessary to enter here into a detailed technical description of the solution which finally evolved from the efforts of generations and which culminated in the works of Apollonius of Perga (c. 200 B.C.), Hipparchus (c. 130 B.C.) and Ptolemy (c. A.D. 150). What matters in our context is the principle on which the celestial phenomena were "saved."

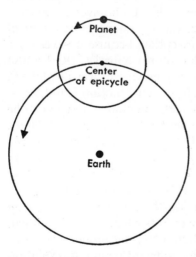

This principle consists in what today would be called a harmonic analysis, an eminently structural procedure. It could be shown that the planetary motions can be described by a combination, or rather superposition, of uniform circular motions consisting of the motion of the planet along the circumference of a circle, called epicycle. The center of the epicycle moves along the circumference of another circle, called the deferent, whose center in turn was either the earth or a point outside the earth, thus making the motion with regard to the earth an eccentric one. This system of deferents and epicycles, each of suitable dimensions and uniform velocities, exhibits a pattern of a definitely stationary character. For the movements which it illustrates are of an inertial type; they are perpetual circular motions equivalent to rest, and their sum total represents a structure which restores to the heavens the pure form of perfect circularity. The elimination of the irregular movements and the restoration of harmony satisfied to a large extent the epistemological needs of the Greek mind. The dynamic question of a causal explanation in terms of forces did not arise because the divine nature of the stars or of the intelligence driving them guaranteed their eternal motion.

The periodicity of the main astronomic phenomena allowed for a rapid advance of both theoretical and observational astronomy and, among other achievements, for a fair precision in foretelling basic celestial recurrences. The structural approach of the Greeks did not constitute any special handicap in the progress of that discipline toward a "prognostic science," although this was fully realized only after the introduction of the dynamical approach. Infinitely more difficult was of course the attempt to rationalize the phenomena of matter, as is known from subsequent developments. Even in the age of dynamics, real advance began only with quantum mechanics in the twentieth century. All the more remarkable is Plato's attempt at a geometrical theory of matter, amplified later by the Neoplatonists, and by Proclus in particular. Plato's sketch of his theory (in the *Timaeus* 53–58) is another conspicuous example of the structural treatment of one sector of reality, in this case the composition of matter and the nature of material change. Plato's aim was to replace the qualitative conception of matter, expressed in the pre-Socratic classification of the four elements fire, air, water, and earth, by a quantitative theory. His central idea, in conformity with the rational attitude of science, was that certain symmetries and regularities must prevail in the structure and modifications of matter which can be expressed by geometrical patterns and thus will "explain" certain phenomena that had before been understood only qualitatively.

What Plato had to account for were, for instance, the great penetrability of fire, i.e., its decomposing faculties, the stability of earth, the transmutability of water into air (i.e., the gaseous state), and vice versa. In order to translate these facts into mathematical language he chose the four perfect ("Platonic") bodies and, in what today would be regarded as a completely legitimate procedure, identified them with the four elements. The tetrahedron symbolized fire, the octahedron air, the icosahedron water, and the cube earth. It can be seen that Plato transposed the perceptible qualities of matter into the structural qualities of geometrical bodies: The piercing faculties of fire are for instance symbolized by the acute angles of the tetrahedron, and the inert nature of earth by the stability of the cube. The decomposition of matter, on the other hand, was symbolized by the decomposition of the bodies into their surfaces which, in the case of fire, air, and water, are equilateral triangles. Plato could thus describe the transition of water into air by means of heat with the help of a simple mathematical formula: One unit of water (20 triangles) is transformed into two units of air (2×8 triangles) and one unit of fire (4 triangles).

These first rudiments of a mathematical approach to chemistry are again significant for the rational procedure of science and particularly for the predominantly structural mode of cognition of the Greeks. Eight hundred years after Plato, Proclus with great ingenuity defended the geometrical theory of matter against the objections made by Aristotle. To the late Neoplatonists it was obvious that what Plato had attempted in the theory of matter was similar in scope to the "saving of phenomena" of the astronomers. It was a rationalization of a group of phenomena through the medium of mathematics or, better still, one of the possible rationalizations in the sense of Plato's words in the *Timaeus* (54a): "If anyone can tell us of a better form than ours for the construction of these bodies, his will be the victory, not of an enemy, but of a friend." This objective attitude of the scientist is echoed in the comments of Simplicius (6th century):

It is possible that the Pythagoreans and Plato did not postulate the triangular constitution of things as something absolute. Their procedure may have been like that of the various astronomers who made hypotheses based on the firm belief that the diversities in heaven are not what they seem to be but that one can save the phenomena by making the basic assumption of a regular and circular motion of the celestial bodies. Similarly the Pythagoreans, preferring in principle the quantitative to the qualitative and shape to quality, chose as elements of the bodies those geometrical forms which are more in the nature of a principle and which are superior for reasons of similarity and symmetry, and which they regarded as sufficient to account for the causes of physical events.[13]

Beginnings of the Dynamical Approach

Only the seventeenth century saw the full emergence of man's dynamical approach to reality. Three of its most conspicuous marks were the invention of the calculus with its central concept of convergence and the limiting process, the use of the time co-ordinate as an independent variable for the description of events, and the introduction of forces as the cause of physical change. Rudimentary beginnings of this mode of thought can be discerned in the Hellenistic period of Greek antiquity; they are embodied in the physical doctrine of the Stoics, which was based on the concept of a dynamic continuum. According to the Stoic theory, the whole universe is filled with a highly tenuous, all-pervading fluid, the *pneuma*, a mixture of air and fire, whose elastic properties make the universe a single, interdependent entity. Physical actions are transmitted from one point to another by the tensional motions of the pneuma, and the interpenetrations of pneuma and matter endow the latter with its various physical properties such as hardness or color.

The Stoic continuum concept led to an extension of the idea of a structure: Only the lower structures, like the stones of a wall or the planks of a ship, are of a static nature; but the hierarchy of structures extends to the realm of organisms where the whole is not merely the algebraic sum of its parts, but where each part has a share in the whole, and there exists a mutual affection between the parts and the whole. The universe, seen as a supreme organic structure, was thus transformed into a field of physical actions where every event in a certain spatial and temporal setting has its effect on other parts, whereby causal transmission takes place through local action, spreading from point to point. While thus a strict determinism was introduced into the world picture there emerged at the same time the idea of force as a physical agent, not that of momentary force of impact and push, already conceived by the atomists, but that of a permanent field of force illustrated by the stresses and tensions of the all-pervading pneuma. The field of force was seen as a "sympathy" between various parts of the universe, and Posidonius (1st century B.C.), for instance, described the tides of the ocean as being in sympathy with the moon and dependent on its positions.

There were far-reaching implications of this dynamical approach to reality for the philosophy of mathematics. One notable example is the replacement of the static definition of a boundary as a fixed limit between two regions by a dynamic one, taking the boundary as a fringe toward which the two regions converge. One can, for instance, regard the surface of a given body as the common limit of the surfaces of a succession of inscribed and circumscribed bodies, forming an infinite series of nested intervals narrowing down to the surface in question: "There is no extreme body in nature, neither first nor last, into which the size of a body terminates. But there always appears something beyond the assumed, and the body in question is thrown into the infinite and boundless."[14] This definition was formulated by Chrysippus, a contemporary of Archimedes (3rd century B.C.), and it is obviously meant as a conceptual step in advance of a static procedure used by the geometricians of that time. When a certain proposition was stated with regard to a curvilinear figure, say a circle, this proposition could sometimes be proved by showing that its contrary did not hold either for any polygon inscribed in or circumscribed around that circle. Chrysippus, in replacing the fixed boundaries by an infinitely converging series, made the first step in the direction of infinitesimal calculus and paved the way for an understanding of the celebrated paradoxes of Zeno.

However, the logical and semantic equipment for the final solution of Zeno's paradoxes was only furnished by the mathematicians of the nineteenth century, two hundred years after the invention of the infinitesimal calculus. Within the conceptual framework of the limiting process, Zeno's paradoxes (e.g., the infinite dichotomy or the flying arrow) cease to be paradoxes as do all the puzzling problems of change which occupied the minds of Plato in the *Parmenides* and of Aristotle in the *Physics*. The mind of the ancient Greeks, adjusted as it was to the structural mode of thought and gathering in the Stoic doctrine the first notions of the continuum problem, could not do better than Chrysippus did in solving the famous paradox of Democritus, which is reported by Plutarch to have been stated as follows: "If a cone were cut by a plane parallel to the base, what must we think of the surface of the sections? Are they equal or unequal? For, if they are unequal they will make the cone irregular, as having many indentations, like steps, and unevennesses; but if they are equal, the sections will be equal, and the cone will appear to have the property of the cylinder and to be made up of equal, not unequal circles, which is quite absurd."[15]

We know today that only the notions of the infinitesimal calculus and especially the dynamic concept of the limiting process can furnish the tools for a satisfactory solution of Democritus' problem. The mathematical argument would run along the following lines: For every given $\epsilon > 0$ one can find a $\delta > 0$ such that if the distance between two parallel sections is smaller than δ, the difference of the areas of both sections will be smaller than ϵ. Chrysippus, grasping the essence of the problem, but being equipped only with the conceptual tools of static mathematics, clad his solution in the form of another paradox, violating the law of the excluded middle. "The surfaces," he said, "will be neither equal nor unequal,"[16] or, as he put it in a similar context, "one surface will be greater but not exceeding."[17] These expressions were obviously coined in the deliberate attempt to describe the process of convergence toward a limit in the static language at Chrysippus' disposal. If the quantities a and $b > a$ differ by a small amount ϵ which is converging toward zero, one may call them "neither equal nor unequal," or one may say that b is greater than a but not exceeding it (i.e., exceeding by a fixed amount). What Chrysippus wanted to express is that the continuum is a dynamic entity which must be conceived in terms of becoming or, alternatively, can only be expressed in terms of being by the violation of the law of the excluded middle.

Finally, Chrysippus' view on time may be mentioned briefly. The difficulty encountered in the mathematical definition of this concept is that on the infinite axis of time the present, the "Now," is represented by a single point. This means reducing to a shadow the only moment which, in contradistinction to the past and the future, is coupled with the immediate awareness of reality. Chrysippus, in analogy to his definition of a body by a limiting process, conceived of the present as the limit of an infinite sequence of nested time intervals shrinking toward the mathematical Now: "He states most clearly that no time is entirely present. For the division of the continua goes on indefinitely, and by this distinction time, too, is infinitely divisible; thus no time is strictly present but is defined only loosely."[18] Hence in conformity with the dynamic conception of continua the present *qua* limit of time is not sharp but forms a fringe covering the immediate past and future. Indeed, we are told by another source that "Chrysippus declared that part of the present is future and part past."[19] We are reminded of Whitehead's conception that the world is made up of events whose temporal sections are not points but "drops of experience." What we perceive as present is "the vivid fringe of memory, tinged with anticipation."

Conclusion: A Scientific and Nontechnical Civilization

The theoretical constructs of Greek science, and of mathematical physics in particular, are distinct characteristics of a logically realistic culture. In this respect the Greeks are undoubtedly the ancestors of the present Western civilization. There are, however, some significant differences within the limits of this definition. The Greek attitude toward reality was a predominantly cognitive one, lacking all the signs of aggressiveness toward nature which in modern times has brought about systematic experimentation and a rapid development of technology. One of the reasons for the fact that Greek civilization was scientific and nontechnical was indicated in this paper: The Greek mode of logical thought was essentially structural and showed only rudimentary beginnings of a dynamic approach. This restriction seems to have grown from deep psychological roots. The Greeks, always careful not to transgress the boundaries of moderation and to avoid *hubris*, were reluctant to interfere with nature and to provoke its revenge. It was further unthinkable that a living organism like the cosmos should be dissected and analyzed by the unnatural methods of experimentation, which consist in the artificial isolation of a narrow section of reality from the integral body of physical events. This tendency was enhanced by the Greek mentality with its definite bias for deductive reasoning, a neglect of induction combined with a lack of interest in applications. The consequences of these limitations were a gradual decline of science in later antiquity when the scientific spirit succumbed to the hostile attitude of the early church to Greek science as part of pagan civilization as well as to Neoplatonism and the influx of Oriental mysticism.

FOOTNOTE REFERENCES

1. Tzetzes, *Chiliades*, VIII 973b.
2. Aristotle, *Metaphysica*, 1025b 32.
3. Iamblichus, *De communi mathematica scientia* (ed. N. Festa), p. 73, l. 22 f.
4. Theophrastus, *Metaphysica*, ch. 1.
5. *Ibid.*
6. Iamblichus, *op. cit.*, p. 34, l. 7.
7. *Ibid.*, p. 93, l. 11 ff.
8. Elias, *Prolegomena* (ed. Busse), p. 28, l. 29.
9. Kant, I., *Metaphysische Anfangsgruende der Naturwissenschaft*, Preface.
10. Aristotle, *Physica*, 192b 13.
11. Philoponus, *De anima* (ed. Hayduck), p. 75, l. 11.
12. Simplicius, *De caelo* (ed. Heiberg), p. 493, l. 2 f.
13. *Ibid.*, p. 565, l. 26 ff.
14. Plutarch, *De communibus notitiis*, 1078e.
15. *Ibid.*, 1079e.
16. *Ibid.*, 1079f.
17. *Ibid.*, 1079d, 1080c.
18. Stobaeus, *Eclogae* (ed. Wachsmuth), vol. I, p. 106, l. 13 ff.
19. Plutarch, *op. cit.*, 1081c.

BIBLIOGRAPHY

On Greek mathematics:

Heath, T. L., *History of Greek Mathematics*, Clarendon, Oxford, 1921.
Struik, D. J., *A Concise History of Mathematics*, Dover, New York, 1948.

On Greek astronomy:

Heath, T. L., *Greek Astronomy*, Dent, London, 1932.
Dreyer, J. L. E., *A History of Astronomy*, Dover, New York, 1953.

On Greek scientific thought in general:

Sambursky, S., *The Physical World of the Greeks*, Routledge, London; Macmillan, New York, 1956.
Sambursky, S., *Physics of the Stoics*, Routledge, London, 1959.
Sambursky, S., *The Physical World of Late Antiquity*, Routledge, London; Basic Books, New York, 1962.

The Theoretical Constructs
of Western Contractual Law JOSEPH C. SMITH

15

Of the many and varied elements contributing to the rise of Western civilization, few have had the impact of Western contractual legal science. In its ancient form, Roman classical and postclassical law, and in its two modern forms, the Continental civil and the common-law systems, this science has had a profound effect upon nearly every aspect of Western culture, and in particular its commercial, political, and religious concepts and institutions; and in recent times its influence has spread throughout all the world with its adoption in various degrees and forms by a vast majority of the earth's population, including many nations such as Turkey and Japan, who have replaced traditional legal systems, centuries old, with either the common or the civil law. The only explanation which satisfactorily accounts for the phenomenon is that these two legal systems contain unique elements found in no other. In order to isolate these elements it is necessary to compare these systems with other legal systems, all of which with the exception of Eastern mediational law, are sufficiently similar that they may be treated as a single unit.[1]

The unique element in Western contractual law can best be illustrated by contrasting its concepts of property and contract with those of other legal systems. The conception of property held by all Western contractual legal systems is that of legal relations existing between the owner of a thing and every other member of the legal system. This relationship, referred to in English law by the term *ownership* and in classical and postclassical Roman law by the term *dominium*, is unique to the legal systems influenced by these Western systems. In legal systems unaffected by Roman or common law, the sensed relationship of physical possession generally has been the basis of the concept of property. In primitive societies a man's personal property such as wearing apparel, ornaments, tools, and weapons were his, not because of any legal conception of ownership, but because of the directly sensed physical connection between the individual and his personal goods, which were often conceived to be a part of him, "a manifestation of his personality."[2] The slaves, flocks, and herds were not owned by the family but were a part of the family unit in the same way as were the children, and the land belonged to a family because they occupied it.

Professor C. W. Westrup in a detailed study, *Introduction to Early Roman Law*, vol. II, *Joint Family and Family Property*, gives a clear analysis of the concept of property of the Romans before their creation of classical Roman law and points out that the concept of proprietary rights or *dominium* did not exist in this period.[3] The relationship between an individual and his property was the physical relationship of possession, which gave rise to an introspected psychological feeling of belonging expressed by the phrase *meum esse*, "this is mine." Professor Westrup further illustrates that this concept was held by all the various Aryan tribes and nations, all of whom had no words in their vocabulary to express the concept of ownership. The early Roman family considered land to be theirs because they occupied it, it was the home of their ancestors who were buried in the soil, and it was the locale of the family hearth containing the sacred fire.[4] Animals, slaves, and children were considered not so much as property but as part of the family, the various parts welded together under the power or *manus* of the *pater familias*.[5]

The concept of *dominium* was not present in Greek law, nor did the Greek vocabulary contain an equivalent word.[6] *Ktēsis*, a verbal noun meaning "possessing," was used to describe the relationship between a person and his property, and the things possessed were often referred to as *ktēmata*, meaning "possessions." This relationship was also described by the term *kratein*, which comes from the word *krateō*, meaning "to lay hold of" or "become master of." The term *chrēma* was usually used to refer to money, and comes from the verb chraō, meaning "to use." The Greek word for estate, oikos, comes from oikeō, meaning "to dwell." The above proprietary concepts illustrate the close relationship between the Greek concept of property and the relations of physical acquisition and possession.

Before the impact of Roman law on the English legal system the word seisin, meaning simply "possession," was the word usually used to describe the relationship between a person and his property.[7] The first recorded appearance of the word owner in the English language is 1340, and the word ownership is not found recorded until 1583, and neither became common legal terminology until the seventeenth century. The only method by which one person could convey property to another was an actual delivery of possession or "livery of seisin." The person seised, even though he had wrongfully dispossessed another of his lands, was the only person who could alienate or convey the land; only his heir would succeed to the property; and it would be his widow, not the widow of the person wrongfully dispossessed, who would be entitled to dower.

The fact that title arose from possession may be further illustrated by a case from the Book of Assizes, where the plaintiff's bill was adjudged bad for pleading that the defendant had stolen and killed his horse, since as soon as the horse was removed from the plaintiff's possession, it was no longer his horse, but that of the possessor.[8]

Inasmuch as we understand the concept of property of any legal system untouched by Roman law to be that of the physical relationship of possession and an introspected feeling of belonging to which it gives rise, property is the result of the physical act of acquisition or creation and is therefore antecedent to the legal system; while in Western contractual law, property, being jural relations, is not merely protected, but is created by the legal system. The issue in the latter systems in an action concerning title is as to which of the two disputants stands in jural relations with everyone else in the legal system in regard to the disputed object, while in the former systems, the issue was generally not proprietary in nature since possession was essential to title, and possession of the disputed object was nearly always with the defendant. The issue was usually instead, whether a wrong had been committed.

In most cases where the dispute concerned a chattel, the issue tried by a court was whether or not a theft had been committed. For instance, in a dispute at early common law in regard to an animal, the claimant would charge the possessor with theft, whereupon the defendant had to prove the charge false either by showing that he had possessed the animal since its birth or that he had purchased it from a third party.[9] If the sale were proved, then the third party became the defendant, was charged with theft, and punished unless he was able to prove possession from birth or a purchase. Eventually someone would be convicted unless it were proved that the animal was purchased on the open market; and where theft was proved the plaintiff would regain the animal upon the basis that any possessor could regain anything taken from him by a thief. A nearly identical procedure was also used by such diversified people as the Babylonians, the Greeks, the Continental Saxons, and the Welsh.[10]

With the divergence of the civil and criminal elements of law in England, theft became a criminal action, and property disputes were tried in trespass, *de bonis asportatis*, the issue being not whether a theft had been committed but whether the defendant had wronged the plaintiff by taking, or disseising him of, his property. Since theft was not an issue, there was no basis upon which the court could return the property to the plaintiff, but damages were given instead. Equally, the action could only be brought against the taker of the goods and not against third parties who later gained possession, since they had committed no wrong. Both the earlier action and trespass could not be brought by a bailor but only by the bailee, since it was from him the goods were stolen or wrongfully taken. While trespass was the common form of action used in disputes concerning chattels, the action of novel disseisin became the most popular method in regard to land. The issue was not as to who owned the land, but whether the defendant had wrongfully disseised or dispossessed the plaintiff, and even a wrongful possessor who had disseised the original occupier could bring this action against the original occupier if he later forcibly regained possession.[11]

Another method of settling property disputes was for the court to ascertain which of the two disputants had the earliest possession, and, if that person could show that he had been wrongfully deprived of possession, then the court would do right by restoring the property to him. But in order to do this it was usually necessary for the court to take or have possession (either literally or symbolically in the case of land) before the action commenced.[12]

A comparison between the concepts of property of these two types of legal systems shows that both deal with people, objects, introspected feelings of belonging, patterns of conduct, physical possession, and the process of legal machinery. The basic difference, however, is that Western contractual law imposes between the person and the object a bundle of right and duty relations which cannot be identified with any of these aspects, while in the systems unaffected by Roman law, every aspect of the concept generally can be referred to physical things, processes, directly sensed relationships, or directly introspected feelings.

An examination and comparison of the concepts of contract equally illustrate the unique element of Western contractual legal science. A contract in Western contractual legal systems is one or, more often, a series of imageless legal relations arising out of acts of agreement or promises between two people; although, as in English law, the word *contract* is often used in a nontechnical sense to refer to the actual operative acts or also to the written document recording them. In his book *Primitive Law* A. S. Diamond points out that this "artificial, technical and theoretical conception" was unknown in ancient non-Roman legal systems, which in most instances knew only transactions of barter and sale.[13] Such transactions are not, however, contracts in the technical sense of Western law, as no legal relations result therefrom.[14] Immediately the transaction is completed the parties have no further relationship to each other. The closest these systems approached the concept of contract was an incomplete conveyance, where one party gave goods but did not immediately receive value in return. Such a transaction, however, did not set up a legal relation between a creditor and debtor, but the nearly universal practice was for the debtor to give a hostage or his own body to insure that he completed the transaction. A failure to pay was considered a wrongful detention of the creditor's property, and a failure to repay a loan, a wrongful detention of the creditor's money.[15] In the early common law, for instance, the action brought for wrongful refusal to surrender a chattel to which the plaintiff was entitled was detinue, while the action for money owed was the closely related action of debt.

Professor J. W. Jones in describing Greek law states:

Despite the obscurity of the not very abundant material which has come down to us, there is good ground for supposing that Greek law, like early Roman and English law, considered sale as essentially an exchange of land or goods for money, a cash transaction giving no right to enforce payment on the one side or delivery on the other. It was a two-sided affair; but there could be no question of any outstanding obligations arising from the simple fact of agreement. In law the sale was complete or it was nothing, and it was not complete until the price had been paid: "paying down the forty minaei, I made the purchase," says a buyer. While Roman and English law eventually came to recognize the binding force of mutual promises, Greek law clung throughout its history to the conception of sale as a purely ready-money business.[16]

Little evidence is to be found of the enforcement of purely executory agreements other than in Western contractual legal systems.[17]

Comparison therefore shows that the unique element in Western contractual legal science is the imageless jural relations which probably exist in no other systems except as they have been influenced by Western contractual law. What is often referred to as a "right" in these systems is merely an introspected feeling of having been wronged, resulting from an interference with a community recognized interest for which the wronged person or the community was allowed to exact a controlled sanction or compensation. A surprising similarity may be found between legal codes from various ages and widely differing cultures. Nearly all follow a basic pattern of listing numerous fact situations amounting to wrongs, with an appropriate penalty or compensation. Even the Greeks, at the pinnacle of their progress, had no conception of a legal right as known in contractual legal science.[18] These legal systems were therefore static and past oriented, since they dealt basically with wrongs and compensation, that is the restitution as far as possible of a previously existing situation which had been wrongfully disturbed. Western contractual legal science, on the other hand, is future oriented and a law of movement concerned with the creation, transfer, and extinction of legal relations and prediction of this future movement.

The Origin of Western Contractual Legal Science

The fact that the uniqueness of Roman legal science lies in its imageless, theoretical conceptions has long been recognized. Savigny, in the early part of the nineteenth century, wrote:

The conceptions and rules of their science do not seem to them to be products of their own creation—they are real beings, with whose existence and genealogy they have become acquainted through long and intimate association. That is why their whole procedure is tinged with an assurance not found elsewhere except in mathematics, and it is no exaggeration to say that they make calculations with their conceptions.[19]

It is as well generally recognized that Roman legal science was the creation of a small group of jurisconsults, who were learned not only in the law, but also in Stoic philosophy, and that the foundation of this science was set out by Q. Mucius Scaevola in his *Ius civile*, a classic treatise of the law, remaining today only in a few scattered fragments.[20] However, the nature of these concepts and their relation to Stoic philosophy has not been clarified until recently.

Professor F. Schulz suggests that the creation of Roman legal science was the result of the introduction of the dialectical method of organizing a body of knowledge into a scientific system by dividing it into genera and species and then ascertaining the principles "governing the kinds and explaining individual cases."[21] Although the Stoics used the dialectical method, this explanation alone does not, however, account for the unique nature of classical Roman law because the mere application of this system would not result in imageless concepts but would merely give a legal system where the law was arranged according to the genera and species of the imageful subject matter of the laws. The beginnings of such arrangements may be found in several early legal systems untouched by Roman law. According to Professor Schulz's reconstruction of the divisions of Q. Mucius Scaevola's *Ius civile*, Scaevola divided the law into four general classifications, the law of inheritance, the law of persons, the law of things, and the law of obligations.²² These divisions are based upon differences in the imageless legal relations rather than differences in classes of the subject matter of the law. For instance, theft and damage of property were included by Scaevola as a part of the law of obligations rather than the law of things. Thus Professor Schulz's explanation still does not account for the existence of the very concepts which make classical Roman law unique, that is, concepts which have no meaning in sensed experience.

Both the nature and origin of these concepts have now been clarified by Professor F. S. C. Northrop, who has shown that the creation of the Western contractual legal science was the result of the Roman Stoic lawyers' introduction of the epistemology, logic, and imageless theoretical forms of Greek physics into their legal system, producing the revolutionary change in Roman law described by Sir Henry Maine as the shift from Status to Contract.²³ Professor Northrop has also shown that the epistemology of legal systems which have not been influenced by Western contractual legal science (except for Eastern mediational law) is that of naive realism and that the Stoic lawyers substituted in its place the epistemology of Greek mathematical physics, which is logical realism.²⁴ He describes the difference between these two epistemologies as follows:

> Realism is the thesis that in knowledge we know an object together with its defining properties and that both are independent of their relation to the observer; in other words we know a public, rather than merely a private, world. Naive realism affirms that we know such a public self in a public world by direct observation. Logical realism affirms, with radical empiricism, that all directly observable items of knowledge are relative. . . . Consequently, while still affirming realism, it rejects the naive realist's thesis that either a public self or any other public object in a public world is directly sensed or introspected, affirming instead that it is knowable only by imageless, speculatively introduced concepts by postulation. . . .²⁵

Like other legal systems whose epistemology was that of naive realism, precontractual Roman law had no conception of legal obligation in the sense of theoretically created rights and duties. Legal liability arose not from a duty but from sensed relationships and directly introspected feelings. Where a person wronged another, there was no question of the other being under a duty to pay compensation, but the legal system channeled the natural desire for vengeance in such a manner that the person wronged would be protected while he or a representative of the community exacted from or upon the wrongdoer the penalty provided by the law, or the legal system would prevent the person wronged from taking vengeance if the wrongdoer paid the compensation. Within the family, all its members were subject, because of the relationship of birth, to the pater familias, who was their only judge, having power to sell their labors, punish them, or put them to death. Liability between heads of families was equally derived from sensed or directly introspected factors, as is reflected in the practice of *nexum*, whereby the debtor made himself liable to the creditor through a ceremony nearly identical to that used for the sale or conveyance of property and in which the debtor became the bondsman of the creditor and subject to literal bonds if he failed to pay.

The legal relations in Western contractual law, however, are not derived from sensed experience but get their meaning from fundamental theoretically created postulates and are what Professor Northrop terms "concepts by postulation," that is a concept, "the meaning of which in whole or in part is not derived from something immediately apprehendable but is constructed or proposed for it by the specific postulates of some deductively formulated theory."[26] Such a relation was referred to as an *obligatio*, which is defined in the *Institutes of Justinian* as a legal bond, *iuris vinculum*,[27] and included both the concept of the right as well as the correlative duty. All laws were a form of *obligatio*,[28] and all *obligationes* arose from a *contractus*,[29] that is, "the concurrence of the wills of the parties, to create an actionable, obligatory bond between them."[30] A *lex publica* was an obligation binding everyone because each was assumed to have agreed to its enactment,[31] and a private contract was often referred to as a law.[32] Thus the legal science of the Stoic lawyers and the legal systems which have sprung from it are termed "contractual." The concept of *contractus* was not a directly sensed or introspected bond, however, but was a theoretically constructed concept arising out of the Stoic concept of the nature of man and the doctrine of free will. This concept of the source of legal obligation, as will be later illustrated, makes possible modern democratic and representative government, and there is no exaggeration in Lord Acton's statement that "It is the Stoics who emancipated mankind from its subjection to despotic rule, and whose enlightened and elevated view of life . . . led the way to freedom."[33]

The Romans never confused the *obligatio* with the acts and words of agreement to which it was annexed, but made the distinction between what they termed the nude or naked pact and the *obligatio* which the law attached to it. The *obligatio* was therefore an imageless theoretically constructed form into which the human being is placed as a material constant. Professor Northrop has shown how these forms were created in Roman law by the use of the concept of the variable of Greek mathematical physics to relate human beings together without reference to sensed qualities of family, tribe, sex, or color. He has further advanced the thesis that the Stoic Roman lawyers used the procedure of Definition 5, Book V, of Euclid to define the meaning of the words "good" and "just" in their legal system by making the human being "an instance of an imageless formal and constitutively constructed and procedurally defined determinate universal law" resulting in the fundamental postulate that

For any act to be good or just, it must be an instance of a formally constructed universal law which applies to any person whatever who implicitly or explicitly assents to it, and in addition the substantive content of this law must be such that if it confers any rights, privileges and duties on one person in the community, it must confer those rights, privileges and duties on any one.[34]

The fundamental division of all actions in classical Roman law into *actiones in rem* and *actiones in personam* furnish strong verification of this thesis. A cursory examination might lead one to think that this is merely a division between property actions and actions in tort and contract in the sense that the former is an action to enforce a right against a thing and the latter, a right against a person; and a few authorities have drawn this conclusion. However, as has been pointed out by many writers, rights in Western contractual law cannot exist against things but are claims against persons upon whom a correlative duty rests. Furthermore, a number of Roman *actiones in rem* such as the *praejudicialis actio* did not involve things,[35] and too, the statement *in rem* is used in the *Digest*, where it could have no possible reference to things.[36]

This division of actions reflects a fundamental division in kinds of rights. Rights in rem are usually referred to as rights against all the world and rights in personam as rights against specific persons. Thus a person who has a proprietary right in relation to a specific object has a right against everyone in the legal system, all of whom are under a correlative duty to refrain from interfering with the object and the owner's enjoyment of it, while a person who has a contractual right has it only against the other party to the contract. This description is not completely accurate, however, since one can only have rights against individuals jointly, but not against everyone in the legal system in mass. This fact was recognized by Professor Hohfeld, who defined a right in rem as "one of a large class of fundamentally similar yet separate rights . . . residing in a single person (or group of persons) but availing respectively against persons constituting a very large and indefinite class of people."[37] This definition also, however, does not accurately describe the right in rem, as the most fundamental characteristic of these relations is that the holder of the duty need not be named, but this definition forces one to name every single person in the legal system as holders of similar duties in order to indicate fully the range of the relation.

The only explanation which accounts for the fact that the duty is the same for, and rests separately and individually upon, everyone in the legal system, but yet does not need to specify every proper-named person to indicate fully the holders of the duty, is that of Professor Northrop, who has shown how the Stoic lawyers substituted the individual (conceived not in terms of a sensed proper-named person, but as an entity variable) in place of the family as the basic unit of the legal system. Thus a right in rem, as explained by Professor Northrop, is a right and duty relationship between two variables where the holder of the right is made determinate and the holder of the duty is universally quantified.[38] To say that a specific person A owns object X is to say that A has a right against "universal" man, or man conceived as a universally quantified variable for whom anyone in the legal system may be substituted, and thus, if A has a right in rem against any one person in the legal system, he has the same right against anyone else.

As the division of legal relations into those in rem and those in personam is fundamental to Western contractual legal science, and since whenever there is a basic change in substantive law a change in procedure is usually necessitated, it is possible to find the approximate period when this science was created by ascertaining the date when Roman procedure was changed to reflect the differences between rights in rem and rights in personam. The form of Roman procedure before the creation of contractual legal science was the *legis actiones*, the earliest and most important of which was the *actio sacramenti*, wherein the parties would challenge each other to stake a wager as to the correctness of their claim, and the question tried was which of the two parties had been correct in their wager.[39] This same procedure could be and was used whether the action was to recover property, a debt, or for compensation.[40]

Under the formulary procedure of classical law, however, all actions were either in rem or in personam.[41] The crux of this procedure was the formula drawn up by the praetor, in which were stated the issues the judex was to decide. The two basic parts of the formula were the *intentio*, which set out the claim of the plaintiff, and the *condemnatio*, delegating to the judex power to condemn or acquit the defendant. The basic procedural difference between an action in rem and an action in personam is that in the former the defendant was not mentioned in the *intentio*, while in the latter he was. An example of an *intentio* in rem is as follows:

Titius be judge. Should it appear that the slave Stichus, about whom this action has been raised, belongs to A.A. in quiritary right,

The *condemnatio* would then follow:

then, unless the slave be restored, whatever be his value, in that, Judge, you will condemn N.N. to A.A.: should it not so appear, you will acquit him.[42]

Whereas the *intentio* of a formula in personam would read:

Titius be judge. Should it appear that N.N. ought to pay 50,000 sesterces to A.A., in that sum,

The *condemnatio* would then follow:

Judge, condemn N.N. to A.A.; should it not so appear, acquit him.[43]

In any action there are usually two questions to be answered: First, whether the plaintiff has the right claimed, and second, whether there has been a breach of that right. Usually the answer to one of these questions is self-evident, and the other forms the main basis of the dispute. If the dispute concerned the existence of a right in rem, then the action would be an action in rem, since the identity of the defendant was irrelevant to the answer to this question. In a property dispute, for instance, the basic issue was not whether the plaintiff had a better claim to the object than the defendant, but whether the plaintiff owned the object, that is had rights in rem concerning it; and the identity of the defendant was irrelevant to the answer to this question, since the duty rested upon anyone in the legal system. If the plaintiff did have such a right, the breach of it was self-evident because the property was usually in the possession of the defendant, who needed only to be mentioned in the *condemnatio*. If, however, the existence of the right in rem was self-evident such as in delictual actions, where if the right exists in the legal system anyone will have it, the basic issue set out in the *intentio* was whether there had been a breach of that right by the specific defendant, who therefore had to be named.

The formulary procedure was introduced into the *jus civile* by the *lex Aebutia*, which, according to Professor Girard, could not have been passed before 149 B.C., and evidences of which begin to appear abundantly during the time of Q. Mucius Scaevola.[44] Since the distinction between *actiones in rem* and *actiones in personam* was made by the time of Cicero, it can be said with a fair degree of certainty that contractual legal science was created in the period of the Scaevolas, which is the same period that, according to Professor Westrup, the concept of ownership first appears.[45]

A most significant reference is made by Aulus Gellius in regard to the *lex Aebutia*, where he records the statement of a lawyer that, "all the ancient lore of the Twelve Tables . . . was put to sleep by the Aebutian law."[46] The only explanation which gives meaning to this statement is that the *lex Aebutia*, by introducing a new flexible procedural system, made it possible for a new type of substantive law to replace the old law of the Twelve Tables.

The capacity of the classical Roman legal system to predict and control the transfer or creation of jural relations and to predicate transfer and creation on future contingent events appears to be the result of the adaptation of Stoic logic to the needs of the legal system. Professor Sambursky states that "the Stoic statement, which simply reads 'every time A is restored B must follow again,' is the first statement on causality on record which introduces the element of recurrence and the idea of reproducibility of a situation B from a situation A. This implies the possibility of the prediction of events. . . ."[47] This basic principle is found illustrated in the concept of title in contractual law. Title to a jural relation is the set of facts upon which the jural relation will come into existence or shift from one person to another. Thus the desired creation or shifting of a jural relation may be achieved through the creation or the production of the factual situation which is equivalent to title.

Stoic logic is also reflected in the presence of hypothetical or contingent and disjunctive propositions in Western legal systems. It is impossible under the early legal systems untouched by Roman law and in the early English legal system to make a gift which would not take effect until some period later than the actual conveyance. To jurists of these legal systems the gift was either given or it was not given; and, if given, then it was the property of the recipient. However, under Roman classical law it was possible for a testator to devise a gift to A if he reaches twenty-five, with the ownership not passing to A until that event, even if it did not occur until many years after the will came into effect through the death of the testator. The achievement of the ability to cause legal relations either to spring into being or shift upon the basis of some future contingency was in all probability the result of the use of the first and the fourth basic Stoic syllogisms propounded by Chrysippus, from which the more complex arguments are compounded.[48] Thus a gift to A if he reaches twenty-five can be justified through the use of the first Stoic form:

> If the first, then the second   (the conditional);
> The first   (its antecedent);
> Therefore, the second   (its consequent).

in the following manner:

> If A reaches twenty-five, then he succeeds to title;
> A reaches twenty-five;
> Therefore A succeeds to title.

the relation or *nexus* between the two parts of the conditional being the free will of the testator. E. Poste, in his commentary accompanying his translation of the *Institutes of Gaius*, recognized that the future passing of title was justified upon the basis of syllogistic logic, but he identified the condition as the middle terms of an Aristotelian syllogism with the title as the major premise and the person as the minor.[49] However, Aristotelian logic is a class logic with classes as variables rather than propositions, and when conditional propositions are substituted for the variables, you get nonsense unless you arrange them in the form of a Stoic syllogism.[50]

A devise such as "to A if he reaches twenty-five, but if he does not reach twenty-five, then to B" reflects the combined use of the first with the fourth basic Stoic form:

Either the first or the second   (disjunctive proposition);
The first   (one of the two disjuncts);
Therefore, not the second   (conclusion).

The devise thus becomes:

Either A will succeed to title or B will succeed;
If A reaches twenty-five, he will succeed;
A reaches twenty-five;
A therefore succeeds;
Therefore B does not succeed.

The first line is the disjunctive proposition of the fourth form, the second line is the conditional of the first form, the third line is the consequence of the first form as well as the disjunct of the fourth form, and the fifth line is the conclusion of the fourth form.

The Introduction of Concepts by Postulation into the Common Law

The historical process whereby the concepts by postulation of Western contractual legal science were introduced into the indigenous legal systems of Europe, resulting in the development of Continental civil law, is clearly recognized and therefore need not be dealt with in this paper. However, as there is some difference of opinion as to the degree to which these concepts have been adopted by the common law, the extent of the influence of Roman law on the English legal system must be examined.[51]

After the disintegration of the Roman Empire in the West, Roman law ceased to be studied in Europe and survived principally through custom. Due to a rediscovery of the *Digest*, which is a compilation of extracts from the writings of the classical jurists, an important revival of this study took place in Northern Italy during the twelfth and thirteenth centuries. Several universities were founded, the most important at Bologna, where scholars from all over Europe came to study law and from where professors were obtained to start the study in other European countries. From the school of Bologna, the Lombard jurist Vacarius was brought by Archbishop Theobald and his clerk, Thomas Becket, who had himself studied law there. Vacarius was appointed a professor at Oxford and was "the first teacher and the real founder of the study both of the civil and of the canon law" in England.[52] In the thirteenth century Roman law was introduced into Cambridge, and both Cambridge and Oxford taught only Roman law down to the seventeenth century.

During the same period Roman law was also brought to England through the medium of the canon law. Mention need only be made of some of the important chancellors and advisors of the kings, all of whom were ecclesiastics, such as Guala Bicchieri, Ricardus Anglicus, William of Drogheda who taught Roman law at Oxford, Henry of Susa, Franciscus Accursii, to show that the effects of canon law were not limited to ecclesiastical matters.

In regard to the strict common law itself in contrast to Equity, Admiralty, and the Ecclesiastical Courts, there can be no question but that the most important channel of Roman law was through the *Tractus de Legibus et Consuetudinibus Anglicanis* of Henry de Bracton (d. 1268), Chancellor of Exeter Cathedral and a justice of the King's Bench. Although Glanville, the principal legal advisor of Henry II, had written a short treatise on English law (in which the influence of Roman law is clear) Bracton's book was the first extensive scientific exposition of the common law, and no English jurist again attempted such a mammoth task until Sir Edward Coke. Although authorities are in conflict as to the amount of Roman law in Bracton's momentous work, the opinion of most scholars is that Bracton introduced the basic forms of Roman law and filled them with common law content;[53] and, where there were gaps in English law, such as in the area of contract, he borrowed extensively from the Roman law, which he obtained principally from the *Summa Institutionum* of Azo, one of the greatest teachers produced by the University of Bologna. Not only did Bracton quote extensively from this book, but according to Professor Güterbock: "Throughout nearly the whole of Bracton's book, we can distinctly trace the scientific influence of Azo's views and doctrines, especially in the definitions and divisions of legal notions and conceptions, which are generally clothed in Azo's words."[54] For the next hundred years the English lawyers "were steeped in Bracton," but during the fourteenth and fifteenth centuries his influence began to wane but was revived again to its highest peak during the sixteenth and seventeenth centuries.

From the middle of the twelfth century to the end of the reign of Edward I, during what has been termed "the Roman epoch of English legal history," the King's judges were mainly ecclesiastics, well trained in canon and Roman law; and Roman law was cited in the common-law courts as primary authority.[55] After this period, when only laymen were appointed to these courts and the education of the legal profession shifted from Oxford and Cambridge to the Inns of Court, a reaction against Roman law set in. It still, however, exercised a direct influence through the courts of equity, the chancellors of which up till the reign of Henry VIII were invariably high church dignitaries trained in civil and canon law, as well as through the admiralty, military, university, and ecclesiastical courts. This influence, nevertheless, was much more subtle than on the Continent. The English jurists, rather than superseding their earlier law with Roman law, adopted the basic premises and the fundamental imageless forms and adapted them to the needs of their legal system, rather than, as on the Continent, adopting both form and content.

Of the many streams through which Western contractual legal science entered English law, that through Bracton is probably the most important. Bracton clearly understood the Roman concept of legal obligation arising from contract rather than from the sensed biological factors of birth, as is evidenced in folios 4a and 4b of his *De Legibus Angliae* where he states that all men by nature are born free and that the legal obligations of serfdom or villeinage are not natural but are forced upon them by the legal systems;[56] and as is also evidenced by his quotation and application of the statement of Papinian that "Lex est . . . communis rei publicae sponsio" (law is the common agreement of the republic).[57] The influence of Bracton partially accounts for the early opposition of the legal profession to serfdom and the part its members played in wiping it out. The extent to which the contractual basis of legal obligation became accepted in English law is evident from the contractual nature of the great constitutional documents (such as Magna Carta, the Petition of Rights, the Bill of Rights, and the Act of Settlement), which have often been described as fundamental compacts or contracts between the crown and the people, and from such documents as the petition presented by the army to Parliament in 1648 asking that a general settlement of peace be "established in the nature of a general contract or Agreement of the people."[58]

Numerous examples of the imageless theoretical forms or concepts by postulation of Western contractual legal science may be found in Bracton. He clearly understood the nature of the *obligatio*, as is illustrated by his reiteration of the distinction drawn in classical Roman law between the naked pact and the imageless legal relation which the law would attach to such an agreement.[59] The Roman concept of ownership is implicit in his writings as is reflected by the distinction he often draws between proprietory and possessory rights,[60] a distinction which is impossible to draw unless ownership is conceived as rights in rem relating people in respect to things.[61] His understanding of the distinction between corporeal rights and the actual physical things which are the objects of the rights, and his comprehension of the use of conditional propositions in controlling the future movement of legal relations, indicates that he understood that contractual law contains many concepts which do not derive their meaning from the senses. It took the legal profession as a whole, however, several hundred years to rid themselves of their naive realism, or what Professor Maitland terms "materialism,"[62] and consequently many of these concepts in Bracton were understood and integrated only gradually into the legal system.

The existence of jural relations in rem, where either the holder of the right or the holder of the duty is conceived as a universally quantified variable, gives rise to two fundamental implications: (1) No law can be passed removing any right in rem from any particular individual or group of individuals without removing it from everyone in the legal system, including those who govern, and (2) those who govern are as equally bound by the duties in rem as is any private citizen. These two implications have given rise to the common-law doctrines of fundamental law or rights, and rule or government of law, and are inherent in Bracton's writing, as is illustrated by his statement made famous by Coke that the king is subject to and under the law.[63]

Although the fundamental postulates of a contractual legal system are in direct conflict to dictatorship and autocratic rule, the Romans were able partially to reconcile their legal theory with their governmental system through the fiction that by an implied contract the people confer upon the emperor all power and authority over them so that his will has the force of law.[64] While the Continent adopted Roman law in a more or less wholesale fashion, including this authoritarian element which was used by the European kings to justify their absolute power, England adopted only the formless, imageless relations and fundamental postulates which were used by the common-law lawyers of the late sixteenth and early seventeenth centuries, and in particular Sir Edward Coke, to limit the power of the monarchy. The great struggle between Parliament, led by Coke, and the Stuart kings, out of which came the famous Petition of Rights, was as to whether the king had the power to arbitrarily imprison persons without trial, and to take people's property without the consent of parliament, or, in other words, it was as to whether the Crown was under a similar duty to respect the rights of an individual in regard to his person and property as was everyone else in the legal system.

In attempting to convince the House of Lords of the lawfulness of the demands made in the Petition of Rights, Coke argued that legal relations, in order to be effective, had to be against everyone in the legal system without exception. He pointed out that if there were just one person in the legal system against whom one's rights did not run, an individual would be in no better position than the villein had been who had rights against everyone in the legal system except his lord.[65] At the time of Coke the law was clear, although often ignored, that the king had no legal power to deprive his subjects of their property without the consent of Parliament. Coke therefore argued that since one's rights in regard to one's property run against everyone in the legal system, his rights in regard to his person would equally do so.[66]

In order to understand Anglo-American democracy and representative government it must always be kept in mind that it is a product of the common law, and to a large extent has been created and administered by common-law lawyers, and is, therefore, based on the fundamental postulates and concepts by postulation of Western contractual law. A comparison of this type of democracy with that of the Greeks, where the concept of an individual having rights against the state was nonexistent,[67] and where equality was thought of only in terms of directly sensed data rather than the theoretical constructed manner of contractual law,[68] shows a striking difference due to the lack of these constructs in Greek political and legal systems.[69]

It is in the field of real property law, as has been shown by Professor Lawson, that the common law became the most logical and scientific, for not only did it adopt the constructs from classical Roman law, but it created new unique constructs which made it superior to that of either classical Roman or civil real property law.[70] The development of this field of law may be traced through four basic steps. The first was the introduction of concepts by postulation into the English legal system, principally through Bracton. The second step was the organizing of real property law into a logical science, clarifying and relating the concepts. This task was carried out in the main by Sir Thomas Littleton in his classic treatise known as *Littleton's Tenures*, which was described by Sir Edward Coke as "the most perfect and absolute work that ever was written in any human science."[71] The third step was the modification of the real property law to fit the newly emerging social order which was replacing feudalism. This was achieved by Sir Edward Coke, who, in his *First Institute of the Laws of England*, commonly known as *Coke Upon Littleton*, used each section of Littleton as a basis for commentary which not only brought Littleton's work up to date, but distilled into a single book the tremendous mass of legal material which had accumulated up to this time. Throughout this work, Coke relied heavily on Bracton, not only as a historical source, but to modernize the existing law, thus completing the last step of the integration into the English system of the concepts introduced by Bracton. The fourth step was the refining and clarifying of the constructs, thus transforming English real property law into an exact science which is so mathematical in its precision that it has often been compared to calculus. This was carried out during the eighteenth and nineteenth centuries by a small group of scholastic lawyers, principally Roman Catholics, who, due to their religion, were unable to practice before the bar and therefore became pure conveyancers, spending most of their time preparing complicated property settlements where, by the use of theoretical constructs, the creation and movement of legal relations could be predicted and controlled far

into the future.[72] Contrary to the usual practice of the common
law, the writings of these men have often been cited by the courts
as authoritative statements of the law in this field.

Analysis of the Principal Concepts
by Postulation of the Common Law

The common law, like all Western contractual legal systems,
consists of imageless jural relations or *obligationes* composed of
four parts, all of which are variables. These parts are: the two
units of the legal system related to each other, the object of the
relation or the thing in relation to which the units are related,
and the content of the relation. They may be symbolically expressed as follows:

$$\overset{\text{(object)}}{\underset{\substack{P \xleftarrow{\hspace{3cm}} P \\ \text{(unit)} \quad \text{(content)} \quad \text{(unit)}}}{\text{x}}}$$

The basic units of the legal system are either actual persons (made
determinate "in terms of imageless, formal, logical properties or
procedural rules rather than in terms of sensed qualities . . .")[73]
or are corporations. The corporation is in itself a legal concept by
postulation and is something entirely separate from the share-
holders, board of directors, or any other directly sensed thing. The
object of the relation may be as well either a directly sensed thing
or a concept by postulation such as, for instance, another jural
relation. The content of a jural relation is of a twofold nature.
Professor Hohfeld, in an analysis which is now standard in most
textbooks on jurisprudence, has divided jural relations, upon the
basis of difference in content, into the following four classes: right
—duty, privilege—no right, power—liability, immunity—disability.[74]

Jural relations can also be divided into those which are in rem
and those in personam. A relation in personam is one in which
both unit variables will be made determinate when filled with content, while those in rem are relations where either one or both
unit variables will be universally quantified. Jural relations in rem
are of three types, and, by using ( ) as the symbol of universal
quantification, may be symbolized thus:

$$\overset{x}{P \longleftarrow \hspace{-3pt}\longrightarrow (P)} \qquad \overset{x}{(P) \longleftarrow \hspace{-3pt}\longrightarrow P} \qquad \overset{x}{(P) \longleftarrow \hspace{-3pt}\longrightarrow (P)}$$

The first type is where the person in whom the relation is vested is related to a universally quantified variable. Such relations are mainly property relations where a determinate person has rights against anyone in the legal system in respect to x. The second type is where the relation is vested in everyone in the legal system, relating them to a determinate person. Examples of such relations are the rights anyone has against the state or specific officers of the state, such as the right to vote or to due process of law. The third type is where both units of the relation are universally quantified variables. The most important relations of this type are those which everyone has against everyone else in relation to their person. While jural relations in rem arise by operation of law, those in personam arise principally through the acts of individuals, either by contract or by committing a breach of a relation in rem, resulting in a secondary right in personam entitling the person in whom it is vested to damages.

Through combining basic jural relations, the legal system is able to create various kinds of compound relations or concepts. Where two units are related by a number of single jural relations, the content of the compound relation may be symbolized thus: $\longleftarrow \hspace{-3pt}\longrightarrow$. One of the most common types of compound relations is the contract, where the two parties are usually bound together by a number of individual relations, and would be symbolized in this manner: $P \longleftarrow \hspace{-3pt}\longrightarrow P$. Both Roman and civil law have a number of contractual forms to work with, while the common law has only one. On the other hand, while the Roman and civil law have few property concepts, the common law has many.

One of the most exceptional and useful concepts developed by the common law is that of the estate, whereby the object of the property relationship is not a sensed thing, but a theoretical construct created by conceiving legal relations on a linear plane of time reaching into infinity and then dividing them into parts of varying time lengths, all of which can be presently owned. If we use the symbol $\Longleftarrow \hspace{-3pt}\Longrightarrow$ to represent a group of jural relations conceived on the plane of time, the jural relations constituting ownership of x would be as follows:

$$P \xmapsfrom{\quad x \quad} (P)$$
$$P \xrightarrow{\hspace{4cm}} (P)$$

An owner, through creating various kinds of estates in his property and through the use of conditional and disjunctive propositions, may control the movement of jural relations in regard to his property from one person to another over a lengthy period of time.

Another important concept, unique to the common law, is that of the trust which a property owner may create by conveying rights of control to a trustee and rights of enjoyment to the cestui que trust, thus creating two parallel ownerships with different content, plus relations in personam binding the trustee and cestui que trust. The relationship can be symbolized as follows:

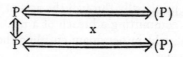

Mention has been made of only a few of the many concepts by postulation in the common law. The civil law contains some concepts which are similar to a number of those mentioned above and many which are different. Such concepts have played an important part in the development of the highly technical, scientific, industrial, and commercial societies of the West by making it possible to predict and control man's relationships with each other in ways impossible under a noncontractual legal system; and it is their presence in Western law which has made it a science.

FOOTNOTE REFERENCES

1. Northrop, F. S. C., "The Comparative Philosophy of Comparative Law," *Cornell Law Quarterly*, vol. XLV, 1960, pp. 617–658; Pringsheim, F., "The Unique Character of Classical Roman Law," *Journal of Roman Studies*, vol. 34, 1944, pp. 60–64.
2. Westrup, C. W., *Introduction to Early Roman Law*, vol. II, *Joint Family and Family Property*, Oxford, London, 1934, pp. 160–172; Beaglehole, Ernest, *Property: A Study in Social Psychology*, Macmillan, New York, 1932, p. 134; Seagle, William, *The History of Law*, Tudor, New York, 1946, p. 51; Hobhouse,

L. T., "Development of the Idea of Property," in Albert Kocourek, and John H. Wigmore (compilers), *Primitive and Ancient Legal Institutions*, Little, Brown, Boston, vol. 2, 1915, pp. 372–380.

3. Westrup, C. W., *op. cit.*, note 2.

4. Fustel de Coulanges, Numa Denis, *The Ancient City, A Study on the Religions, Laws, and Institutions of Greece and Rome*, Doubleday, Garden City, New York, 1956, pp. 60–72.

5. Noyes, C. Reinhold, *The Institution of Property*, Longmans, New York, 1936, p. 51; Morey, William C., *Outlines of Roman Law* (2nd ed.), Putnam's, New York, 1914, p. 281.

6. Vinogradoff, Paul, *Outlines of Historical Jurisprudence*, Oxford, London, vol. 2, 1922, p. 198.

7. Joüon de Longrais, F., *La Conception Anglaise de la Saisine du XIIe au XIVe Siècle*, Jouve, Paris, 1924; Maitland, F. W., *The Collected Papers of F. W. Maitland*, H. A. L. Fisher (ed.), Cambridge, London, vol. I, 1911, pp. 329–384 and 407–457; Van Caenegem, R. C., *Royal Writs in England from the Conquest to Glanville*, Selden Society, vol. 77, B. Quaritch, London, 1959, pp. 306–316; Pollock, Frederick, and F. W. Maitland, *The History of English Law*, Cambridge, London, vol. 2, 1952, pp. 1–183; Holdsworth, William, *A History of English Law* (5th ed.), Methuen, London, vol. 3, 1923, pp. 88–101, 351–360.

8. Ames, J. B., "Disseisin of Chattels," *Harvard Law Review*, vol. 3, 1889–1890, p. 24.

9. Laughlin, J. Laurence, "The Anglo-Saxon Legal Procedure," in *Essays in Anglo-Saxon Law*, Little, Brown, Boston and London, 1876, p. 206; Pollock, Frederick, and F. W. Maitland, *The History of English Law*, *op. cit.*, note 7, p. 157; Henry G. Richardson, and G. O. Sayles (eds.), *Select Cases of Procedure Without Writ under Henry III*, Curia Regis Roll no. 131, Selden Society, vol. 60, 1941, B. Quaritch, London, pp. 24–25.

10. Edwards, Chilperic (ed.), *The World's Earliest Laws*, Code of Hammurabi, Watts, London, 1934, sections 9–13, p. 17; Godfrey R. Driver, and John C. Miles (eds.), *The Babylonian Laws*, Clarendon, Oxford, 1952, pp. 95–105; Plato, *Laws* 11; Laughlin, J. Laurence, "The Anglo-Saxon Legal Procedure," *op. cit.*, note 9, p. 206; Kocourek, Albert, and John H. Wigmore, *Sources of Ancient and Primitive Law*, Little, Brown, Boston, vol. 1, 1915, "Laws of Howel Dda," pp. 542–543.

11. Van Caenegem, R. C., *Royal Writs in England from the Conquest to Glanville*, *op. cit.*, note 7, pp. 283–290.

12. Gaius, 4. 17; Polybius 12. 16; Pollock, Frederick, and F. W. Maitland, *The History of English Law*, *op. cit.*, note 7, p. 38.

The Court could, however, award temporary possession to one of
the disputants after taking sureties.

13. Diamond, Arthur S., *Primitive Law* (2nd ed.), Watts, London,
    1950, p. 392.
14. Jolowitz, H. F., *Historical Introduction to the Study of Roman
    Law*, Cambridge, London, 1932, p. 164; Corbin, Arthur L., "Offer
    and Acceptance, and Some of the Resulting Legal Relations,"
    Yale Law Journal, vol. 26, 1917, p. 171.
15. Jolowitz, H. F., *Historical Introduction to the Study of Roman
    Law*, op. cit., note 14, pp. 162 and 165; Paton, George W., *A
    Text-Book of Jurisprudence* (2nd ed.), Clarendon, Oxford, 1951,
    p. 37; Seagle, William, *The History of Law*, op. cit., note 2, p.
    252.
16. Jones, John W., *Law and Legal Theory of the Greeks*, Clarendon,
    Oxford, 1956, p. 228.
17. Seagle, William, *The History of Law*, op. cit., note 2, p. 256.
18. Jones, John W., *Law and Legal Theory of the Greeks*, op. cit.,
    note 6, pp. 151 and 217.
19. Quoted in Schulz, Fritz, *Principles of Roman Law*, Clarendon,
    Oxford, 1936, p. 36.
20. Arnold, E. Vernon, *Roman Stoicism*, Cambridge, London, 1911,
    p. 384; Schulz, Fritz, *History of Roman Legal Science*, Clarendon,
    Oxford, 1946, pp. 62–63, 81; Jolowitz, H. F., *Historical Introduc-
    tion to the Study of Roman Law*, op. cit., note 14, p. 90; Wolff,
    Hans J., *Roman Law*, Oklahoma, Norman, 1951, p. 100.
21. Schulz, Fritz, *History of Roman Legal Science*, op. cit., note 20,
    p. 62.
22. *Ibid.*, p. 95.
23. Maine, Sir Henry S., *Ancient Law*, Murray, London, 1912, p. 174.
24. Northrop, F. S. C., "The Comparative Philosophy of Compara-
    tive Law," op. cit., note 1, p. 617.
25. Northrop, F. S. C., *Philosophical Anthropology and Practical
    Politics*, Macmillan, New York, 1960, pp. 31–32.
26. Northrop, F. S. C., *The Complexity of Legal and Ethical Ex-
    perience*, Little, Brown, Boston, 1959, p. 207.
27. Justinian *Institutes* 3. 13. 1.
28. McIlwain, Charles H., *Constitutionalism, Ancient and Modern*
    (rev. ed.), Cornell, Ithaca, New York, 1947, p. 50.
29. *Digest*, 5. 1. 20.
30. Berger, Adolf, *Encyclopedic Dictionary of Roman Law*, American
    Philosophical Society, Philadelphia, 1953, p. 413.
31. *Digest*, 1. 3. 1.
32. *Digest*, 2. 15. 14; D. 1. 7. 34; D. 2. 14. 7; Gaius, 3. 145.

33. Acton, John E. E. D., *The History of Freedom and Other Essays*, Macmillan, London, 1922, p. 24.
34. Northrop, F. S. C., "The Comparative Philosophy of Comparative Law," *op. cit.*, note 1, p. 656.
35. Justinian *Institutes* 4. 6. 13.
36. *Digest*, 4. 2. 9; D. 44. 4. 2.
37. Hohfeld, Wesley N., *Fundamental Legal Conceptions*, Yale, New Haven, 1923, p. 72.
38. Northrop, F. S. C., "The Comparative Philosophy of Comparative Law," *op. cit.*, note 1, pp. 649–650.
39. Laws of the Twelve Tables, Tab. 1. 1, 2; Gaius, 4. 13–17; Sohm, Rudolph, *The Institutes of Roman Law* (3rd ed.), Oxford, London, 1907, p. 230.
40. Gaius, 4. 15, 16.
41. Justinian *Institutes* 4. 6. 1.
42. Muirhead, James, *Historical Introduction to the Private Law of Rome* (3rd ed.), A. & C. Black, London, 1916, p. 327.
43. *Ibid.*, p. 325.
44. Girard, Paul F., *Mélanges de Droit Romain*, Recueil Sirey, Paris, 1912, pp. 67–174.
45. Westrup, C. W., *Joint Family and Family Property*, *op. cit.*, note 2, pp. 160–161.
46. Gellius, Aulus, *The Attic Nights of Aulus Gellius*, III, 16. x. 1–6.
47. Sambursky, S., *Physics of the Stoics*, Routledge, London, 1959, p. 54.
48. Mates, Benson, *Stoic Logic*, California, Berkeley, 1961, pp. 67–74.
49. Poste, Edward (ed. and trans.), *Gai Institvtiones; or, Institutes of Roman Law by Gaius* (4th ed.), Clarendon, Oxford, 1904, p. 342.
50. Mates, Benson, *Stoic Logic*, *op. cit.*, note 48, pp. 2–3.
51. See generally: Sherman, Charles P., *Roman Law in the Modern World*, Baker, Voorhis, New York, vol. I, 1937; Vinogradoff, Paul, *Roman Law in Medieval Europe* (2nd ed.), Clarendon, Oxford, 1929, pp. 97–118; Scrutton, Thomas E., *The Influence of the Roman Law on the Law of England*, Cambridge, London, 1885; Holdsworth, William, *A History of English Law* (4th ed.), Methuen, London, vol. 2, 1936, pp. 133–149, 176–178, 202–206; Pollock, Frederick, and F. W. Maitland, *The History of English Law*, Cambridge, London, vols. I and II, 1952, pp. 111–135; Spence, George, *The Equitable Jurisdiction of the Court of Chancery*, Lea & Blanchard, Philadelphia, vols. I and II, 1846–1850.

52. Holdsworth, William, *A History of English Law*, op. cit., note 7, p. 147.
53. For this problem, see generally: Güterbock, Carl E., *Bracton and His Relation to the Roman Law*, Lippincott, Philadelphia, 1866; F. W. Maitland (ed.), *Select Passages from the Works of Bracton and Azo*, Selden Society, vol. 8, B. Quaritch, London, 1895; Plucknett, T. F. T., *Early English Legal Literature*, Cambridge, London, 1958, pp. 42–79; Kantorowicz, Herman, *Bractonian Problems*, Jackson, Glasgow, 1941; Vinogradoff, Paul, *Roman Law in Medieval Europe*, op. cit., note 51, pp. 101–118; Woodbine, George E., "The Roman Element in Bracton's De Adquirendo Rerum Dominio," *Yale Law Journal*, vol. 31, 1921–1922, p. 827; Holdsworth, William, *A History of English Law*, op. cit., note 51, pp. 267–286.
54. Güterbock, Carl E., *Bracton and His Relation to the Roman Law*, op. cit., note 53, p. 52. See also Maitland, F. W., *Bracton's Note Book*, Cambridge, London, vol. I, 1887, p. 9.
55. Sherman, Charles P., *Roman Law in the Modern World*, op. cit., note 51, p. 360.
56. Bracton, Henry de, *De Legibus Angliae*, f. 46. See also f. 4.
57. *Ibid.*, f. 2a.
58. Cobbett, William (ed.), *Parliamentary History*, Bagshaw, London, vol. 3, 1808, p. 1263.
59. Bracton, Henry de, *De Legibus Angliae*, op. cit., note 56, ff. 99–100b.
60. *Ibid.*, f. 3.
61. Van Caenegen, R. C., *Royal Writs in England from the Conquest to Glanville*, op. cit., note 7, pp. 306–316.
62. Maitland, F. W., *Collected Papers*, op. cit., note 7, pp. 372–373.
63. Bracton, Henry de, *De Legibus Angliae*, op. cit., note 56, f. 5b. See also f. 34.
64. Justinian *Institutes* 1. 2. 6. See also McIlwain, Charles H., *Constitutionalism, Ancient and Modern*, op. cit., note 28.
65. Howell, Thomas B. (ed.), *A Complete Collection of State Trials and Proceedings*, Longman, Hurst, Rees, Orme & Brown, London, vol. 3, 1816, pp. 128–129.
66. *Ibid.*, pp. 78, 130, and 132.
67. Fustel de Coulanges, Numa Denis, *The Ancient City*, op. cit., note 4, p. 223.
68. Aristotle, *Politics* iii, 13 and vi, 2.
69. Aristotle, *Politics*; Plato, *Republic*.
70. Lawson, F. H., *Introduction to the Law of Property*, Clarendon,

Oxford, 1958, and *The Rational Strength of English Law*, Stevens, London, 1951.
71. Hargrave, Francis, and Charles Butler (eds.), *Coke Upon Littleton*, Small, Philadelphia, vol. I, 1853, p. xxxvi.
72. Pollock, F., "Holdsworth's *History of English Law* by W. S. Holdsworth, vols. VII and VIII," *Journal of the Society of Public Teachers of Law*, 1926, p. 37; Lawson, F. H., *A Common Lawyer Looks at the Civil Law*, Michigan Law School, Ann Arbor, 1955, p. 69; Holdsworth, William, *History of the English Law* (2nd ed.), Methuen, London, vol. 7, 1937, p. 384.
73. Northrop, F. S. C., "The Comparative Philosophy of Comparative Law," *op. cit.*, note 1, p. 650.
74. Hohfeld, Wesley N., *Fundamental Legal Conceptions, op. cit.*, note 37, p. 36.

BIBLIOGRAPHY

Noncontractual Legal Systems

Aristotle, *Politics*.
Attenborough, Frederick L., *The Laws of the Earliest English Kings*, Cambridge, London, 1922.
Beaglehold, Ernest, *Property: A Study in Social Psychology*, Macmillan, New York, 1932.
Bonner, Robert J., *Lawyers and Litigants in Ancient Athens*, University of Chicago, Chicago, 1927.
Bonner, Robert J., and Gertrude Smith, *The Administration of Justice from Homer to Aristotle*, University of Chicago, Chicago, 1938, vols. I and II.
Diamond, Arthur S., *Primitive Law* (2nd ed.), Watts, London, 1950.
Driver, Godfrey R., and John C. Miles (eds.), *The Babylonian Laws*, Clarendon, Oxford, 1952.
Fustel de Coulanges, Numa Denis, *The Ancient City*, Doubleday, Garden City, New York, 1956.
Jones, John W., *Law and Legal Theory of the Greeks*, Clarendon, Oxford, 1956.
Jolowitz, H. F., *Historical Introduction to the Study of Roman Law*, Cambridge, London, 1939.
Kocourek, Albert, and John H. Wigmore, *Sources of Ancient and Primitive Law*, Little, Brown, Boston, 1915.

Kocourek, Albert, and John H. Wigmore, *Primitive and Ancient Legal Institutions*, Little, Brown, Boston, 1915.

Laughlin, James L., in *Essays in Anglo-Saxon Law*, Little, Brown, Boston, 1876.

Maine, Henry, *Ancient Law*, Murray, London, 1912.

Noyes, C. Reinhold, *The Institution of Property*, Longmans, New York, 1936. (Courtesy David McKay Co.)

Plato, *Laws*.

Plato, *Republic*.

Seagle, William, *The History of Law*, Tudor, New York, 1946.

Vinogradoff, Paul, *Outlines of Historical Jurisprudence*, Oxford, London, vols. I and II, 1920–1922.

Westrup, C. W., *Introduction to Early Roman Law*, Oxford, London, vols. I–V, varying dates, 1934–1954.

Western Contractual Legal Systems

Bracton, Henry de, *Tractus de Legibus et Consuetudinibus Angliae*, G. E. Woodbine (ed.), Yale, New Haven, 1940.

Buckland, W. W., and Arnold D. McNair, *Roman Law & Common Law* (2nd ed.), Cambridge, London, 1952.

Coke, Edward, *The First Part of the Institutes of the Laws of England*, Small, Philadelphia, 1853, parts I to IV.

Corpus Iuris Civilis, Samuel Parsons Scott (trans.), Central Trust Co., Cincinnati, Ohio, 1932.

Fearne, Charles, *An Essay on the Learning of Contingent Remainders and Executory Devises* (7th ed.), Butterworth, London, 1820.

Poste, Edward (ed. and trans.), *Gai Institvtiones; or, Institutes of Roman Law by Gaius*, Clarendon, Oxford, 1904.

Gulliver, Ashbel G., *Cases and Materials on the Law of Future Interests*, West, St. Paul, Minn., 1959.

Güterbock, Carl E., *Bracton and His Relation to the Roman Law*, Lippincott, Philadelphia, 1866.

Hart, H. L. A., *Definition and Theory in Jurisprudence*, Clarendon, Oxford, 1953.

Hohfeld, Wesley N., *Fundamental Legal Conceptions*, Yale, New Haven, 1923.

Holdsworth, W. S., *A History of English Law*, Methuen, London, 1923.

Jolowicz, H. F., *Historical Introduction to the Study of Roman Law*, Cambridge, London, 1939.

Jolowicz, H. F., *Roman Foundations of Modern Law*, Clarendon, Oxford, 1957.

Kocourek, Albert, *Jural Relations* (2nd ed.), Bobbs-Merrill, Indianapolis, 1928.

Lawson, F. H., *Introduction to the Law of Property*, Clarendon, Oxford, 1958.

Lawson, F. H., *The Rational Strength of English Law*, Stevens, London, 1951.

Lawson, F. H., *A Common Lawyer Looks at the Civil Law*, University of Michigan Law School, Ann Arbor, 1955.

McIlwain, Charles H., *Constitutionalism, Ancient and Modern* (rev. ed.), Cornell, Ithaca, New York, 1947.

Maitland, F. W. (ed.), *Select Passages from the Works of Bracton and Azo*, Selden Society, vol. 8, B. Quaritch, London, 1895.

Maitland, F. W., *The Collected Papers of F. W. Maitland*, H. A. L. Fisher (ed.), Cambridge, London, vol. I, 1911.

Northrop, F. S. C., *The Logic of the Sciences and the Humanities*, Meridian, New York, 1959.

Northrop, F. S. C., *The Complexity of Legal and Ethical Experience*, Little, Brown, Boston, 1959.

Northrop, F. S. C., *Philosophical Anthropology and Practical Politics*, Macmillan, New York, 1960.

Pollock, Frederick, and F. W. Maitland, *The History of English Law*, vols. I and II, Cambridge, London, 1952.

Schulz, Fritz, *History of Roman Legal Science*, Clarendon, Oxford, 1946.

Schulz, Fritz, *Principles of Roman Law*, Clarendon, Oxford, 1936.

Schulz, Fritz, *Classical Roman Law*, Clarendon, Oxford, 1951.

Van Caenegem, R. C., *Royal Writs in England from the Conquest to Glanville*, Selden Society, vol. 77, B. Quaritch, London, 1959.

Wambaugh, Eugene (ed.), *Littleton's Tenures*, Bryne, Washington, D.C., 1903.

Status and Contract
in Primitive Law E. ADAMSON HOEBEL

16

This paper undertakes to deal with the significance of Sir Henry Maine's distinction between the Law of Status, as a characterization of ancient and primitive societies, and the Law of Contract, as a characteristic of later Roman law and of those social systems which have been strongly influenced by it. Circumstance has forced a delay in the preparation of this paper and has given me the advantage of access to the contributions of other authors in this volume. As a consequence, the substance and argument of this paper reflect, in considerable degree, response to the stimulus of other papers closely related to the topics on which I write (notably, those of Professors Northrop and Smith).

It is wholly true, as Professor Northrop has specified, that cultural anthropology is still largely in the natural history stage of scientific development and that even the work of those of us who have moved in the direction of formulation of postulational sets of given cultures "is not to be confused with the achievement of a cultural anthropology that has arrived at the stage of logically realistic, deductively formulated theory."[1] Anthropologists, especially the British and American, were, throughout the first half of this century, naively and even callowly proud of their radical empiricism and naive realism as supposed hallmarks of genuine scientific objectivity. They spurned the "speculative" deductive theoretical formulations of earlier generations of culture historians

284

and anthropologists as empirically unsound and quite without worth.

However, it is one thing for anthropologists to insist that their discipline must be founded upon observed data derived from real societies scientifically observed and something less than justifiable to insist that theory is baneful, or, as Kluckhohn reported the mental state of American anthropologists in 1939, "to suggest that something is 'theoretical' is to suggest that it is slightly indecent."[2] Fortunately, such intellectual infantilism has at long last been outgrown, but its inhibiting effects have indeed retarded the scientific maturation of cultural anthropology and are responsible for the condition which Professor Northrop rightly asserts needs correcting. Most anthropologists of today, I believe I am right in reporting, will accept Professor Northrop's injunction "that to shift one's epistemology and science from a naive realistic to a logically realistic theory of knowledge and scientific method is as important for the humanities and cultural sciences as it is for the natural sciences."[3]

In the development of a scientific theory of culture, it is still, as always, important that the theory be built of theoretical possibles within the rubrics of which the data of radically empirical findings may properly be ordered, if our goal is to achieve operationally based findings upon which to effect, according to our goals, more satisfactory cultural systems. This is the thesis, in contrast to that of Hans Kelsen, advanced by Professor Northrop. It is, as we see it, the approach of greatest potential usefulness, for as demonstrated by the contributions of several of the other conference participants, it is the method of productive science that has distinguished the Greco-Roman-Occidental epistemological traditions. The Kelsenian "pure science" of logical positivism produces a system of theoretical possibles "without social content or significance . . . without flesh, blood or bowels."[4] We are seeking a theory of culture that transcends naive realism without total abandonment of the "radically empirically known and relativistic data."[5]

One reason we are still bumbling and fumbling in the development of anthropological theory is that we have not successfully developed adequate taxonomic systems for the classification of societal types. And, failing this, we are unable to go beyond piecemeal formulations of significant abstractions. We have not yet been able sufficiently to order our exceedingly rich and complex data in manageable meaningful categories from which we may generate the intellective formulations that will stimulate the creative birth of an all-embracing deductively formulated theory based upon the minimal set of theoretical possibles. Professor Northrop notes that my own recent comparative study of primitive law systems made use of a deductive method to state natural history descriptive findings re the normative legal statics of a group of primitive societies.[6] But an anthropological colleague wrote of the same work that "it lacks a central thesis, or rather . . . it contains so many different theses that no one of them remains central."[7] In other words, while we are able to achieve some measure of success with variegated hypotheses of probable validity, we fall short of a capacity to shape a deductive minimal set theory for our area of interest.

It seems to me, however, that anthropology must enjoy a natural growth through painstaking development of meticulously tested middle-level generalizations (even though based upon relatively inchoate theories) before its practitioners will possess adequate materials on the basis of which they can move into maturation of effective, deductively formulated theory. The great leap can be made only with solid underfooting.

The argument that has been made for the crucial role of the Greek invention of a *systematic* mode of logically realistic thought, its utilization in the development of Western science, and, through the Roman Stoics, in the shaping of Western law is impressive. Its implications for future development of the science of culture and a universal world culture are equally so.

The discussion that now follows is intended only as refinement of the historical analysis of the case for the thesis under consideration, not as contrary argument. Here enters Sir Henry Maine. Both Professors Northrop and Smith rest their discussions solidly upon Maine's formula "that the movement of the progressive societies has hitherto been a movement *from Status to Contract*"[8] in which, "Starting, as from one terminus of history, from a condition of society in which all the relations of Persons are summed up in the relations of Family, we seem to have steadily moved towards a phase of social order in which all these relations arise from the free agreement of individuals."[9] Professor Northrop rightly interprets Maine's concept of Status as meaning "the specific sense of being determined by naive realistically conceived, natural history biological properties fixed by one's genealogical table at one's birth" with the result that "a person's rights and duties are determined at birth by his naively realistically sensed sex, primogeniture, or lack of it, of birth, and color of skin racial ancestry of breeding in the ancestral joint family and in the tribe";[10] and Contract (in Maine's sense) means "what the Stoics called 'cosmopolitan man' . . . [whereby] the moral and legal person is . . . the logically realistic *any one* . . . individual."[11] Maine's formula is phrased as a very broad generalization which more recent anthropological research confirms in the large. Professor Smith, however, in his paper, and Professor Northrop, to a lesser degree, seem to read into it an "all-or-none" quality which it is improbable that Maine intended or anthropological data justify. Legal and moral relationships are presented as being *exclusively* either Status (kin and biologically based) or Contract (ideationally based on theoretically created rights and duties). Professor Northrop's Chapter 12 shows that Asian societies developed under the Great Traditions of Confucian, Buddhist, and Hindu thought and moved from Status to the procedural device of mediation, rather than to Contract.[12] In concert with Professor Smith, he sees the movement toward contract as the product of Roman Stoic thought; Professor Smith even more explicitly denies the historical existence of the abstract intellective concept necessary to Contract-type law and morality in all systems "unaffected by Roman law."[13] "Comparison," he writes further on, "therefore shows that the unique element in Western contractual legal science is the imageless jural relations which probably exist in no other systems except as they have been influenced by Western contractual law."[14] The base of comparison upon which such a statement rests is much too narrow to have full empirical validity. It continues the scholarly method of Maine without regard to what has been learned about a wide gamut of primitive societies in the hundred years of natural history anthropology that have followed Maine. Significant as Maine's work remains to this day, it was even in its time lamentably parochial, for as Redfield has written

he thought that the early Graeco-Roman and early Hindu materials were more representative of human societies than they are. . . . Maine asked materials on Rome and Greece to tell him what the first social condition of mankind was, and we now know that the materials are not of a sort that would answer that question.

The reader of the book [*Ancient Law*] will not find a single reference to any non-literate people surviving into modern times. . . . In short, Maine has nothing to say, in any particular, about custom and law in non-literate, tribal or subtribal communities. . . . The chapters on the development of contracts and of criminal law are based almost entirely on Roman history.[15]

Redfield's stricture is also almost perfectly appropriate to Diamond's *Primitive Law*. Authoritative as is Diamond's work with reference to archaic and medieval codes, he shows little interest in contemporary legal studies of tribal law and in his volume cites only sixteen older ethnographies of primitive cultures.

To follow Maine too closely can lead to misleading conclusions, for again anthropologists will agree with Redfield's observation:

A comparison of the general conclusions Maine reached regarding law and custom in European and Asiatic Indian societies with the law and custom that we now know to characterize non-European primitive peoples, while acknowledging the worth, for the comparative student of society, of some of Maine's more fruitful findings, will point out cases in which Maine's conceptions of ancient law are quite inapplicable to the actual primitive societies that we know today and which are, in certain respects, inapplicable to any human society.[16]

The major misconceptions are: (1) the assumed prior universality of patriarchal, patrilineal social organization with corporate submergence of all individual members with the whole; (2) an unawareness of the widespread existence of nonkinship intratribal groupings (such as men's clubs, or fraternities) many of which are free associations so far as membership is concerned; (3) the assumed universality of *themistes* and their priority over custom; (4) a failure to appreciate the extent of criminal law in many primitive systems, the very kind of law which most readily engenders the concept of universal obligation; and (5) the actual, even if sporadic, occurrence of free contract in primitive systems.

(1) Maine's first assumption inflates the relative importance of Status as it shapes the conception of Legal Man in non-Western and archaic societies. Modern research shows that unilineal descent groups are indeed the central unit of social structure in many types of societies. The most recent and extensive comparative

analysis by a highly competent scholar (Professor David F. Aberle) shows that more than one third (36 percent) of the selected sample in Murdock's "World Ethnographic Survey"[17] of 564 societies are bilateral, lacking either matrilineal or patrilineal kinship groups. Forty-four percent are patrilineal, 15 percent matrilineal, and 5 percent duolineal.[18]

Very few contemporary anthropologists utilize the concepts patriarchal or matriarchal because anything approximating the *patria potestas*, on the one hand, or "rule by women," on the other, is so rare as to be exceptional, and where these do exist, they are independent variables not to be confused with the more common descent groups utilizing one unilineal principle or the other. This point, while of great ethnological significance, is not of critical importance for our major concern here, except as it signifies (along with the actual natural histories of many social systems) that Family is not so persistently structured as Maine had it, especially not patriarchally.

(2) R. H. Lowie first demonstrated in 1927 the great significance of men's associations (military societies) in the legal culture of North American Plains Indians.[19] Llewellyn and Hoebel,[20] Richardson,[21] and Province[22] subsequently specified it in behavioral detail with materials that show that individual behavior measured against universal norms rather than kinship status were the determinant factors in all matters affected by the military societies. Data from a number of African and Melanesian societies reveal similar phenomena.

(3) On the priority of capricious *themistes* over custom, held by Maine, it is sufficient to give accord to Redfield's statement without further comment: "A society in which there is no custom, and in which conflicts are solved or wrongs are punished solely by individual pronouncements that have no reference to general principle is, to put it plainly, unthinkable to a modern student."[23]

(4) The issue of Maine's failure to appreciate the *extent* of criminal law in many primitive systems brings us back to the heart of our problem, and so requires somewhat more extensive discussion.

Maine's position was summed up thus:

Now the penal Law of ancient communities is not the law of Crimes; it is the law of Wrongs, or, to use the English technical word, of Torts. . . .

If therefore the criterion of a *delict*, wrong, or *tort* be that the person who suffers it, and not the State, is conceived to be wronged, it may be asserted that in the infancy of jurisprudence the citizen depends for protection against violence or fraud not on the Law of Crime but on the Law of Tort.[24]

Herein is set forth the second of Maine's great positive formulations, closely related to the doctrine of priority of Status over Contract. Its emphasis is upon process and less upon structure than is his more famous First Principle, although, obviously enough, processes do not operate divorced from structures. But it is through procedure alone that we are able to discern whether an offense is conceived by the people concerned as a private injury (primarily) or a delict against the *societas per se*. I qualified "private injury" with a parenthetical "primarily," because where legal norms are regularized, the injured-man-qua-prosecutor is vested with the privilege-right of enforcing the law, and, as has been demonstrated for a number of primitive societies, he (and his kin group) receive indirect and, in some systems, direct support from the remainder of the population. The private prosecutor remains the representative of the general social interest as well as his own.

Explicit crimes are directly identifiable when a designated agent (individual or group), not itself directly injured by the act, moves in the name of the society to apply legal sanctions. Thus, even for the lowly Australian aborigines, as Hart writes, ". . . the literature, for example, is full of evidence that crimes (as distinct from torts) are punished by individuals acting as representatives of the community in that their acts override kinship loyalties and ignore kinship ties."[25]

Most criminal law by its very nature is built upon the concept of the moral and legal person as "the logically realistic any one individual," as Professor Northrop has so aptly put it. The criminal is one who attempts to put himself outside the universality of the logically realistic construct.

Space does not allow of detailed demonstration, but one or two cases may be indicated. The Cheyenne Indians had a universal rule imposing an obligation on every member of the tribe to refrain from individual hunting during the time of the communal hunt. It was physically enforced by the military society in charge of the hunt of the season. One extreme individualist, Sticks Everything Under His Belt, publicly announced the rule would not apply to him. All the civil and military chiefs convened to consider the situation. In the words of a well-informed Cheyenne, "This was the ruling they made: *no one* could help Sticks Everything Under His Belt in any way, *no one* could give him smoke, *no one* could talk to him. . . . The chiefs declared that if *anyone* helped him in any way that person would have to give a Sun Dance."[26] In due time, the culprit's brother-in-law formally announced he was putting on a great Sun Dance as a means of settling the situation through which the outcast could be reinstated within the system.

Inasmuch as Professor Northrop has demonstrated that

No radical empirical or naive realistic theory of the meaning of ethical and legal language can answer the question of how one passes from the legal obligation of the majority to be judged by the statutes which they approve to the legal obligation of everyone else to be so judged. Only a logically realistic theory in which to be an individual citizen means to instance the formal properties of a logically realistic relation . . . that is universally quantified tautologically can do so.[27]

We must conclude that these primitive people are thinking not in terms of Status but of Contract.*

To reinforce the point, one further instance may be cited. Among Plains Indians favorite horses were, indeed, privately possessed and conceived as extensions of the owner's personality. *Friends* could borrow horses. It was a Status relationship. Among the Cheyennes, *A* borrowed *B*'s horse, in *B*'s absence, leaving his personal bow and arrow in evidence and security. He did not return with the horse. *B* appealed to his military society for procedural guidance, saying, "I want you to tell me the right thing." The chiefs of the society settled the immediate issue to the satisfaction of all concerned. They then moved on, moreover, to shift

* In the discussion of this inference by Professor Hoebel, Professor Northrop referred to Peano's Fifth Postulate for arithmetic to illustrate a logically realistic universal proposition, i.e., one that is not merely universally quantified, but also analytically and, therefore, tautologically so, as distinct from a naive realistic universal proposition in which the universal quantification is present but not tautologically so. Then, Professor Northrop suggested that the inferences Professor Hoebel draws (1) from the anthropological evidence of himself, Redfield, and Murdock with respect to Professor Smith's paper, and (2) from this quotation from Professor Northrop's paper, do not follow. The anthropological examples meet the first condition for the existence in a culture of a logically realistic legal rule, i.e., universal quantification, but not the second, namely, that the universal quantification follows analytically from the imageless formal properties of the relatedness of the terms. (Symposium Chairman's footnote.)

the legal obligation from a naive realistic to a logically realistic footing, pronouncing, "Now we shall make a new rule. There shall be no more borrowing of horses without asking. If any man takes another's goods without asking, we will go over and get them back for him. More than that, if the taker tries to keep them, we will give him a whipping."[28]

They had postulationally specified a "universally quantified logically realistic law R." A later Cheyenne case showed in action the manner in which the R related to the f^1 instance. A notoriously delinquent horse "borrower" was tracked down for three days, beaten, and stripped, and the horses returned to their owner by the members of a military society other than the one that had originally promulgated the rule.[29]

There are unnumbered primitive societies without criminal law. But it is manifestly evident that the number in which universal criminal law exists is greater. Within these latter, however, it is true that legal norms based upon Status qualities rather than Contract qualities are predominant. The relative dominance of the one with respect to the other is a highly variable factor related to many and complex features of culture, including social structure.

The shift from Status to Contract is an ideological transformation in the conception of social and legal man. In the history of human societies the interaction of intellective ideas and social structure has always been, and will remain, reciprocal. The burden of the argument of this paper is that the seeds of logical realism are to be found in the soil of many non-European primitive cultures and that the contrast of Status as against Contract legal forms is not one of mutual exclusiveness but of degree. The great achievements of the Romans, following the Greeks, is that they *systematized* logical realism for social purposes, whereas primitive peoples and the Status-oriented civilizations did not. The fact that the seeds of logical realism are historically widely scattered, even if sporadically, should enhance the prospects for the wider realization of the freeing effects of Contract type of legal order.

FOOTNOTE REFERENCES

1. Northrop, F. S. C., "Toward a Deductively Formulated and Operationally Verifiable Comparative Cultural Anthropology," in

Northrop, F. S. C., and Helen H. Livingston, *Cross-Cultural Understanding*, Harper & Row, New York, 1964, p. 204.

2. Kluckhohn, Clyde, "The Place of Theory in Anthropological Science," *Philosophy of Science*, vol. 6, 1939, p. 333.
3. Northrop, F. S. C., *op. cit.*, note 1, pp. 217–218.
4. Simpson, Sidney P., and Ruth Field, "Law and the Social Sciences," *Virginia Law Review*, vol. 32, 1946, p. 862.
5. Northrop, F. S. C., *op. cit.*, note 1, p. 285.
6. Northrop, F. S. C., *op. cit.*, note 1, p. 201.
7. Hart, C. W. M., "Review of E. A. Hoebel, *The Law of Primitive Man*," *American Anthropologist*, vol. 58, 1956, p. 566.
8. Maine, Henry S., *Ancient Law* (3rd Amer. ed.), Holt, New York, 1879, p. 165.
9. *Ibid.*, p. 163.
10. Northrop, F. S. C., *op. cit.*, note 1, p. 217.
11. *Ibid.*
12. *Ibid.*, p. 218.
13. Northrop, F. S. C., and Helen H. Livingston, *Cross-Cultural Understanding*, *op. cit.*, note 1, p. 258.
14. *Ibid.*, p. 259.
15. Redfield, Robert, "Maine's *Ancient Law* in the Light of Primitive Societies," *The Western Political Quarterly*, vol. 3, 1950, p. 576.
16. *Ibid.*, pp. 578–579.
17. Murdock, George P., "World Ethnographic Sample," *American Anthropologist*, vol. 59, 1957, pp. 664–687.
18. Aberle, D. F., "Matrilineal Descent in Cross-Cultural Perspective," in David M. Schneider, and Kathleen Gough (eds.), *Matrilineal Kinship*, California, Berkeley, 1961, p. 665.
19. Lowie, Robert H., *The Origin of the State*, Harcourt, Brace, New York, 1927.
20. Llewellyn, Karl N., and E. A. Hoebel, *The Cheyenne Way: Conflict and Case Law in Primitive Jurisprudence*, Oklahoma, Norman, 1941.
21. Richardson, Jane, *Law and Status Among the Kiowa Indians*, Monographs of the American Ethnological Society, Augustin, New York, vol. I, 1940.
22. Province, John R., "The Underlying Sanctions of Plains Indian Culture," in F. Eggan (ed.), *Social Anthropology of North American Tribes*, University of Chicago, Chicago, 1937.
23. Redfield, Robert, "Maine's *Ancient Law*," *op. cit.*, note 16, p. 580.
24. Maine, Henry S., *Ancient Law*, *op. cit.*, note 9, pp. 358, 359.

25. Hart, C. W. M., "Review of E. A. Hoebel," etc., *op. cit.*, note 8, p. 567.
26. Llewellyn, Karl, and E. A. Hoebel, *The Cheyenne Way*, *op. cit.*, note 21, Case 3, pp. 9–12. (Italics added.)
27. Northrop, F. S. C., *op. cit.*, note 1, p. 215.
28. Llewellyn, Karl, and E. A. Hoebel, *The Cheyenne Way*, *op. cit.*, note 21, p. 128. (Italics added.)
29. *Ibid.*, Case 2, pp. 6–9.

Three

Experimental Criteria for Distinguishing
Innate from Culturally Conditioned
Behavior IRENÄUS EIBL-EIBESFELDT

17

During his studies on the taxonomy of ducks, Heinroth[1] discovered behavior patterns that were constant in form and thus character-istic for a species or even for larger systematic units and could, therefore, be used for taxonomic purposes. He called them "*artei-gene Triebhandlungen*," and Lorenz,[2] "*Instinktbewegungen*" or "*Erbkoordinationen*," which has been translated into English as "fixed action patterns." A number of investigators have demon-strated their taxonomic value. Reviews of this subject were given by Lorenz, Mayr, Tinbergen, and Wickler.[3] By means of depriva-tion experiments it has been shown that fixed action patterns de-velop even in animals raised in isolation and prevented from exer-cising the behavior pattern in question. The term *innate* was, therefore, applied to them.

Recently a number of investigators (Birch, Hebb, Lehrman, Schneirla, and Riess[4]) have criticized the ethological way of ap-proach and especially have questioned the analytical value of the deprivation experiment. Their argument is focused upon the fact that one can never deprive an animal of all possible sources of information. It is always put in an environment which acts upon it, and it might even learn in utero or in the egg. This is certainly true but does not yet justify the conclusion that the term *innate* is of no analytical value at all. In assuming this, the critics of ethology overlook the all-important fact that behavior is adapted to certain environmental situations. It mirrors the environment, so to speak, and if one does not accept this as a given fact, as vitalists used to do, one has to explain this adaptedness, which must have been developed at some time or other. Whenever this took place, information concerning the environmental data must have been fed into the organism at that time. This, as Lorenz[5] emphasized, can happen in two ways: (1) by trial and error learning by the individual, in active interaction with the environment, and (2) by interaction of the species with the environment during phylogeny.

Both ways involve acquisition of information. In the latter case, the information is stored in the genome of the species and decoded during ontogeny.

By means of a deprivation experiment we are in a position to check if a certain adaptive behavior pattern owes its adaptedness to individual learning or to phylogenetic adaptation. One can always deprive an animal of specific information about certain environmental data to which its behavior is clearly adapted. If afterward in the testing situation it still surprises us with the adaptive behavior pattern, then we can state that the adaptedness was brought about during phylogeny. It is *phylogenetically adapted* behavior, in contrast to *acquisitionally adapted* behavior, which owes its adaptedness to individual learning.

Let me give two examples. In autumn we can observe the European squirrel hiding nuts. After it has plucked a hazelnut it descends to the ground and searches there for a while, usually until it has found the base of a large tree trunk, where it starts to dig a little hole with the forepaws (digging, 1). Into this hole it deposits the nut (depositing, 2) and tamps it down with a short sequence of rapid blows with the snout (tamping, 3). This done, it covers the hole with loose earth by sweeping movements of the forepaws (covering, 4) and finally presses the earth down (packing, 5). Every adult squirrel does this with the same stereotyped sequence of movements.

If a squirrel were to learn nut-hiding behavior, it would need a lot of specific information to do so. If the mother does not instruct the young animal, it would have to learn by itself that something, which it has somehow by chance hidden in the ground, helps it over periods of food shortage, and it would have to learn the right way to do this, by trial and error.

One can easily deprive an animal of all possibility of learning this behavior by interaction with the specific environmental situation, by raising it on a diet of liquid food in a wire mesh cage, in which there is no possibility of digging.

This was done with eighteen European squirrels (*Sciurus vulgaris L.*). At an age of two to three months these squirrels were given open hazelnuts which they ate. After satiation none of the squirrels simply dropped the nut, but all started to search for a hiding place. Five of these that were given a large pan filled with sand hid the nut with the full sequence of the above-described patterns (1–5). Others had no opportunity to dig. These animals carried on a longer search. They looked at the floor of the cage and the room and were much attracted by vertical obstacles, at the base of which they frantically started scratching as if digging a hole. The corners of the room proved especially attractive and here three animals deposited their nuts, going through all five movements. The rest also hid their nuts, but only performed the first three movements. This is sometimes the case with experienced animals, as a sign of fatigue, when they have hidden several nuts in succession or when the situation does not allow digging, as in our case. When provided with a pan filled with sand, all the latter experimental animals except one started to hide the nut, using the complete sequence of movements.

The fact that all squirrels hid their first nut, performing the first three movements, and a great number even carrying out all five movements, clearly shows that these adaptive behavior patterns are available to the animals like ready-made tools. The fact that three animals which had no opportunity to really dig in sand performed the covering movements after depositing the nut, although no earth had been dug up, demonstrated that this adaptive behavior is at least partly internally coordinated.

The component activities of digging, placing, nose-pushing, covering, and packing down follow one another in a fixed sequence, and not because each element changes the releasing situation and thus activates a new behavior. Even when the animal has not dug up anything, it places the nut and, after nose-pushing, it covers the nonexistent hole and packs down nonexistent earth. The nose-pushing, which follows placing of the nut, could be released by an external stimulus (the nut). But it occurs only in the appropriate situation. Normally an uncovered nut releases a picking up. We may, therefore, presume that the entire sequence follows an inherited program that once being activated by a certain stimulus situation can run off even without further support from external stimuli. For a detailed discussion, see Eibl-Eibesfeldt.[6]

The size of innately coordinated units varies greatly. Generally, in mammals only rather short movement sequences, like gnawing or levering in the nut opening technique of the squirrel, described below, are given to the species as fixed action patterns. But, in the case of the nut hiding, we seem to be confronted with a highly complicated innate coordination. Not only the single movements one through five seem to be available to the animals as ready-made tools, but also their sequence is at least in part laid down by an inherited program. The animal furthermore does not need to learn when to perform, but has an a priori knowledge of the releasing stimulus situation.

Certainly it is an interesting example of an adaptive behavior pattern which owes its adaptedness not to individual learning, but to phylogeny. The motor patterns are available to the animal like ready-made tools. They develop their function as many organs do, i.e., without functional practicing, but rather by a process of decoding genetically acquired information during ontogeny. This does not mean that learning does not play any role in the later elaboration. Inexperienced squirrels, when covering the nut after depositing it, often do not perform at exactly the right place, and the nut remains uncovered. Seeing the nut still uncovered, the animal often corrects and orients its movements toward the nut. The orientation of the animal toward the nut is perfected by experience. In case nothing is dug up, the animal, after making the covering movements, often takes the nut again and tries to bury it at another place. Soon the squirrels learn where it is really possible to hide a nut. Squirrels, as well as agoutis (*Dasyprocta aguti*), show reactions of discomfort when they "bury" their food on the solid floor. Seeing the food still uncovered, agoutis shake their front legs or scratch themselves frantically with one hind leg, which they also do if one tries to feed them with hot potatoes, on which they can burn themselves.

In dealing with behavior patterns we have to be aware of the fact that different levels of integration can be observed. In the case of nut hiding we have at the highest level a coordination composed of the above-described acts one through five. But each of these acts, e.g., the digging, is again composed of smaller acts, as the lifting of one forepaw, extending it, scratching on the floor, and so forth, and we can continue further down this hierarchy. We must, therefore, always define our level of operation.

It may well be that the sequence of acts at a high integrational level is genetically controlled, but in the developmental mechanics of one or several acts at a lower integrational level learning enters. Thus we have not excluded, in our experiments with nut hiding, the possibility that the coordination of antagonistic muscles, on a lower level of integration, is learned, perhaps, in utero. Although we do not know, therefore, this part of the developmental mechanics, we can say that, on the level of nut hiding, the functional sequence is genetically coordinated, even if acts at a lower integration level, in later investigation, prove to be acquired coordinations. This seems to be one point that has not been made clear yet, but is important to avoid a misunderstanding.

If, on the other hand, behavior patterns are integrated by learning into functional units, then we call these units "acquired coordinations." Very often we observe that the animals are adapted to learn certain specific skills rapidly. Such innate learning dispositions are phylogenetic adaptations too. Some receptoral apparatus must have evolved, in such cases, which "tell" the animal when a certain behavior fulfills its biological function. Observations indicate that fitting is rewarding, nonfitting, the reverse. This way animals often learn the appropriate use of innate behavior patterns. Rats have a number of nest-building movements available as fixed action patterns. Their appropriate sequence, however, has to be learned.[7] At the beginning of nest building an inexperienced rat may push with the forepaws after it has carried in only one piece of nesting material. The behavior normally fulfills the function of forming a mold, but at this early stage of nest building it cannot fulfill this function and the pushing animal often performs in the air. The activity soon fades away, whereas it seems reinforced when enough nesting material is available. In this way the animals learn the appropriate sequence, which is, in its high complexity, an acquired coordination that comes with the help of an inherited learning disposition and is thus genetically adapted.

Another example can be demonstrated in the development of the nut-opening technique of squirrels (*Sciurus vulgaris L.*). Adult squirrels open nuts with a very characteristic technique. In the middle of the flatter curved side they gnaw a furrow toward the top of the nut and another one just opposite. Then they insert the lower incisors like a lever and open the nut in two halves. Young ones do not show this work-saving technique, but gnaw fissures all over the nut. So do adult squirrels deprived of the experience of nut opening.

It is most interesting to study the process by which the squirrels learn the best technique by themselves. The first indication of learning is shown when the gnawed fissures run mostly parallel to each other from the base to the top. If one examines the structure of the nut, one will find that the fibers of the wood run from the base to the top, and it is easier for the squirrel to gnaw parallel to them instead of perpendicularly. Furthermore, one finds that the gnawed fissures are more and more confined to the flatter side of the nut, where the teeth of the squirrel get a better grip, especially as there is a slight groove, which they finally follow exclusively. Thus, the structure of the nut channels the activity of the squirrel in a certain way. Following the way of least resistance, it automatically comes to one specific technique, which nearly all squirrels develop in the end.

Many squirrels develop the above-mentioned technique, and an observer not studying the ontogeny might be misled into assuming it to be a species specific innate behavior pattern. But sometimes, though rarely, individual squirrels develop techniques of nut opening different from the one described. One inexperienced squirrel opened the first nut in a short time by gnawing a hole at the base. This success determined her further behavior and blocked the way to the development of the best technique. The animal stuck to the method of gnawing a hole at the base, perfecting this technique. Eventually, it did not gnaw many furrows but learned to gnaw only a few at approximately right angles so that the squirrel was able to break a piece of nutshell out of the nut. Finally it shifted this technique to the softer top of the nut.

From the very beginning one observes that the squirrel attempts to insert the lower incisors in the furrows and tries by levering movements to crack it open. This, of course, only works when the furrows are placed in a certain way. Successful cracking seems rewarding. In a series of experiments still in progress, squirrels raised on a liquid diet were given hazelnuts which were emptied and the shells were then glued together. These they learned to open. The performance of the motor pattern of gnawing and splitting apparently was reinforcing enough for the development of an efficient opening technique.

For opening nuts the squirrel is given only two behavior patterns, gnawing and cracking, and the special disposition to learn an efficient technique. It is easy to understand why it is not given a complete inborn technique, for every sort of nut needs a different one to which the squirrel must adapt. It would be a difficult task, indeed, to outfit the animal with so many different techniques a priori.

In the development of the nut-opening technique we were confronted with an example of a behavior that was learned on the basis of an innate learning disposition and few innate motor coordinations. The drumming habit in chimpanzees comes about similarly. All male chimpanzees develop the habit of drumming against resounding objects as a way of display. The motor pattern, however, varies individually. While one male has the habit of kicking the iron door of the cage with one foot, the other does it with the palms of his hands. Here we might hypothetically assume that a template—the innate releasing mechanism (IRM) —is given to the animal prior to any experience against which the behavior is checked and learning channeled this way. This would be another example of a genetically adapted behavior which in its coordination is learned.

That an innate, phylogenetically acquired teaching mechanism channels learning during ontogeny so that species specific behavior is acquired has furthermore been demonstrated in birds. Chaffinches raised in isolation in soundproof chambers develop a song of a certain length and a certain number of notes that have to be considered as a fixed motor pattern. This innate song lacks the differentiation in three stanzas characteristic of the song of normally raised adults. The experiments of Thorpe[8] demonstrated that this must be learned. Only if the young are able to listen to the song of another member of their species can they learn the species specific pattern. They do not imitate, however, any other species and, given an opportunity to listen to different songs, they will pick out that of their own species to imitate. Their phylogenetically acquired teaching mechanism tells them which song to imitate; they have an innate knowledge of which is the correct song. There are other species of birds which are less restricted and imitate a great variety of different songs, and still others that have all their call notes given, without needing to learn them.

A number of observations show that man, too, although most of his behavior is learned and formed by tradition, has a given outfit of innate behavior patterns. In detail they have been studied in the neonate.[9] Innate patterns are the sucking response, the breast-seeking automatism, smiling, crying, and a number of reflexes. The fact that babies, born deaf, start to burble like normal ones at a certain age indicates that the urge to use the vocal apparatus is inborn, too. The uniformity of many mimical expressions throughout mankind of different races and cultures and the finding of homologous patterns in anthropoids indicate that they are fixed action patterns, although the proof has been given only for the smiling response.[10]

Besides innate abilities to act with a given motor pattern, students of animal behavior found evidence for an innate "knowledge" of biologically relevant situations. There are phylogenetically acquired adaptations on the receptor side or afferent sector which show that even the inexperienced animal reacts with specific motor responses only to a very few stimuli or stimuli configurations out of the many stimuli it perceives. Experiments with test animals have shown that in many such cases the animal reacts to very few "sign stimuli," which characterize nevertheless the biologically adequate situation in which the adaptive behavior is to occur. An inexperienced toad (*Bufo bufo*) snaps at every small moving object, even pebbles, while it ignores an insect which is sitting quietly. A clawed toad (*Xenopus laevis*), newly metamorphosed in deprivation, tries to catch moving dots of light projected against the wall of a tank or a jet of water directed against its body.[11] It soon learns to react more selectively after experiencing unpalatable objects. The sign stimuli are supposed to act upon a hypothetically assumed afferent apparatus (IRM) which only at the reception of specific stimuli gives way to a certain behavior. This innate recognizing is something different from the abilities as expressed in the fixed action pattern. Both form a functional unit, as a fixed action pattern is always released by certain key stimuli.

Lorenz assumed that the knowledge of certain mimic expressions is inborn in man, as he reacts blindly to very crude dummies of mimical expressions.[12] Often human behavior might be checked by an innate learning disposition based on such innate releasing mechanisms. This would explain a number of similarities in greeting ceremonies, submissive postures, and display behavior. Although they show great cultural variation, one easily recognizes common features in all of them. In displaying himself, man always tries to make himself larger, and, by coloration, ornaments, and noisy behavior, more impressive. Submission is the antithesis. One tries to be inconspicuous, to make oneself smaller by bending the head, or even falling prostrate to the ground. Such common features indicate that human behavior is not ad libitum flexible, but that certain behavioral traits are laid down in the genome of our species, partly determining the cultural development. The evaluation of chance experiments and the comparative study of human behavior will in time provide us with the needed information to illuminate this point.

In mammals deprivation experiments have shown that adaptive behavior occurs which owes its adaptedness to phylogeny and not to individual learning. Many of these adaptive behavior patterns are fixed action patterns, which means that the well-coordinated playing together of the muscle actions at the observed level is not a result of individual learning. These fixed action patterns form the skeleton of the behavioral outfit of the species. For a convenient shorthand description we also call these innate patterns, not excluding per *definitionem* the possibility that some sort of learning enters at some stage of the development, as long as this learning does not include an interaction with the specific environmental situation to which the behavior is adapted, but occurs at a different level of integration. Besides these innate motor patterns phylogenetic adaptations also occur on the receptor side. Inborn responses to specific stimuli or stimuli configurations have been demonstrated, as well as specific inborn teaching mechanisms or learning dispositions that channel learning in certain pathways.

FOOTNOTE REFERENCES

1. Heinroth, O., "Beiträge zur Biologie, namentlich Ethologie und Psychologie der Anatiden," *Verhandlungen des 5. internationalen Ornithologen-Kongresses*, Berlin, 1910, pp. 589–702.
2. Lorenz, K., "Über die Bildung des Instinkbegriffes," *Die Natur-*

wissenschaften, vol. 25, 1937, pp. 289–300; "Vergleichende Bewegungsstudien an Anatiden," *Journal für Ornithologie, Supplement*, vol. 89, 1941, pp. 194–293; "Phylogenetische Anpassung und adaptive Modifikation des Verhaltens," *Zeitschrift für Tierpsychologie*, vol. 18, 1961, pp. 139–187.

3. Mayr, E., "Behavior and Systematics" in A. Roe and G. G. Simpson (eds.), *Behavior and Evolution*, Yale, New Haven, 1958, pp. 341–362; Lorenz, K., "The Comparative Method in Studying Innate Behavior Patterns," in *Physiological Mechanisms in Animal Behavior*, Symposia of the Society for Experimental Biology, Cambridge, London, 1950, pp. 221–268; "The Evolution of Behavior," *Scientific American*, vol. 199, December, 1958, pp. 67–78; Tinbergen, N., *The Study of Instinct*, Oxford, London, 1961; Wickler, W., "Ökologie und Stammesgeschichte von Verhaltensweisen," *Fortschritte der Zoologie*, vol. 13, 1961, pp. 303–365.

4. Birch, H. G., "The Pertinence of Animal Investigation for a Science of Human Behavior," *American Journal of Orthopsychiatry*, vol. 31, 1961, pp. 267–275; Hebb, D. C., "Heredity and Environment in Mammalian Behavior," *British Journal of Animal Behaviour*, vol. I, 1953, pp. 43–47; Lehrmann, D. C., "A Critique of Konrad Lorenz's Theory of Instinctive Behavior," *Quarterly Review of Biology*, vol. 28, 1953, pp. 337–363; "On the Organization of Maternal Behavior and the Problem of Instinct," in P. P. Grassé (ed.), *L'Instinct dans le Comportement des Animaux et de l'Homme*, Masson, Paris, 1956, pp. 475–520; Riess, B., "The Effect of Altered Environment and of Age on the Mother-Young Relationships among Animals," *Annals New York Academy of Science*, vol. 57, 1954, pp. 606–610; Schneirla, T. C., "Interrelationship of the 'Innate' and the 'Acquired' in Instinctive Behavior" in P. P. Grassé (ed.), *op. cit.*, pp. 387–452; "Instinctive Behavior, Maturation—Experience and Development," in B. Kaplan and S. Wapner (eds.), *Perspectives in Psychological Theory, Essays in Honor of Heinz Werner*, International Universities Press, New York, 1960, pp. 303–334.

5. Lorenz, K., "Phylogenetische Anpassung und adaptive Modifikation des Verhaltens," *op. cit.*, note 2.

6. Eibl-Eibesfeldt, I., "Angeborenes und Erworbenes in Verhalten der Säuger," *Zeitschrift für Tierpsychologie*, vol. 20, 1963.

7. Eibl-Eibesfeldt, I., "The Interactions of Unlearned Behavior Patterns and Learning in Mammals" in CIOMS, *Symposium on Brain Mechanism and Learning*, Montevideo, Blackwell, Oxford, 1961, pp. 53–73.

8. Thorpe, W. H., "The Learning of Song Patterns by Birds, with

Especial Reference to the Song of the Chaffinch Fringilla Coelebs," *The Ibis*, vol. 100, 1958, pp. 535–570.

9. Ahrens, R., "Beitrag zur Entwicklung des Physiognomie und Mimikerkennens," *Zeitschrift für Experimentelle und Angewandte Psychologie*, vol. 2, part I, 1953, pp. 412–454; *ibid.*, vol. 2, part II, pp. 599–631; Koehler, O., "Das Lächeln des Säuglings," *Die Umschau*, vol. 54, no. 11, 1954, pp. 321–324; Peiper, A., "Menschenkind und Affenjunges," *Experientia*, vol. 17, 1961, pp. 529–538; Prechtl, H., "Die Entwicklung und Eigenart frühkindlicher Bewegungsweisen," *Klinische Wochenschrift*, vol. 34, 1956, pp. 281–284; "The Directed Head Turning Response and Allied Movements of the Human Baby," *Behaviour*, vol. 13, 1958, pp. 3–4; Prechtl, H., and W. Schleidt, "Auslösende und steuernde Mechanismen des Saugaktes," *Zeitschrift für Vergleichende Physiologie*, vol. 32, part I, 1950, pp. 257–262; *ibid.*, vol. 33, part II, 1951, pp. 53–62.

10. Spitz, R., "The Smiling Response: A Contribution to the Ontogenesis of Social Relations," *Genetic Psychology Monographs*, Journal Press, Provincetown, Mass., vol. 34, 1946, pp. 57–125.

11. Eibl-Eibesfeldt, I., "Die Verhaltensentwicklung des Krallenfrosches (Xenopus laevis) und des Scheibenzünglers (Discoglossus pictus) unter besonderer Berücksichtigung der Beutefanghandlungen," *Zeitschrift für Tierpsychologie*, vol. 19, 1962, pp. 385–393.

12. Lorenz, K., "Die angeborenen Formen möglicher Erfahrung," *Zeitschrift für Tierpsychologie*, vol. 5, 1943, pp. 235–409.

Distinguishing Differences of Perception from Failures of Communication in Cross-Cultural Studies[*] DONALD T. CAMPBELL

18

This paper has two goals: to report on the results of a cross-cultural comparison of susceptibility to optical illusion, and to discuss a problem in applied epistemology indicated in the title. First I shall present evidence of substantial cultural differences in a basic psychological process. This evidence will be presented confidently, as though there were no methodological problems. And I do, in fact, believe these to be "real" differences, i.e., potentially demonstrable by a large variety of methods. Next I shall present the practical efforts which we took to ensure optimal communication of the task, and our means of sifting out instances where the task was misunderstood. With these concrete illustrations before us, I shall ask the more general question: How can we discriminate between misunderstanding and disagreement? How can we tell when we are communicating well enough to know that we see things differently?

Ethnic Differences in Optical Illusion

These are preliminary results from a wide-reaching cooperative effort started in 1956[1] and soon to be presented in monographic detail elsewhere.[2] The study began as a debate between the late Professor Melville Herskovits and myself. Herskovits had long been

* The research reported in this paper has been supported by the Program of African Studies, Northwestern University, the late Melville J. Herskovits, Director.

an articulate advocate of cultural relativism.[3] While sympathetic to this perspective, I argued that cultural relativism presumed the biological homogeneity of culture-learning man, and that this biological homogeneity would include the basic perceptual and learning processes. On the basis of experience in Africa, Herskovits was quite sure we would find differences in visual perception. As it turned out, he was right, and fortunately so, for differences are more fun to report than samenesses.

There were, of course, good psychological as well as anthropological grounds for expecting differences. As we stated in the test manual:[4]

Not only will the findings be of interest for those concerned with the comparative study of culture, they will also contribute to the theory of perception, particularly with respect to the role of experience. Currently there are a number of lines of development in the theory of visual perception which create a new interest in the nativist-empiricist controversy. There is new evidence which emphasizes the role of early visual experience in setting the base for adult perceptual processes. Clearly relevant to this topic would be findings on perceptual illusions among peoples whose visual worlds are quite different from that of the European.

If cross-cultural differences in extent of illusion are found, the initial explanatory effort would be focused on differences in the usual visual environment. For this reason, it is very important that details of the visual environment of each group be recorded on the form provided. Such details include the typical form of houses, the maximum distance at which objects are typically viewed, whether or not vistas over land or water occur, typical games, skills, artistic training, and other aspects of culture that might affect habits of inference from line drawings.

Two cultural factors are apt to be of particular significance for this investigation. In the carpentered Western world such a great proportion of artifacts are rectangular that the habit of interpreting obtuse and acute angles as rectangular surfaces extended in space is a very useful one. Such an inference pattern would generate many of the line illusions here tested. In a culture where rectangles did not dominate, this habit might be absent. Similarly, elliptical retinal images are interpreted as circles extended in the third dimension. This inference pattern might be absent where objects are truly elliptical in cross-section.

Another cultural factor which might be related to illusions is two-dimensional representation of three-dimensional objects. Perspective drawing is a most pervasive feature of Euroamerican culture. It is a substantial feature of the visual world from childhood on. Children in this culture from a very early age attempt to make representations of this kind themselves. The techniques or conventions involved may be related to the habits of inference which some illusions illustrate.

These and other considerations lie behind the inventory of the visual environment which is included with the respondents' record sheets.

Our test figures were assembled in a compact 5″ by 7″ booklet of 71 pages printed on washable Eastman paper. Professor Herskovits distributed these booklets and the accompanying record sheets to volunteer collaborators in Africa and elsewhere. Over the past six years some 20 ethnologists have cooperated in administering the booklets to some 1800 persons. In 1960, Marshall Segall, the psychologist who actually designed the booklet, spent a year in Africa and there administered the tests to some 350 persons. An anthropology graduate student administered the tests in a door-to-door survey of 200 persons in Evanston, Illinois (U.S.A.), to provide our main European culture sample. Figures 1 and 2 show results for adults on the two illusions providing the largest differences.

While it is not appropriate to our purpose to focus on the details, some interpretive comments are in order. Our faith in the differences found is increased by noting general similarity to the findings of Rivers at the turn of the century.[5] He found the Todas (India) and the Murray Islanders (Torres Strait, New Guinea) less subject to the Müller-Lyer illusion than Englishmen and more subject to the horizontal-vertical illusion. His mode of testing was quite different from ours, and in fact we had suspected that his might offer possibilities of confusing random responding with the absence of bias.

The Müller-Lyer data of Figure 1, the differences found by Allport and Pettigrew,[6] and the parallel results from the Sander parallelogram illusion in the present study lend themselves to an explanation in terms of the visual environment which we call the "carpentered-world" hypothesis. What we mean by this is perhaps most easily shown by the Sander parallelogram (Figure 3). In this illusion, the bias is to judge the left diagonal as longer. In the dominant theory of the optical illusion tradition,[7] this bias is understandable as a tendency to perceive the nonorthogonal parallelogram as a rectangular surface extended in space. In the carpentered Western culture such an inference habit has great ecological validity.[8] For we live in a culture in which straight lines abound, and in which perhaps 90 percent of the acute and obtuse angles formed on our retina by the straight lines of our visual field are

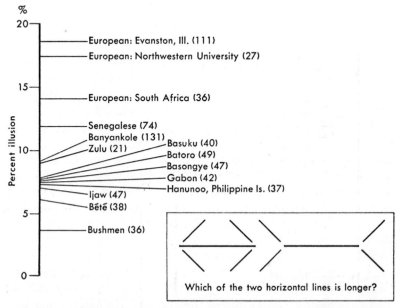

FIGURE 1. Müller-Lyer illusion. *Note:* The percent illusion is the percent by which the arrowhead horizontal (left in the illustration) exceeds the tailed horizontal (right) when they are judged equal. The number of cases upon which the mean is based is indicated in the parenthesis (adult data only). Most of the larger gaps are statistically significant; e.g., both the South African Europeans and the Senegalese differ significantly from all other groups, as do the Bushmen. The Banyankole differ significantly from the Ijaw.

realistically interpretable as right angles extended in space. For those living where man-made structures are a small portion of the visual environment, and where such structures are constructed without benefit of saw, plane, straight edge, tape measure, carpenter's square, spirit level, chalk line, surveyor's sight, and plumb bob, both straight lines and "real" right angles are a rarity. As a result, the inference habit of interpreting all acute and obtuse angles as "really" right angles extended in space would not be learned (or, if innate, would be extinguished).

The application of this inference habit to the Müller-Lyer illusion is not unequivocal, but I am convinced it is tapping the same process symptomized in the Sander parallelogram. Correlational

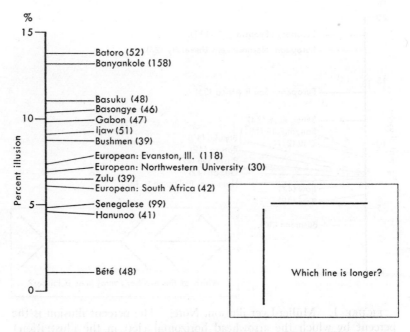

FIGURE 2. The horizontal-vertical illusion. *Note:* The percent illusion is the extent to which the horizontal exceeds the vertical when the two are judged as equal. With regard to group differences, the Banyankole are significantly different from all lower groups, the Basuku from the Ijaw, the Evanstonians from the Ijaw and the Senegalese, the Bété from all other groups, and so on.

data support this. Following Brentano[9] in applying this orthogonalizing concept to the Müller-Lyer, consider the diagonals pulled into rectangularity with the horizontals by turns around their own centers. This would compress the horizontal in the arrowheaded figure and would stretch it in the tailed figure. Or following Thiéry[10] the horizontal is the front edge of a box or tipped sawhorse in the arrowhead figure and the inner back edge in the tailed figure. If the back edge, it is farther away and has to be "really" longer to subtend the same visual angle or retinal projection. (You may or may not be able to confirm that the horizontal line which appears longer also appears farther away.) While these illustrations are not entirely convincing to me, and while the situation doubtless involves other processes, I do regard it as probable that the illusion is to a considerable degree a by-product of an inference habit of interpreting acute and obtuse angles as really right angles. Note that these European scholars, although totally unaware of group differences in optical illusions, in their effort to explain the normal European case provided a theory which committed them to predicting less illusion in other environments.

On these grounds, we should also expect rural–urban differences

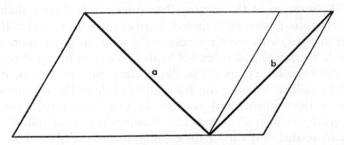

FIGURE 3. Sander parallelogram: Which of the two diagonals, *a* or *b*, is longer?

within our own culture, and cold climate vs. warm climate differences too, insofar as severe winters force children to spend more of their time in a carpentered visual environment. Possibly, the significant difference between Evanstonian and South African Europeans is explainable upon the two bases of urbanism and climate.

The interpretation of the illusion as a learned habit of inference is complicated by the frequently confirmed age trends for the illusion within the European culture.[11] Data from a separate sample of Evanston children, but using our same booklets,[12] show the following progression in mean percent of illusion for age groups from 4 years to 9 years: 27%, 23%, 22%, 20%, 19%, and 17%. This age trend is confirmed for almost all cultures, although culture-to-culture differences are in general larger for children than for adults. The simplest application of our theory would have expected European adults, having had the longest influence of the culture, to have had more illusion than European children. The outcome is thus puzzling and complicating.

For the purposes of this conference the stimulus value of puzzling cross-cultural data is fully as great as that of well-understood data, and I should perhaps attempt no further explanation. However, my favored resolution at the moment is this: European children have fully mastered visual-locomotory coordination by the age of two or three. The inference habits useful in reaching for objects and locomoting around them are well established by that age. Soon thereafter they have also mastered the European inference conventions of *reading* two-dimensional drawings in terms of three-dimensional solids and displays. At this stage they are naive realists, unaware of the sensory data from which their real-object inferences have been constructed. Further maturation makes them more analytic, with greater access to the sensorial given, more able to hold the inferential processes in abeyance so as to report on the specific stimulus components. Supporting this development of analytic skills is learning the transmitter's role in the communication of three-dimensional content in two-dimensional drawing. (In order to construct perspective drawings one must inhibit perspective-related illusions, reduce "object constancy," and so on. Thouless[13] has demonstrated that artists are more able to free themselves from these constancies. The implication that trained artists should be less subject to the Müller-Lyer illusion remains to be tested.) Thus from a learned peak of acute-obtuse-inference illusion, our European children gradually and in part unlearn it or learn to hold it partially in abeyance for certain tasks. The habitant of an uncarpentered world has never learned the inference-habit to as strong a degree. The notion that cultural differences in perception are to a considerable part tied up with our European conventions and great experience with regard to the two-dimensional representation of three-dimensional messages is supported by Hudson's[14] study of the dramatic misunderstandings which persons from uncarpentered worlds can make of European perspective drawings, and of the influence of both education and cultural isolation upon such inferences for both Africans and Europeans living in South Africa.

The cultural differences in the Müller-Lyer, the Sander parallelogram, and the rotating trapezoid[15] might suggest interpretation in terms of Northrop's typology of realistic vs. radical empirical aesthetic modes of perceiving.[16] Thus the European habitants of the carpentered world might be interpreted as realistically constructing from the sense data hypothetical entities, and, in so doing, failing to note, or falsifying, the empirically given. On the other hand, the inhabitants of natural landscapes perceive the stimulus cards in a radical empirical aesthetic mode. Lacking a pressure to interpret the given realistically, they can report accurately upon what is empirically given and hence are free from the illusion. However, this is not necessarily how Northrop would interpret the data, recognizing as he does the universality of a naive realistic mode. Further, there are other data which contradict so general an interpretation. Beveridge[17] and Thouless[18] report that for judgments of tilted circles and ellipses, natural-visual-environment peoples have greater object-constancy (phenomenal regression to the real object) than do Europeans. In the terms of the present discussion, on these tasks they show a stronger tendency to construct real objects from the sense data than do Europeans. In conclusion, my favored interpretation of the cultural differences in the Müller-Lyer illusion is to assume for both groups naive realistic inference habits and to locate the differences in the specifics of the inference habits supported by their particular visual ecologies. (Note to anthropologists: I am using "ecology" in the mode of Brunswik to refer to the typical totality of environment, both man-made and natural.) In regard to this specificity, it is of interest to note that Beveridge[19] found that judgments of the gravitational vertical made by Africans were less influenced by misleading rectangular cues from a tilted room than were judgments made by Europeans.

Figure 2 shows the results of a quite different illusion in which the error is to exaggerate the length of the vertical line. It provides a quite different ordering of peoples, and new puzzles of interpretation. In our Evanston children's data for the horizontal-vertical no age trends at all are present. For the noncarpentered peoples, insofar as there are trends, children tend to have more of the illusion. I probably do not have as good an interpretation of these data as for the Müller-Lyer. Again, for the purposes of this conference, we can profit from interesting differences even though they remain unexplained. However, here also the students of optical illusions in explaining the normal (European) case provided a basis for predicting cultural differences. Woodworth[20] states the theory concisely: "A short vertical line in a drawing may represent a relatively long horizontal line extending away from the observer. The horizontal-vertical illusion can be explained by supposing the vertical to represent such a foreshortened horizontal line." Sanford[21] cites Hering[22] and Lipps[23] as hypothesizing "an unconscious allowance for foreshortening, acquired through preponderating experience with squares lying in planes inclined with regard to the plane of vision."

Consider a man who stands on a flat plain, into which crisscrossed furrows have been plowed. Compare the retinal extensions of furrows which cross his line of sight from left to right with those which extend away from him. Relatively, those that extend away from him are much more foreshortened. They have a much shorter retinal extension per ground-measured yard. Further, the furrows extending away from him along his line of regard are represented on the retina as vertical lines. For such a person, there might be great ecological validity in the inference habit of interpreting vertical linear extensions as greatly foreshortened lines in the horizontal plane extending away along the line of regard. Such an inference habit would have less validity for a person living in a rain forest in which the largest real surfaces in the visual regard were in fact vertical and in which tree trunks and hanging vines were the commonest source of vertical lines. Here the foreshortening of what comes to be represented as the visual vertical would be absent, the inference habits different, and the susceptibility to the horizontal-vertical illusion less. Canyon dwellers should be similar.

On such a continuum of environments, it might be reasonable to assume that the European indoors-dwellers, for whom vertical walls are as frequent as floors, would be intermediate. As an interpretation of Figure 2, it is comforting to note that the Bété, at the bottom, have a jungle environment, and that the Batoro and Banyankole live in high open country. But in detail, the data do not fit well. The Bushmen of the flat deserts should be at the top; the Zulu should be much higher. The Gabon, Ijaw, and Basongye much lower, and so on. If this ecology is a factor, as I do believe it is, it is obviously only one of many factors.

The "ecological validities" of various inference-habits in various cultures need not, of course, be left at the conjectural level. Brunswik[24] pioneered in the statistical sampling of visual environments to ascertain "ecological cue validities," of the *Gestalt* principles of organization. Similar studies should be made to replace our conjectures about the culturally varying cue validity of retinal verticals and acute and obtuse angles. While this has not been done, all of our cooperating anthropologists filled out, for their cultures, an "Inventory of the Visual Environment," which covered natural vistas, types of human artifacts (houses, containers, furniture, and so on), and traditions in representational art.

Practical Efforts to Assure Task Comprehension

The control details which I am going to discuss are products of common-sense considerations. They are routine mediational details which are usually compressed into fine print or left out of research reports altogether. Yet in such operational specifics lie the frontiers of epistemology. On what grounds does an experimenter decide whether an unexpected recording is a new phenomenon or an instrumentation error? What model of the philosophy of science will account for the substantial portion of the "data" which every experimenter disregards and fails to report?

Consider an extreme form of our cross-cultural task: Suppose that we parachuted an anthropologist and a test booklet into a totally isolated New Guinea tribe and that the anthropologist had first to learn the language without the help of an interpreter. The process of language learning would then become a part of the operations which we would have to detail. It would become obvious that no person ever learns another's language perfectly; that the existence of "interpreters" should not be taken for granted; that here is a problematic situation in which the cues and presumptions of communication need to be specified. It turns out that the anthropologist's main cue for achieved communication is similarity between the response of the other to a stimulus and the response which he himself would make. Disagreement turns out to be a sign of communication failure. How then can disagreement on an optical illusion test item be taken instead as a difference in perceiving the world? This is the focal problem justifying the somewhat tedious presentation of the administrative details in what follows.

COMPREHENSION CHECKS. The instructions to the anthropologists read in part:

It is essential that the data be collected under as standardized conditions as possible, and that all deviations from these procedures be recorded. The location and dimensions of the working area should permit display of the figures at a distance of four feet from the respondent, at his eye-level, and in a plane perpendicular to his line of vision. Lighting conditions should permit comfortable viewing of the drawings.

Once rapport has been established, the experimenter should, insofar as cultural and semantic factors permit, conform to the following procedure:

Have respondent sit in appropriate position. Instruct him as follows:

"I am going to show you some drawings and ask you questions about them." Show page 1 (Figure 4). "What is the color of this line?" Point to red line. "What is the color of this line?" Point to black line. "Which line is longer, the red or the black one?" Note: in all of the comparisons, the respondent, if possible, is to be forced to choose one line as longer, equal judgments not being allowed, unless rapport is seriously threatened. If equal judgments have to be accepted, modify the record sheets accordingly. Show page 2 (Figure 5). "Which of these two red lines is longer?" Record. Repeat page 2 procedure with pages 3 and 4. (Pages 1 through 4 are intended as comprehension checks. If the responses to these drawings are not correct, further efforts with that respondent may be considered a waste. If he demonstrates comprehension, the session should be continued.)

Thus on these first four items, if the respondent did not respond as the anthropologist would have, it was assumed that translation or comprehension or cooperation had failed. Yet on the subsequent items, we are prepared to accept such discrepancies in response as signs of differences in perception. What canons of applied epistemology are implicitly being invoked? The fourth check item is particularly relevant, for it is in the form of a Müller-Lyer drawing. How do we know the illusion is not causing the wrong response? It would take a 500-percent illusion to produce it, while strongest of the test items designed for scoring is 50 percent. We find it incredible that cultures or persons exist for whom the illusion is that strong. We prefer to say that they did not understand the task or were unwilling to cooperate or were blind and guessing. Are the grounds for this incredulity epistemologically legitimate?

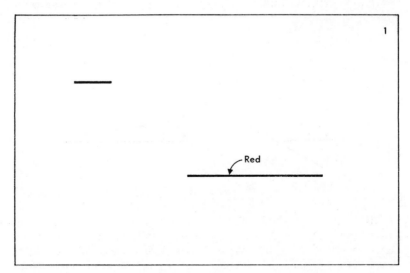

FIGURE 4. Test item 1 from the booklet (comprehension check).

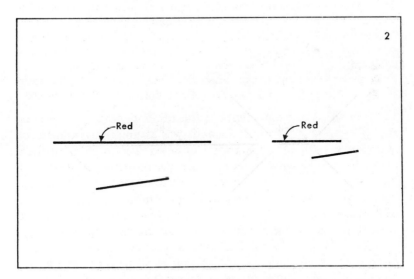

FIGURE 5. Second inspection page (comprehension check).

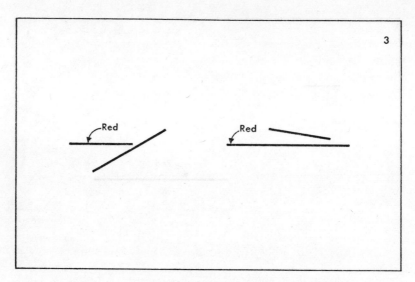

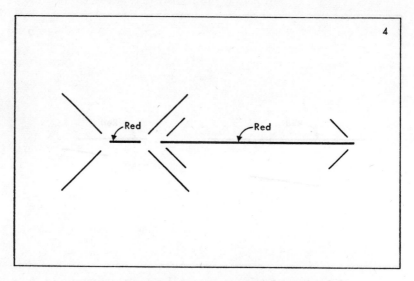

FIGURE 6. Third task page (comprehension check).

FIGURE 7. Fourth task page (comprehension check).

Or are they merely evidence of the ethnocentric bigotry of a Westerner?

OPTIMIZING THE COMMUNICABILITY OF THE DRAWINGS. In the traditional form of the illusion, the parts of the drawing are all connected, and one asks, "Which horizontal line is the longer?" (Figure 8.) Such an assignment involves a number of European

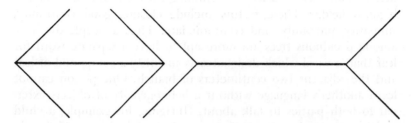

FIGURE 8.   Traditional form of the Müller-Lyer illusion.

linguistic conventions which are unlikely to be widely shared. The term *line* itself may have no counterpart in many languages. Or, if it does it seems doubtful that the counterpart would imply only straight line, with an implicit end boundary where bends occur. To make sure that the comparison was not one of total figures including the distracting arrowheads and feathers, to make more certainly "thinglike" the things being compared, we separated the parts, producing a discontinuous line. We further printed the lines to be compared in red and the distractors in black (Figure 9). We

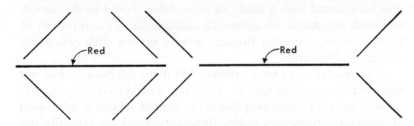

FIGURE 9.   Modified type of Müller-Lyer figure employed.

could now ask, "Which of the two red lines is longer?" no longer needing to designate horizontal. We knew that these changes weakened the illusion substantially, but we felt that the increased certainty of communication was more important.

Behind these decisions lies a theory relating communicability to entitativity.[25] The more entitative or thinglike an object, the more likely is a language to have a separate word designation for it, the earlier in childhood will the word be learned, and the more dependably will it be translated correctly by an interpreter. A good beginning set of criteria for entitativity is contained in Wertheimer's famous set of factors determining the organization of an ambiguous field.[26] These factors include closure, good continuity, similarity, proximity, and common fate. Thus a people dwelling among deciduous trees are more apt to have a separate word for leaf than a word which designates as an entity a compound of leaf and the adjacent two centimeters of branch. One person cannot learn another's language without a heterogeneity of objects external to both parties to talk about. (Imagine, for example, a child and his mentor in communication only by telephone.) These objects edit and discipline the emergent language in terms of their "talkaboutableness," their entitativity. The learner's basic approach is a series of guesses that objects which he can differentiate and identify are similarly differentiated and named by the mentor. He learns the language only insofar as there are sufficient of these third-party objects present to edit his guesses. Even for those born into a culture, this is an unfinished business, best achieved in the areas of greatest use and most entitative designata. For the problem at hand, we would have felt that the test task would have been still more certainly communicated had the design been represented by sticks instead of lines. By using magnetized wires on an iron background such a mode of presentation could be developed, and with the added advantage of enabling the demonstration of the comparison intended through picking up one stick and laying it alongside the other.

MULTIPLE ITEMS IN MIXED ORDER.   When a respondent does not understand an assignment or does not wish to comply, he frequently prefers pseudocompliance to outright refusal or admission of ignorance. Responses under these conditions are typically not random, but instead are characterized by irrelevant regularities. Thus a noncomprehender might always pick the one on the right or the line with the arrowheads or might alternate left and right, possibly changing his rule of response halfway through, and so on. We wanted such irrelevant sources of order not to be confounded with the regularities of interest. For this reason, we represented each illusion by a number of separate drawings. The two types of figures were alternated randomly from left to right. The order of items was mixed in terms of degree of difference between the comparison lines. The ten Müller-Lyer pages had the following order-characteristics, in terms of the location of the tailed figure on the right or the left, and the percentage by which the arrowheaded line exceeded the tailed line in length: L, 30%; L, 0%; R, 20%; L, 25%; L, 5%; L, 40%; R, 45%; R, 10%; L, 50%; R, 15%; R, 35%; R, −5%. Because the orders were set down at random, the raw data sheets were nearly impossible to interpret. For analysis, we transformed the data into an orderly arrangement, using a 1 to indicate an illusion-supported response (i.e., choosing the tailed line as longer). Typical response patterns would look like this:

Item Illusion %	−5,	0,	5,	10,	15,	20,	25,	30,	35,	40,	45,	50
Presentation order	12	2	5	8	10	3	4	1	11	6	7	9
Illusion-supported response	R	L	L	R	R	R	L	L	R	L	R	L
Typical Evanstonian	1	1	1	1	1	1	0	0	0	0	0	0
Typical Bushman	1	1	0	0	0	0	0	0	0	0	0	0

Where the data turn out to have consistent patterns of this sort, the patterned orderliness of both sets convinces us that the task is comprehended and that the two persons differ in their perceptions. But had the two rows been of this form:

Evanstonian	1	1	1	1	1	1	1	1	1	1	1	1
Bushman	0	0	0	0	0	0	0	0	0	0	0	0

our interpretation would have been less decisive. A most plausible hypothesis would have been that both misunderstood the task but in different ways. Had we still felt that visual perception was the explanation, we would have wanted to add many more test items at both ends until we had the two patterns agreeing at both extremes.

We had no such cases as these last two. But we did have cases that could not be interpreted, for which no statement of threshold seemed possible. Here are some Evanston cases:

1	1	0	0	0	1	0	1	1	1	1	1
1	0	0	0	0	1	1	1	0	1	1	0
1	0	0	1	1	0	1	0	0	0	0	0

For such nonscale types, our preferred interpretation was failure of communication or instability so extreme that perceptual performance could not be summarized. In the data reported in Figures 1 and 2, such cases have been eliminated. In borderline instances, the decision becomes arbitrary. For the analyses presented, a very strict rule has been used—only perfect cases and cases with a single reversal, i.e., cases like these:

Perfect	1 1 1	0	0	0	0	0	0	0	0	0		

Perfect
1 1 1   0 0 0 0 0 0 0 0 0
1 1 1   1 1 0 0 0 0 0 0 0
1 1 0   0 0 0 0 0 0 0 0 0

One reversal
1 1 1   0 1 0 0 0 0 0 0 0
1 1 0   1 0 0 0 0 0 0 0 0
1 1 1   0 1 1 1 0 0 0 0 0

By these strict standards, 10 percent of the Evanston cases were lost, 22 percent of the Bushmen, 18 percent of the European South African, 9 percent of the Basongye, 65 percent of the Zulu, and so on.

Discarding cases is dirty business, rightfully suspect.[27] Leaving in obvious error, in varying amounts from culture to culture, is also bad. I do believe we take the path most common to science (although not to social science) by eliminating the nonscale, communication breakdown cases. Note a special problem of test design: *random* responding (or responding to irrelevancies) can often produce a *systematic* bias. It will, for example, make a person appear more stupid on an intelligence test. Because of the location of our items relative to the general illusion threshold, random responding would lead to an increase in the number of illusion responses, particularly for a low-illusion group. As it turned out, none of the good cases produced 1s on the three extreme items (40, 45, and 50 percent). These three items thus come to serve as additions to the four comprehension checks. Similarly all cases gave a 1 to the −5-percent item, where, indeed, this was the correct response, the illusion effect being combined with a true difference in the same direction.

Fortunately, the decision to discard cases is not a crucial one in the present instance. The percentage of lost cases shows no correlation with the magnitude of the illusion ($r = -.04$, N of 16 cultures). Further, within all groups, when all cases are pooled, there is a steady decrease in the percentage of 1s as one moves from the

—5-percent item toward the 50-percent item. This recurrence of a common pattern assures us that in general there has been a communication of the task, plus an over-all similarity in function. And when we use all cases, scoring even the most errorful by the number of 1 responses, the cultural differences persist in essentially the same form and level of statistical significance.

Epistemological Considerations

We must not underestimate the fundamental nature of these practical problems and research decisions. *In essence, we could only observe differences in perception because these differences were small. Had any of our groups perceived in a radically different way from ourselves, we could not have determined that fact.* We could not have distinguished between total failure of communication and total difference in perception. In the end, it is because in great bulk we perceive alike (respond alike) that we can note small differences in perception. The total context of agreement provides the firm platform from which we can note a particular, localized discrepancy. This supporting context of agreement includes that extensive basis of similar perceptions, similar classifications of substance into reidentifiable discrete objects, which has made the learning of the other's language possible. Lacking this, communication fails. Analogously, the blind person and the color-blind person never fully learn English. But they share enough common contours and hypothesized entities to learn that they perceive differently from the rest of us.

To repeat, were a culture to perceive in a radically different way, we could not confirm communication and hence could not ascertain perceptual differences. In emphasizing this we have endorsed the tenability of a cultural and linguistic solipsism. Arthur Child, one of the very few technically trained philosophers to have examined problems raised in the sociology of knowledge,[28] in an important though obscurely published paper has demonstrated with Malinowski's data the extreme difficulty of ascertaining that the members of another culture perceive things differently.[29] But like the present writer, he does not believe these difficulties are in all instances insurmountable.

I have used the phrase "applied epistemology" to specify the intended range of problems and quasi solutions. If when asked "How do we come to know?" the epistemologist answers "Knowledge is impossible," he has answered a different question, which involves different criteria for knowing, from what the asker had in mind; for the question asker used the word so that instances of knowing and ignorance and false belief all occurred and could in some instances in practicable degree (but without logical certainty) be discriminated. Applied epistemology would ask how these discriminations between ignorance and truth and falsehood are made when in practice they do get made. The solipsist's point is conceded: Any knowledge of externals or pasts or other minds is hypothetical. In further concession, applied epistemology becomes the "epistemology of the other one," a discrimination between error and accurate knowing on the part of other knowers than oneself. In further concession, it is anticipated that in many, or perhaps most, situations, the presence or absence of knowledge will be unascertainable. Discrimination may only be possible in rare conditions, such as are created in the experimental laboratory.

Emphasizing the problems of solitary-person-at-one-moment solipsism throws into light some neglected features of cultural-linguistic solipsism. Frequently those making the point of the linguistic and cultural determination of how the world is perceived have implicitly presumed that language learning within the culture is *perfectly* achieved. Further, the necessity of a stably structured physical world as a precondition of language teaching has been neglected. The physical discriminanda available to the children of any society are also available to the anthropologist. Of course, such discriminanda exist in far greater number than any language uses, and an adult conditioned to the culture of one society has the disadvantage of having to learn to disregard well-learned discriminations while attending to the subtleties given prominence in another. But the fact that novel languages can be learned to a considerable degree by an adult sets limits for linguistic relativism which are far short of a complete linguistic solipsism.

Applying this to our cross-cultural perceptual data, we accept the fact that were the differences greater, we could not have learned of them, and we recognize the possibility that someone may come along with a plausible rival hypothesis which will explain the differences obtained without invoking a difference in perceptual process. In the meantime, we have attempted to eliminate such plausible rival hypotheses as we had available, including the hypotheses of failure of communication, response sets, and so on.

Within the area of applied epistemology, our methods illustrate one important general principle: Discrepancy can be noted and interpreted only against the background of an overwhelming proportion of nondiscrepant fit, agreement, or pattern repetition. This principle is found in operation in knowledge processes as varied as binocular vision and astronomy. Again and again in science, the equivocal interpretations are available: separate entity vs. same entity changed, moved, or perceived from a different perspective. And in all such instances where the second interpretation occurs, it is made possible by the overwhelming bulk of stable nonchanging background. Consider the reidentification of a single planet on successive nights, plus the inference that the planet migrates in an eccentric backtracking manner. Had Jupiter been the only star in the sky, this might never have been documented, certainly not by a nomadic people. Had all the stars been planets, it would also have gone unascertained. Had the oscillations in the locations of the fixed stars been so great as to subtend several degrees of visual angle, the backtracking would not have been observed. It was the recurrent "fixedness" of 99.9 percent of the stars which made the wanderings of the few planets interpretable as such. Similarly for binocular resolution, as illustrated in the stereoscope. If the great bulk of the detail in the two stereoscope pictures is similar, then minor discrepancies provide a gain in three-dimensional inference; the hypothesis becomes tenable that each eye is seeing the "same" thing from different angles. If all details differ, binocular resolution does not take place, and specific discrepancies are unused and unnoted. The more general point has been well made by Lorenz,[30] and I have expressed it in greater detail elsewhere.[31]

Analogous Problems in Diagnosing Aspects of Culture

A naive realistic approach to anthropology would assume that cultural differences were objectively directly available for any and all observers to "see." There would be no awareness of methodological problems, no recognition of the problematic character of knowing about another culture. Such an innocent epistemology could survive neither the experience of extensive fieldwork nor the comparison of interpretations between students of "the same" culture. As in other fields, the rejection of naive realism is made first by a move to complete subjectivity, to a radical empirical epistemology. At this stage, there is recognition of the fact that knowing involves the knower, is shaped by his characteristics. This recognition goes to the extreme of rejecting any other component, i.e., of denying all objectivity to knowledge. The stage of logical realism (or critical realism, or hypothetical realism, or corrigible realism) shares with radical empiricism an emphasis on the subjective relativity of all knowing. It shares with naive realism the aspiration to objective knowledge, invariant over points of observation or instruments. But it recognizes that such constructions will be fallibly known, through a process of hypothetical models only indirectly confirmed. The conditions of confirmation will never provide certainty and will often be totally lacking. From this point of view, scientific knowledge is not immediately available for the asking, but requires very special settings. It is a part of the assignment of this conference to consider the degree to which such special conditions are, or can be made, available in the study of the philosophies of cultures.

We must emphasize that the achievement of logically realistic science in any given area is exceedingly problematic. We should not at all rule out the conclusion that in the comparative study of the philosophy of a culture, these conditions are lacking.[32] In this case, the radical empirical extreme is certainly to be preferred to the naive realistic. This is how I understand Professor Maquet's pessimistic conclusion in his paper in this volume. In the bulk, our conference discussion failed to confront this important challenge, failed in effect to countenance the possibility of this conclusion. While I do not regard it as inexorable, I do accept Maquet's reasons and agree that only very special conditions will make him wrong.

THE NECESSITY OF A BASE OF SIMILARITY IN SPECIFYING DIFFERENCES. The major conclusion from the optical illusion study was sort of a "postulate of impotence," that only under the very special condition of great perceptual similarity could one diagnose the particular nature of a perceptual difference; that had the differences been much greater they could not have been distinguished from total failure of communication. It is my thesis that this is not only unavoidably so for the optical illusions task, but is also so for all instances in which it has been learned that one culture differs in a specified manner from another. My methodological recommendation is that this anchoring base of similarities, usually left unconscious, be made explicit at least in methodological examples. This must remain an empty challenge without detailed analyses by anthropologists of instances in which they have successfully diagnosed specific cultural differences. Our informal and unreported discussions in this conference provided beginning examples, however. Professor Ehrenfels pointed out that the Tibetans stick out their tongues to symbolize friendly greeting, whereas for Europeans, the gesture symbolizes contempt. It is argued here that this diagnosis would have been impossible without a similarity in the meaning of the context of behaviors, such as the fighting or friendly sharing that followed. Ehrenfels also described the initial conditions in which he observed that the Bulgarians indicate assent by a horizontal wagging of the head, not a vertical one. As a traveler asking if indeed this road leads to such a city, his respondents indicated that he was correct both verbally and by head gesture. Had they used only the head gesture he would not have had the context of similarity in which to anchor the striking conclusion that the head gesture was being used in reverse.

Professor León-Portilla in conversation described the great difficulty in determining the meaning of the Aztec words for body parts because of the different conceptual segmenting involved. He agrees that the successful translation achieved (the successful instances of learning *how* they classified *differently*) was only made possible by the fact that many of the body-parts-segments were conceived similarly, including classifying human protoplasm into person-segments and within these the distinctions among arm, leg, head, and body. He reports that a similar situation exists in the study of Aztec religious concepts. The great array of similar religious concepts (emphasized in his paper in this volume) make possible the comprehension of certain religious concepts quite foreign to our way of thinking. (These latter are better represented in León-Portilla's full-length presentations—their strangeness makes their presentation require more space than does a familiar trait and thus makes them inconvenient as illustrations in a short chapter.)

Similar postulates of impotence, assertions of limits to the possible achievement of objective knowledge, can be found in other papers in this book, although again, understressed in our discussions. Hockett has emphasized both the value of striving for an "inside view" of the philosophy of a culture and at the same time the impossibility of doing more than approximating it. MacKay, in his meaty section "Failure of Communication," says clearly that a brain which has mapped a certain environment becomes a biased machine for mapping another environment. The "trapped universal" concept of McCulloch and Northrop has a similar import. The perceiving organism is not a passive blotter, but instead an active, shaping filter. Furthermore, the form of the filter is a product not only of inherited structure but also of past use. Braitenberg's drumskin analogy for memory carries a similar lesson. These limitations are particularly binding for anthropology, where human minds provide the major instrument both for observation and for confronting theory and data.

IDENTIFYING "THE SAME" TRAIT IN DIFFERENT CULTURES. A recurrent problem in the comparative study of culture is that of identifying corresponding cultural items in two societies.[33] Analysis of this problem shows that it again requires the anchoring of the specific by a context. And concomitantly a limitation is placed upon its successful achievement. As Professor Northrop has repeatedly made explicit, our thinking on such matters may be biased by the carry-over of the atomistic radical empiricism of British associationism. In this instance it leads us to the anticipation that culture-elements are more certainly identifiable than culture complexes. The reverse is in fact the case.

An analogy may help. Consider the task of identifying corresponding dots of black of which two copies of a newspaper photograph are built. The task is impossible if the dots are taken singly, but becomes more possible the larger the area of the photographs available. Insofar as particular elements can be matched it is only because of the prior matching of the wholes. Similarly for matching elements between languages. A given word cannot usually be translated by a single word when it is in isolation, but can be when it is a part of a sentence or a speech. A paragraph is more accurately translated than a word. To the extent that the translation of a word is anchored, it is because the paragraph of which it is a part has been successfully translated.

In a similar way, it takes acquaintance with the larger cultural context to identify the appropriate parallel or classificatory assignment of any particular cultural item. This context dependence correspondingly removes the possibility of certainty and makes ever present the possibility of erroneously alleging cultural differences as a result of mismatching.

TRIANGULATION THROUGH THE OWN-CULTURE BIAS OF OBSERVERS. The achievement of useful hypothetically realistic constructs in a science requires multiple methods focused on the diagnosis of the same construct from independent points of observation, through a kind of triangulation.[34] This is required because the sense data or meter readings are now understood as the result of a transaction in which both the observer (or meter) and the object of investigation

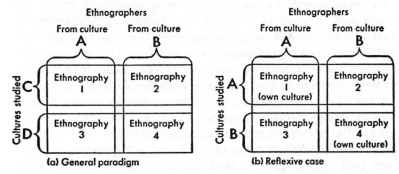

FIGURE 10. Multiple-ethnography schedules to extricate the ethnographer-contributed content from the culture-studied content.

contribute to the form of the data. With a single observation at hand, it is impossible to separate the subjective and the objective component. When, however, observations through separate instruments and separate vantage points can be matched as reflecting "the same" objects, then it is possible to separate out the components in the data due to observer (instrument) and observed. It turns out that this disentangling process requires both multiple observers (methods) and multiple, dissimilar, objects of study.[35]

Applied to the study of the philosophy of a culture, this implies that our typical one-observer one-culture study is inherently ambiguous. For any given feature of the report it is equivocal whether or not it is a trait of the observer or a trait of the object observed. To correct this the ideal paradigm might be as shown in Figure 10 (a). In the most general model, two anthropologists from different cultures would each study a third and fourth culture. Of the four ethnographies resulting, the common attributes in ethnographies 1 and 3 not shared with 2 and 4 could be attributed to ethnographer A, the common attributes in 2 and 4 not elsewhere present to ethnographer B. Looking at row consistencies in the figure, the common attributes in ethnographies 1 and 2 not present in 3 and 4 could be attributed to culture C as "objectively" known. Attributes common to all four ethnographies are inherently ambiguous, interpretable as either shared biases on the part of the ethnographers or shared culture on the part of the societies studied. Note the desirability in this regard of comparing ethnologists with as widely differing cultural backgrounds as possible. Insofar as the ethnologists come from the same culture, the replication of results becomes more a matter of reliability than validity, as these terms are used in discussions of psychological tests. Were such a study carried out by using four ethnographers, two from each ethnographer cultures A and B, studying separate villages of cultures C and D to avoid interference and collusion, then the attributes unique to any one of the ethnographies would be attributable to an equivocal pool of village specificities within its culture, to personality specifics of the ethnographer, and interaction of specific ethnographer culture and studied culture. (If only one ethnologist were used from each culture, and if each of the two studied in turn the same village in the target cultures, then the features unique to any one of the four ethnographies would be equivocally due to ethnographer-culture interactions, time-order effects in which the ethnographer reacted differently to his second culture, time-order effects in which the society reacted differently to the second student of it, historical trends, and interactions among these.) The presence of these indeterminacies should neither be suppressed nor be allowed to overshadow the great gains in understanding which such multiple ethnographer studies would introduce.

While multiplicity of both ethnographer cultures and cultures studied is ideal, it would also be a great gain to achieve only the upper half of Figure 10(a), i.e., two ethnographer cultures focused on the study of a single target culture. In all such triangulations, we again face the paradox of inability to use differences when these so dominate as to make it impossible to match the corresponding aspects of the reports being compared. The necessity of this common denominator provides one justification for Hockett's advocacy (in our discussion) of including material and behavioral cultural details even in ethnographies focused on the determination of the philosophy of the cultures.

Another version of the multiethnographer, multiple-target design is that in which two cultures study each other, as diagramed in Figure 10(b). Usually the focus is on ethnographies 2 and 3, A's report on B and B's report on A. Implicitly, however, A's description of A and B's description of B are contained as bases of reference. There is probably some scientific value to be gained from such reports, even at the level of mutual stereotype sets or of reputational consensus from neighboring peoples.[36] Once the evaluative component (each tribe viewing itself as best) is removed, such mutual stereotype sets show remarkable agreement in confirming the direction of group differences.

Summary

Evidence has been presented demonstrating wide cultural differences in susceptibility to optical illusions. Inspection of the methodological details shows that the demonstration of these specific differences is dependent upon a great preponderance of similarity in perceptual processes. Had the cultures differed in all aspects, the differences in perception could not have been distinguished from failures of communication.

Analogously, it is asserted that a similar limitation exists in the description of cultural differences of other sorts. The recommendation is made that reports on cultural differences make more explicit the cultural communalities which provided the contextual anchoring for the interpretation of differences.

The general methodological theme of contextual matching as the basis for identifying particulars is also applied to the problems of identifying comparable culture traits in cross-cultural studies and removing the bias of the ethnographer's own culture in multiethnographer studies.

FOOTNOTE REFERENCES

1. Herskovits, Melville J., Donald T. Campbell, and Marshall H. Segall, *A Cross-Cultural Study of Perception*, The Program of

334 Cross-Cultural Understanding

African Studies, Northwestern University, Evanston, Ill., 1956. (Instruction manual and test items.)

2. Segall, Marshall H., Donald T. Campbell, and Melville J. Herskovits, "Cultural Differences in the Perception of Geometric Illusions," Science, vol. 139, 1963, pp. 769–771; The Influence of Culture on Visual Perception, Bobbs-Merrill, Indianapolis, Ind. (in press).

3. Herskovits, Melville J., Man and His Works, Knopf, New York, 1948, pp. 61–78; "Tender and Tough-Minded Anthropology and the Study of Values in Culture," Southwestern Journal of Anthropology, vol. 7, 1951, pp. 22–31; "Some Further Comments on Cultural Relativism," American Anthropologist, vol. 60, 1958, pp. 266–273.

4. Herskovits, Melville J., Donald T. Campbell, and Marshall H. Segall, "A Cross-Cultural Study of Perception," op. cit., note 1, pp. 2–3.

5. Rivers, W. H. R., "Introduction" and "Vision," in A. C. Haddon (ed.), Reports of the Cambridge Anthropological Expedition to the Torres Straits, Cambridge, London, vol. II, part I, 1901; "Observations on the Senses of the Todas," British Journal of Psychology, vol. 1, 1905, pp. 321–396.

6. Allport, Gordon W., and Thomas F. Pettigrew, "Cultural Influence on the Perception of Movement: The Trapezoidal Illusion among the Zulus," Journal of Abnormal Social Psychology, vol. 55, 1957, pp. 104–113.

7. Sanford, E. C., A Course in Experimental Psychology, part I; Sensation and Perception, Heath, Boston, 1908.

8. Brunswik, Egon, Perception and the Representative Design of Psychological Experiments (2nd ed.), University of California, Berkeley, 1956.

9. Brentano, Franz, "Über ein optisches Paradoxen," Zeitschrift für Psychologie und Physiologie der Sinnesorgane, vol. 3, 1892, pp. 349–358; vol. 5, 1893, pp. 61–82.

10. Thiéry, Armand, "Ueber geometrisch-optische Täuschungen," Philosophische Studien, Engelmann, Leipzig, vol. 11, 1895, pp. 307–370; vol. 12, 1896, pp. 67–126.

11. Pintner, Rudolf, and Margaret M. Anderson, "The Müller-Lyer Illusion with Children and Adults," Journal of Experimental Psychology, vol. 1, 1916, pp. 200–210; Wohlwill, Joachim F., "Developmental Studies of Perception," Psychological Bulletin, vol. 57, 1960, pp. 249–288.

12. Campbell, Donald T., and Solveig Cedarloo Wenar, "Perceptual and Cognitive Bias in Children" (in preparation).

13. Thouless, Robert H., "Individual Differences in Phenomenal Regression," *British Journal of Psychology*, vol. 22, 1932, pp. 217–241.

14. Hudson, W., "Pictorial Depth Perception in Sub-cultural Groups in Africa," *Journal of Social Psychology*, vol. 52, 1960, pp. 183–208.

15. Allport, Gordon W., and Thomas F. Pettigrew, "Cultural Influence on the Perception of Movement: The Trapezoidal Illusion among the Zulus," *op. cit.*, note 6.

16. Northrop, F. S. C., *Philosophical Anthropology and Practical Politics*, Macmillan, New York, 1960.

17. Beveridge, W. M., "Racial Differences in Phenomenal Regression," *British Journal of Psychology*, vol. 26, 1935, pp. 59–62; "Some Racial Differences in Perception," *ibid.*, vol. 30, 1939, pp. 57–64.

18. Thouless, Robert H., "A Racial Difference in Perception," *Journal of Social Psychology*, vol. 4, 1933, pp. 330–339.

19. Beveridge, W. M., "Some Racial Differences in Perception," *op. cit.*, note 17.

20. Woodworth, Robert S., *Experimental Psychology*, Holt, Rinehart & Winston, New York, 1938, p. 645.

21. Sanford, E. C., *A Course in Experimental Psychology*, *op. cit.*, note 7, p. 238.

22. Hering, Ewald, *Beiträge zur Physiologie*, Engelmann, Leipzig, 1861–1864, p. 355.

23. Lipps, Teodore, "Aesthetische Faktoren der Raumanschauung," *Beiträge zur Psychologie und Physiologie der Sinnesorgane*, Voss, Hamburg and Leipzig, 1891, pp. 219–307.

24. Brunswik, Egon, and J. Kamiya, "Ecological Cue Validity of Proximity and other Gestalt Factors," *American Journal of Psychology*, vol. 66, 1953, pp. 20–32.

25. Campbell, Donald T., "Common Fate, Similarity, and other Indices of the Status of Aggregates of Persons as Social Entities," *Behavioral Science*, vol. 3, 1958, pp. 14–25.

26. Wertheimer, Max, "Untersuchungen zur Lehre von der Gestalt, II," *Psychologische Forschung*, vol. 4, 1923, pp. 301–350; Woodworth, Robert S., *Experimental Psychology*, *op. cit.*, note 20, p. 625; Campbell, Donald T., "Common Fate, Similarity, and other Indices of the Status of Aggregates of Persons as Social Entities," *op. cit.*, note 25.

27. See Kruskal, William H., "Some Remarks on Wild Observations," *Technometrics*, vol. 2, 1960, pp. 1–3, for an introduction to the technical literature on the problem.

28. Child, Arthur, "The Theoretical Possibility of the Sociology of Knowledge," *Ethics*, vol. 51, 1941, pp. 392–418; "On the Theory of the Categories," *Philosophy and Phenomenological Research*, vol. 7, 1946–1947, pp. 316–335; "The Problem of Truth in the Sociology of Knowledge," *Ethics*, vol. 58, 1947, pp. 18–34.

29. Child, Arthur, "The Sociology of Perception," *Journal of Genetic Psychology*, vol. 77, 1950, pp. 293–303.

30. Lorenz, Konrad, "Gestaltwahrnehmung als Quelle wissenschaftlicher Erkenntnis," *Zeitschrift für Experimentelle und angewandte Psychologie*, vol. 6, 1959, pp. 118–165. Translated in *General Systems*, Yearbook of the Society for General Systems Research, vol. 7, 1962, pp. 37–56.

31. Campbell, Donald T., "Methodological Suggestions from a Comparative Psychology of Knowledge Processes," *Inquiry*, vol. 2, 1959, pp. 152–182; "Pattern Matching as an Essential in Distal Knowing" in K. R. Hammond (ed.), *Probabilistic Functionalism: The Psychology of Egon Brunswik*, Holt, Rinehart & Winston, New York (in press).

32. Campbell, Donald T., "The Mutual Methodological Relevance of Anthropology and Psychology," in F. L. K. Hsu (ed.), *Psychological Anthropology*, Dorsey, Homewood, Ill., 1961, p. 340.

33. Sears, R. R., "Transcultural Variables and Conceptual Equivalence," in B. Kaplan (ed.), *Studying Personality Cross-Culturally*, Harper & Row, New York, 1961, pp. 445–456; Norbeck, E., D. E. Walker, and M. Cohen, "The Interpretation of Data: Puberty Rites," *American Anthropologist*, vol. 64, 1962, pp. 463–483.

34. Campbell, Donald T., and Donald W. Fiske, "Convergent and Discriminant Validation by the Multitrait-Multimethod Matrix," *Psychological Bulletin*, vol. 56, 1959, pp. 81–105; "Methodological Suggestions from a Comparative Psychology of Knowledge Processes," *op. cit.*, note 31.

35. Campbell, Donald T., and Donald W. Fiske, "Convergent and Discriminant Validation by the Multitrait-Multimethod Matrix," *op. cit.*, note 34.

36. Campbell, Donald T., and Robert A. LeVine, "A Proposal for Cooperative Cross-Cultural Research on Ethnocentrism," *Journal of Conflict Resolution*, vol. 5, 1961, pp. 86, 91.

Four

The Relevance of Neurophysiology
for Anthropology

19

HOCKETT: We have agreed to go a little more deeply into neurology and into the connections between what had been said on that score and the other things with which we are concerned; and then work, in what we feel will be a natural direction from that, into the problem of free will. The logical person to start is Dr. McCulloch.

MCCULLOCH: The first point is that, in looking at a nervous system at any moment, we see activity going on. So we set up a model in which what is going on at any time can be described as a consequence of a sharply previous event. These systems, no matter how they came to be what they are, must act as prescribed by the model. I think all physiologists feel that there is noise in the works. There are disturbances that go on, but the nervous system is remarkably well built to compete with these difficulties.

Let's think of it as a physical system of the postulated kind. My brain is to me a postulate. It is ordinarily thought of as a vivid realistic object. The great difficulty we've had in neurophysiology is that that notion just hasn't worked. What we lacked, to make the next step, was a hypothetical relation, that is, a circuit theory of the nervous system. For that, the neuron may be made out of flesh and blood or ceramics and vacuum tubes. The circuit action in the crucial sense is going to be the same. I would say *the* great example of such a purely postulational affair in biology, the only place where it can be said to be critical, is in genetics, where the genes were such postulated entities. Today people are trying to make out of the genes another affair, as if they were dealing with a visible chromosome where they have a naive realistic picture in mind. What they fail to take into account is that in doing it, they are still working in terms of postulated entities, which are what we call coded entities. The crucial problem in our genetics is to find that code. It is not going to be a hunk of matter. You probably can't point at it and say "This one." This is the critical thing. So our move in neurophysiology has been the introduction of definitely postulated entities of the right kind.

Now, point one: There is no trouble with it at the level of physics, no trouble with it at the level of theory. I don't mean that it is all solved, please. There are plenty of little details everywhere you turn, and there are going to be very great technical difficulties.

Point two: A very large fraction of the neurons in our heads are involved primarily in housekeeping. Sometimes something which grew up with primarily a housekeeping function has become utilized, or specialized, for something different. You see this in the cerebellum, which began as a very simple arc between the two vestibular mechanisms and became a correlating device which is able to pick signals out of a noise. It is greatest in all the creatures which use it for navigation. It began as a very simple housekeeping affair.

HOCKETT: *Housekeeping* is such a lovely term that I think you should tell us what you mean by it.

MCCULLOCH: Maybe an example would be best. The basal ganglia program the motions of the body on the body—not on the outside world. The Parkinsonian patient, when he tries to eat, shakes, and his food flies all over the place instead of getting into his mouth. About ten years ago Paul Yakalev took two of these Parkinsonians, neither of whom could feed himself. They sit there happily . . .

HOCKETT: Feed each other and it worked?

MCCULLOCH: Each feeds the other. No trouble. That is, the system which was running in each patient, building the action on itself so to speak, had failed. The other system was working in relation to something outside. This is what I would call the difference between a housekeeping affair in programed movement and its use externally. O.K.? The part of the nervous system, the so-called reticular formation, is such that if you plant it in an animal where it can grow, it will grow a thalamus and a cortex. The reverse is not true. If you transplant only the upper structures, they don't carry the specifications for building what they need by way of a reticular formation. So, if you want a generalized picture, there is, in the central nervous system, a core, which has the property of specifying what is to grow. It also specifies how it is to be used. And that particular formation, once it began, has never relinquished control over the other structures. One way or another, it has retained the power to commit the whole organism. I say, "This is the place where the homunculus is hiding at the present time." It will be reduced some time to proper kinds of circuits before we get through.

Now, what does it do with the cortex? That depends upon what its business is at the moment. It grows a cortex to pull out invariants of certain kinds in this world, say pull out a tune. It doesn't need a cortex to pull out a pitch, it can do that without one, but it does need it to pull out a tune or a chord. With us, it needs it to pull out shape, regardless of size. Even in the monkey, it is not necessary for measuring total luminous flux. The monkey can tell brighter from dimmer, so to speak, more light from less light, without a cortex. We can't.

HOCKETT: When you speak of growth, your reference is to phylogeny, is it not?

MCCULLOCH: No, sir, transplant! You take the midbrain containing the bulk of the reticular formation and plunk it elsewhere into the beast and it proceeds to develop to some extent a thalamus and a cortex. It is a rudimentary cortex in such a beast, but it is there. How far up in the vertebra scale we can carry it, no one knows yet. This is the work of Dr. D. P. Nieuwkoop.[1]

Now, when you try to go from the simple job of pulling out specific qualities in the world and shipping that information back down to be used by the rest of the system, in a thing like speech, you have a great deal of difficulty at a somewhat different level from the one I have been talking about. The act is symbolic. Most acts of the nervous system are the sending by the entities of a message, derived internally, to this place, that place, and the other. The event that it is about is something which simply triggered it, so that in a certain sense you have always been dealing with signals.

But now in speech you are dealing with signals of another kind.

Take such a thing as number and make the crucial distinction: the numbers one through six, for many organisms including man, are just plain discernibles. Seven is very rarely so in man. You just don't see seven. By the time you've got to seven, you've begun to count. The greatest natural number is six. I would say it is given for you. One through six are gifts of your system, but the minute you go to seven, you've instituted a procedure. In instituting that procedure, in creating for yourself number, you have made something that you literally cannot see. You cannot see nine, you cannot see eleven. You've instituted a procedure called counting—putting things into one-to-one correspondence.

Speech is this kind of procedure for pretty nearly everybody. The sound you make has to be given a meaning for you by some sort of a procedure. When you ask "Where do we look for such things in the nervous system?" thanks to Professor Gallavardin, we do have information about it which is most surprising. Typically it happens with crack-steppers, handwashers, filing clerks, train starters, tally keepers, those with the habit of doing things several times to make sure there is no error. In this group of human beings, when changes in circulation of blood through the brain begin, say in the forty-fifth to the fifty-fifth year, this checking process tends to take on a life of its own, and it often gets very noisy—so noisy that the guy is hearing a voice telling him "Yes, you have counted it right," "Yes, you did lock the door." But when this gets too noisy, the man loses his job and then lands with us, the neurophysiological psychiatrists. These patients have been studied rather carefully for the last sixty or seventy years. Some discover that if they keep a pebble in their mouth, others that if they are eating, the voice is silent. This group of patients have visible or palpable motions going on at the time: their mouths and throats move. The patterns of these motions have been studied.

Finally, Gallavardin made beautiful electrical measurements, and you could, in these, recognize the different themes, but you had to correlate them first with what the patient told you he had just heard. But you could correlate the electrical patterns with what the patient said he heard.

One of Gallavardin's patients suffered from an eternal chicken, and it got so noisy that he lost his job, and he insisted that something be done. He was sent up by Gallavardin; surgery was done, and it silenced the eternal chicken. Now, the interesting thing is this. The motor path comes down out of one part of the cortex for these things, the auditory cortex is sitting off on the side of the head, and the path of return goes into a well-defined angle between two grooves in your brain. The bilateral removal of this area did not produce an aphasia, except momentarily. The man could still speak, perhaps not as well as before. The path, in other words, was over the motor system outward and back over the sensory system into that sensory area, and from there across, over into the auditory system. This gives you the kind of elaboration which you must look for when you deal with such an act of speech.

The difference between our brains and those of the primates is largely in two areas, one of which, lacking the other, is concerned principally with the recognition of those objects which are had through more than one sensory modality. The other region is the one forward, which is concerned principally with the elaboration of performance over long time schedules. We do not yet know any way to look at a cell in this brain and say "Either here or there" and "This has something specific to do with speech." We only know that these are the areas which have to be elaborated for speech.

Having passed to the problem of speech, we have passed to the possibility of setting up verbal behavior which is related, over the meanings of things, that can give you the structures in a thought process of a kind which introduces an essential novelty like number. And I don't mean the numbers one through six. But how it's done, for heaven's sake, we do not know. If we did, we would be well on our way into psychiatry.

MACKAY: Could you summarize that, McCulloch, in one sentence each?

MCCULLOCH: Yes. Point one: We think of a nervous system as a state-determined system. Point two: We think about it in terms of postulated neurons, components, and their relations, to obtain an abstract circuit theory which should be the same regardless of the stuff out of which the components are made. Point three: The bulk of the brain is concerned with housekeeping. Point four: Decisions committing the whole organism are usually made by a relatively small central portion known as the reticular formation. This has never lost control of the more specialized portions for pulling out the shapes, sizes, chords or whatnot in its receptive field. It can even grow the necessary apparatus. Finally, Point five: When we come to speech, we have symbolism at a superordinate level to the symbolizing activity which is always going on in the nervous system. But that superordinate level utilizes sounds, marks on paper, whatnot, motor performances of some sort which have a very complicated path back to the brain. The crucial sectors of the brain, not for the closure of this act, but for the elaborations which make possible the postulated world, are the relatively new sectors of our brain. The new posterior sector is concerned with objects which can be had over more than one sensory modality, and the new sector forward with the elaboration of acts over a long time. If we knew that physiology, we would be well on our way in psychiatry.

NORTHROP: Your second statement has to do with why we don't naively sense our nervous system and have to postulate in that connection. Why did you have Pitts working with you on this?

MCCULLOCH: Because I had difficulty at the mathematical level not knowing enough of the behavior of closed loops from a purely theoretical standpoint. That looks very simple as one looks back at it, but I assure you it was anything but. It required a familiarity with modular mathematics which I did not have. Pitts then cleaned up all that was fuzzy in my way of thinking. The paper was extra hard to write because we were all up against Carnapians, and the early Carnapian symbolism is so clumsy that when I read the paper today, I have to scratch my head to figure out what the proof was. It was an inappropriate terminology. So to speak, we were trying to do long division with Roman numerals.

NORTHROP: The second question is: What is the difference between what is done when a naive realistic universal is abstracted, from what is done when a logically realistic universal is constructed?

MCCULLOCH: If you hear the word cow, you have a naive realistic notion of it. You've just heard cow. It was something there that just had that quality, and it's patent to you right there in your world. But the moment you go to use the word cow, the word itself has become a thing for you which, though you may have heard it only once, is given for all time. It's the same whether it is written on paper, or heard in your ear, or translated into another language, or something else. Somehow the word has got this quality for you. It is, so to speak, because you can make it at will that it has to come to you every "Saturday night to be paid" that obtains the power of conveying a generality which is completely missing in the kind of generality that you have with green, or square, or something that has a sensed effect. It has not gotten that by abstraction. It's gotten that because it serves, it can be made, it can convey, and this is the crucial turnover. It's the reason why we keep finding the word *logos* cropping up. It is of the essence of the word that this is done.

MACKAY: Isn't the short answer that we don't know anything about the neurological correlates of the distinction between those two?

MCCULLOCH: No, and I don't believe you could ever find it by looking into an organism. Just as I don't believe you could find consciousness there, if consciousness is the agreement of witnesses. I think an organism is the wrong place to look. If you have to go to a world in which you have organisms, their environments, and the interactions between them, no looking at the system is going to give you a bona fide answer. It can't. The nature of the question is such that it will be a specious problem.

HOCKETT: Let me insert something at this point. When people pass from a discussion of individual behavior, cast in terms of neurophysiology, to the topic of human social behavior and language, they make a ninety-degree turn of which they are often unaware.

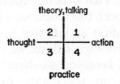

Notice the labels on the diagram. The "thought-action" axis and the "theory-practice" axis are in one sense similar: Each scale provides for a distribution of events as relatively more "implicit" or more "explicit"; but in fact they are orthogonal. Individual behaviors of a single person must be located in both scales. Thus, I can talk out loud (quadrant 1); or I can talk silently to myself—can "think in words" (quadrant 2); or I can drive a car (quadrant 4); or I can close my eyes and imagine the motions and sensations of driving a car (quadrant 3).

The horizontal axis is relevant for the discussion of the way in which the nervous system integrates and coordinates the behavior of an individual. The vertical axis is relevant for the discussion of the way language and other systems of communication integrate and coordinate the behavior of a community. However, at least for human beings, even the behavior of the *individual*—past infancy— must be discussed with full awareness of both axes. To try to handle everything with just the horizontal axis is to miss the sense of man's nature as a social animal.

MACKAY: I wonder if it would help the nonphysiologists if we could get clearer the relevance (and nonrelevance) of physiology to anthropology. I wonder if we would agree that at the moment physiology is pretty well entirely at the *receiving* end of the partnership. Interesting questions may be raised for physiology by the data of the anthropologist; but in the other direction, I can see scarcely anything of the sort we've been discussing bringing much light to anthropology. One of the few exceptions that I know is the comparison of the natural brain rhythms of different races— native South Africans versus Afrikaners, for example.[2] It was not too exciting, but there were differences.

In this sort of area it seems conceivable that physiology might provide classificatory tools like Don Campbell's tests. But as for *explanatory* tools, my impression is that the anthropological value of neural network theory and physiological details of the sort we have been discussing is negligible and promises to be little greater for a long time to come. That may be extreme!

BRAITENBERG: I respect this position which you, MacKay, call extreme, but if it did reflect an inherent restriction of the explanatory power of neurophysiology, I think we should all give up studying the brain. In fact, however, we have just recently been animated by new enthusiasm, to be sure, more on the grounds of some new theoretical insights rather than of experimental results. It is painfully evident that we have no answer to the question Professor Northrop has posed, as to whether we know the difference between the neurophysiological happenings which accompany the abstraction of naive realistic universals on one hand and of logically realistic universals on the other. But we do now understand the question—it would have had almost an ironic ring to it until a few years ago—and we must grant the philosopher the right to ask the neurophysiologists to answer it, since we have claimed, following McCulloch and Pitts, that we may describe neurons as propositions, as I have tried to show in my paper. This in turn allows us to think of research on the brain as a new kind of experimental epistemology, as the only kind, in fact, that will eventually be able to state with full assurance how it is really done.

MACKAY: May I just say for clarification that there's nothing I've just said which opposes what you've just said.

BRAITENBERG: No. But I know from private conversations that what I have just said seems shocking to many people here, and it may well be too bold, as long as our knowledge of the thinking mechanism in the brain is as meager as it actually is. But I would like to point out that we have gone a good deal beyond the biologists of the last century who said things that seem shocking even to us, such as the slogan of the secretion of thought from the brain and other such conceptual aberrations. An outgrowth of one of them, the trend to limit the study of the brain to "localization of function," is still alive: The brain is pictured as a set of neatly separated boxes; a similar collection of subdivisions of the mind is borrowed from the psychologists and represents the set of "function"; then each function is mapped on a particular anatomical box; and that is supposed to be all the neurologist can do.

As recently as ten years ago a famous neurologist presumptuously stated that the "empirical scientist" may indicate the place and time of the physiological phenomena accompanying psychological events, but he must be forever agnostic about the nature of the connection between the two. Progress beyond such agnosticism was mainly due to technical progress, simply because microelectrodes (which were introduced in 1949) permit one to record any one of the hundred million or so neurons which make up one of the older anatomical "boxes." Their firing patterns appear to be just about as complex as we would expect, considering the vast combinatorial possibilities offered by their number. When it was realized that anything sufficiently complex could carry a language, however evolved it may be, there was sufficient ground for the optimism which I have just mentioned.

I will admit that we have hardly understood one word of the language of neuronal activities in terms of the languages proper; I will even say that we are not too sure of the alphabet, but a language it is, carrying images from the senses—where their coding is fairly clear—through the brain to the motor organs—where it becomes again almost understandable. In this sense I must say that I could not fully appreciate the "ninety-degree turn" which

Dr. Hockett experiences when the conversation goes from cerebral mechanisms to language, as he has stated some time ago.

HOCKETT: May I throw out a counterchallenge?

BRAITENBERG: Yes.

HOCKETT: I don't believe in either one! What you have said in terms of my diagram is that we can study the epistemology of an organism by studying the brain.

BRAITENBERG: Yes.

HOCKETT: Let me throw out, as a counterchallenge, that the anthropologist can more fruitfully study the epistemology of a community of people by studying this segment at the top of the vertical axis, which is language and other communicative behavior. Regardless of what kind of physiological structure is inside their skulls—or in their big toes—it carries the necessary circuitry.

NORTHROP: I agree with all three points which you, MacKay, and Braitenberg have made and want to try to put one of them more sharply. If the anthropologist didn't come from a culture—

HOCKETT: I would like to try to imagine that!

NORTHROP: —then recent neurophysiology might contribute little more to anthropology than what MacKay has suggested. To me, however, the neurophysiological contribution becomes very important the moment you look philosophically at contemporary anthropologists and other social scientists and their culture.

Let me take the problem of the difficulty people have in recognizing that logically realistic concepts aren't given through the senses. I believe this goes back to the fact that in the modern world, still trapped in people's brains, is the *tabula rasa* theory of the knower. Once you admit the knower to be a *tabula rasa* or, as Aristotle did, mere formless matter, before it gets knowledge, then it follows of necessity that no concept we have can gain its meaning in any other way than through the senses. Now, what these neurophysiologists make us aware of is that we are not bringing a *tabula rasa* to the incoming sensory data. We're bringing, among other things, a neurophysiological net with a certain logic built into it. If this is the case, then knowledge has to be a synthesis of the built-in structure of the nervous system and the incoming data on its sensory side. In this inherited or built-in sense, the logic of one's nervous system is an a priori, just as the logic built into a calculating machine is its a priori.

But this leaves out the ideological and more important cultural part of the story. In any calculating machine there is always its built-in logic, and there may also be programed-in logics and other normative procedural instructions. The former is the innate part of the calculating machine's behavior, the latter its culturally conditioned component which can, so to speak, be brainwashed out.

There is also the matter of memory, including its persisting ideas. In both psychology and philosophy people said, "Never can you find or construct a logically realistic, neurophysiological correlate of directly introspected memory or its ideas." Such is what Bergson said. This conclusion rested, not on the *tabula rasa* theory, but on the theory that the only possible neurophysiological system was a nonteleologically mechanical one and also that it was impossible to construct a logically realistic, neurophysiological correlate of remembered ideas. To me, the importance of Braitenberg's point and the logically constructed McCulloch-Pitts theory of trapped universals is that they show these traditional assumptions to be false.

Unfortunately, however, these old, now outmoded "trapped universals" still persist in the minds of countless public officials and, it should be added, social scientists. This persistence shows in the fact that too many of them still believe that purposeful behavior, remembered ideas, and the various types of meaning to which MacKay referred in his paper are of no causal significance in the understanding of their subjects. Then, the meanings people put on the facts, and, *ipso facto*, the cultural philosophies of the anthropologist, will always be dismissed as insignificant and causally irrelevant.

In short, the point I am trying to make is this: Everyone, the anthropologists included, is in a culture, and he is bringing certain covert, past scientific, and philosophical ideas to everything that he listens to or does. Consequently, both MacKay's and Hockett's points must be supplemented with that of Braitenberg if the old, covert, and erroneous scientific and philosophical assumptions are not to make what they say ineffective.

MACKAY: Northrop has brought out positively the first point that I was trying to make negatively. If our anthropological colleagues want to squeeze the juice out of current neurophysiology for their present purpose, it amounts to little more than this one general principle, that the in-built logic of a brain inevitably conditions its owner's perceptual framework. What I want to guard against is any suggestion that Northrop's point is dependent on current speculative physiology. The McCulloch-Pitts theory, for instance (as I know McCulloch would agree), makes no claim to physiological realism and stands in history as an "existence theorem" rather than a description of the actual brain. It would be a disaster, I think, if anthropologists were to start founding anthropological arguments explicitly on the McCulloch-Pitts theory.

CAMPBELL: We haven't really had a humanistic social scientist speak here. But I would like to emphasize one way that Braitenberg's point should shock the typical humanistic social scientist. The bulk of them are still essentially dualistic in having a concept of mental substance which is not physical. This was best portrayed early in our seminar with the homunculus model of conscious experience, according to which in our brains there is a little homunculus watching a television screen and then with a kind of free will (not the kind of free will that MacKay is going to talk about) deciding arbitrarily how to respond. This dualism connotes a discontinuous nervous system. Now, clearly physiology, particularly in the experiments in which we control conscious experience by cortical stimulation, has removed that gap in the middle of the conceptual nervous system, so that what the homunculus perceives on the screen and how he decides to act become in themselves determined. It's in this sense that the state-determinedness of mental processes is important. Moreover, if we go back to the part of MacKay's paper to where he talks about misunderstandings, it must be emphasized that learned habits of knowing can put the same kind of restrictions on the knowing process as would, for example, an innate color blindness. If there are habits, these are substantial physical, physiological. If there are learned differences in ways of perceiving, these are substantial, just like the inherited components. There is thus a kind of a physiological isomorphism for every differentiation in conscious experience, whether due to learned or innate determinants. We can no longer accept a dualism that implies an arbitrary indeterminacy at the middle of the brain—where consciousness precedes action.

HOCKETT: The indeterminacy is spread all over, though.

CAMPBELL: Yes.

MCCULLOCH: I would like to go on from this to clear up a distinction which I think is crucial between what I will call society and what I will call culture. I think that's got to become clear.

Most of the information theory is concerned with notions of what goes into this distinction. When you try to apply it to the nervous system, you run up against the problem of working with defective components. When you have to work with defective components, and they are dying in us all the time, you have to design your circuit so that the function from input to output continues despite the death or misbehavior of the particular components. No circuit of the kind that runs through a thing like the cerebral cortex could continue to operate *if* you could assign uniquely a function in terms of input–output to any particular neuron. It must be something carried profitably so that the component, which is at one time participating in one particular chore and at another time moving in another, and the role that it will play will change even in that one function according to what is being carried on elsewhere. With respect to cooperative phenomena in biological systems, we are still *miles* from having a decent theory, and I would not like anybody to think that I or Pitts or anyone else thinks that in setting up our theory we were trying to do anything more at the time than to establish an existence proof, namely, to show that if a nervous system has the right kind of connection of neurons, as simple as those postulated neurons, postulated connections, it could compute any number that a Turing machine could compute. It's an existence proof, and the main function of it was to put man back into nature, to put the thinking process back into the physical world. Once that is done, there is no reason why you can't make use of this in explaining the origins of societies or cultures, but I fear we are a long way from the goal as to cultures.

MACKAY: Can I put it positively the other way? It seems to me that what you and Pitts did in your paper was to disprove the "postulate of impotence," which was the only cogent basis for vitalism: I mean the view that no mechanical process could mediate the functions exercised by the human organism, so the human organism could not be explained by mechanical principles.

HOCKETT: May I expand that? This disproves at one stroke the most cogent argument of the vitalists in biology and of the mentalists in the study of human beings and human society.

JAHN: What is life is not explained by this.

HOCKETT: That's right. I think it's really the other way.

NORTHROP: Let me put this point positively in another way.

Every item in the McCulloch-Pitts model might turn out, with further investigation of the brain, to be wrong. It wouldn't alter the situation one iota. All that had to be done to dispose of the vitalist's thesis, that a mechanically causal neurophysiological correlate of introspected ideas and memory is impossible, was to present one theoretically possible mechanical model to the contrary, and this the McCulloch-Pitts theoretical construct accomplishes. Whether the brain instances this particular model or some other or, as is likely, a combination of it and other mechanical ways is of secondary importance.

MACKAY: Yes. Jahn has brought out an ambiguity. When I mentioned vitalism, I was referring only to the theory that in the brain there must be some nonphysical forces active to explain mental activity. I wasn't referring, of course, to the question of the nature of living matter. I agree, McCulloch said nothing about that.

CAMPBELL: But there are analogous handlings which make life perfectly compatible with the materials of inorganic substance.

HOCKETT: That's a separate problem.

CAMPBELL: Yes. But, there are analogous positions.

HOCKETT: Well, I don't know that there has been an existence proof of the same kind. That's the real issue.

MCCULLOCH: Will you please try to put for us the distinction which I think we both feel, a gap between our ways of thinking of society and of culture?

HOCKETT: The individual organism behaves as his genes dictate, but his patterns of behavior are modified because of the physical realities of his environment. Among those physical realities are the bodies and behavior of surrounding members of the same species. Insofar as the individual's acquired habits are conditioned by the bodies and behavior of surrounding members of the same species, we could say that the individual is learning from them. Insofar as the conditioning behavior of the surrounding members was itself learned in this same way, we have what some anthropologists call *cultural* learning or just *culture*, or what some ornithologists call *tradition*. I prefer the latter term, since anthropologists greatly overwork the word "culture" anyway. Tradition, then, is a biological mechanism of phylogenetic continuity and change, alongside the genetic mechanism; and it appears variously in the animal world, by no means exclusively with human beings. Human tradition has become especially complex and flexible because of the development of language, itself transmitted largely by tradition, which enables many lifeways to be passed down "symbolically" rather than by tutelage in actual conditions. As Childe points out, it is safer to tell the young how to deal with a bear than to try to teach them only when there is a live bear at hand.

SAMBURSKY: I want to come back to Mackay's discussion of vitalism versus the explanation of life by mechanical or neurophysiological concepts. This does not mean yet that consciousness has been explained and free will is involved in consciousness too.

MACKAY: This we will certainly come to.

CAMPBELL: On this point, however, it may not mean that consciousness is explained, but it does mean that we are close to, and are committed to, finding a physiological process correspondent to each of the subtle differentia in consciousness, as in the *Gestalt* psychology concept of isomorphism. This is similar to Feigl's synthetic identity solution to the mind–body problem. Many of us with physiological leanings are committed to a kind of synthetic identity proposition where each of the differentia in conscious experience will eventually be found to have corresponding differentia in the physiological function. The work of Penfield, using electrical cortical stimulation of conscious patients, with his ability to repeatedly control the content of their conscious experience by moving a probe over the surface of the cortex, is dramatic evidence of this close tie-in.

SAMBURSKY: This does not yet explain the uniqueness of inner experience; it remains unique for me even if the event I experience repeats itself under similar circumstances. Inner experience will not enter the mathematico-physical equations which one day may give a complete description of life. Leibniz has seen this very clearly, and what he has said means the following, if you express it in modern terms: If the dimension of a computer, having all the faculties of a human brain, is enlarged so that you can enter it like a factory, you will only find wirings, electronic parts, and everything that corresponds to your equations, but consciousness will not be found there.

BRAITENBERG: Just one moment. I should like to continue in my role of the simple-minded optimist. Let me hope that we will some day have a good mathematical theory of the brain and that we will be able to anchor it in a good theory of biological evolution, in the sense that we shall be able to prove that such and such a brain, for instance a human brain with all its capacity of speech, and so on, will necessarily arise. In a similar way by that time I am sure we will be able to let the whole theory of the evolution of biological objects logically follow from our knowledge of the inanimate physical environment. I could see that my task would then be to demonstrate to you how in such an environment, through evolution as well as development of language, an automaton would arise which could tell me that it has an inner experience of a particular kind, not quite matching anything it can observe in another of its kind, and which you may well call "consciousness."

HOCKETT: Which still doesn't answer the problem.

MCCULLOCH: May I say this? I think we are using the word "consciousness" in a very strange sense. To my mind, as a physician, I think of consciousness as an agreement of witnesses and not something to be found in any one head. I would be much happier with a word like "awareness." It is not at all the same notion.

But quite apart from that, if I look inside the head of somebody who sees green, I don't expect to find green running around inside his head! The impulse won't be green. I see no reason why one should deny awareness to a sufficiently complicated structure—awareness of things external to itself, awareness of its internal state, and so on. I think there is no reason why this attribution should be something we hold as unique to living systems—they happen to be the only systems having it with which we are familiar. There is no reason why we can't make one that will report "Yes, I'm feeling too hot in my umph." "Yes, I'd better open the window, or turn on the cold water," or something. Internally or externally, if you use this test, if you think you know what is being done informationwise, and you can state it in a finer and less ambiguous manner, I can build the machine to do it. That's the point. It must be finite. It must be unambiguous. I don't think there is any problem of awareness other than this.

MACKAY: I agree entirely with McCulloch here. There is no possibility of specifying behavior which a machine can't reproduce, if you take "machine" in the sense of a logically specifiable construction. But this behavioral problem is not, I think, the same as the problem of awareness. There remains a conceptual distinction between *reporting* and *uttering the sounds* which have for us the significance of a report; and it's not clear to me that any behavioral test could meet the need we feel for that distinction.

HOCKETT: Lying is possible.

MACKAY: Having said this, let me emphasize that I see no barrier in principle to our producing (artificially begetting as it were) an organism which could be conscious as we are. I'm only saying we wouldn't be able to prove it so by any behavioral test.

CAMPBELL: You are in this only agreeing, however, with the philosophers who recognize that this is also impossible from one human being to another.

MACKAY: That's right, of course. I have elaborated elsewhere[3] the argument that the step is one of commitment and not one of deduction. The big question then is, under what circumstances would it be rational for us to commit ourselves to an artificially begotten organism in the same way as we do to a naturally begotten human being?

FOOTNOTE REFERENCES

1. Nieuwkoop, P. D., "Investigations on the Regional Determination of the Central Nervous System," *The Journal of Experimental Biology*, vol. 24, 1947, pp. 145–183; "Origin and Establishment of Organization Patterns in Embryonic Fields During Early Development," *Proc. Koninkl. Nederl. Akademie van Wetenschappen*, Amsterdam, Series C, vol. 58, no. 2, 1955, pp. 219–227; no. 3, 1955, pp. 356–367.
2. Mundy-Castle, A. C., B. L. McKiever, and T. Prinsloo, "A Comparative Study of the Electro-Encephalograms of Normal Africans and Europeans of Southern Africa," *International Federation of Electro-Encephalography and Clinical Neurology*, vol. 5, 1953, pp. 533–543.
3. MacKay, Donald M., "The Use of Behavioural Language to Refer to Mechanical Processes," *British Journal for the Philosophy of Science*, vol. 13, 1962, pp. 89–103.

20

MACKAY: Human freedom is often felt to be imperiled by mechanistic theories of brain function. Is this the case?

To clear the ground, let us go in imagination to the fullest extreme of determinism in the nineteenth-century sense of the word. Suppose we have in front of us somebody (whom I will call Joe Smith) whose brain is open to us in full detail. We can look at all the works, and they are physically determinate. We are isolated from Joe by a one-way screen, so that it is quite impossible for any of our activity to influence him. Suppose that all of us are led by scientific calculation to the prediction that Joe will choose an apple rather than an orange out of the dish in front of him, where there is one apple and one orange. Let me now raise the question which I think is fundamental. This prediction of ours—can we say that it is *certain?*

What do we mean by certain? Among other things, I think if we want to say that a prediction is certain, we mean that anyone who disbelieves it is in error, and anyone who believes it is correct; or another way of putting it is that it is mandatory on all members of the linguistic community. Now the snag, of course, is that we haven't considered Joe. If Joe is a member of the linguistic community, we've got to face the question: Would Joe be correct if he believed our prediction? Whether he hears of it or not, is it mandatory on him as on anyone else? It doesn't take much insight to realize that if our prediction presupposes that Joe does not hear it, it would be invalidated by Joe's even being offered it, simply because Joe's brain would then be in a different state from the one presupposed when we calculated it. Furthermore, there exists a class of cases in which no attempt on our part to allow for the effects of our prediction on Joe could converge. In other words, *no valid prediction exists* in the common calculus that is binding upon both Joe and us.

This, I think, is the logical oddity about what we call free choice. I suggest that it doesn't depend on any mechanical oddity in our brains. What we have to recognize is rather that *choosing* is an event of a unique sort, such that no universally valid prediction of it exists in our common calculus.

Let us now add an important qualifier. This does not mean that there is only a chaotic relation between the physical state of Joe's brain and what Joe may do. On the contrary, we have assumed a one-to-one relation. In other words, corresponding to whatever "outside" view we have of Joe's choosing, there is only one story from Joe's side (though a different one) which would correctly describe his mental processes.

What I'm suggesting, therefore, is that we here face a kind of epistemological principle of relativity. It's quite analogous to the principle of relativity in physics, whereby if two individuals, A and B, differ in their relation to an event, for example by moving with different velocities, then, in order that A should rightly believe what he does, the expression of his belief must differ from that of B. For example, the question may be which of two events, P and Q, occurred first. In relativity theory, if A and B are moving with relative velocity, it is possible for one observer to see Q before P and the other to see P before Q.

In other words, what I'm suggesting is that this view of the genuine freedom of an individual's choice does not mean the abandonment of objectivity. What it does imply is that objectivity must be attached to judgments of the *validity of believing*, rather than to judgments of the *truth of propositions*. We may rightly be certain that Joe will choose an apple. But we have to admit, in fact to insist, that this does not mean that "*it* is certain" that he will; for Joe wouldn't be right to believe this. Nevertheless, there is a transformation such that, corresponding to our "outside" account of Joe's choosing, only one account will be valid for Joe.

The sum of this, then, is that it is fallacious to suppose that determinism in brain mechanism implies determinateness of choice. It's a very curious logical situation—for me the nub of the mystery of what it is to be a human agent. The mystery is not a mere puzzle in the scientific sense of something to be resolved by more data. It is the irreducible oddity, to us, of needing two mutually validating, but different, accounts to do justice to human agency. In the sociological-anthropological context, this has the odd consequence that there are quite a number of generalizations which can validly be made about "any" member of the community, which nevertheless would be systematically invalid for *any one* member of that community to believe as applied to himself. Even sociological determinism does not undermine the genuineness of human freedom.

HOCKETT: This has a beautiful corollary in the limitation of social science that is built into it by the fact that *all* science must by definition be public. Any observation of a social scientist is expressed as some sort of statement. But the subjects of the social scientist's observations are humans, specialists in the reception and interpretation of statements. The statements of the social scientist cannot be secret, or the public nature of science is violated. But if they are not secret, they can feed back to his subjects and alter their subsequent behavior in unpredictable ways.

SAMBURSKY: It means that the rules of scientific prediction do not apply to the person itself who makes predictions, because his own self is for him a singularity in the field of determined events.

MACKAY: And it means further that all the members of an *interacting* group are indeterminate to one another.

SAMBURSKY: Planck once wrote a paper on free will and determinism where, as a believer in free will, he looks at the problem from the logical point of view. He said that the possibility of determining the actions of a living being become greater the greater the gap between your intelligence and his. Determination becomes thus logically impossible for my own actions. Again, from a temporal perspective, I can discover the whole causal nexus of my seemingly impulsive actions, but this perspective is missing at the moment when I act. I might at this moment be in a terrible rage and smack somebody's face. Months after this, I may be able to see the causes that led me to that, but in principle I'm not able at this moment to see them.

HOCKETT: Well, this is an operational definition of free will.

MACKAY: Yes. There's one very important point which follows, if I'm right. Even though in retrospect you can show Joe Smith a movie of the brain data which led you correctly to make the prediction, Joe is not retrospectively entitled, on this basis, to change his mind and say "Oh, I see I wasn't free after all." To say that would imply that *at the time* he would have been correct to believe the data in the movie. But, of course, we've seen that he wouldn't, because his believing would have rendered them out of date. Thus even in retrospect one cannot validly adopt a deterministic view in the sense of negating one's earlier belief. All one can do is, so to speak, to increase the dimensionality of one's view and in some sense sympathize with the outside observer's view of what went on, without adopting it *in place* of one's earlier belief.

HOCKETT: May I remind you of a very beautiful aphoristic way of expressing this that Anatol Rapoport invented? You have to make it in the first person singular. To the extent that I can predict my own behavior, I speak of free will; to the extent that I can predict the behavior of something else, I speak of determinism.

MACKAY: I wouldn't say predict.

HOCKETT: He said it this way.

MACKAY: Well, then, I am reluctant to accept it, because surely to predict something is to set up an expectation for it; and I would say that logically expectation is an *alternative* to decision. If I have to decide something, then it's something for which expectation would be logically inappropriate. If I expect something, then it's something about which I have no decision to make.

HOCKETT: He obviously meant something more general than you choose to by the term *predict*.

MCCULLOCH: I might just add that Gödel was delighted and said, "The consequences of a decision cannot be among its causes."

NORTHROP: I'd like to ask whether Don MacKay's theory is the Stoic theory. If I understand the Stoic theory, it is that every fact is deterministically caused; but, there is one thing, however, with respect to which we are free, and this is assent to any belief about what the facts are. The fact that you, MacKay, brought in the word *believe* suggests that your theory is identical with that of the Stoics.

SAMBURSKY: The Stoics said that if a freely falling stone could think, it would believe that it falls of its own free will. Seen from the inside, I have a choice at any moment; but seen from the outside, I am completely determined.

MACKAY: That's just what I want to deny. It is not seen from outside that *I* am completely determined; what's seen from outside, or rather what's valid for the outsider, is that *my bodily processes* are determined. That is not logically the same thing. If it were, it would lead to the suggestion "Well, you're free to believe what you like, but perhaps you are in error in believing what you like." My point is that the agent is not in error in believing what he does; that the "outside" data do not establish what is "really" the case, in such a sense that he's in error in believing that his choice is undetermined.

CAMPBELL: This argument is a subtle one, and I think we will later remember that it was very valuable and may not be able to pinpoint it; therefore, I would like to suggest a MacKay reference, "On the Logical Indeterminacy of a Free Choice."[1] I can report that this paper was relevant to a discussion between Professor Smith and myself on the relation between psychiatry and law. Currently most psychiatrists find themselves unable to testify on the deliberateness of a given person's intentions in committing a murder, and so on. The concept of responsible choice found in law is lacking in current psychiatry. But it may not be lacking in the cybernetically corrected psychiatry of twenty years from now, and we may find a model of human decision behavior which justifies some of the "superstitious" characteristics of the common law such as guilt and intent. Is this a fair statement about our discussion?

SMITH: Yes, except I wouldn't classify the concepts of guilt and intent as "superstition."

MACKAY: One of the things I had most in mind when writing was indeed the argument "It ain't my fault, it's my glands."[2]

CAMPBELL: This general point has relevance to our interest in a physiological epistemology. In attempting a biological or psychological epistemology, I have restricted myself to an "epistemology of the other one," to borrow a phrase from Max Meyer, an early German-trained behaviorist who had the slogan "the psychology of the other one." I think it is very important, if we are going to have a kind of experimental epistemology, that we recognize it has an important difference in its aspirations from much of the epistemology in the Cartesian tradition in that it only aspires to be an epistemology of the *other* one.

SAMBURSKY: I should still like to put the question from the operational point of view. I can predetermine the actions of an animal which is on a much lower level of intelligence than I am. I can arrange things so that I can predict what it will do. But this becomes more and more difficult the more the animal approaches my own intelligence. That leads finally to the singularity of myself applying the causal laws to myself.

MACKAY: If I do understand you, I am not sure that I agree. I would say that this increase in the difficulty of prediction is, from our philosophical point of view, not fundamental. It simply means that you need to get your hands on more and more determining factors in order to make a successful prediction in complete detail. There's a world of difference between prediction and decision.

HOCKETT: Your exposition is in the traditional terms of determinism and free will. I would like to hear somebody relate what you have said about those to indeterminacy.

MACKAY: You mean Heisenberg indeterminacy?

HOCKETT: That generic sort.

MACKAY: I must say that in spite of all the brain does to insure stability of function, I'm prepared to believe that every now and again in the cell population there may be events whose occurrence, because of a sort of convergence of slight indeterminacies, is both significant and unpredictable from the physical data. But I would associate this, if anything, with spontaneity and creativeness and imaginative mental activity rather than the exercise of what we call a sober, free choice.

SAMBURSKY: How do you fit complementarity in this? Is not introspection complementary to action? The moment I decide to act, I have to put an end to my train of thought.

MACKAY: I like it better as an image than an argument. I think the logical concept of complementarity, freed of its particular associations in physics, has quite a wide application to situations which demand more than one "linguistic projection" for completeness.[3] But I'm worried by the way in which people tend to assume that when you talk of complementarity, you are deducing something by analogy from physics. This, I think, would be quite illegitimate.

SAMBURSKY: I agree.

HOCKETT: I'm not so sure. We may have, rather, two manifestations in seemingly very different realms of something which is actually more basic. The relationship that has been described between determinism and free will may stem from such elementary physical facts as locality and spatiotemporal separation, plus the fact that information can get from one place to another only by being *transmitted*—which takes time. To some extent, what happens next *here* depends on what is happening now *elsewhere*. But one can know what is happening now *elsewhere* only by receiving signals from elsewhere, and the receipt *here* of such signals is part of what is to happen next *here*. This is relativistic indeterminacy. It occurs to me that the indeterminacies found by the quantum physicists in the behavior of elementary particles may stem from the same thing.

MCCULLOCH: I would like to disagree with you on that. I think this is an entirely different kind of difficulty. It is neither such affairs as we run into from the scatter of the threshold, let's say, that determines whether or not an impulse will arise, or the time at which it arises, or what not. Thermal noise does not answer for it. Nor is it the essentially Tychastic one that you have in the letting go of a particular atom of a particular kind in time. Indeterminacy here is of an entirely different kind.

HOCKETT: The burden of proof is on you. . . . Well, I'm trying to think about that. I'll store it for later.

CAMPBELL: One of the achievements of cybernetics is providing a model in which in some sense the consequence appears as the cause in that there has been a template for a goal and a discrepancy signal has been used to modify behavior to reduce discrepancy.

MCCULLOCH: This is much closer to the egocentric particular in all descriptions. It is inherent in the problem. It is not a matter of noise in the works or something of that sort. It would make noise responsible for a new idea, just as radiation is certainly responsible for enlargement of mutations.

HOCKETT: Well, I think it's inherent in the problem because of the structure of the physical world of which we are a part. That would be my point. I think this can be shown, though certainly not by me in the next two minutes!

MACKAY: It might be simpler to consider the problem of description instead of prediction. Suppose I want to describe exhaustively the state of my own brain. I'm in the same old logical dilemma—like chasing my own tail. Suppose now in dialogue with another I seek to describe the state of *his* brain. By virtue of the dialogue relationship, this becomes impossible too. In other words, in dialogue the other also is fundamentally and logically, and not just empirically, unspecifiable. I take this to be at least one dimension of the mystery of persons to one another. A person in dialogue with me becomes a mystery to me in such a way that it *makes no sense to want* a full description of him as a thing. I think our respect for his choices as free and undetermined reflects our awareness that he cannot be to us a fully specified thing insofar as we are in dialogue with him. To reduce him to the isolated status in which he becomes fully specifiable would be to cut the dialogue. He would then be no longer "one of us."

Here I think we see the operational meaning of respect for a man's dignity. It requires one to open oneself to him for this kind of reciprocal relationship, in which he can get his hand on my controls, so to say, and I can get my hand on his, in such a way that we become irreducibly one system. In that situation, he ceases to be a specifiable entity to me. If I adopt a one-way relationship so that I can manipulate him, but he has no grip on me, then this both makes him predictable to me and makes impossible the kind of dignity that I'm talking about.

HOCKETT: But you would not be willing to say that to experiment with a physical system is to conduct a dialogue with it?

MACKAY: Well, no. The difference between the physical indeterminateness of electrons and the logical indeterminateness of human agents, of course, is that an electron is not a member of our linguistic community, so the problem is not the same. Even if there are unspecified disturbances due to our interaction, this doesn't give electrons the kind of mystery that another cognitive being has for us.

HOCKETT: Does anyone want to summarize what we have said today? The Chairman is not going to attempt it—unless I close by telling you the story about the Chinese emperor who developed a passion for Chinese boxes—that is, nests of boxes—and decided that he was going to make his life work the accumulation in a single room of all the Chinese boxes in the world. He sent his scouts out to collect them. A rather foolish prime minister pointed out to him that when he had all the Chinese boxes in the world in one room, the room itself would be a Chinese box. The prime minister was executed, but the emperor never smiled again.

FOOTNOTE REFERENCES

1. MacKay, Donald M., "On the Logical Indeterminacy of a Free Choice," *Mind*, vol. 69, 1960, pp. 31–40.
2. MacKay, Donald M., "Brain and Will," *The Listener*, vol. 57, May 9th and 16th, 1957.
3. MacKay, Donald M., "Complementarity, II," *Aristotelian Society Proceedings*, Supplementary vol. 32, 1958, pp. 105–122.

Some Practical Implications

21

NORTHROP: What are the practical implications for anthropology? Since Mr. Klausner was the one who suggested this topic, I'll call on him first.

KLAUSNER: Thank you. I would like to make a few comments that have occurred to me after reviewing the discussions of this conference. *Cross-Cultural Understanding: Epistemology in Anthropology* is, I think, a most basic problem for those concerned with the introduction of technological change. At the same time, there is the problem of the preservation of human dignity, as Professor MacKay has elucidated it.

What is the anthropologist's role in this context? As I see it, it is—one—to help identify the needs within the community as expressed by the community itself and—two—present the various modernization alternatives available to that community and the consequences attendant on such changes. As one looks at the history of the introduction of technological changes, or modernization, there are several methods which have been used. I would suggest that, on the basis of this conference, the role of the anthropologist should be points one and two above. The decision of what change should be accepted must come through group discussions in the community in question in order to preserve the dialogue between the educator and the community, and thus human dignity. It is also through this process that the best chance for achievement of effective change is provided. This is the basic methodology which is behind the fundamental education and community development processes, where one does not introduce change from above, but, through group dynamics, effects an understanding on the part of the villagers themselves of their needs and sets in motion the process of decision making and implementation of change on the part of the villagers.

Assuming that this can be done, then the anthropologist has another role. It is to point up the most appropriate and effective channels existing within the community for the introduction of this agreed-upon change. This leads to the issues of an understanding of the expressed value structure, of the epistemology of the culture, of the implicit cultural forms of that value system, or hierarchy, to use the term of Professor Northrop. It is the anthropologist's function to identify this epistemology, to make it known to the organization and groups involved in the introduction of technological change.

Now, I think we would all agree that the change should be introduced with as little destruction, disorganization, and sacrifice to the system and with as little economic, social, and cultural disruption as possible. That there will be disruption, I think we would all agree. But, again, it is the anthropologist's role, as I see it as it has developed in the discussions we've had here, to point up the ways and means that will result in as little initial disruption as possible. The anthropologist also should point up, to both the villagers and those technicians responsible for the introduction of change, the consequences such technological change will bring to the value system and to the implicit cultural forms of that system. In many cases, the village communities may themselves see those consequences. In many cases, they may not. Even if they are pointed up, the village communities may not still appreciate them either intellectually or emotionally. Nevertheless, it is the responsibility of the anthropologist to point up the consequences to the system.

Technological change, when it is brought, implies an epistemological view, a philosophical basis that can, and often is, in conflict with the value systems of that society. With the introduction of technological change, there will inevitably be a subtle and, in some cases, a gross change in the value system and in the cultural forms, whether it is a question of family, economy, social relations, and so on. I think we can preserve the unity of the culture and human dignity, and yet have as little destruction as possible, by engaging in this dialogue among the educators, technicians, anthropologists, and villagers—not imposing the technological change on the villagers in question.

I view it of high priority to encourage anthropologists, who understand the processes involved in the determination of a philosophy of culture, such as we have been discussing for the past ten days, to undertake applied research work for national governments, the United States Government, and international agencies in the terms of points one and two above. Likewise, it is of high priority for those national governments, international agencies, and the United States Government to encourage anthropologists to work for and with them. This is a two-way street, and I must say there has not been too much communication on this rather lonely thoroughfare.

JAHN: What Mr. Klausner has just said is, for me, not one job, but two separate jobs. The first is that of the educator and the second that of the person having the task of introducing a change. But this is not at all the job of the anthropologist. In the first place, the anthropologist is there to understand and to be the mediator for mutual understanding. If, in the course of the work, an educator seems to be necessary, that is another, completely different job. I feel a danger in mixing these two roles. Otherwise anthropology would become a tool of Western culture to change people, which is certainly not what it is meant to be.

KLAUSNER: I meant to specify these as two separate roles. I was thinking of the educator as taking anthropological training from one who understands the processes in question. I would agree with the qualification just made.

EHRENFELS: While agreeing generally with the preceding statements, I would like to point up two distinct fields which offer standard examples for defective understanding of, and a destructive attitude towards, cultures other than our own. One is highly theoretical, the other highly practical. On the theoretical side, I think that a certain region of beliefs of philosophical content in non-European societies is *judged* before it is adequately represented. We can only understand concepts if we get at their best and most complete representation; not their worst or least complete.

As an example, the theory in astrology is that planets do not cause changes on the earth, but they are, so to say, the hands of a clock moved by a third agency. By reading the movements of the various clock hands, we may come to understand corresponding terrestrial streams of changes. According to this theory, the naming of a particular planet, such as, for instance, Venus, is not at all a chance product of human imagination, but an expression of the intuitive or otherwise achieved understanding of an inner cause-and-effect context, or affinity, between the hand of the clock—that is, the planet—and the nature of the terrestrial movement to which it corresponds. Also, according to this theory, if we see two celestial bodies in opposition, the astrologer interprets this event *not* as directly causing conflicts on earth, but as indicating two terrestrial streams of forces, moving in opposite directions, and thus expects some particular clash to happen *in terram*. As the understanding of this method implies the identification of planets, precious stones, symbolic colors, or animals with aspects of the human character, we arrive at an understanding of the holistic theory behind astrology. I do not propose to say that this is a correct theory or hypothesis, nor to defend its point of view. But I think we should at least try to understand the underlying philosophies of astrology, numerology, geomancy, or whatever it be. This is one field in which I feel that many otherwise nonethnocentric anthropologists still tend to dismiss an inadequately represented philosophy, instead of getting at its most appropriate, and hence best, representation.

The other application is in a very different field. It is the anthropologist's attitude, for example, to European forms in etiquette, particularly clothing. I think it is a unique phenomenon which happened at the end of the nineteenth and beginning of the twentieth centuries that one type of clothing, such as we are wearing here, is considered all over the world as the only proper and decent one. This is a generalization which never happened before in history. On the contrary, when the British first came to India they tended to adopt Indian clothing to a certain extent. According to Somerset Maugham's descriptions, some of the administrators still did so in the twentieth century, when wearing the sarong in Malaya. Now Asian or African students feel that wearing their own national dress is a disgrace to their honor and prestige. I think that in this field of "applied ethnocentrism," anthropologists could still do a lot to clarify the position by making people realize, in Europe as well as overseas, that there is no absolute value attached to any particular type of clothing, or otherwise institutionalized forms of outward appearance.

MACKAY: Thinking back to what Jahn was just saying, it seems to me impossible to dissociate knowledge from power. Therefore, willy-nilly, anthropology, insofar as it is scientific, does place a tool in our hands. This, of course, raises the question: By what criteria do we as scientists interested in this area (I include myself) decide the ethical validity of the application of the tool that we are fashioning? Have we many? Are the criteria decided by the light of nature? Are we here naively realistic? Or have we any logically realistic concepts to guide the applied anthrolopogist as well as the theoretical anthropologist?

SMITH: Do you mean the anthropologist in his task as educator?

MACKAY: Well, I mean the sort of thing that Bill Klausner told us about. Here is a culture. We, from our point of view, see it as deficient. The people are probably perfectly content, though they may wonder whether they are missing something. We form judgments, by virtue of our investigations, that they are lacking this, this, and this, and the best we can do for them is this, this, and this. Unscrupulous persons in this position could manipulate the situation in ways that we as human beings would disapprove of. What is it that stops us from being unscrupulous? Is it purely an emotional factor, or are there any principles that we can extract as guide principles for applied anthropology, analogous, for example, to the Hippocratic oath in medicine?

HOEBEL: Do we agree that the ultimate purpose of anthropology is to acquire a knowledge of man in society to the end that we may modify society more satisfactorily to fulfill the purposes of man as we may define them? In other words, anthropology is not just to study man for curiosity's sake, but to make it possible for us effectively and intelligently to manipulate human cultures.

NORTHROP: Might I try to reformulate this point? Previously we have been asking purely descriptive questions: What is the philosophy of a culture? Now, are you asking, How do we evaluate the coming together of two cultures with different hierarchical value systems? If they are incompatible, how does one evaluate which one gives way? Is this the question you are asking?

MACKAY: That's one half of it. The other half, which is inseparable in practice, but theoretically different, is: Granted that you

do decide which ought to give way, how do you settle which methods are ethically permissible in displacing it? You used the word
manipulate. There are many philosophers who would say that the
one thing you can't do compatibly with human dignity is to manipulate people. Manipulation, in the sense of making them into
pawns, is just ethically bad. Maybe we don't agree, but that's the
kind of question which it seems to me is inescapable.

MAQUET: On these two matters we must clearly distinguish
the question of knowledge and the question of values. Anthropology is a pursuit of knowledge. Thus, the problem of values of anthropologists is not a question which is linked to the position of
the anthropologist as such. As a human being he has values and
chooses to use his knowledge in one way or another. It is the same,
I think, with the question of assessing the value of different cultures. It is going outside the scope of anthropology to try to judge
other cultures. For instance, MacKay said, "We, from our point of
view, see it as deficient." I, as an anthropologist, never felt like
that, and I do not think we can fairly insist on that point. We
may be asked by different governments to use our knowledge, but
that is another question. Then we are acting as experts and, as
human beings, may or may not accept the aims of these governments.

KLAUSNER: On this point, I think it should be noted when you
say "we," you'll find, in the practical application of this throughout
Asia, that what happens is that it is the national governments, that
is, those in power in the capitals, who are largely Western-edu-
cated, who are demanding these technological changes. Whether
these national political leaders are fully cognizant of the implications of these changes is another question. I think it is the anthropologist's role to make them cognizant.

It is not we (the aid organizations) going in and telling them
what they are deficient in, but it is they coming to the organizations and asking for this or that change. I'm not sure (and this is a
question that deserves continuing study) whether the villagers are
at a similar level of rising expectation. It certainly is true for the
capital group, but we must be careful before we generalize and
apply this state of expectation to the villagers.

In other words, regarding the first question about this conflict,
I don't think there is any question of which ought to give way—
one is going to give way. I think technological change is going to

come to these governments because *they* are requesting it.

In regard to the second question, about the preservation of human dignity, I think such dignity can be achieved through the educator and technician, schooled by the anthropologist, who do not impose technological decisions upon the villagers, but rather work and live intimately with the villagers and lead them to carry out their own discussions, identify their own needs, and make their own decisions for planning and action, hopefully after considering the alternatives open to them and the probable consequences of their action as outlined by the anthropologist. In this way, human dignity will be preserved and effective change brought about.

HOCKETT: Let me return to Professor Maquet's remarks. At one time I should have agreed with him. I no longer do. Ethnographic field work necessarily involves human confrontation, and in any human confrontation ethical issues arise and must be faced. These issues need have little to do with governmental or colonial policy. I have no general solution to these ethical issues, but I have one suggestion. The anthropologist might envisage his function largely as that of establishing and maintaining channels for clear cross-cultural communication—on the basis of the ethical *meta*-decision that clear communication is in the long run always desirable.

YAMAMOTO: As Mr. Jahn pointed out, there is a role of mediator. But when cultures meet and change, the values are also affected. The anthropologist himself might be changed. I would like to make just two points. One is the importance of the study which creates real ethical problems. This is the study deeply rooted in values. Here is one value, here is another value. We have been facing different values. This confrontation of values happens all the time in cultural contacts. Then come the questions of which is higher, which is more widely acceptable, and so on. But while this could not be answered objectively, the actual contacts produced the change of values. This change is to be studied.

The second is the relative viewpoint of human values. We have these values. But we are challenged by people of other values. This relative view is important for the anthropologist as interpreter or mediator. It is indispensable in order to get deeply into the problems of other people's minds. Dynamic, movable, and relativistic views of values may be useful. Perhaps we must trace the historical change of values.

MCCULLOCH: Let's take one simple example from my field of

psychiatry. I'm convinced that in Haiti, psychiatry for the neurotic is at least as good as it is anywhere else I know in the world and certainly better than in the United States. Haiti is very interesting for this reason. The social upper crust are still largely French in their thought processes, the rest still African. You give the latter a saint, and the saint is fitted right into their old ways. Their Voodoo handles neuroses beautifully. When it comes to psychoses, for which they would need the ideas of physics, chemistry, physiology, anatomy of the brain, they know enough to turn to the psychiatrist, who is of the upper crust and has our Western type of ideas. This is a happy solution and a very rugged one. If you went to Haiti and tried to change it, you would get nowhere. I think one of the fundamental criteria here is that when a thing is working well, you just about can't influence it.

JAHN: I want to go back to Professor MacKay's question. His first point was, what is the position of the anthropologist between two cultures? My answer may sound rather dogmatic, but I apply it only to myself. It is not our job only to find deficiencies in other cultures. Our job is to find out, by comparison with other cultures, the deficiencies in our own. This means that we must never be in the role of educator, but in the role of learner; not of teacher, but of pupil. If then, by our presence, they want to change, it's their free choice, and not our right to force them to anything. It is our free choice as well to learn where we have to change our own consciences. Thus we are in the second problem Professor MacKay has formulated—the moral part.

It is already certain that our limitation is that we say that something in another culture is defined by our moral system alone or can be defined by our moral system. We must respect the value systems in another culture so that we will not in advance say a human sacrifice, or even cannibalism, is wrong. It might be right in the context of another culture. It might even be their moral. If that is so, it means that we have to see our own culture in the light of another one. It is not just a problem of who gives way, but who learns from whom. Thus in time of cultural contacts, both cultures give way. They will find out some of their own deficiencies and will learn what can be added.

MACKAY: I think this point of humility needs stressing, though I think one must not confuse open-mindedness with empty-mindedness. Could we clarify the first of the points that Bill Klausner made, namely, that the anthropologist's function is to identify the needs of the community? I take it we mean by this not to decide ex cathedra what the needs are, but rather to listen and regard things as needs when you can get agreement from the community. This is difficult, because in the medical context, which Warren McCulloch has rightly suggested as a parallel, the doctor may sometimes neglect his responsibility if he takes the need of the patient to be only what the patient himself thinks it to be. It's not obvious to me that anthropologists can shrug off that responsibility and say "I'll only take it as a need if they do so."

The second thing that worries me is the word *appropriate*. The applied anthropologist must point out, presumably to the government, the most "appropriate" channels for the introduction of change. Here it seems to me we need the hardest thinking. Appropriate relative to what value? For example, suppose that the most "appropriate" way would require disclosure of a tribal secret which the anthropologist has promised not to disclose. Isn't there a real, though limited, analogy with psychiatry in getting into the confidences of a culture? If you are in a similar ethical position of a doctor and a patient, isn't there a need for a code of practice for the anthropological practitioner, for the same reason?

MAQUET: I think that there is a distinction between the psychiatrist and the anthropologist in the sense that I always understood that the psychiatrist was there to cure people. In MacKay's conception, when he says "What the people think they need is perhaps not what they really need," he is making anthropology into a kind of social therapy.

MACKAY: We are talking about applied anthropology, which is, I take it, in part social therapy.

LEÓN-PORTILLA: I think that here we are thinking of anthropologists coming from the air who would get some people to change their values and way of life. But I don't think that this is the case. Today we have tremendous cross-cultural contacts, let's say in Thailand or Africa or Latin America. For centuries you have had this cross-cultural contact occurring spontaneously, very often in a barbaric way. Today some governments want to introduce their own changes—new highways, education, sanitation, many other things. Here is perhaps where the social anthropologist or the applied anthropologist by knowing precisely the particular situation of these groups and not trying to modify their values, but *knowing* these values, could help to make these cultural contacts less violent. Instead of disintegrating these groups, the anthropologist could help to integrate into the other cultures the new technical improvements. Technical changes can't be stopped because they are actual things. Economics are entering, roads are being built. This is the philosophy we have developed in Mexico through Dr. Caso and Dr. Gamio. Social applied anthropology is planning how these improvements should be made, not judging them as better or worse.

NORTHROP: Could you specify what is the criterion they use to decide which is the best possible method?

LEÓN-PORTILLA: First, they followed Gamio's idea of the integral approach. They have experts in the various fields working with social anthropologists for one or two years to get an acceptable picture of this area and the situation there. For example, you have a community, living for years and years around a Spanish town very similar to a market town. The anthropologists consider this community and think how the new improvements should be made without producing frictions—new schools established, what subjects are to be taught, how physicians could understand the Indian mind, and so on. Once all these facts are collected, centers are located through which all governmental action is channeled. Thus the action coming from the government would be adapted to the particular conditions. Little by little, instead of disintegration, the new techniques are integrated into the old way of life. Some people might prefer to lose many of their old ways, some might not; some prefer to speak their own language, some do not. We would not insist that they should speak it. It's up to them because they are human individuals. This is generally the philosophy that has been developed in Mexico.

NORTHROP: Mr. Jahn sharpened an issue, I think, when he stated that there are two roles—the listening and the teaching. He took the position in favor of the listening role. Does anybody want to say something about the teaching role?

SAMBURSKY: It was very clearly brought out that there are two functions of anthropology—the cognitive and the social. I believe it is very difficult to apply some ethical standards to the cognitive procedures; they have to be applied to the social function. In the process of knowledge, you can apply only certain pragmatic standards. You need to proceed with a method of investigation that does not block further knowledge—for instance, tactlessness. One of our members here will not give away the archaeological secret because he knows it might hamper further contact with the people who disclosed it to him. That is a pragmatic approach, which is the correct approach.

MACKAY: Surely his reason for not giving away his information is not that it would hinder contact in the future, but because he would be breaking his promise?

HOEBEL: It's both. I ask myself the question: If I am never going back, then does the obligation to my fellow scientists supersede the obligation to the Indians? I say pragmatically that as long as there is any possibility of my return to the Pueblo, I will not make this revelation. When it is clear that I am not going back, then I will consider whether or not I can break the promise in terms of other obligations.

With respect to Jahn's observation, in my own experience as a field ethnographer, the student-learning role is the most successful for evoking response from the people whose culture I am trying to study. I, however, would go beyond this with Redfield and say that I think anthropologists are full of self-deception when they deny cultural ethnocentrism to themselves and try to tell us that we are not evaluating cultures as better or worse, but merely taking them in their own terms.

Let's begin by suggesting that we always have to ask ourselves the question: What are our cultural commitments as anthropologists? As anthropologists and scientists we have worked very hard to develop objectivity and to train our membership to look at cultures without condemning them. But as anthropologists we are human beings, which leads us to the question of what are the bounds to the definition of the society to which we are committed. Professor Northrop's book *Ideological Differences and World Order* is concerned with the ordering of a world society, and, as I understand it, ideological differences are cultural phenomena that stand in the way of a world order. At any rate, there are certain differences that have *got* to be resolved if we are going to structure a world society in which we will not subject humanity to self-destruction through the application of what the physical scientists and technologists have been developing.

There is a man named Putnam who writes and speaks for the White Citizens' Council in the South. In a series of pamphlets

and speeches he reiterates over and over again the thesis that integration of the races in the U.S. is a conspiracy launched by anthropologists and made possible only by anthropological poisoning of
the nation's mind. He tries to document this and cites anthropological literature. Anthropologists in the United States do have quite
a solid position on the matter of integration, and it's true they use
their science, and everything they can marshal from their science,
to give support to integration in attempting to impose on the
Southern states a way of life that is not theirs. We anthropologists
have no great respect for the dignity of the segregationist aspects
of the way of life as conceived by the traditionalist white South-
erner. I think you all applaud us for it because you agree with us.

Extended a bit further with respect to the Pueblos, Llewellyn
and I were invited *in* to do our research because the Pueblos were
having certain difficulties with the courts in the state of New
Mexico, in particular, and, potentially, with the Supreme Court of
the United States. The Pueblos are organized as monolithic, autocratic theocracies which use the most repressive measures possible
to prevent deviation from the Pueblo way of life. In Zuni Pueblo,
for instance, as described by Watson Smith and John Roberts, between 1880 and 1890, there are written records of fourteen cases of
individuals who were strung up on a frame in the Pueblo plaza and
beaten with clubs and stones by the Bow Priests until they confessed to deviationalism. If they didn't confess, they were beaten
to death. This is a system which runs all through the Pueblos, one
way or another, albeit today such patterns of control have gone
underground.

Among the particular Pueblos I studied, the method was to
stand anyone suspected of deviationalism in a sacred cornmeal
circle three feet in diameter. The war chief or war priest of the
society undertook the inquisition. He stood with a drawn bow and
arrow. The questions were put one after another day and night
and day and night until the individual confessed and recanted.
If he fainted and fell outside the circle without confessing, the
arrow was driven through his heart and he was killed. I cannot say
that it is done exactly this way today, but this has been done in the
past, and we do know that individuals still disappear. The Pueblo
also used the cat-o'-nine-tails, unless it were a serious deviation
that was being punished. At present when the public schools open,

the Pueblo governor gets all the little children in front of him and says that his whip is the authority of the Pueblo for the time they are in school. "My authority is transmitted to the teachers. If you do not behave and the teacher complains, I will use the full force of authority."

We were invited in by these authorities to help them with their litigational problems in relation to the courts of New Mexico and the United States federal courts and also to study the procedures and substance of the Pueblo legal system in order to serve as expert witnesses should litigation be taken to the state or federal courts. We could thus demonstrate that there is a legal system operating among these Pueblos. It is not a vacuum into which the courts of the state can step. So far so good. This could be done without any commitment.

However, while doing such work one finds the young men are very restive under this type of a system. They have served in the U.S. Army, been around the world, have learned something of other possibilities and potentialities and of other ways of organizing human society, wherein individuals are allowed to achieve some of their aspirations without having to go through twenty to thirty years of rising to the position of the high priest who controls the system. These young men want a more direct, and what we call more democratic, system. The anthropologist can either report that the young men are restive and would like to reorganize the system or honestly confess, as I do, that I admire and have great empathy for the Cheyenne system and loathe the Pueblo system. That is, I have certain concepts of what constitutes a decent society that does lend dignity to the individuals in it. I must recognize that the criteria are within me, but these are criteria which, if put to the ultimate test, I think I'd die for. In the concept of the dignity of man, about which we have been talking, can we arrive at a logically realistic scientific concept of this dignity which gives us some sense of assurance that we are actually contributing to (if you don't like the word *manipulating*) the construction, invention, and development of human systems, thus making it possible more adequately to satisfy the fullest potentials of the decent aspirations of humanity and to eliminate those that don't? This is what I see applied anthropology as being.

NORTHROP: Do I take it that the sense of this dialogue is that you can't escape the evaluative judgment question as well as the descriptive? Coming back to Mr. Jahn's question, is it sufficient merely to listen?

JAHN: No, and I feel quite like you, Hoebel, and have often been called into the same position. When I was in Africa, I wanted to learn. Suddenly I was asked to give some instruction. That put me in the position of Mr. Klausner as a teacher, but I would not do it without being asked, even if I might detest what some people do.

MACKAY: Our discussion seems to me to reflect a confessed ethical chaos. Perhaps some Foundation should be asked to call another conference, on the ethical presuppositions of the practice of anthropology.

HOCKETT: I think there is a need for a sound ethical basis.

NORTHROP: I think we ought to have another distinction here. We are all agreed that you have to go to education to get at the values, but are you satisfied that you don't have to go to education even to get at description? As this conference was called to determine the descriptive problem, I think we ought to face this first. The evaluative problem arises later. What do you want to describe in education?

JAHN: I went to Africa to find out the value system of the Africans and describe it for Europeans. I did this. Later my book *Muntu* was translated into English and French. I was then confronted with the situation where somebody approached me and said, "Now the Africans in this country are using your book to learn how to behave ethically." This is the discrepancy between what you want to do and what you are really doing. You cannot escape it.

NORTHROP: Do you think you only have to learn the non-Westerner's culture to do the descriptive problem correctly, before you reach an evaluative judgment? Do you merely have to listen to *his* culture? What else do you have to do?

HOEBEL: Lest you get the impression that I, as a practicing anthropologist, feel that one must have the aim of social modification, I say that I agree with David Riesman who said that the anthropologist does a much better job than the political scientist, and certainly the sociologist, in leading us to an understanding of political and social processes because anthropologists do not have political and social reform as their primary aim. Sociologists, wanting to reform the society, condemn and precommit themselves too soon. The anthropologist's commitment is more remote and, we hope, more effective in the long run.

SMITH: I would like to postulate the proposition that there is a responsibility to encourage certain changes in the thinking of peoples of other cultures. Most cultures have accepted Western technology and legal and political institutions, or are now introducing them and requesting aid in this transition. As Professor Northrop has pointed out, the acceptance of Western "gadgets" without a basic understanding of the technology upon which they are based results in inefficiency and confusion. Similarly, Western legal and political institutions, without an understanding of the basic postulates and principles from which they are derived, can become tools of dictatorship or rule by small military groups. The fundamental theoretical and conceptual differences between the American, English, and various European legal and political institutions should be pointed out and clarified. If this is done, peoples in cultures which are in the process of transition will be in a better position to select the type of Western institutions which will further the goals of human dignity and will enable them to better adapt the compatible parts of their own systems to the adopted institutions.

NORTHROP: Would you say that part of the descriptive job is not merely to acquaint the natives with what you are doing, but also to acquaint them with, or educate them to, the mentality and assumptions of the new system? This is just descriptive. You haven't evaluated either one. That is up to the natives.

JAHN: In the case of a request, I agree. In the case they do not request it, I do not agree at all. Regardless of what you tell them, even if there would be chaos, they will have to learn by their own experience. We cannot claim that we have done better. Very recently in Germany we had the most cruel kind of system. We have no moral right at all to impose anything on another people. They just wouldn't take it. It would put us in a very bad position, in morals as well as in international politics. We deal with grown-up people and should not abuse power to enforce something on them. All we should do is to be honest in explaining in the most correct way possible what we are asked to explain and hope that it will help one side or the other. We must realize that the deficiencies are not only on their side, but on ours as well.

MAQUET: I want to say that Smith's statement implies a knowledge of the integration of a culture that we do not yet have, I am afraid. Because new nations have chosen a Western type of technology, it does not mean that they have chosen the economic organization of free enterprise. They can also have an Eastern, in the sense of a Communist, economic organization. When an African government adopts Western technology, its choice does not necessarily imply a preference for the Western type of economic organization. Now, when we go into other sections of a culture, we find a still larger choice. For instance, in political organization, they can have the British parliamentarian type of government, or a one-party system. In the field of religion, they can have, compatible with Western technology, Christianity, atheism, Islam, or new syncretistic cults which are reinterpretations of their old religious traditions. So you see, we are not so sure that, when we leave the solid ground of technology, we know what is good for another people. There is a large gamut of possibilities because there is no connection of necessity, only of congruence, between, let's say, technology, a certain system of economics, a particular system of government, a specific religion, and so on.

EHRENFELS: I would like to support this statement of Maquet by drawing attention to one fact and that is the example-giving implication of the mere presence of technologically advanced individuals or groups. If, in a non-European society, a number of Russian or Chinese technologists settle down, the majority of people in this community will identify technological progress with the day-to-day behavior pattern as much as with the doctrines of the technologists. The same will happen if they are American or European or any other experts; or, for that matter, anthropology teachers. This specific quality of example-setting is answered without wishing or wanting to do so. It is a factor which I think we should take up.

YAMAMOTO: I am rather doubtful about this. If the man is a really devoted Hindu and strictly follows the traditional epistemology, it seems to be impossible for him to be an anthropologist in the sense we understand here. It would be the same for a devoted Shintoist, I believe. Naive realistic or radically empirical epistemology could not be used for the study of logically realistic culture.

NORTHROP: I think this raises the question, when you get trapped universals from two different systems: Which are the ones that are compatible or incompatible? That distinction is very important.

YAMAMOTO: Study of social groups might be possible, but not for philosophy or values.

MACKAY: I think we underrate the capacity of the human mind to maintain incompatible postulates. Remember the story of the scientist who was found to have a horseshoe over his door. They asked him, "You don't believe in these things, do you?" "No," he said, "but they say it works whether you believe in it or not."

MCCULLOCH: One practical suggestion. In medicine one may not disclose anything confidential concerning his patient. Had that information perished with the physician receiving it, medicine would not yet have achieved what it did in the days of Hippocrates. The great art was to keep a record available to other physicians and *not* available to the public. Thus medicine went ahead with an excellent relation to its patients. Unfortunately, in the case of psychiatry, this has never been possible. With the advent of Public Health measures, more and more physicians have been swept into a position of having to report disease and having to persuade or enforce decisions on other people. The normal procedure in medicine is for no doctor to say anything about his patient. I should think that there would be no fundamental block to creating in anthropology a secrecy such as exists in medicine.

HOCKETT: I think that is impossible because it is contrary to the basic requirement that science be public. However, we might propose that the scientific information made public be only generalizations, from specific facts that are kept private on the grounds of another kind of ethics—the kind that prevents the medical practitioner from revealing the troubles of his individual patients. Yet such "privileged" facts must be open to any fellow scientist who needs access to them. One cannot have a secret society of anthropologists.

MACKAY: Even in medicine it is possible to report cases publicly, provided that the particular individual is well enough camouflaged. What needs to be publicly available to science is not the story of that individual, but only those generalizations or abstractions that his story supports, to which his personal identity is irrelevant. Is there any reason why anthropology should not accept a similar discipline?

Index

Abélard, Peter, 188
Aberle, David F., 289, 293
Accursius, Franciscus, 269
Acton, Lord, 262, 279
Adrian, 185
Africa, 7, 66, 170, 209, 210, 221,
    222, 309, 310, 368, 373, 378,
    380
  Sub-Saharan, 6, 55–69
Afrikaners, 346
Agnosticism, 347
Ahrens, R., 307
Alcmeon of Croton, 183–184
Alembert, Jean Le Rond d', 165 n.
Alexandria, 184
Alexandrian period, 237
Algebra, Greek, 238
Al-Hazen, 221
Allport, Gordon W., 310, 334, 335
Altekar, A. S., 122
Ambalavasi caste, 107
Ames, J. B., 277
Anderson, Arthur J. O., 54
Anderson, Margaret M., 334
Anglicus, Ricardus, 269
Animism, 55, 82, 87, 89–92
Anthropologist, role of, 16, 20–22,
    365–379, 381
Anthropology, 5, 18–19, 24–26, 30,
    170, 178, 202, 284–286, 288,
    289, 317, 330, 339–355 passim,
    365–381 passim
  applied, 369, 373–374, 377
  British, 284
  comparative, 25, 210
  cultural, 3–4, 6–8, 10–11, 93, 103,
    194, 196, 198, 200, 201–202,
    203–205, 210, 284, 285
  deductive, 22–25, 30
  ethics in, 365–381 passim
  materialistic, 26–27
  natural history, 287

Anthropology (Continued)
  naive realistic, 327
  nonethnocentric, 368
  purpose of, 369–371
  sociological, 358, 373–374
  theoretical, 369
  in the United States, 7, 284–285,
    376
Anuman Rajadhon, Phya, 92
Apollo, 26
Apollonius of Perga, 246
Arabs, 106
Archaeology, 36
Archimedes, 242, 250
Ardhanarishvara, 115–116
Aristotle, 158, 180, 181, 183, 184,
    188, 211, 219, 240, 242, 244,
    245, 248, 250, 253, 280, 281,
    348
Arithmetic, 238
  Greek, 239–240
Arnold, E. Vernon, 278
Art, African, 57, 65
  Greek, 239
Ashby, W. Ross, 189, 193
Asia, 35, 70, 209, 218, 220, 368, 370
Assam, 105, 106, 107, 108, 109, 111,
    113, 114
Astrology, 78, 367–368
Astronomy, 327
  Greek, 241, 244–248
  mathematical, 241, 244–245
Atman-that-is-Brahman, 220
Atomists, 180, 183, 249
Attenborough, Frederick L., 281
Austin, William M., 144
Australian aborigines, 290
Ayocuan, 45, 50
Azcapotzalco, 43
Azo, 269–270
Aztecs, 36–38, 42–48
  religion, 329

Bachman, Hedwig, 122
Balandier, George, 104
Banerjea, J. N., 122
Bantu, 56
Banyankole, 316
Barbosa, Duarte, 106, 122
Barenne, Dusser de, 186
Bashō, 98
Basongye, 316, 324
Batoro, 316
Beaglehole, Ernest, 276, 281
Bechert, H., 123
Becket, Thomas, 269
Beethoven, 137
Behavior, adaptive, 298–300, 305
  culturally conditioned, 297–305
    passim
  goal-directed, 148, 162–164
  innate, 297–305 passim
Benares, 219
Benedict, Ruth, 26, 31, 94
Bengal, 107, 115
Berger, Adolf, 278
Bergson, 349
Bété, 316
Beveridge, W. M., 315, 335
Bhakti cult, 115
Bicchieri, Guala, 269
Bigelow, Julian, 148, 160, 178, 186
Billing, H., 179
Bintu, 57–58
Biology, 186, 195, 339, 347, 351
Biophysics, 148–149
Birch, H. G., 297, 306
Blei, 116–117
Boethius, 188
Bologna, 269
Bolshevik Revolution, 203
Bonner, Robert J., 281
Book of Assizes, 256
Bracton, Henry de, 269–271, 273,
  280, 282
Brahmanism, 82, 87–92, 105, 108,
  110
Brain, anatomy of the, 372
Braitenberg, Valentino, 4, 5, 200, 201,
  213, 330, 346–348, 349, 350,
  353–354
Brazil, 62
Brentano, Franz, 312, 334
Bringi, 116
Brunswik, Egon, 315, 316, 334, 335
Buckland, W. W., 282

Buddha, the 74, 86, 89, 90–91, 221,
  228, 229, 233, 234
Buddhism, 7, 70–71, 80, 85–86, 113,
  115, 209, 218, 220–221, 227,
  228, 232–235
  in Burma, 233
  Hinayana, 71, 232
  Hindu, 107, 119
  in Japan, 98, 121
  Mahanikaya, 79
  in Thailand, 70–92
  Theravada, 71
  Zen, 97
Bulgarians, 329
Burma, 7, 107, 209, 223–235
Bushmen, 316, 324
Butler, Charles, 281

Calculus, 5, 242, 249
  infinitesimal, 250–251
Callicles, 239
Cambridge University, 200, 269, 270
Campbell, Donald T., 4, 204, 214,
  333, 334, 335, 336, 346, 350,
  352, 355, 360, 362
Cannon, 185
Cantlie, Keith, 123
Cantor's theory, 214
Carnapians, 344
"carpentered-world" hypothesis, 310
Cartesians, 361
Caso, Alfonso, 52, 53, 374
Caton, 185
Causality, naive realistic, 220
Césaire, Aimé, 66, 68
Ceylon, 121
Chaitanya, 115
Chandra, Moti, 123
Chattopadhyaya, Deviprasad, 123
Chemistry, 248, 372
Cherry, Colin, 178, 179
Cheyenne Indians, 290–292
Chicomóztoc, 43
Child, Arthur, 325, 336
Childe, V. Gordon, 353
China, 7, 51, 93, 209, 218, 380
Christianity, 62–63, 121, 171
  in India, 114, 116
Chrysippus, 250–252, 267
Cicero, 266
Cobbett, William, 280
Cohen, M., 336
Coke, Sir Edward, 269, 271–273, 282

Communication, human, 170
science, 4–5, 162, 163, 164–165,
178, 200
theory of, 162–178
Concept by intellection, defined, 230
Concept by intuition, 229–230, 232
defined, 229, 234
Concept, logically realistic, 348
Concept by perception, 230–231, 232
defined, 230
Concept by postulation, defined, 229–
230, 232, 262
Confucianism, 209, 218, 220
Congo, 7
Consciousness, 345, 353–355
Continuum, aesthetic, 234–235
undifferentiated, 221, 235
Conze, Edward, 92
Corbin, Arthur L., 278
Correlations, epistemic, 207–208
Cosmology, 244
Cranganore, 115
Cree Indians, 132
Cuauhtitlan, 39
Culhuacan, 43
Culture, African, 55–69, 289, 315,
378
American, 310, 380
Aryan, 209, 255
Asian, 51, 221, 287
Aztec, 329
Buddhist, 230
English, 103, 310
European, 36, 51, 66, 103, 109–
110, 237, 288, 310, 313–316,
329, 380
Greek, 113, 252
Indian, 67, 109–110, 219, 288
Japanese, 93
logically realistic, 252, 380
Melanesian, 289
non-Aryan, 208–209
non-Western, 194, 208
philosophy of, 98, 328
Polynesian, 67
Western, 94, 98, 111, 120, 194,
209, 254, 309, 311, 367, 379–
380
Cybernetics, 4–5, 147, 153, 158, 186,
362

Dahomey, 60–61
Dandy, 181

Darwinian theory, 149
Dasgupta, Shashibhusan, 123
Democracy, 272
Democritus, 183, 209, 211, 250–251
Descartes, René, 184, 185, 209
Determinism, 356, 358, 359–362
Dhamma, the, 82–83, 85
Diamond, A. S., 258, 278, 281
Dibble, Charles E., 54
Dionysus, 26
Diop, C. A., 66, 68
Dogon, 15
Dravidians, 106
Dreyer, J. L. E., 253
Driver, Godfrey R., 277, 281
Duns Scotus, 188
Durga, 115
Durgapur, 107
Dynamics, deductively formulated,
199–200
laws of, 242
theoretical, 198

East Pakistan, 107
East-West Philosophers' Conference,
208
Ecology, 315, 316
Economics, 198
Communist, 380
Thai, 77
Western, 380
Edward I, 270
Edwards, Chilperic, 277
Ehrenfels, U. R., 7, 122, 123, 329,
367–369, 380
Eibl-Eibesfeldt, Irenäus, 4, 300, 306,
307
Einstein, 3, 5, 8–10, 11, 12, 195,
197, 198, 199, 204, 211, 222
Electromagnetics, of Maxwell, 9, 196
Elias, 253
Elmore, W. T., 123
Empedocles, 182
Empiricists, 180
Asian, 220
Energy, law of conservation of, 181
Engineering, 186
Entities, coded, 340
postulated, 340
Epistemology, 3–11, 98, 103, 183,
186, 196–197, 198, 205–206,
211, 228, 261, 285, 308, 317,
327, 347, 348, 357, 360, 366
applied, 318, 325–327

Epistemology (Continued)
  Asian, 218, 220
  Buddhist, 218
  Cartesian, 361
  Confucian, 218
  defined, 5, 8, 206
  experimental, 180–192, 360–361
  Greco-Roman-Occidental, 285
  Hindu, 218
  Kantian, 203, 214
  naive realistic, 380
  physiological, 360
  radical empirical, 328, 380
  Western, 229
Ethiopia, 121
Ethnocentrism, 321
  cultural, 375
Ethnography, 125–127, 129, 130–131,
  140, 141, 331–333, 371, 375
Ethology, 297
Euclid, 195, 196, 221, 239, 240, 263
Europe, 35, 95, 269, 309, 368
Evanston, Ill., 310, 313, 315, 323–
  324

Far East, 210
Fawcett, F., 123
Fearne, Charles, 282
Feedback, 148
  negative, 148
Feigl, 353
Field, Ruth, 293
Fisher, H. A. L., 277
Fiske, Donald W., 336
Florid Wars, 44
Forbes, 185
Forest Tiyyas, 107
Fourier, 170
France, 95
Franklin, Benjamin, 203
Free will, 4, 353, 356–364 passim
Frobenius, Leo, 62, 68
Fustel de Coulanges, Numa Denis,
  217, 277, 280, 281

Gabon, 316
Gabor, D., 179
Gaius, 277, 278, 279
Galileo, 209, 238
Gallavardin, 342
Galvani, 185
Gamio, 374
Gardner, Martin, 161

Garibay K., Angel Ma., 52, 53, 54
Garo, 105, 106–107, 108, 114, 116–
  117, 121
Garo Hills, 106
Gellius, Aulus, 279
Genetics, 339–340
Geometry, Greek, 238–240, 250–251
Germany, 379
Gibbs, Willard, 5
Girard, Paul F., 266, 279
Glanville, 269
Gödel, 188, 190, 359
Gopalakrishnan, M. S., 123
Gough, Kathleen, 293
Grassé, P. P., 306
Great Britain, 106
  Act of Settlement, 271
  Bill of Rights, 270–271
  Parliament, 272
  Petition of Rights, 270, 272
  House of Lords, 272
Greece, 288
Greenberg, Joseph H., 68
Greenwich observatory, 218
Griaule, Marcel, 15, 68
Guatemala, 45
Güterbock, Carl E., 269, 280, 282
Gulf of Mexico, 37
Gulliver, Ashbel G., 282
Gurdon, P. R. T., 123

Haddon, A. C., 334
Haiti, 62, 372
Hammond, K. R., 336
Hantu, 56
  -forces, 58–59
Hart, C. W. M., 290, 293, 294
Hart, H. L. A., 282
Hartline, Haldan K., 151, 160
Hargrave, Francis, 281
Harvard University, 7, 233
Hearn, Lafcadio, 93
Heath, T. L., 253
Hebb, D. C., 297, 306
Heidegger, 56
Heinroth, O., 297, 305
Heisenberg, 361
Helmholtz, 186
Hellenistic period, 249
Henry II, 269
Henry VIII, 270
Henry of Susa, 269
Hering, Ewald, 316, 335

Herskovits, Melville J., 308–309, 310, 333, 334
Hindemith, 137
Hinduism, 107, 113, 114–116, 119, 121, 220–221
  nondualistic Vedantic, 209
  Vedantic, 220
Hipparchus, 246
Hippocrates, 182, 183, 381
Histology, 186
History, Roman, 288
Hobhouse, L. T., 276–277
Hockett, Charles F., 5, 7, 15, 68, 144, 214, 330, 332, 339, 340, 341, 345, 348, 349, 350, 351, 352, 354, 355, 359, 361, 362, 363, 371, 378, 381
Hoebel, E. Adamson, 7, 201, 204, 289, 291, 293, 294, 369, 375–377, 378
Hohfeld, Wesley N., 264, 274, 279, 281, 282
Holdsworth, William, 277, 279, 280, 281, 282
Honolulu, 208
Howell, Thomas B., 280
Hsu, Francis L. K., 104, 336
Hudson, W., 314, 335
Huehuetéotl, 37
Huexotzincas, 38
Huexotzinco, 45, 50
Huitzco, 39
Huitzilopochtli, 43, 44, 47
Human dignity, preservation of, 365–366
Hume, 10, 11, 158, 220
Hutton, J. H., 123

Iamblichus, 241, 243–244, 253
Ijaw, 316
Imana, 18
India, 7, 51, 106, 119, 121, 209, 220, 223, 310, 368
  Fertile Crescent, 119
  Hindu Succession Act of June, 1956, 119, 121
  philosophy in, 105–122
  South, 6, 105, 107, 111, 116, 119
    ethnology in, 106
    religion in, 114–117
Indians, see under specific types
Indeterminacy, 361–363
Indonesia, 121, 221
Information, defined, 164–165

Information theory, 351
Innate releasing mechanism, 303
Inns of Court, 270
Ise, Imperial Shrine, 101
Islam (religion), 116
Italy, 60–61, 268–269
Itzcóatl, 46
Iyer, L. K. Ananthakrishna, 122

Jahn, Janheinz, 6, 68–69, 351, 367, 369, 371, 372, 374, 375, 378, 379
James, William, 221
Japan, 7, 93–104, 142, 209, 218, 254
  Institute of Statistical Mathematics, 99, 104
  National Institute of Statistical Mathematics, 95
  religion in, 94, 96, 97, 98, 103
Java, 221–222
Jefferson, 203
Jolowitz, H. F., 278, 281, 282
Jones, J. W., 258, 278, 281
Joüon de Longrais, F., 277
Jowei, 107
Jupiter, 246, 327
Justinian, 278, 279, 280

Kagame, Alexis, 66, 68
Kakati, Banikanta, 123
Kamiya, J., 335
Kannikkar, 107
Kant, 200, 203, 214, 244, 253
Kantorowicz, Herman, 280
Kaplan, B., 306, 336
Karve, Iravatti, 123
Kelsen, Hans, 285
Kepler, 183, 184
Kerala, 105, 106, 107, 108–110, 111–115, 119
Key (caste), 107
Khasi, 105, 106–112, 114, 116–117, 121
Khasi Hills, 107
Kindaichi, Haruhiko, 98, 104
Kintu, 56, 57–58, 60–61, 62, 63, 65–66
Klausner, William J., 7, 66, 68, 365–367, 369, 370, 372, 378
Kleene, 201
Kluckhohn, Clyde, 3, 5, 6, 8, 10–11, 12, 15, 202–203, 204, 285, 293
Knowledge, cardiocentric theory of, 181

Knowledge (Continued)
    haemic theory of, 180–183
    nervous theory of, 183–188
Kocourek, Albert, 277, 281, 282, 283
Koehler, O., 307
Krishna, 115
Kruskal, William H., 335
Kubie, 190
Kuhlenbeck, 193
Kuntu, 56, 59–60, 65–66
Kuruchar, 107
Kyūshū University, 95

Landahl, H. D., 161
Language, 6, 22, 133, 143, 197–198,
    203–205, 208–209, 291, 322,
    325, 326, 347–348
    African, 55
    Aryan, 194, 203–204, 208, 211,
        220
    Buddhist, 221
    Burmese, 223–230, 232
    Chinese, 223
    development of, 173
    English, 127, 129, 130, 133, 137,
        203, 208–209, 224, 225–226,
        256
    Hindu, 221
    learning, 317
    Náhuatl, 36, 43, 49, 50
    Pali, 71 n., 74
    Sanskrit, 105, 219, 220
    semantic, 195
    Stoic, 216
    Tibeto-Chinese, 223
    use of, 24, 25
    Yoruba, 62
Latin America, 373
Laughlin, J. Laurence, 277, 282
Law, 360
    Adat, 221
    Aebutian, 266
    African, 63–64
    Babylonian, 257
    Buddhist, 218
    canon, 269–270
    Cheyenne Indian, 290–292, 377
    civil, 254, 268, 270, 272, 275–276
    common, 218, 254, 255, 257–258,
        271–274, 275–276, 360
        English, 269–270
    Confucian, 218
    Continental, 254, 268, 270, 272

Law (Continued)
    of contract, 103, 217–218, 284,
        286, 287, 288, 292
        Western, 209, 218, 254–276
    criminal, 288, 289–290, 292
    English, 254, 256–259, 267–273
    European, 268
    Greek, 255–256, 257, 258–259,
        273
    Hindu Aryan, 218
    logical realistic, 215–216
    mediational, 254, 261
    naive realistic, 215, 217, 221
    of the Plains Indians, 291
    primitive, 284–292
    problem of induction in, 215
    Pueblo Indian, 376–377
    radical empirical, 215
    Roman, 217, 254, 255–256, 258–
        273, 275, 284, 287
    Saxon, 257
    of Status, 217–218, 221, 261, 284,
        286, 292
    Stoic, 261, 262, 263, 264
    Thai, 77
    of tort, 289–290
    of the Twelve Tables, 266, 279
    in the United States, 203
    Welsh, 257
    Western, 286, 287
Lawson, F. H., 273, 280, 281, 283
Legal positivism, 285
Lehrman, D. S., 297, 306
Leibniz, 353
Leiden, 184
León-Portilla, Miguel, 6, 52, 54, 67,
    68, 329, 373–374
Lettvin, Jerome Y., 151, 160, 193
LeVine, Robert A., 336
Lin Yutang, 236
Linguistics, 125–130, 131, 133–134,
    138, 204
    European, 321
Lipps, Teodore, 316, 335
Littleton, Sir Thomas, 273
Llewellyn, Karl N., 289, 293, 294,
    376
Locke, John, 211
Logan, William, 123
Logic, 6, 10, 19, 23, 152, 153–154,
    261
    Aristotelian, 267–268
    Greek, 286
    mathematical, 5

Logic (*Continued*)
Stoic, 266–268
symbolic, 5, 155, 157, 158, 197, 204–205
Logical realism, 26, 102, 103, 197, 206–207, 209–218, 221, 261, 292, 328
defined, 206, 210
Lombard, Italy, 269
Lorenz, K., 297, 298, 304, 305, 306, 307, 327, 336
Lowie, Robert H., 289, 293
Lull, Raymond, 158
Lullian machine, 157–158
Lyngngam, 106

McCarthy, J., 161
McCulloch, Warren S., 4, 148, 151, 153, 154, 160, 161, 188, 193, 200, 201, 330, 339–345, 346, 350–351, 352, 354, 359, 362, 371, 373, 381
McCulloch-Pitts theory, 4, 153–155, 156, 188, 189, 349, 350, 351, 352
McIlwain, Charles H., 278, 280, 283
MacKay, Donald M., 4, 5, 67, 68, 178, 179, 190, 200, 201, 330, 343, 345, 346, 347, 348, 349–350, 351, 352, 353, 354–363, 364, 365, 369, 370, 372–373, 375, 378, 381
McKiever, B. L., 355
McNair, Arnold D., 282
Magara principle, 57, 58, 63
Magendie, 185
Magna Carta, 270
Magnus, Rudolf, 186
Maine, Sir Henry, 217, 261, 278, 282, 284, 286–290, 293
Maitland, F. W., 271, 277, 279, 280, 283
Malabar, 114
Malaya, 368
Malinowski, 325
Mandalay, 231
Mapillais, 114
Maquet, Jacques J., 7–8, 31, 202, 203, 205, 328, 370, 371, 373, 380
Margenau, Henry, 208
Marinos, 244
Mars, 246
Marx, 103

Mates, Benson, 279
Mathematical physics, 3–4, 8, 10, 11, 198, 200, 202, 211, 230, 243
Greek, 261, 263
non-Aristotelian Western, 6
Western, 209, 211
Mathematics, 5–6, 213, 215, 250
Egyptian, 240
Greek, 239–244, 250–251
modular, 344
Platonic, 240
pure, 197, 205
Maturana, H. R., 151, 160
Maugham, Somerset, 368
Maw Syn Jri, 111
Maxwell, 9, 196
Mayr, E., 297, 306
Meaning, concept of, 165–168
Mechanics, Newtonian, 9, 196, 200
Medicine, African, 63–64
ethics in, 381
Hippocratic, 180, 369
Thai, 76–77
Meditation, 233
Meiji, 102
Mendel, 181
Menon (caste), 107
Mercury, 196, 245
Metaphysics, 211
Mexico, 45, 374
Ancient, philosophy of, 35–52
Indians of, 36, 53
pre-Columbian, 35, 52
Spaniards in, 35, 37
Valley of, 37, 43
Mexico City, 38, 39
Mexico-Tenochtitlan, 44
Meyer, Max, 360
Michelson-Morley experiment, 9
Miles, John C., 277, 281
Minami, Hiroshi, 99, 104
Morey, William C., 277
Morse radio signals, 173
Motion, Aristotelian law of, 242
Mount Xicócotl, 39
Muduvar, 107
Müller, Max, 219
Müller-Lyer illusion, 310–312, 314–315, 318, 323
Muirhead, James, 279
Mundy-Castle, A. C., 355
Muntu, 56–57, 58, 59–61, 62, 63
Muramatsu, Tsuneo, 95, 104

Murdock, George P., 69, 289, 291, 293
Murray Islanders, 310
Music, Pythagorean theory of, 241, 242
Muslims, 107, 121
    Malayalam, 107
Mysticism, Oriental, 252
Mythology, Greek, 56

Naga, 88
Nagoya University, 95
Nahuas, 38
Nahuas-Texcocans, 38
Náhuatls, 37, 38, 43, 45, 46–48
    See also Language and Philosophy
Naive realism, 26, 102, 197, 209–210, 211–212, 213, 215, 218, 219–221, 228, 229, 232–233, 261, 284, 285, 287, 291, 314, 315, 328
    defined, 206, 210
Nakamura, Hajime, 98, 104
Nambiar, 107
Nambisan, 107
Nambudri Brahmans, 108
Nayars, 106, 107, 111
Neoplatonists, 240, 241, 243, 247, 248, 252
Nervous system, 339–344, 348, 350–351
    circuit theory of the, 339
    logic of, 348–349
Neural network theory, 346
Neurology, 339, 347
Neurons, 347
Neurophysiology, 4–5, 153, 200, 339–355 passim
New Guinea, 310, 317
New Mexico, 376, 377
Newton, 9, 10, 195–196, 199, 209, 218, 238, 242, 244, 245
Nezahualcóyotl, 45
Nieuwkoop, P. D., 341, 355
Niger valley, 15
Nirvana, 72, 85, 221, 233, 234–235
Nó, Lorente de, 190
Nommo, 56–57, 58, 59–60, 61, 62, 63, 64, 67
Nonohualcas, 39
Norbeck, E., 336
Norbeck, Edward, 104
North Malabar Mapillais, 107
Northrop, F. S. C., 11, 12, 18, 19, 23, 29, 31, 50, 92, 102, 192, 222, 226, 228, 229–231, 234–235, 236, 261, 262, 263, 264, 276, 278, 279, 281, 283, 284, 285, 286–287, 291, 292, 293, 294, 315, 330, 335, 344, 346, 348–350, 351–352, 359, 365, 366, 369, 374, 375, 377–378, 379, 380
Noyes, C. Reinhold, 277, 282
Number, natural, 342
    Pythagorean theory of, 238
NTU, 56, 60–61, 65, 66–67

Occam, 196
Occam's Razor, 195
Occident, 210
Oedipus complex, 16
Olorun, 56, 58, 61–62
Ometéotl, 38, 40 n.
Omeyocan, 40, 42
Ontogeny, 298, 300, 302, 303
Optical illusion, 329
Optics, geometrical, 149, 151, 183, 242
    neural, 149–152
Orisha, 57
Ornithology, 352
Oxford University, 269, 270

Padu, 231
Pahlavi script, 223
Pakistan, 121
Pánuco River, 37
Papinian, 270
Paracelsus, 181
Parkinson's disease, 340
Parvati, 115, 116
Pasteur, 182
Paton, George W., 278
Peano, 215
Peano's Fifth Postulate, 214, 291
Peiper, A., 307
Penfield, 353
Perception, theory of, 309
Perception tests, cross-cultural, 4, 204, 308–327 passim
People of the Sun, see Aztecs
Pettigrew, Thomas F., 310, 334, 335
Philoponus, John, 245, 253
Philosophy, 3, 5–6, 8, 10, 14, 17–18, 30, 349
    Aristotelian, 27, 244

Philosophy (*Continued*)
  cultural, 4, 6, 13–14, 17–19, 22, 26–30, 203
  African, 55–67 *passim*
  Buddhist, 57, 232–235, 287
    See also Buddhism
  Burmese, 223
  Confucian, 287
  defined, 202
  European, 56
  expressed, 28–29
  Greek, 42, 218, 292
  Hindu, 42, 114, 116, 287
    See also Hinduism
  humanistic, 200
  implicit or covert, 15–18, 28–29
  Kantian, 200
  Milesian, 237
  Náhuatl, 36, 37, 43, 49–51, 67
  Platonic, 26, 244
  Pythagorean, 57, 244
  Roman, 218, 292
  Roman Stoic, 217, 261, 286–287
  of the Ruanda, 18, 21–22, 29
  of science, 8, 207, 208, 317
  Stoic, 48, 260, 262–263, 287, 359–360
  Western, 14–15, 16, 23
Phonemics, 126, 127, 167
  English, 137
Phylogeny, 298, 300, 305, 341
Physics, 8, 9, 24, 125, 194, 195, 196, 197, 208, 211, 340, 357, 361, 372
  of Einstein, 5
  Greek, 261
  modern, 4
  of Newton, 9
  quantum, 362
  relativity theory, 357
  theoretical, 244
Physiology, 180, 181, 186, 339, 346, 350, 372
Pillai (caste), 107
Pillai, Elamkulam P. N. Kunjan, 124
Pintner, Rudolf, 334
Pitts, Walter H., 151, 153, 160, 161, 188, 189, 190, 193, 201, 344, 346
Plains Indians of North America, 289, 291
Planck, 358
Plato, 209, 239, 240, 241, 242, 243,
  244, 245, 246, 247–248, 250, 277, 282
Platonists, 211, 240, 242
Playfair, A., 124
Plucknett, T. F. T., 280
Plutarch, 250, 253
Poduval, 107
Poetry, African, 64–65
Pollock, Frederick, 277, 279, 281, 283
Polybius, 277
Polynesia, 221
Porphyry, 188
Portuguese, the, 106
Posidonius, 249
Poste, E., 267, 279, 282
Prechtl, H., 307
Prediction, causal, 356–364 *passim*
Pringsheim, F., 276
Prinsloo, T., 355
Proclus, 240, 244, 247, 248
Protestantism, 63
Province, John R., 289, 293
Psychiatry, 202, 360, 372, 373, 381
Psychology, 178, 347, 349, 353
  experimental, 159
Ptolemaic system, 241
Ptolemy, 246
Pueblo Indians, 375, 376–377
  Zuni, 376
Putnam, 375
Pylus, 182
Pythagoreans, the, 238, 240, 241–242, 248

Quantum mechanics, 196, 199–200, 201, 247
Quetzalcóatl, 38–41, 43, 45

Rachewiltz, Boris de, 69
Radical empiricism, 26, 102, 103, 197–198, 209–211, 213, 215, 218, 219–221, 226, 228–229, 231, 233, 235, 261, 284, 285, 291, 315, 328
  British, 330
  defined, 206, 210
Radin, Paul, 11, 202, 203, 204
Rajput, 119
Ramon y Cajal, 186
Rangachari, K., 122
Rangoon, University of, 233
Ranson, 190
Rapoport, Anatol, 359
Rashevsky, 193

Ratliff, Floyd, 160
Realism, 315
  defined, 210, 261
Reality, Greek physical, 237–252
  passim
  nature of, 26, 29
Redfield, Robert, 287–288, 289, 291, 293, 375
Reichardt, Werner, 151, 160
Reichenbach, 208
Relativism, cultural, 309
  linguistic, 326
Relativity, Einstein's theory of, 199
  General Theory of, 196
  Special Theory of, 8, 9, 10, 196
Religion, 380
  in Western Europe, 103
    See also under specific types
Richardson, Henry G., 277
Richardson, Jane, 289, 293
Riesman, David, 378
Riess, B., 297, 306
Rivers, W. H. R., 310, 334
Robbins, Lionel, 198
Roberts, John, 376
Robertson, Donald, 54
Roe, A., 306
Roman Catholicism, 62
Roman Catholics in England, 273
Roman Empire, 268
Rome, 288
Rorschach tests, 94
Rosenblueth, Arturo, 148, 160, 178, 185
Royal Society of Medicine, 185
Ruanda (country), 20, 21–22
Ruanda, the, 7, 15, 18–19, 20, 30
Rules of correspondence, 208
Russell, Bertrand, 5
Russia, 186, 203, 380

Sahagún, Fray Bernardino de, 36, 45–46, 53, 54
Saint Thomas, 211
Samantham (caste), 107
Sambursky, S., 4, 6, 201, 209, 253, 266, 279, 353, 358, 359, 361, 374
Samoa, 135
Sander, 310
Sander parallelogram, 312–313, 314
Sanford, E. C., 316, 334, 335
Saturn, 246
Savigny, 260

Sayadaw, Ledi, 235
Sayles, G. O., 277
Scaevola, Q. Mucius, 260–261, 266
Scheduling, 129–132, 135
Schilpp, Paul A., 11, 12, 222
Schleidt, W., 307
Schneider, David M., 293
Schneirla, T. C., 297, 306
Schulz, F., 260–261, 278, 283
Science, 198
  Buddhist, 218
  Confucian, 218
  deductively formulated, 195–196, 198
  defined, 8
  Greek, 209, 212–213, 237–245, 248–250, 251–252
  Hindu, 218
  logically realistic, 328
  natural, 196, 200
  natural history, 194–198, 204, 207
  Platonic, 238, 247–248
  pre-Socratic, 247
  Stoic, 209, 249
  Stoic Roman, 217
  Western, 286
    empirical, 194
Scott, Samuel Parsons, 282
Scrutton, Thomas F., 279
Seagle, William, 276, 278, 282
Sears, R. R., 336
Sechenov, 185
Segall, Marshall, 310, 333
Séjourné, Laurette, 54
Seler, Eduard, 54
Semantics, 164
Senghor, Léopold Sédar, 66, 68
Shakti, 115–116
Shango, 61
Shannon, Claude E., 143, 144, 161
Sheffer, H. M., 195
Sherman, Charles P., 279, 280
Shintoism, 98, 209, 218
Shiva, 115–116
Siam, see Thailand
Simplicius, 248, 253
Simpson, G. G., 306
Simpson, Sidney P., 293
Smith, Gertrude, 281
Smith, Joseph C., 4, 201, 209, 284, 286, 287, 291, 360, 369, 379, 380
Smith, Watson, 376
Social science, 8, 202, 358

Sociology, 378
Sociology of knowledge, 325
Socrates, 239
Sohm, Rudolph, 279
Solipsism, 326
Sonlun Meditation Center, 233
Sonlun Sayadaw, 233
Sorokin, P. A., 26, 29, 30, 31, 203
South Africa, 314
South Africans, 346
   European, 313, 324
Southeast Asia, 7
Species, law of conservation of, 181
Speech, 341–344
Spence, George, 279
Spencer, 103
Spitz, R., 307
Statics, deductively formulated, 199–200
   legal, 201
Sticks Everything Under His Belt, 290–291
Stobaeus, 253
Stoics, 211, 217, 249, 250
   See also Philosophy
Struik, D. J., 253
Sumner, 10
Symbolism, Carnapian, 344

Takakusu, J., 227, 236
Tambiah, H. W., 124
Tamils, 115
Taut, Bruno, 94
Tecamachalco, 45
Tecayehuatzin, 45, 50
Teleology, 148–149, 186
Tempels, P., 26, 31, 69
Tennō worship, 94, 96
Teotihuacán, 37 38
Texcoco, 43, 45
Tezcatlipocas, 42, 45
Thailand, 7, 66, 70–92, 121, 209, 373
   Ministry of Education, 76
Theobald, Archbishop, 269
Theology, 211
Theophrastus, 184, 242–243, 253
Thiéry, Armand, 312, 334
Thomas, Jr., William L., 210
Thorpe, W. H., 303, 306
Thouless, Robert H., 315, 335
Thurston, E., 122
Tibet, 51, 329
Time, concept of, 218–220

Time, concept of (Continued)
   African, 58–59
   Buddhist, 227–228
   Burmese, 224–225, 227, 232
   Greek, 251
   logical realistic, 218
   cyclical theory of, 232
   unilinear notion of, 103
Tinbergen, N., 297, 306
Tlacaélel, 44, 46
Tlaxcallans, 38
Tloque-Nahuaque, 42
Todas, 310
Tōkei Sūri Kenkyūjo, 104
Toltecs, 36, 38–45, 47
Torres Strait, 310
Trubetzkoy, 137 n.
Tula, 38, 43
Turing, 189
Turing machine, 189, 351
Turkey, 121, 254
Twadell, W. F., 142
Tzetzes, 253
Tzincoc, 39

United Kingdom, 95
   See also Great Britain
United States, 95, 182, 367, 372
   federal courts in, 377
   integration in, 276
   political system of, 203
   Supreme Court, 217, 376
   White Citizens' Council, 375
Universals, logically realistic, 344, 346
   naive realistic, 344, 346
   trapped, 4, 148, 191–192, 201–202, 349, 380
Ushijima, Yoshitomo, 95, 102–103, 104
Uttley, A. M., 159, 161

Vacarius, 269
Vaillant, George C., 54
Vaishnavism, 115
Values, cultural, 367–373, 375
Van Caenegem, R. C., 277, 280, 283
Vedas, the, 219
Velayudhan, P. V., 123
Venus, 245, 368
Vinci, Leonardo da, 184
Vinogradoff, Paul, 277, 279, 280, 282
Virpat Malayalar, 107
Vishnu, 115
Vision, binocular, 327

Vitalism, 351–352, 353
Vos, George de, 101, 104

Walker, D. E., 336
Wambaugh, Eugene, 283
Wapner, S., 306
Weaver, Warren, 144
Wenar, Solveig Cedarloo, 334
Wertheimer, Max, 322, 335
West Germany, 95
Westrup, C. W., 217, 255, 266, 276, 277, 279, 282
Whitehead, 5, 187, 191, 192, 201, 207, 208, 252
Wickler, W., 297, 306
Wiener, Norbert, 147, 148, 160, 178, 186
Wigmore, John H., 277, 281, 282
William of Drogheda, 269
William of Occam, 188

Win, Khin Maung, 4, 7
Wittgenstein, Ludwig, 157, 161
Wohlwill, Joachim F., 334
Wolff, Hans J., 278
Woodbine, George E., 280
Woodroffe, Sir John, 222
Woodworth, Robert S., 316, 335
World view, see Philosophy
World War I, 203
World War II, 94, 102
Wun, U, 223, 236

Yakalev, Paul, 340
Yamamoto, Tatsuro, 7, 371, 380, 381
Yemaya, 61

Zeno, 250
Zeno's paradoxes, 250
Zulu, 316, 324
Zuordnungsdefinitionen, 208

Format by Faith Nelson
Set in Linotype Electra
Composed and printed by York Composition Co., Inc.
Bound by Haddon Craftsmen
HARPER & ROW, PUBLISHERS, INCORPORATED